# Privacy-Respecting
# Intrusion Detection

# Advances in Information Security

## Sushil Jajodia

*Consulting Editor*
*Center for Secure Information Systems*
*George Mason University*
*Fairfax, VA 22030-4444*
*email: jajodia@gmu.edu*

The goals of the Springer International Series on ADVANCES IN INFORMATION SECURITY are, one, to establish the state of the art of, and set the course for future research in information security and, two, to serve as a central reference source for advanced and timely topics in information security research and development. The scope of this series includes all aspects of computer and network security and related areas such as fault tolerance and software assurance.

ADVANCES IN INFORMATION SECURITY aims to publish thorough and cohesive overviews of specific topics in information security, as well as works that are larger in scope or that contain more detailed background information than can be accommodated in shorter survey articles. The series also serves as a forum for topics that may not have reached a level of maturity to warrant a comprehensive textbook treatment.

Researchers, as well as developers, are encouraged to contact Professor Sushil Jajodia with ideas for books under this series.

### Additional titles in the series:

*SYNCHRONIZING INTERNET PROTOCOL SECURITY (SIPSec)* by Charles A. Shoniregun; ISBN: 978-0-387-32724-2

*SECURE DATA MANAGEMENT IN DECENTRALIZED SYSTEMS* edited by Ting Yu and Sushil Jajodia; ISBN: 978-0-387-27694-6

*NETWORK SECURITY POLICIES AND PROCEDURES* by Douglas W. Frye; ISBN: 0-387-30937-3

*DATA WAREHOUSING AND DATA MINING TECHNIQUES FOR CYBER SECURITY* by Anoop Singhal; ISBN: 978-0-387-26409-7

*SECURE LOCALIZATION AND TIME SYNCHRONIZATION FOR WIRELESS SENSOR AND AD HOC NETWORKS* edited by Radha Poovendran, Cliff Wang, and Sumit Roy; ISBN: 0-387-32721-5

*PRESERVING PRIVACY IN ON-LINE ANALYTICAL PROCESSING (OLAP)* by Lingyu Wang, Sushil Jajodia and Duminda Wijesekera; ISBN: 978-0-387-46273-8

*SECURITY FOR WIRELESS SENSOR NETWORKS* by Donggang Liu and Peng Ning; ISBN: 978-0-387-32723-5

*MALWARE DETECTION* edited by Somesh Jha, Cliff Wang, Mihai Christodorescu, Dawn Song, and Douglas Maughan; ISBN: 978-0-387-32720-4

*ELECTRONIC POSTAGE SYSTEMS: Technology, Security, Economics* by Gerrit Bleumer; ISBN: 978-0-387-29313-2

*MULTIVARIATE PUBLIC KEY CRYPTOSYSTEMS* by Jintai Ding, Jason E. Gower and Dieter Schmidt; ISBN-13: 978-0-378-32229-2

*UNDERSTANDING INTRUSION DETECTION THROUGH VISUALIZATION* by Stefan Axelsson; ISBN-10: 0-387-27634-3

*Additional information about this series can be obtained from*
http://www.springer.com

# Privacy-Respecting Intrusion Detection

by

Ulrich Flegel
*University of Dortmund*
*Germany*

 Springer

Dr. Ulrich Flegel
University of Dortmund
Department of Computer Science
44221 DORTMUND
GERMANY

Ulrich.Flegel@CS.Uni-Dortmund.DE

Privacy-Respecting Intrusion Detection by Ulrich Flegel

ISBN   978-1-4419-4175-6          e-ISBN   978-0-387-68254-9


Printed on acid-free paper.

9 8 7 6 5 4 3 2 1

springer.com

# Contents

**Part I Introduction and Background**

1    Introduction .............................................. 3

2    Authorizations ........................................... 9

3    An Architectural Model for Secure Authorizations .......... 13

4    Traditional Security Objectives ........................... 27

5    Personal Data Protection Objectives ....................... 31

6    Technical Enforcement of Multilateral Security ............. 43

7    Pseudonyms – A Technical Point of View .................... 47

8    An Architectural Model for Pseudonymous Authorizations .. 55

9    Comparing Architectures .................................. 65

10   Audit Data Pseudonymization ............................. 77

**Part II Set-based Approach**

11   Requirements, Assumptions and Trust Model .............. 91

**12 Modeling Conditions for Technical Purpose Binding** ......... 97

**13 Cryptographic Enforcement of Disclosure Conditions** ....... 103

**14 The Mismatch Problem** ..................................... 109

**15 Operational Pseudonymization and Pseudonym Disclosure** ... 115

**16 Extensions** .............................................. 123

**Part III Application to Unix Audit Data**

**17 Unix Audit Data** ......................................... 137

**18 Syslog** ................................................. 141

**19 Instantiating the Set-based Approach for Syslog Audit Data** . 147

**20 Implementation: Pseudo/CoRe** ............................ 159

**Part IV Evaluation**

**21 APES: Anonymity and Privacy in Electronic Services** ....... 171

**22 Evaluating the Design Using Basic Building Blocks** ......... 177

**23 Evaluating the Performance of the Implementation** ......... 187

**Part V Refinement of Misuse Scenario Models**

**24 Motivating Model Refinements** ............................ 199

**25 Models of Misuse Scenarios** .............................. 203

**26 Pseudonymization Based on Serial Signature-Nets** .......... 229

**27 Pseudonym Linkability** ................................... 233

**28  Pseudonym Disclosure** ....................................... 247

**Summary** ...................................................... 283

**A   Threshold Schemes for Cryptographic Secret Sharing** ....... 285

**References** ................................................... 287

**Index** ....................................................... 303

# List of Figures

3.1 A classification of properties ................................ 14

3.2 Relationships between property statements and entities ......... 17

3.3 Verification of property statements .......................... 17

3.4 Basic model ............................................... 18

3.5 A classification of property attributes ....................... 20

3.6 Converting property attributes ............................. 20

3.7 Relationships between security objectives and property attributes 22

3.8 Relationships between the subject, its interests and its privileges . 22

3.9 The authorizer obtains a referenced certificate ............... 24

3.10 The authorizer forwards the service request to the service ....... 24

3.11 The authorizer sends an authorization to the service ........... 24

3.12 The certifier forwards the service request to the authorizer ....... 24

5.1 Concepts of the German Census Decision ..................... 35

8.1 Unilateral security: accountability ........................... 60

8.2 Unilateral security: management anonymizes .................. 60

8.3 Multilateral security: certification of pseudonyms ............. 61

8.4 Multilateral security: authorization of pseudonyms ............ 61

8.5 Multilateral security: pseudonymization of audit data .......... 62

8.6 Purpose binding of controlled pseudonym disclosure ........... 62

11.1 Trust and control in the architectural model of our approach ..... 92

12.1 An example abstract event .................................. 99

12.2 Decision tree for assigning disclosure contexts and weights to
feature types............................................. 102

14.1 A mismatch: a set of incompatible shares matches a secret ....... 110

15.1 Associations and dependencies between conceptual elements ..... 116

15.2 Data flow between the pseudonymizer and the reidentifier ....... 117

16.1 Data flow between the extended pseudonymizer and reidentifier .. 124

16.2 Simplified architectural model due to an extension ............. 127

17.1 Solaris audit components ................................... 138

18.1 Sample Syslog audit records ............................... 142

18.2 Parts of a sample Syslog audit record ...................... 142

18.3 Pseudonymizing Solaris audit data.......................... 145

19.1 Syntactical concepts in a sample Syslog audit record ........... 148

19.2 A sample Syslog audit record .............................. 151

19.3 A pseudonymized Syslog audit record with pseudonymity-layer
data .................................................... 151

19.4 Trust and control in the architectural model of the applied
approach ................................................ 153

19.5 Architectures integrating pseudonymization with Syslog ........ 156

22.1 Decomposing our approach into building blocks ............... 179

23.1 Performance measurements of the cryptographic components..... 189

23.2 Performance measurements of the pseudonymizer .............. 191

23.3 Server statistics: number of audit records generated per hour..... 194

23.4 The day when FTP went wild............................... 194

25.1 Symbols for (non)-consuming edges ......................... 211

25.2 Symbols for types of places ................................ 212

25.3 Symbols for transitions and transition labels with an example .... 213

25.4 Symbols for events and tokens as well as token bindings ........ 215

25.5  Marking before any transitions occur ......................... 218

25.6  Marking after two transitions occurred ....................... 219

25.7  Marking after all activated transitions have occurred ........... 220

25.8  An example serial signature-net ............................. 223

25.9  Emulating disjunctions ..................................... 224

25.10 Emulating conjunctions and spontaneous transitions ........... 225

25.11 Emulating repetitions ...................................... 226

26.1  Trust and control in the architectural model of the fine-grained
      approach ................................................. 230

27.1  Linkability requirements graph for a serial signature-net ........ 239

27.2  Example operation of the pseudonymizer (only linkability) ....... 244

27.3  Example operation of the analysis engine (only linkability) ...... 245

28.1  Disclosure requirements graph for a serial signature-net ........ 253

28.2  Example disclosure contexts with scheme descriptions .......... 264

28.3  Example disclosure contexts with instantiated threshold schemes . 265

28.4  Example operation of the pseudonymizer (linkability and
      disclosure) ............................................... 274

28.5  Example operation of the analysis engine (linkability and
      disclosure) ............................................... 280

# List of Tables

9.1  Summary of architecture properties .......................... 65

10.1 Summary of the properties of selected approaches ............. 80

13.1 Application of Shamir's threshold scheme for secret sharing ...... 107

14.1 Properties of the proposed mismatch handling approaches ....... 111

19.1 Mapping observations from abstract events to Syslog events ..... 149

21.1 Basic anonymity building blocks............................. 174

22.1 Basic anonymity building blocks used in our approach .......... 182

23.1 Default values for the parameters and how they were varied ..... 190
23.2 Influence of the key length on encryption and secret sharing ..... 192
23.3 Influence of the communication technique .................... 192
23.4 Maximum number of audit records generated per second ........ 195

25.1 Semantic requirements for models of misuse scenarios .......... 207
25.2 Semantic requirements met by signature-nets ................. 221
25.3 Semantic requirements met by serial signature-nets ............ 227

# Foreword

Computer and network security is an issue that has been studied for many years. The *Ware Report*, which was published in 1970, pointed out the need for computer security and highlighted the difficulties in evaluating a system to determine if it provided the necessary security for particular applications. The *Anderson Report*, published in 1972, was the outcome of an Air Force Planning Study whose intent was to define the research and development paths required to make secure computers a reality in the USAF. A major contribution of this report was the definition of the reference monitor concept, which led to security kernel architectures. In the mid to late 1970s a number of systems were designed and implemented using a security kernel architecture. These systems were mostly sponsored by the defense establishment and were not in wide use.

Fast forwarding to more recent times, the advent of the world-wide web, inexpensive workstations for the office and home, and high-speed connections has made it possible for most people to be connected. This access has greatly benefited society allowing users to do their banking, shopping, and research on the Internet. Most every business, government agency, and public institution has a public facing web page that can be accessed by anyone anywhere on the Internet. Unfortunately, society's increased dependency on networked software systems has also given easy access to the attackers, and the number of attacks is steadily increasing. These attacks result in the disclosure and/or destruction of sensitive data, productivity loss, and large financial losses. Therefore, there is a need to protect our computers and networks from attack.

For many years the goal of the security community was to build systems that were 100% secure. In the early days of computing when standalone systems were used by one user at a time, computer security consisted primarily of physical security. That is, the computer and its peripherals were locked in a secure area with a guard at the door that checked each user's identification before allowing them to enter the room. Unfortunately, as computers and computer applications got more complex and thousands, and even millions, of systems were connected to one another, protecting these networked systems became a daunting task. Even with the most advanced protection, computer systems are still not 100% secure. In fact, most security experts agree, that, given all of the desirable user features, such as network connectivity, the goal of having a completely secure system will never be achieved. Since systems that are 100% secure cannot be built, it is necessary to use other approaches to protect computer systems from misuse and attacks. One approach is to develop intrusion detection techniques and systems to discover and react to computer attacks. Intrusion detection systems analyze the actions performed by users and applications looking for evidence of malicious activities. This usually requires user behavior to be recorded in audit data.

The incredible growth in the use of the Internet also resulted in an increase in the number of privacy vulnerabilities. As users were given online access to their bank accounts, health records, and shopping portals, the demand for more user friendly interfaces increased. To make these systems more user friendly, personal information, such as shopping preferences, and even credit card and social security numbers, were collected and stored on the systems. Unfortunately, the same information that is used to make access more efficient and user friendly is also accessible to the attackers. As a result, the number of attacks aimed at accessing personal data has also increased dramatically. These attacks range from the release of embarrassing personal information to identity theft and personal financial losses.

The issue of privacy, like computer security, has been studied for many years. In 1977, the Privacy Protection Study Commission issued a report entitled *Personal Privacy in an Information Society*. The issue of privacy is also not new to the computer security community. In 1980 when the IEEE Security & Privacy Symposium began, *Privacy* was a prominent part of its name. Unfortunately, the reality is that for many years the conference only paid lip service to privacy. In 1980 only 1 of the 19 papers presented at the conference was a privacy paper. In 1981 the count was 0 of 18, and in 1982 it was 1 of 20. It is only in the last few years that privacy has come to the forefront of the security community. In fact, there are now many computer science conferences that are primarily concerned with privacy issues.

The relationship between intrusion detection and privacy is particularly interesting. In order to analyze the actions performed by users and applications intrusion detection systems need to collect and retain data about a user's behavior. In contrast, privacy is concerned with the right of individuals to determine if, when, how, and to what extent data about themselves will be collected, stored, transmitted, used, and shared with others. Clearly there is a tension between these two. That is, to do a good job of detecting malicious behavior an intrusion detection system needs to collect personal information, but to protect an individual's privacy the amount and type of data collected must be controlled. One approach to easing the tension between the accountability needed for intrusion detection and the protection of personal data is the use of anonymity. That is, approaches that anonymize personal information to protect a user's privacy must be adapted.

This book addresses the tension between personal privacy and security. The author proposes a balance between the security objective of accountability and the privacy objective of anonymity. The solution put forth is the concept of *technical purpose binding*. The idea is to pseudonymize audit data in a way that allows misuse detection to be performed as efficiently as if it were using the original audit data. The binding also allows the original personal data to be recovered only when malicious behavior is detected and a response is necessary. The result is privacy respecting intrusion detection.

Richard A. Kemmerer
Computer Science Department
University of California, Santa Barbara
Santa Barbara, April 2007

# Acknowledgements

As is probably true of most technical books, this one owes a great many thanks to many individuals who have helped me in various ways. Several people have stimulated or influenced some of the technical content in this book or even contributed technical results, for which all the credit is due to them.

This book was written during my time as research associate at the University of Dortmund in the research group of Joachim Biskup. He inspired this work from the beginning and believed in its importance. I benefited greatly from his considerable experience in the field. Without his patient guidance, his broadmindedness and his generous support this book would not have been possible.

In particular Michael Meier's expertise on and experience with misuse detection was most valuable for developing the last part of this book. During countless meetings around workshops and conferences and during several visits in Dortmund and Cottbus we discussed the expressiveness of models for misuse detection. Our fruitful collaboration culminated in a general framework for modeling misuse scenarios.

I am also grateful to my former colleague Frank Müller, who studied the mismatch problem in detail and came up with a novel approach for share invalidation, which is described in the second part of this book. My thanks go also to Heike Neumann for influential discussions on mismatch avoidance, to Stefan Köpsell for pointing out the importance of share invalidation, and to Yücel Karabulut for sharing his views on authorization models.

During my work on this book numerous people encouraged and supported me and I am grateful to all of them. I resist the temptation of assembling an exhaustive list, since it is foreseeable that it would be incomplete.

Ulrich Flegel
Dortmund, May 2007

# Part I

# Introduction and Background

The first Part gives an introduction to this book and provides the background for the proposed solutions. Chapter 1 motivates this work and briefly characterizes all Parts of this book. Starting from authorizations in the real/physical world Chap. 2 derives conditions for trust and control for an appropriate architectural model for secure authorizations. Such a model is presented in Chap. 3. The notion of security captured by the model is examined in Chap. 4, ascertaining that the aspect of user privacy is poorly supported. Privacy aspects are examined in detail in Chap. 5. A balance of the conflicting security objective of accountability and of the privacy objective of anonymity is proposed in Chap. 6 on the basis of pseudonyms. Legal aspects are considered as the foundation for the proposed approaches, and the main assumptions for legal audit data analysis and pseudonym disclosure are identified in Chap. 6. The more technically inclined aspects of pseudonyms are investigated in Chap. 7. In Chap. 8 pseudonyms are integrated with the architectural model from Chap. 3. The distinct architectures possible in the model are compared in Chap. 9, and it is shown, how the model can be used to classify privacy-enhancing technologies (PETs). Related work on PETs is separated into loosely and closely related work. A comparison of closely related work is given in Chap. 10 and selected approaches are described in some detail. Finally, the distinction of our approaches from existing work is distilled in Chap. 10.

# 1

## Introduction

Along with the growing dependence of our society on information technology systems (IT), issues regarding IT security are becoming more urgent. While until recently in practice primarily preventive safeguards were deployed, it becomes more and more apparent that IT security cannot be achieved by prevention alone. Rather, preventive safeguards and reactive aspects need to complement one another.

To be able to react to violations of a given security policy, one needs to detect such violations in the first place. We acknowledge that violations of security policies may come in many forms, however, for the remainder of this book we subsume such violations under the term of *misuse*. While the history of scientific research on the detection of misuse goes back to the seminal work of Anderson in 1980 [5], only recently software for detecting misuse is widely available and in use. Such software systems are commonly denoted as *intrusion detection systems* (IDSs).[1] While commercial IDS products are available today, they notoriously stay behind the expectations of their users. Hence, research in this area is an ongoing effort of the scientific community that has been strongly intensified during the recent years. Nowadays, there are even two international conferences devoted to this area, annually bringing together leading scientists and experts (RAID[2] since 1998 [57] and DIMVA[3] since 2004 [95]).

---

[1] Commercial vendors nowadays are marketing their software as *intrusion prevention systems* (IPS). This term denotes an IDS that is supposed to respond to detected misuse attempts by disrupting the ongoing misuse attempt. Such automated response is a doubled-edged sword, if it relies on unauthenticated data, possibly resulting in self-inflicted denial of service.

[2] Annual International Symposium on Recent Advances in Intrusion Detection

[3] Annual International Conference on Detection of Intrusions, Malware & Vulnerability Assessment

While today the importance of detecting misuse and appropriately responding to detected misuse is widely acknowledged[4] and many scientists devote their work to better detection capabilities, the interplay of intrusion detection with the privacy of IT system users is largely neglected.

The interplay of intrusion detection and privacy stems from the working principle of IDSs, which observe activity occurring in the IT system, record these observations in *audit data* and analyze the collected audit data to detect misuse. Advanced IDSs search the audit data for certain patterns of audit records, and to do so, must be able to correlate audit records by means of certain features in the audit data. In other words, it is necessary that the IDS can link certain features in distinct audit records by the content of the features. These features are said to be *linkable*.

System activity is mostly driven by user activity, such that observations recorded in audit data almost necessarily document user behavior. As a result of the analysis methods used and certain international standards for generating audit data, this data mostly contains identifying features of the system users. Hence, audit data contains personal data of the system users.

In most western countries personal data is protected by privacy law. Users desire and expect their personal data to be protected against collection and processing, unless authorized by the user himself or by law. Hence, the collection and processing of audit data for intrusion detection conflicts with the expectation and the rights of the system users. This conflict calls for a solution providing an acceptable balance between the privacy of the users and the interests followed by introducing an IDS.

An approach to balancing these interests is replacing identifying features in audit data with *pseudonyms*. The IDS analyzes *pseudonymized* audit data, such that the privacy of the users is not affected. To sustain the IDS's capability to analyze the pseudonymized audit data, a certain amount of linkability must be retained in the audit data, such that audit records can be correlated by means of pseudonymized features. However, the more pseudonyms are (transitively) linkable in the audit data, the larger is the working surface of an attacker to link pseudonyms to some identifying feature or to draw conclusions about the activity of certain users. Hence, it is desirable to reduce *pseudonym linkability*. If pseudonym linkability is technically reduced to the amount necessary for misuse detection w.r.t. to a given set of misuse scenario models, the pseudonym linkability is said to be *technically bound to the purpose of analysis for misuse detection*.

When the IDS detects some misuse, an appropriate response may involve the original identifying features that were concealed by the pseudonyms. The process of recovering the original feature concealed by a pseudonym is denoted as *pseudonym disclosure*. Certainly, it is desirable to allow only the disclosure of the

---

[4] The German Informatics Society (GI) in 2002 even founded the special interest group *Security – Intrusion Detection and Response* (SIDAR) focusing on this topic.

pseudonyms of users, who are involved in a detected misuse scenario. If pseudonym disclosure is technically limited to the pseudonyms involved in a detected misuse scenario, the pseudonym disclosure is said to be *technically bound to the purpose of misuse response*.

Since Fischer-Hübner's seminal work in 1993 [79], which provides a basic approach, no significant progress has been made in this area, despite a growing need for working solutions. Previous work does not reduce pseudonym linkability and notoriously does not limit pseudonym disclosure, alas, rendering the effort of pseudonymization basically useless.

This work is primarily motivated by the urgent need for and the gaping lack of working solutions in this area. This book introduces the concepts of *technical purpose binding* for pseudonym linkability and pseudonym disclosure and presents novel, secure and workable solutions to pseudonymize audit data to be analyzed for privacy respecting misuse detection.

There are basically two fundamentally distinct approaches to intrusion detection, distinguished by the behavior that is modeled as a reference for detecting misuse. If an IDS uses models of normal behavior e.g. of users, programs, or protocols, to detect deviations from these models, then the detection approach is denoted as *anomaly detection*. If an IDS uses models of attacker behavior, i.e. models of *misuse scenarios*, to detect misuse, then the detection approach is denoted as *misuse detection*. The distinguishing properties of these fundamentally different approaches are well understood and documented in detail in many publications, e.g. in the book by Krügel et al. [131]. This book investigates audit data pseudonymization for misuse detection. Similar solutions as proposed in this work may also apply to anomaly detection.

## 1.1 Overview

This book is structured in five parts. The first Part comprises this introduction and provides the background for the technical solutions. The second Part is devoted to presenting a coarse-grained approach for pseudonymizing audit data. The third Part demonstrates how the approach can be applied to audit data of operational systems in practice and describes an implementation. In the fourth Part the soundness of the approach is informally analyzed and the performance of the implementation is experimentally evaluated. After having demonstrated the soundness and usefulness of the coarse-grained approach, a fine-grained approach is developed in the fifth Part. The book concludes with a summary of the key contributions and conclusions.

An appendix provides the necessary background on threshold schemes for cryptographic secret sharing. Several figures in this book use graphical elements of the Unified Modeling Language (UML). The books of Rumbaugh, Jacobson and Booch may serve as a useful reference [21, 192].

**Part I: Background**

The background of this text is introduced step-by-step, while developing an architectural model for secure authorizations. The model is used to derive fundamental requirements for our solutions, and to review related work.

Starting from authorizations in the real/physical world Chap. 2 derives conditions for trust and control for the architectural model, which is developed in Chap. 3. The notion of security captured by the model is examined in Chap. 4, ascertaining that the aspect of user privacy is still poorly supported.

The missing privacy aspects are examined in detail in Chap. 5, and a balance of the conflicting security objective of accountability and of the privacy objective of anonymity is proposed in Chap. 6 on the basis of pseudonyms.

The legal aspects of pseudonyms for the protection of personal data are considered as the foundation for the solutions presented in this book. The main assumptions for analyzing pseudonymized data and for pseudonym disclosure are identified in Chap. 6. Binding pseudonym disclosure to a legal purpose is a central concept for the protection of personal data.

The more technically inclined aspects of pseudonyms are investigated in Chap. 7, introducing the concept of technical purpose binding of pseudonym disclosure and pseudonym linkability. Pseudonyms are integrated with the architectural model in Chap. 8.

For the extended model criteria are derived in Chap. 9, which are used to compare distinct architectures that are possible in the model. An architecture where audit data is pseudonymized after being generated provides a pragmatic and yet secure solution, while coming at low deployment costs when compared to other architectures. The solutions presented in this book leverage this advantageous architecture.

Also, the model is used to review related work, distinguishing loosely and closely related work. Closely related work implements the aforementioned architecture. Chapter 10 compares closely related work, and reviews selected approaches in some detail. Finally, the distinction of our solutions from existing work is distilled in Chap. 10.

**Part II: Set-based Approach**

Part II is devoted to a coarse-grained approach for pseudonymizing audit data, where the pseudonym disclosure is subject to technical purpose binding.

First, in Chap. 11 the assumptions, requirements and the trust model of the approach are derived from Part I. Second, a set-based framework for modeling conditions for the purpose binding of controlled pseudonym disclosure is defined in Chap. 12. Third, Chap. 13 demonstrates how the modeled disclosure conditions can be securely enforced by cryptographic means.

A new problem emerges due to the way we apply a certain cryptographic primitive. The so-called mismatch problem is described, analyzed and solved in Chap. 14. Chapter 15 ties together the developed solutions and informally provides an algorithm implementing the set-based approach. Eventually, Chap. 16 presents extensions to the approach, some of which will be used in Part III.

## Part III: Application to Audit Data

This Part demonstrates how the approach from Part II can be applied to audit data of operational systems in practice.

Chapter 17 gives on overview of the relevant concepts of audit data and of an audit architecture. The widely-used audit service *syslog* is described in the some detail in Chap. 18, and it is shown in Chap. 19 how the approach from Part II can be instantiated for *syslog*-style audit data. An according implementation called *Pseudo/CoRe* has been developed and is briefly described in Chap. 20.

## Part IV: Evaluation

Part IV evaluates the design of the set-based approach and the performance of the implementation *Pseudo/CoRe* from Part II and Part III, respectively.

For the evaluation of the design we use the basic building blocks for anonymity defined in the project *Anonymity and Privacy in Electronic Services* (APES) [71]. In Chap. 21 we introduce the APES project and motivate the use of basic building blocks for anonymity. In Chap. 22 we decompose our design into basic building blocks for anonymity and consider the remaining building blocks for further improvement. The informal evaluation indicates that the design is sound with respect to the given requirements and that it contains no deficiencies.

We also evaluate the performance of the implemented toolset *Pseudo/CoRe*. The performance evaluation in Chap. 23 demonstrates that the implementation is able to handle real-world audit data volumes in practice.

## Part V: Model Refinement

Part V refines the modeling framework for pseudonym disclosure conditions defined in Part II and provides appropriate solutions for audit data pseudonymization. Due to the general nature of the refined modeling framework the results are widely applicable to existing and future misuse scenarios and IDSs.

Two limitations of the coarse-grained pseudonymization approach developed in Part II and implemented in Part III are identified in Chap. 24. It is proposed to develop a superior approach for fine-grained pseudonymization that is tightly bound to models of misuse scenarios used by IDSs.

An appropriate Petri-Net-based framework for modeling misuse scenarios is presented in Chap. 25. Based on a carefully restricted version of the framework an approach to fine-grained audit data pseudonymization is introduced in Chap. 26.

The issues of pseudonym linkability and pseudonym disclosure are investigated in detail in Chap. 27 and Chap. 28, respectively. By exploiting knowledge in given models of misuse scenarios (from the given knowledge-base of an IDS), pseudonym linkability and pseudonym disclosure are tightly tailored to the models and to the analysis algorithm of the IDS.

# 2

# Authorizations

Section 2.1 motivates to examine trust and safeguards for authorizations by using examples from the real, i.e. physical, world in order to develop an analogous model for authorizations in the digital world, starting with an example of real-world authorizations in Sect. 2.2. Necessary conditions for trust and control are considered in Sect. 2.3. The constructions used in Sect. 2.2 are mapped to constructions in the digital world in Sect. 2.4 and elaborated as a model for secure authorizations in Chap. 3.

## 2.1 From the Real World to the Digital World

Many safeguards in the digital world mimic safeguards in the real/physical world. The reason probably is that safeguards are necessary if the actors do not trust each other. However, at the end of the day, trust is finally anchored in the real world.

In the following, we consider trust and safeguards in the real world to understand the models presented in this Part. The models in turn help us to classify and distinguish available privacy-enhancing technologies in the digital world and to infer their properties. While the exposition in the first seven Chapters of this Part has a wide scope, the models are developed to focus on audit data pseudonymization.

## 2.2 Visiting the Zoo – Example Real-world Authorizations

Using an example it is shown how we deal with trust in the real world. In the following, we describe the case of a student who wants to visit the zoo. In the example the zoo serves as a service provider offering free admission to students. Non-students might feel tempted to defraud the zoo by pretending to be a student in order to obtain free admission. Hence, the personnel at the zoo ticket booth is instructed not to trust statements that customers make about their own property as a *student*. For customers it is thus insufficient claiming to be a *student*, also because the ticket booth personnel cannot verify the statement without considering supporting documents. Instead, it is required to show a valid student ID.

The student ID is used as a certified property statement that assigns the name of the subject of the statement to the property *student*. The name of the university is stated as the agent that is responsible for the correct assignment. An embedded picture indicates that the subject name actually is the name of the person visually matching the person on the picture. Finally, the property statement comprises information regarding its validity, e.g. expiry, and features of genuineness that are expensive to counterfeit. At the ticket booth a certified property statement is accepted, if: it is a student ID, as a matter of policy the issuing university is trusted to generate useful property statements, the person on the picture visually matches the presenting person, the student ID has not yet expired and looks "genuine".

If the student ID is accepted at the ticket booth, the presenting person is authorized to pass the zoo entrance. The presenting person receives the service-specific property *authorized for zoo entrance*. At the zoo entrance, again, it is insufficient claiming to be *authorized for zoo entrance*. The lack of trust, again, is reasonable, since anyone could defraud the zoo by cheating in order to pass the entrance for free. Therefore customers that are *authorized for zoo entrance* receive an admission ticket at the ticket booth. This authorization comprises a ticket number, the statement that it *authorizes for zoo entrance*, identifies the issuing ticket booth, validity information, such as features of genuineness that are expensive to counterfeit[1] and expiry. The ticket is accepted at the zoo entrance if: the stated ticket booth is trusted to issue tickets only to persons that are *authorized for zoo entrance*, the ticket number looks "plausible", the ticket authorizes to pass the zoo entrance, it has not yet expired and looks "genuine". Note, that the ticket contains no information to authenticate the presenting person, i.e. it is transferable. Further possibilities for cheating are hinted at by the apostrophes ("...").

If the admission ticket is accepted at the zoo entrance, the student may enter the zoo. Right in the front is a sign that specifies behavior that is by policy prohibited in the zoo. Most notably, it is prohibited to tease the monkeys, since they may take revenge using banana peel projectiles. It is highly unlikely that anyone will responsibly certify that the student will avoid all prohibited behavior, i.e. that the student has the property *policy-compliant-behavior*. Thus, for the time being, the zoo trusts that the visitors stick to the rules. At critical areas (at the monkey

---

[1] That is, the cost of counterfeiting the validity information is higher than the admission price.

house) the zoo may put a guard in place. The guard observes the behavior of the visitors and reacts if he detects a violation of the zoo policy.

## 2.3 Trust and Control

Section 2.2 describes two situations where service-specific *givers* (here: zoo ticket booth, zoo entrance) give something. The process of giving is subject to conditions over properties as defined by the policy of the giver (here: *student, authorized for zoo entrance*). If the *taker* can put the *giver* at a disadvantage by cheating w.r.t. the properties required by the *giver*, the *giver* cannot rely on the respective property statements of the *taker*. Instead, the *giver* wishes to verify by himself the required properties of the *taker*. Only then he knows that the *taker* enjoys the required property, and the *giver* himself can assign the property to the *taker*. In case the *giver* cannot carry out the verification by himself, he needs to trust a third party (here: university, zoo ticket booth) to carry out the verification, to assign the property statement to the *taker* and to provide it with features of genuineness that are expensive to counterfeit (here: student ID, admission ticket), i.e. to responsibly certify the property statement. Using appropriate property statements the third party trusted by the *giver* may delegate the verification and certification to other parties that it trusts. Delegation and licensing are not within the scope of this text, however, they integrate seamlessly with the models we present [18, 19, 125].

Since the *taker* may be interested in corrupting the process of certification, he must not be able to control the trusted third party. Specifically, only the trusted third party must be able to provide the property statements that it certifies with features of genuineness. If these requirements are satisfied, the *giver* can trust that the required property in a certified property statement exists and is correctly assigned to the *taker*.

In some environments or applications it is impossible or not intended to employ property verification preventively, e.g. to enforce compliance of behavior with a certain policy. In these environments or applications, taking will be prohibited or sanctioned if the property *policy-compliant-behavior* is violated. That is, for the time being, the *giver* needs to trust that the *taker* enjoys the required property and he may observe (here: guard) the *taker's* behavior at critical areas (here: monkey house) to detect violations of the policy.

## 2.4 Real-World Counterparts in the Digital World

In the digital world the preventive property verification using certified property statements corresponds to access control, e.g. using a public key infrastructure

(PKI). Also in the digital world it is not always useful or possible to preventively verify all properties, such as policy compliance of behavior of the users or processes of an IT system. However, the IT system can record the observable behavior in the form of audit data, which can be analyzed w.r.t. policy violations, e.g. using intrusion detection systems (IDS) [147, 3, 6].

# 3

---

# An Architectural Model for Secure
# Authorizations

Chapter 2 motivated trust issues and safeguards for authorizations in the digital world. In this Chapter an appropriate architectural model for secure authorizations is presented. The notion of security supported by the model is further examined in Chap. 4.

In the following, an architectural model for secure authorizations is introduced. The model generalizes from the hybrid PKI model of Biskup and Karabulut [18, 19, 125] by abstracting from PKI-specific technology. The exposition focuses on the parties that are communicating directly with the service user. Licensing, delegation and the various modes of interaction, as defined by Biskup and Karabulut, are not described, they work just as in the hybrid PKI model [18, 19, 125]. The model for secure authorizations is already prepared for the extensions we make for pseudonymization in Chap. 8.

In the digital world neither the corresponding entities of the real world, nor their properties are visible. Therefore *entities* (see Sect. 3.1) of the real world are represented by so-called *principals* in the digital world, and their real *properties* (see Sect. 3.2) are encoded by *property attributes* that are visible in the digital world. The relationship between an entity and its properties is expressed by *property statements* in the digital world (see Sect. 3.3), where the *validity* of the association of a principal with a property attribute is based on cryptography and on private parameters of the agent that is responsible for the certification of each property statement (*responsible agent*). The *authentication* of the presenter of a property statement, i.e. the process of verifying that the *subject* of a property statement corresponds to its presenter, is based on cryptography and on private parameters of the subject. At the end of the day, the question whether a digital property statement really represents properties of an entity in the real world, can only be decided w.r.t. individually and subjectively justified belief, i.e. *trust* enjoyed by the responsible agent.

The basic model for authorization architectures and the corresponding control requirements are introduced in Sect. 3.4, as well as the verification of and references to property statements. In the same Section, the model, the three phases of service utilization and the accompanying property attribute conversion are described in detail. Finally, in Sect. 3.5 some versions of the basic model are motivated by example architectures that are relevant in practice.

## 3.1 Entities and Properties

In the proposed model individuals, computers and other players in a distributed IT system are denoted as *entities*. A *principal* is a bit string that is unique within its scope of application and it is associated with an entity to serve as its surrogate. An entity can enjoy *properties*, which in turn may be used in conditions in authorization policies, and are taken into account during the trust evaluation. Biskup and Karabulut distinguish characterizing and administrative properties [18, 125] (see Fig. 3.1). While the first characterize the users, the latter describe the responsible agents in the case of licensing and delegation. Administrative properties and corresponding property attributes, as well as property statements are not considered here, they integrate with the authorization model as described by Biskup and Karabulut [18, 19, 125].

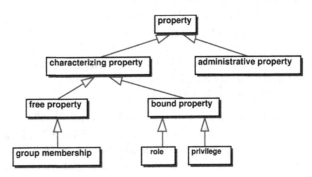

**Fig. 3.1.** A classification of properties (cf. Fig. 3.5)

## 3.2 Certification and Authorization

According to Biskup and Karabulut [18, 125], we can classify characterizing properties as free and as bound properties. (see Fig. 3.1).

*Free properties* are enjoyed by entities independently of any services, e.g. personal data, technical features, abilities, (group-)memberships, etc. A free property does not directly express a service-specific authorization. The terms *certification* and *certificate* in the model denote the process and the result, respectively, when a responsible agent certifies a statement about free properties in its role as a *certifier*. In Sect. 2.2 the student ID is a certificate, which expresses the certified statement about the free property *student*.

*Bound properties* express an authorization relationship between an entity and a specific service, e.g. the zoo admission ticket. Thus, bound properties are specific to a certain service and they imply a specific authorization to use that service, e.g. by means of an authorizing role. In the model the term *authorization* denotes the process and the result, when a responsible agent certifies a statement about bound properties in its role as an *authorizer*. In Sect. 2.2 the zoo admission ticket is an authorization, which expresses the certified statement about the bound property *authorized for zoo entrance*.

## 3.3 Property Statements

A *responsible agent* (cf. Sect. 2.3, here the university or the zoo ticket booth) verifies that a *subject* entity enjoys certain properties and certifies a statement under one of his own principals, such that the statement assigns a principal of the subject to property attributes that correspond to the verified properties of the subject. The association of the subject principal with the presenting entity is verifiable by means of authentication data. A property statement also contains verifiable data concerning the validity of the statement, where the data can only be generated by the responsible agent and practically cannot be counterfeited. Note, that certified property statements come in different forms, such as static documents (e.g. certificates [18]) or as traces of interactive protocols (e.g. anonymous credentials [34]).

A property statement comprises the following *components* (see Fig. 3.2 and Fig. 3.3):

responsible agent: a principal of the entity, which is responsible for verifying that the subject entity enjoys the properties under consideration and that the subject principal belongs to the subject entity. This component indicates the responsible agent to the recipient of the statement.[1] If the recipient trusts this agent (see 'trust expression' in Fig. 3.7), he can trust that the agent correctly set the following associations up:

- the subject principal is correctly associated with an entity;
- the entity actually enjoys the properties that are expressed by the property attributes.

---

[1] The agent component may be omitted, if the responsible agent is known, e.g. if the property statement is directly received from the responsible agent via an authenticated channel (see 'A4' in Fig. 3.9 and 'A3' in Fig. 3.12, as well as 'C1' in Fig. 3.10, 'B3' in Fig. 3.11 and 'C1' in Fig. 3.12).

Additionally, this component can be used as a reference to property statements about the responsible agent. In more complex scenarios these property statements need to be considered for licensing and delegation [18].

validity: public parameters for cryptography. This component allows to verify the validity of the property statement and of its technical features, such as guaranteed uniqueness, transferability, the ability to disclose hidden information, etc. (see Sect. 7.4).[2] The verification may be carried out on demand using an online protocol, or it may be carried out offline, such as for referenced property statements. The validity component must be generated using private parameters of the responsible agent, such that the component can only be generated by the responsible agent.

authentication: public parameters for cryptography. This component serves as a proof that the property statement belongs to the presenting entity.[3] The proof is usually generated using an online protocol. The authentication component must be generated using private parameters of the subject entity as well as fresh challenge values chosen by the recipient, such that the component can only be generated by the subject entity as an individual answer to the individual challenge values.

attributes: expressing the set of properties enjoyed by the subject entity, about which a statement is made.[4] This component supports the decision process of the recipient, based on his security policy (see 'property attribute expression' in Fig. 3.7).

subject: a principal of the subject entity (also denoted as *subject principal*). This component supports the linkability of different transactions that correspond to the same property statement (see 'query context' in Fig. 3.8), e.g. to establish reputation that is associated with this principal.[5]

To be able to generate the authentication and validity components, private parameters of some parties must be used. We assume that the private parameters

---

[2] The validity component may be omitted, if the property statement is received directly from the responsible agent via an authenticated and secure channel (see 'A4' in Fig. 3.9 and 'A3' in Fig. 3.12, as well as 'C1' in Fig. 3.10, 'B3' in Fig. 3.11 and 'C1' in Fig. 3.12).

[3] The authentication component may be omitted, if the presenting entity has already been authenticated by a responsible agent, which sends the property statement together with the service request via a secure channel to the service (see 'C1' in Fig. 3.10 and Fig. 3.12). In that case the service trusts the responsible agent for the correct authentication of the presenting entity.

[4] The attributes component may be omitted, if the responsible agent always certifies the same a priori known set of properties.

[5] The subject component is always included, if a property statement needs to be referenced (see Sect. 3.4.2) (see 'A4' in Fig. 3.9 and 'B3' in Fig. 3.11). It may be omitted if the property statement is not referenced and if the property statement does not need to be linkable.

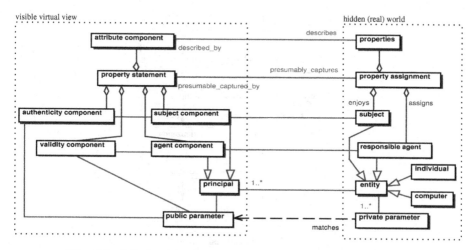

**Fig. 3.2.** Relationships between property statements and entities

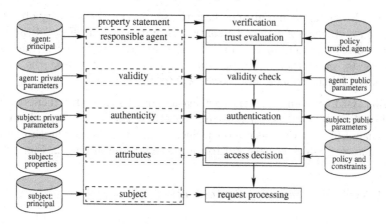

**Fig. 3.3.** Verification of property statements

have been securely distributed beforehand and are appropriately safeguarded. Similar assumptions hold for the public parameters used for the verification of the authentication and validity components.

## 3.4 Architectures and Control Requirements

From Sect. 3.3 follows that the components of certified property statements primarily support security objectives of the service providers. Considering this together with the implications from Sect. 2.3 we require that the user as subject entity must not be able to control the certification, the authorization and the service. Accordingly the fat light grey frames in Fig. 3.4 (and Fig. 3.9 to Fig. 3.12)

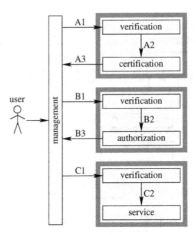

**Fig. 3.4.** Basic model

enclose the system components where the service-related security objectives are enforced and which must not be controlled by the user. In Fig. 3.4 (and Fig. 3.9 to Fig. 3.12) the solid arrows indicate the flow of certified or verified property statements, or of their corresponding references.[6] In the text the arrows are referenced by their identifiers (here: 'A1' to 'C2').

Section 3.4.1 explains how the verification of property statements works (see 'verification' in Fig. 3.4), whereas Sect. 3.4.2 describes how references to property statements fit into the basic model. Section 3.4.3 examines the three phases of service access, which correspond to the three fat grey frames in Fig. 3.4.

### 3.4.1 Verifying Property Statements

In the basic model depicted in Fig. 3.4 the recipient of a certified property statement verifies the statement (see 'verification' in Fig. 3.4) starting with determining the responsible agent (see 'certification' or 'authorization' in Fig. 3.4) from the homonymous component of the statement. First, the recipient decides whether he trusts the agent w.r.t. the verification of the properties expressed by the attributes component and w.r.t. the correct association of the property attributes to the principal of the entity which enjoys the corresponding properties (see 'trust evaluation' in Fig. 3.3 and 'trust base' in Fig. 3.7). Subsequently, the recipient determines by means of the validity component, whether the property statement is valid (see 'validity check' in Fig. 3.3). Then, the recipient authenticates the presenting entity using the authentication component, i.e., he checks whether the presenting entity corresponds to the subject component (see 'authentication' in Fig. 3.3). Eventually, the recipient interprets the property attributes

---

[6] We assume that the service answer does not include statements about the properties enjoyed by the user. Hence, the service answers are not shown in the model.

according to his policy (see 'access decision' in Fig. 3.3 and 'property attribute conversion' in Fig. 3.7).

### 3.4.2 Referencing Property Statements

In the versions of the model depicted in Fig. 3.9 and in Fig. 3.11 the user obtains merely a reference to a property statement (see 'A3' in Fig. 3.9 and 'B4' in Fig. 3.11) that he forwards to the recipient (see 'B1' in Fig. 3.9 and 'C1' in Fig. 3.11). A property statement reference comprises the following components:

subject: subject principal of the corresponding property statement.

supply: information, where the corresponding property statement can be obtained.[7]

The recipient receives the referenced property statement from the responsible agent (see 'A4' in Fig. 3.9 and 'B3' in Fig. 3.11).[8]

### 3.4.3 Phases and Property Attribute Conversion

The players depicted in Fig. 3.4 (and in Fig. 3.9 to Fig. 3.12) are the user-side management, a certifier, an authorizer and a service.

The utilization of a service can be broken down into the following three phases:

1. The user has his relevant properties certified (see 'A1', 'A2' and 'A3' in Fig. 3.4).
2. Presenting his relevant certificates the user is authorized for the utilization of the service (see 'B1', 'B2' and 'B3' in Fig. 3.4).
3. Presenting the authorization the user can utilize the service (see 'C1' und 'C2' in Fig. 3.4).

This sequence of phases can be regarded as a multi-level conversion of property attributes (see Fig. 3.6). Accordingly, property attributes can be classified in analogy to Fig. 3.1, with the supplement that convertible attributes and finally bound property attributes are distinguished (see Fig. 3.5).

---

[7] The supply component may be omitted, if the supplier is known a priori.

[8] If the recipient obtains the corresponding property statement via an authenticated and secure channel, and if the recipient trusts in the security of the responsible agent and supplier, the responsible agent component and the validity component may be omitted from the property statement (see 'A4' in Fig. 3.9 and 'A3' in Fig. 3.12, as well as 'C1' in Fig. 3.10, 'B3' in Fig. 3.11 and 'C1' in Fig. 3.12).

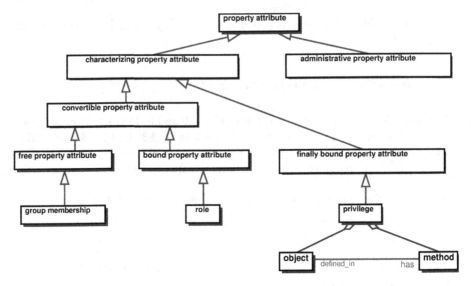

**Fig. 3.5.** A classification of property attributes (cf. Fig. 3.1)

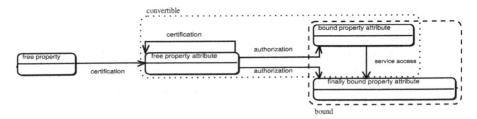

**Fig. 3.6.** Converting property attributes (see Fig. 3.5)

## Management

The management is controlled by the user. It interacts with other players, and based on the policy of the user, and aiming at satisfying the requirements of the service or responsible agent (see the policies in Fig. 3.3 as well as 'property attribute expression' and 'trust expression' in Fig. 3.7), it chooses property statements and information that are/is suitable for the respective interaction.

## Certifier

The certifier usually operates independently of the services. It associates free properties to users by issuing certificates (see 'free property attribute' in Fig. 3.7). The policy of the certifier expresses the conditions that must be met by the user for certification (see 'property attribute expression' in Fig. 3.7). On the one hand, the certifier may convince himself in the real world that the user enjoys the required properties (see 'free property' in Fig. 3.6). On the other hand, the certifier may accept a certificate that has been issued by another certifier (see 'free property attribute' in Fig. 3.7) and may infer that the user enjoys the property to be certified (see 'property attribute conversion' in Fig. 3.7). The certifier issues a certificate (see the arrows labeled with 'certification' in Fig. 3.6), which does not necessarily need to be represented digitally. Where appropriate, the subject obtains merely a reference to the certificate (see Fig. 3.9).

**Authorizer**

On behalf of the service the authorizer associates the user with service-specific authorizations (see '(finally) bound property attribute' in Fig. 3.7). Accordingly, a service is usually closer related to the authorizer than to any certifier. The policy of the authorizer expresses the conditions that must be met by the user for authorization (see 'property attribute expression' in Fig. 3.7). On the one hand, the authorizer may accept certificates about free property attributes (see 'free property attribute' in Fig. 3.7). On the other hand, the authorizer may interpret and accept bound property attributes as free property attributes that are bound to other services. The authorizer converts (see 'property attribute conversion' in Fig. 3.7) the acceptable free property attributes into service-specifically bound property attributes, e.g. into roles, which the service finally binds to privileges, or into property attributes that are already finally bound to privileges, such as capabilities. Subsequently, the authorizer grants an authorization to the user (see the arrows labeled with 'authorization' in Fig. 3.6),[9] which is always digitally represented, because the service needs to verify it in the digital world. Where appropriate, the subject obtains merely a reference to the authorization (see Fig. 3.11).

In the case where all required certified property statements are digitally available and the authorization can be decided digitally, the authorizer may forward the authorization together with the user's service request via a secure and authenticated channel directly to the service (see 'C1' in Fig. 3.10 and Fig. 3.12).[10] From the user's point of view the authorizer and service appear to be merged into one entity.

---

[9] An authorizer may interpret bound property attributes as free property attributes, and it may convert them into (finally) bound property attributes. Before conversion, in Fig. 3.6 the property attributes are interpreted from the point of view of the converting entity. Hence, in Fig. 3.6 exists no authorization arrow starting from bound property attributes, since these are interpreted as free property attributes during the authorization.

[10] If the service trusts the authorizer to correctly authenticate the user, then in addition to the validity and responsible agent component also the authentication component may be omitted from the authorization.

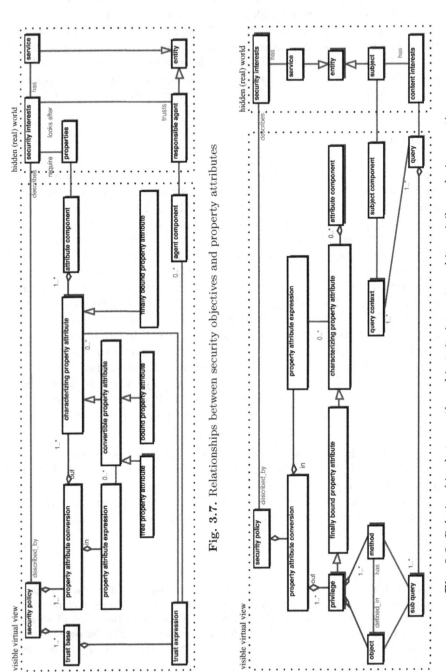

**Fig. 3.7.** Relationships between security objectives and property attributes

**Fig. 3.8.** Relationships between the subject, its interests and its privileges during run time

**Service**

The service may receive the authorization and the service request/query (see 'attribute component' and 'query' in Fig. 3.8) simultaneously or at different times. The security policy of the service expresses the conditions that must be met by the user for service utilization (see 'security policy' in Fig. 3.8). The service accepts (digital) authorizations and may check additional conditions that do not refer to the authorizations as such, e.g. conditions w.r.t. the time stamp of the reception of an authorization. The authorizations have the form of capabilities and privileges, respectively (see 'finally bound property attribute' in Fig. 3.7), which the service compares with the requested access privileges (see 'privilege' and 'sub query' in Fig. 3.8).

Alternatively, the service receives service-specifically bound property attributes (see 'characterizing property attribute' in Fig. 3.8) and converts them according to its policy into corresponding privileges (see 'privilege' and 'property attribute conversion' in Fig. 3.8).

## 3.5 Example Architectures

In the following, we indicate how the model maps to existing systems by giving some well-known examples.

The basic model as given in Fig. 3.4 can be used to model the authorization architecture of Kerberos (as described by Gollmann [107], Sect. 10.2.1): The management corresponds to the client, the certifier corresponds to the *authentication server*, the authorizer corresponds to the *ticket granting server*, and finally the service corresponds to the server.

The upper part of Fig. 3.9 can be used to model the deferred acquiring of a certificate, such as it occurs when an email user agent asks a PKI directory for the signature verification key certificate required for verifying the digital signature in an email (see 'A4' in Fig. 3.9). Note, that the certification part in Fig. 3.9 may also be combined with the model versions in Fig. 3.10 and Fig. 3.11.

As depicted in Fig. 3.10 the authorizer and the service may be merged. The user sends his service request together with the required certificates to the authorizer/service (see 'B1' in Fig. 3.10). This version models the data sources of an information mediator [18].

The model version depicted in Fig. 3.11 can be used to model the password-based authorization that is traditionally wide-spread in practice. Based on the certificate about his organizational affiliation (see 'B1' in Fig. 3.11) the user obtains from the IT system administrator (authorizer) the reference to his authorization in the form of an account name (subject principal, see 'B4' in Fig. 3.11). The authorization comprises the components 'subject', 'authentication' and 'attributes'

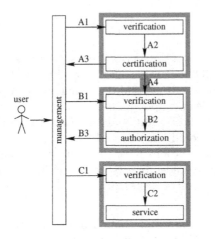

**Fig. 3.9.** The authorizer obtains a referenced certificate

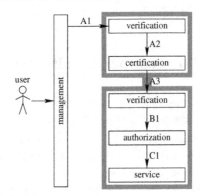

**Fig. 3.11.** The authorizer sends an authorization to the service

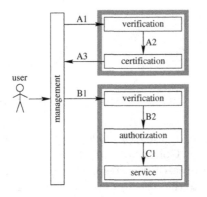

**Fig. 3.10.** The authorizer forwards the service request together with the authorization to the service

**Fig. 3.12.** The certifier forwards the service request together with the certificate to the authorizer

and is directly brought into the IT system (service) by the administrator (see 'B3' in Fig. 3.11). The private parameter for authentication is the password that the administrator initially entrusts the user with.

In the model version depicted in Fig. 3.12 the certifier could model an IPSEC node that receives IP packets (service requests) from the user and that provides them with an authentication header (certificate). The authentication header comprises the components 'responsible agent', 'validity' and 'subject'. By doing so, the IPSEC node certifies that the request (or better: packet) originates from within the address range for which it is authoritative. If the destination node receives the IP packet, its IPSEC stack verifies the authentication header (authorizer) and may or may not allow the IP packet to be handed upwards in the TCP/IP stack towards the addressed process (service).

# 4

# Traditional Security Objectives

In Chap. 3 a model for secure authorizations was introduced. The notion of security captured by this model supports requirements of users and service providers. IT systems and the services they are hosting need to meet certain expectations regarding dependability, safety and security. In the following, we consider traditional security objectives, such as confidentiality, accountability, availability, etc. The high-level definitions of security objectives are commonly known, for example from textbooks by Gollmann [107], Sect. 1.1 or Eckert [72], Sect. 1.2. While the notions captured by the various definitions may vary in detail, here we are rather concerned with the expectations of people w.r.t. IT services on a higher lever.

Section 4.1 roughly describes the high-level expectations of service users and how they motivate security objectives of the service providers. The intrinsic security objectives of service providers are described in Sect. 4.2, and how they may go further than users would like them to. For this text, the focus of security is narrowed down to audit data for misuse detection in Sect. 4.3. Section 4.3.1 describes the common use of audit data in practice.

The privacy aspects of security, particularly w.r.t. audit data, and the conflict between traditional security objectives of service providers are examined in detail in Chap. 5.

## 4.1 Expectations of Users

The users of an IT service expect that the service is provided in a dependable and secure way, such that the service is always available and delivers the results according to the functionality as announced by the service provider. The users expect that the service works properly, regardless of possible threats, such as malfunctions of parts of the system, deliberate attacks or human error. This high-level expectation of users translates to the task of the service providers, to take appropriate measures, such that their service is eligible to be used by people. The service providers will not only follow these high-level objectives to please their users, naturally the providers also are inherently interested in protecting their systems and investments.

On the one hand, service providers are interested in the same security objective as their users. On the other hand, the security objectives of the service providers may go further than that and might conflict with further security requirements of the users, in particular with their expectations regarding privacy and protection of their personal data.

## 4.2 Requirements of Providers

As stated in Sect. 4.1, the provider of a service is interested in certain security objectives to protect his investments and business. The providers use preventive safeguards to reduce vulnerabilities and to avoid threats. Exemplary safeguards are firewalls and virtual private networks, i.e. access control and cryptography, respectively.

The preventive nature of many safeguards is illustrated in the following, using the example of access control based on property statements (see Sect. 3.3). In many situations trust relationships are established in the real world, but represented and evaluated in the digital world (see 'responsible agent' component in Sect. 3.3). Before a property statement is accepted, its validity is verified (see 'validity' component in Sect. 3.3), and it is verified, whether it is the subject of the statement, who presents the statement (see 'authentication' component in Sect. 3.3). When a property statement has been verified, the properties represented by the statement are matched against the access policy (see 'attributes' component in Sect. 3.3).

As far as these preventive safeguards are concerned, they protect the security interests of both, the service providers and the users. However, as in the real world, preventive safeguards in the digital world do not shield IT systems from all digital threats. It is therefore useful to be able to detect system compromises and to collect sufficient data about the situation to be able to react appropriately.

It could be argued that collecting data to improve the system protection is also in the interest of the users. Considering the linkability of property statements as an example (see 'subject' component in Sect. 3.3), the linkability could be used to analyze service accesses w.r.t. misuse, or it could be used to establish a reputation system. The users surely appreciate the additional security and the information about the reliability of potential business partners.

Nowadays, property statements are usually tied to some person-identifying feature, such as the name of the subject of the statement. Thus, information collected about service activity and user activity clearly is personal data. If personal data of users is collected, the individual rights of the users and the potential of misuse of personal data must be weighted against the criticality of the service and the effects of its failure. While for some very critical services the users would accept that their personal data is collected, for other services this would not be the case. Also, the users might not know, what data is collected about them and how it is used (possibly against them).

In a time when customer relationship management (CRM) also includes the notion of collecting, analyzing and exploiting consumer profiles, it is not far-fetched, if users suspect that their personal data might not only be used to pursue the user's security objectives, but also to realize far more extensive objectives of the service provider, which are in conflict with the user's desire for privacy. These issues are discussed in Chap. 5.

Data about user activity can be collected at various layers of an IT system. Most operating systems already provide for such data collection at the system level in the form of audit data. Intrusion detection systems instrument the system with probes to collect further audit data. The focus of this book is on audit data for misuse detection. In Sect. 4.3 and Sect. 4.3.1 audit data and its uses are introduced.

## 4.3 Surveillance Using Audit Data

To detect misuse or malfunctions of a service, one needs to collect and analyze information describing the relevant and current behavior of the service. Such data is often called monitoring data, log data or audit data. In the following we use the term audit data also synonymously for monitoring data and log data. *Audit data* is the data that a service (possibly instrumented with a probe) collects about activity, which is observable in the system, and which is relevant for the purpose of audit data analysis. See Sect. 12.1.1 for a more technically inclined definition of audit data as an ordered set of audit records describing events. Example *syslog* audit data is given in Sect. 18.1, and Sect. 19.1 shows how abstract events, as defined in Sect. 12.1.1, map to *syslog* audit data.

Most modern operating systems offer comparable audit components, e.g. AIX, BSDs, HP-UX, Linux, Solaris, Windows-NT and its descendants. All of these record the identity of the originator of an event or at least identifying features of users [75, 178]. Audit components specifically designed for compliance with the Trusted Computer System Evaluation Criteria (TCSEC) (C2 or higher) [37, 38] or the Common Criteria (FAU_GEN1.2 and FAU_GEN2) [53] are required to record information identifying the originator of an event. Hence, all of these audit components record personal data. The implications for user privacy are discussed in Sect. 5.7 and Sect. 5.4.3 considering German privacy law.

Many IDSs leverage audit data provided by the operating system. To complement their view of the current situation, IDSs instrument the service system with probes and collect additional audit data, e.g. from the TCP/IP stack or from the network interfaces. IDSs analyze the audit data in an automated fashion and control what audit data is retained and what is discarded. In addition, most service providers collect and archive extensive amounts of audit data also for manual inspection, e.g. for after-the-fact forensics, or just "to be on the safe side" in the case of litigation. Section 4.3.1 describes the most common security-related objectives that service providers follow, when collecting audit data.

### 4.3.1 Audit Data Related Security Objectives of Providers in Practice

A study of the US National Science Foundation (NSF) [183, 184] yields that audit data is collected and analyzed in practice to provide secure (44%), efficient and stable services. In nearly all surveyed organizations audit data was collected for these reasons (96%). The majority of the service providers would like to collect even more (detailed) audit data (59%). From the perspective of the service providers this does not happen due to lack of time (57.7%), insufficient technical resources (50%) and other factors (38.5%), but only a small proportion of service providers accounts this to organizational data processing policies (11.5%), personal ethical principles (9.6%), or pertinent law (7.7%). Most providers tailor audit data collection to their local needs w.r.t. searching and analysis (82%).

Facing suspected misuse, nearly half of the service providers have already monitored their users without informing them and without a priori having requested the users' permission to do so (42%). Nearly all service providers archive audit data for later forensics or to be able to provide a stable system (82%). Roughly a quarter of all service providers keeps archived audit data for longer than two months (22%).

# 5

## Personal Data Protection Objectives

In the preceding Chapters the exposition was focused on the security objectives of the service providers. As motivated in Chap. 4, such safeguards are also in the interest of the service users. In particular, the users can benefit from the reliability of secure services. In the following, the perspective is extended to also comprise the user requirements for personal data protection, particularly pseudonymity, serving the right to *informational self-determination*.

Section 5.1 motivates the need for privacy or personal data protection in the digital world. Section 5.2 distinguishes the protection of privacy or personal data from rather traditional security objectives. Protection of privacy or personal data is expected by the users (see Sect. 5.3) and required by pertinent law. Section 5.4 scratches the surface of the legal aspects and concepts for the protection of privacy or personal data. Section 5.5 motivates, why laws and user expectations alone are not sufficient for privacy protection. Section 5.6 surveys the principles for technical enforcement of the protection of privacy or personal data. Section 5.7 argues that safeguards are a double-edged sword and investigates this aspect for audit data. In Chap. 6 a notion of multilateral security is developed w.r.t. audit data, integrating traditional security objectives and privacy objectives.

## 5.1 Why Personal Data Protection?

In the digital world the importance of privacy related security objectives is growing. First, on-demand services in contrast to broadcast services need to understand the information needs of their users; so the users disclose them to the on-demand service. Second, compared to business transactions in the real world, in the digital world more parties are involved in the transactions, which can draw inferences from the personal data of the users. Third, in the digital world the threat of unnoticed passive eavesdropping (of personal data) is increased compared to the real world. Finally, digitally captured personal data can be efficiently and arbitrarily stored, processed and correlated with data from other parties.

Today, users already leave a multitude of traces when accessing services in the digital world [207]. Some parties such as Internet service providers or web email service providers already have access to the personal data of very large user populations. Large scale surveillance of activity in the digital world could be installed much more cost-efficiently than surveillance of activity that remains in the real world, but outside the digital world. In fact, currently there is a trend in many EU member states to oblige telecommunication providers to collect and retain telecommunication data, such that it can be efficiently retrieved by law enforcement agencies [69, 198].

## 5.2 Distinction from Traditional Security Objectives

There is a noteworthy difference between traditional security requirements (e.g. integrity) and privacy requirements for personal data protection. This difference can be illustrated using an exemplary message being sent from a sender to a recipient. Many traditional security objectives consider attackers as a third party, which has no established relationship with the sender or the recipient/processor of the message. This attacker model assumes in particular that the attacker is unknown to the victims. In contrast, personal data usually is (possibly necessarily) disclosed within the scope of accessing some service. In that case, the attacker model includes the recipient of the personal data, which usually is known to the sender.

The preventive effect of the pertinent legislation can be assumed to be low w.r.t. unknown attackers or attackers, with no interest in sustaining a relationship with the victim. Consequently, technical safeguards that are controlled by the potential victims are considered a high priority. As for traditional security objectives, such safeguards are also useful for the protection of personal data. However, some services inherently require the disclosure of personal data, such that the data is available to a potential attacker, i.e. the service as the recipient. Yet, in this case the service is keen not to impair his relationship with the sender, e.g. by his own misconduct. Moreover, the recipient or attacker is known, whereby the legal momentum gains additional significance.

Summarizing, the legitimate recipient of personal data is motivated to protect the personal data in the interest of sustaining a good relationship with the data subject and to avoid sanctions. As a result, to be able to comply with the user expectations, the recipient needs to provide technical safeguards, even though from the view of the sender such safeguards are less preferable than sender-controlled safeguards. When comparing sender- and recipient-controlled safeguards, we find that the latter exhibit specific advantages, such as cost-efficient deployment (see Sect. 9.1).

Thus, alongside with the customer relationship management the privacy law poses a considerable motivation for the service providers to deal with technical measures for the protection of personal data. In the following, both sides will be examined. Specifically for the statutory aspects this book takes a technological point of view and cannot provide legal advice.

## 5.3 Expectations of Users

In the real world we find several socially accepted anonymous services, such as anonymous hotlines for counseling and advice, anonymous elections, anonymous telephone calls using cash or pre-paid cards in phone booths, and last but not least, anonymous purchase of merchandise by using cash. People expect to be able to carry out these transactions anonymously also in the digital world. Several studies demonstrate that Internet users and customers value their privacy also in the digital world [163, 179, 1, 116, 189, 39].

Consequently, the lack of anonymous access alternatives can keep users from accessing a service. The majority of customers would not use recent technologies, if they had to risk that their personal data would be collected and processed for other purposes than agreed upon beforehand [65]. Another study concludes that more users would conduct commercial transaction in the digital world, if the services could be accessed under pseudonyms [114].

The users predominantly look favorably upon the concept of *anonymity on the Internet* and associate it with the protection of personality and freedom [31]. This is also reflected by the strong concern about third party surveillance and profiling [179, 31]. Nevertheless, merely 4% to 5% of the respondents use an anonymization service, which can presumably be attributed to a lack of information [31, 179]. The percentage of users that would use an anonymization service increased to 76%, after the users looked into the subject in the course of the survey [31]. A further survey shows that the usage of anonymization services already faded to the daily routine of sophisticated users with the intent of avoiding profiling by providers of the services that they access via the anonymization service [208].

## 5.4 Requirements of Pertinent Legislation

In the following, the relevant terms, concepts and principles for the design of technical safeguards for the protection of personal data are introduced, specifically with a focus on pseudonymous authorizations and audit data. Section 5.4.1 introduces the terms of privacy and informational self-determination. The fundamental concepts generally in use for protecting privacy are described in Sect. 5.4.2.

Section 5.4.3 examines audit data related issues in German privacy law, whereas Sect. 5.4.4 briefly comments on the broader perspective of harmonizing the privacy law of member states of the European Union.

### 5.4.1 The Right to Informational Self-determination

The first know vague definition of *privacy* was given by Warren and Brandeis: "the right to be alone" [220]. The most common definition of privacy in current use is the one by Westin and it already suggests a notion of informational self-determination: "Privacy is the claim of individuals [...] to determine for themselves, when, how and to what extent information about them is communicated to others" [222]. In this text the informational aspect of privacy is focused, particularly as it is postulated in the so-called Census Decision (CD, Volkszählungsurteil in German) of the German Federal Constitutional Court (Bundesverfassungsgericht in German) as a right to informational self-determination [66].

In this book we often refer to German law related to privacy because it strongly influenced the European directive 95/46/EC [76]. The objective of this directive is the harmonization of the law of EU member states concerning privacy (see Sect. 5.4.4). Fischer-Hübner provides a broader and at the same time more detailed survey on privacy laws [80].

The right to informational self-determination is derived (see C II 1a in CD [66]) from the basic rights of human dignity (Art. 1 (1) German Constitution, Grundgesetz/GG in German [28]) and the right to free development of personality (Art. 2 (1) GG [28]), so that it forms one of the highest legal values. It permits the individual to determine on principle himself on the disclosure and use of his personal information.

### 5.4.2 Fundamental Concepts of Personal Data Protection

The constitutional right to informational self-determination cannot be considered to be unlimited or absolute, since it can be in conflict with other rights or legal values (see Chap. 6). Also, it seems hardly possible to participate in society without revealing any personal information.

As a result, exemptions from this right are assigned for *legal purposes* that are in a predominant public interest. Being restrictions of the right to informational self-determination (s. C II 2 in CD [66]), exemptions have to be permitted by a constitutional law, which, according to the *principle of the rule of law*, must follow the *principle of clarity of the law* and the *principle of proportionateness* (s. C II 1b in CD [66]). That is, according to the principle of clarity of the law, any restricting law has to make clear under which conditions and to what extent restrictions on the constitutional right are permitted. According to the principle of proportionateness, a measure affecting a constitutional right must be

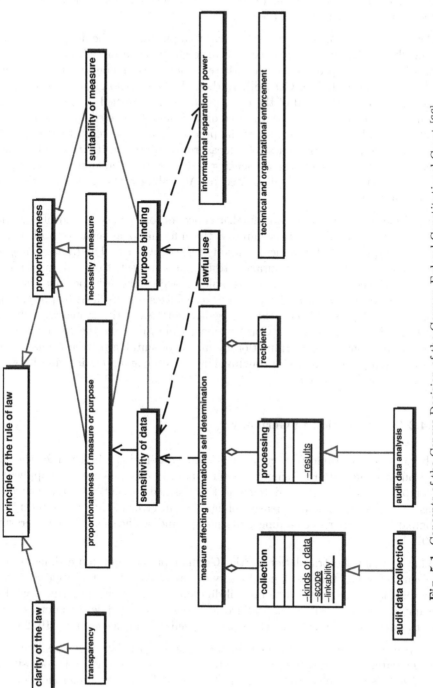

**Fig. 5.1.** Concepts of the Census Decision of the German Federal Constitutional Court [66]

*necessary*, *suitable* and *proportionate*, i.e., in proper relations w.r.t. the purpose that is pursued by means of the measure.

The proportionateness of a measure w.r.t. to a purpose can be judged by considering the sensitivity of the concerned personal information. The German Constitutional Court proclaimed that there is no a priori non-sensitive personal information (s. C II 2 in CD [66]). Rather, the *sensitivity* of personal information results from the kind of the measure, from the pursued *purpose*, as well as from the *kind* and *scope* of the collected data, from its processibility (i.e. linkability), and finally from the *results* of the processing and the respective *recipients*. To judge the proportionateness of a measure, the data sensitivity is determined and fixed. Operationally, the influencing factors, in particular the pursued purpose, are made public and committed to. Accordingly, this concept is denoted as *purpose binding*.

In the German census decision further concepts for the protection of personal data are introduced: the transparency, the informational separation of power, and the requirement for implementation of the protection. The *transparency* results from comprehensive assurances to the data subject, to be informed about aforementioned measures and to be able to access the own personal data in that process. The *informational separation of power* is installed to prevent the correlation of personal data that is legally and necessarily stored by different parties. Finally, the German Constitutional Court requires the enforcement of the informational self-determination by means of suitable *technical and organizational safeguards*. Figure 5.1 roughly illustrates the main relationships between the introduced concepts.

### 5.4.3 The Situation in Germany

The pertinent German privacy law postulates a default prohibition for the collection, storage and processing of personal data. In the presence of an applicable exemption by law or of the data subject's informed consent, the data controller has to comply with comprehensive obligations in favor of the data subject, e.g. compatible use (purpose binding), information and notification, as well as erasure [191, 198].

What renders the translation of the German privacy law more difficult into action, is the fact that the kind of a service determines the set of applicable acts and ordinances, which in detail entail different requirements and sanctions. For example, an email service is classified as a tele-service, while a content service on the web (web server) is a tele-service as well as a media-service [119, 26].

The privacy acts categorize personal data either as stock data, as usage data or as billing data. In contrast to the other data categories the storage and processing of *stock data* is not subject to temporal restrictions [119]. For example, the property statements introduced in Chap. 3 belong to this data category.

An example for *usage data* is the individual service request of a service user. The collection, processing and storage of usage data is restricted to the (personal) data that is necessary for service provision and it is allowed only during the duration of the service usage. Usage data usually relates to persons, e.g. if it contains the IP address of the user's machine or the name of the user's access account [198, 140, 106, 183, 184, 119, 134, 26, 205].

As a result, the common practice of service providers collecting usage data in the form of audit data is a problem [198, 106]. The collected audit data frequently documents the service access characteristics and thus, also the service-related behavior of the users. Audit data usually is collected and stored for future use, aiming at misuse detection in order to assert the rights of the service provider and to hold attackers accountable [184] (cf. guard and intrusion detection in Sect. 2.2 and Sect. 2.4). Audit data can be collected at various points in the model from Chap. 3. In this text only the audit data collected by the service is considered.

Data, which the service provider immediately depends on for billing his services, is denoted as *billing data*. The billing data is the subset of the usage data that is relevant for billing the accessed service. The billing model determines, which data can be legally collected, stored and processed [106]. Usually it is not necessary for the billing to collect complete user access traces. For example, if the billing model is a flat rate, in principle no usage data should be required for billing [198]. Thus, billing data alone in general is not useful for misuse or intrusion detection. Moreover, billing data that is related to persons is subject to erasure after a short time limit [119].

Organizations frequently offer their employees services for working and business purposes. If the private utilization of these services is tolerated by the organization, collecting audit data may infringe the employees' right to informational self-determination. Additionally, according to German labor legislation the works or staff council has the right to co-determination, if a system is about to be introduced that can be used or abused for monitoring the employee performance [26, 204]. If the services accessed by the employees collect and store audit data or usage data, various alternatives for analysis are enabled, also w.r.t. employee performance [198].

As a result from the complex statutory situation and from the restrictions imposed by privacy laws concerning the collection, storage and processing of personal data, the law-abiding introduction of audit data driven safeguards, such as IDSs, remains an intricate endeavor [120].

### 5.4.4 European Harmonization

The main objective of directive 95/46/EC [76] of the European Union (EU) is the protection of privacy as a fundamental right. The directive aims for a uniformly high minimum standard of privacy protection to avoid restrictions on the free flow of personal data between EU member states, which is one essential enabler for further European economic development (see considerations 3, 5, 7–9 in directive 95/46/EC [76]).

The rationale of the data protection provisions required by the directive is oriented along a combination of the principles as introduced in Sect. 5.4.2, which are found in the privacy law of various EU member states. However, the directive was mainly influenced by the German system [80].

By means of the directive, a harmonization of the national privacy law of the majority of the EU member states has been achieved. Article 25 of the directive imposes restrictions on the transborder data flow, resulting in economical pressure on third countries that is useful to motivate them to establish an adequate privacy protection level. Anyhow, due to cultural, political and historical diversity a complete international harmonization cannot be expected. The approach of the USA may serve as an example. Instead of a comprehensive privacy law the USA prefer a self-regulation approach with some private sector specific law. Due to the lack of facilities for control and enforcement the self-regulation approach remains inadequate [80].

## 5.5 Necessity of Technical Enforcement

Digitally available information can be stored, aggregated or correlated with other information in a cost-efficient way. Normally, the data subject does not notice if his personal data is copied and passed on. After a misuse it is hard or impossible for the data subject to produce proof of the misuse. Even if the misuse can be proven, the data subject may suffer an irreversible damage because data, once publicized, e.g. on the Internet, practically cannot be retracted. Also in the course of transborder flow, personal data may leave the jurisdiction of a country with a high level of protection of data protection.[1]

Also, even if the data subject trusts the service provider and the owner of the hosting IT system, disguised system components, i.e. trojan horses, cannot be ruled out, which may copy and forward personal data to unauthorized third parties. Moreover, most IT systems may have so far unknown vulnerabilities, enabling unauthorized third parties to access the personal data on the vulnerable system.

The aforementioned problems demonstrate that laws alone are insufficient to protect personal data effectively. This motivates the need for technical safeguards that preferably are controlled by the respective data subjects. Nevertheless, technical safeguards must be embedded in a legal framework. Also, the data controller still has the obligation to adhere to national privacy law. Even though safeguards that are controlled by the data subjects are most preferable, the data controller's

---

[1] As remarked in Sect. 5.4.4, a global harmonization of privacy law cannot be expected.

obligation remains and cannot be shifted to the data subjects by referring them to user-controlled safeguards.

## 5.6 Principles of Technical Implementation

Aiming at the protection of the informational self-determination of the individual, national data protection acts (e.g. the German Federal Data Protection Act [29]), international privacy directives (e.g. the EU Directive on Data Protection [76]), the Guidelines of UN and OECD, as well as voluntary privacy codes and standards devise various principles for the handling of personal data. In the following, the common principles are introduced, as far as they are relevant for the technical implementation of informational self-termination.

Personal data should be collected and processed in a fair and lawful way. The principle of *fairness* comprises the principle of transparency, accuracy and default prohibition. *Transparency* can be achieved by comprehensive *information* and *notification* of the data subject, e.g. regarding automated decision processes, the data controller, the scope, the purpose, the right to data access and correction.

Transparency also helps to achieve data *accuracy*. The data subjects have a right to *access* their personal data and to *correct, erase* or *block* incorrect or unrightful data. These options should ideally already be implemented in the systems that are under the control of the data subject (e.g. in the user-controlled management component in the model from Chap. 3), if they store personal data, which later can be passed on by the system. The system could assist the data subject by automating the clearance for personal data to be passed on, based on the situation, e.g. the data recipient's privacy policy, and on the user-controlled privacy policy.

The principle of *default prohibition* of collection of personal data requires that an *exemption by law* permits or the data subject himself gives his *informed consent* to collect the personal data. The management of digitally declared and informed consent should be implemented by the data controller in a legally effective way. Note, that informed consent implies the requirement for transparency.

The technical realization of the introduced fairness aspects are not further considered in this text. Rather, the text in the following focuses on aspects of *data quality*, which subsume the concepts of necessity and purpose binding (see Sect. 5.4.2). The concept of *necessity* implies that, if possible, a service must be accessible anonymously, i.e. personal data must be processed by the service in anonymous form, and anonymous payment must be accepted. The service users must be informed about the available anonymous access and payment options. Ideally, these options are by default pre-selected for the user.

The concept of necessity comprises the principles of *data avoidance* and *data reduction*. The latter can be implemented by means of data aggregation, coarsening, anonymization, pseudonymization or erasure after fulfillment of the purpose or after mandatory time limits. Personal data can be avoided if it is not collected or if it is collected only in the necessary minimal amount, and/or in anonymous or pseudonymous form. *Purpose binding* can be achieved by fixing the legally permitted or consented purpose and the processing possibilities. The respective results are bound to that purpose. Likewise, in certain environments the collection of personal data can be technically controlled (cf. the user-controlled management component in the model from Chap. 3).

## 5.7 Duality of Safeguards

While safeguards can be used to protect personal data, they can also be at odds with the very same objective. Personal data that is collected by safeguards for security reasons may also be used for purposes that are incompatible with the purpose originally followed with that safeguard. Considering some examples, in the following this conflict is illustrated and in Sect. 5.7.1 and Sect. 5.7.2 it is elaborated for the collection of audit data.

Property statements that identify the user in the subject component (see Sect. 3.3), reveal a part of the user's activity and possibly his physical location, when being used for service access. Within an organization this data can be consolidated for example in an employee location profile, which could be used to monitor employee performance.

A property statement identifying the user additionally describes his properties and (possibly) authorizations in the attributes component. These attributes commonly can be observed by many users, who do not need to know this information.

One standard safeguard for data availability are regular data backups. The personal data on the less recently used backup media may not be up to date, i.e. incorrect. Although the data subjects have the right to rectify incorrect personal data, they predominantly in practice do not have that option w.r.t. data backups.

Audit data such as used for intrusion detection on the one hand supports the integrity protection objective of the service provider. On the other hand, the audit data usually contains personal data and therefore collecting that data affects the informational self-determination of the users who do not violate any security objectives of the service provider. Although almost all users play by the service provider's rules, they are affected by this restriction. Audit data containing personal data could be used to monitor employee performance, to analyze the employee activities, or possibly even to profile employee personalities [204]. It is known that employee awareness of such provisions increases the work stress and adversely affects employee productivity and satisfaction [118].

### 5.7.1 Personal Data Protection Problems with Audit Data

A study of the US National Science Foundation (NSF) on audit data [183, 184] yields that system administrators (as employees of a service provider) have an overly technology-centered view on authorizations in the systems they manage. They fall for the common misconception that they are (officially, legally, morally, etc.) authorized to perform all those activities in a system, for which they are technically authorized by the access control mechanisms.

Unfortunately, the technically enforced authorizations that are required to provide for sustained and secure operation of an IT system, mostly exceed the authorizations that are preferable from the view of privacy and personal data protection. Hence, privacy objectives for the most part are not technically enforced and remain in the realm of guidelines, laws and user expectations. The gap between not technically enforced privacy objectives and technically enforced reliability or security objectives gains momentum due to the following factors:

- The technically enforced authorizations usually allow the system administrators in a mean of 1.6 steps to identify the person from given audit data.

- System administration is sometimes carried out by green men, such as students.

- System administration employees may change roles and responsibilities, but the technically enforced authorizations commonly are not updated or revoked.

- Often, new employees are not briefed about privacy-related authorization restrictions that are not technically enforced. Mostly, there are no guidelines documenting such restrictions.

### 5.7.2 Principles of Technical Implementation Violated by Audit Data in Practice

The survey of the NSF [183, 184] identifies all direct sub-aspects of the three main privacy principles *fairness*, *data quality* and *safeguards* for technically implementable data protection as being endangered by the existence of audit data.

Fairness: First, the principle of fairness calls for transparency, which as the survey shows, prevalently is not established. Second, without transparency it is hardly possible to achieve accuracy of the collected personal data. And third, system administrators frequently do not consider the default prohibition concerning personal data collection, because they do not realize that audit data contains personal data.

Data quality: Due to the lack of guidelines for the processing of personal data, purpose binding is not adhered to. Shortage of manpower and time resources[2] usually discourage the immediate analysis of audit data that has been collected and stored. This practice runs contrary to the principle of necessity, in particular to the principle of data reduction.

Safeguards: The safeguards of widely spread commercial off-the-shelf (COTS) operating systems are ineffective, because the systems are configured for daily operation such that the system administrator's authorizations always enable him to undermine the confidentiality, integrity and availability of (personal) data collected, stored and processed by the system. Guidelines clarifying the official limits to the broad technically granted and enforced authorizations of the administrators, are commonly missing.

The concerns regarding audit data driven safeguards are summarized in the survey as follows. "The security concerns regarding computer systems and networks [...] constitute fertile ground for the development of increased surveillance technologies. Another driving force is the desire to extend the technologies to their outer limits." [184]

---

[2] Shortage of manpower and time are a common justification to neglect security and privacy issues. As with everything, whether this justification holds, is a matter of the priorities defined at the executive level of the organization.

# 6

# The Challenge:
# Technical Enforcement of Multilateral Security

As motivated in Chap. 4 and Chap. 5, there is an inherent conflict between the individual user who is interested in personal data protection or anonymity, and the potential misuse victims, e.g. the service providers, who are interested in accountability, which could be required to claim compensation. Obviously, the simplest solution is to give up one of the requirements in favor of the other requirement.

If only the security objectives of the service provider are accounted for, this also holds for the certification and authorization (see Fig. 3.4 and Fig. 3.9 to Fig. 3.12). Eventually, all components of certified property statements support primarily the security objectives of the service provider. Such a scenario does not inspire the user's confidence in the protection of his anonymity by the certifier, authorizer or service, particularly if the subject component in property statements identifies the individual user. Depending on the nature of a given service, the user will more or less reluctantly employ such property statements (see Sect. 5.3).

If only the anonymity interest of the users is enforced, this also holds for the certification and authorization. In such a scenario the service providers cannot have confidence in the complete protection of their security objectives. Given the nature of the service, the provider will or will not be willing to accept this risk.

Obviously, following such a simple approach we can easily create scenarios where users and services will not interact. As the discussion of Fiedler and Rossnagel [77, 190, 78] demonstrates, a solution that satisfies the involved parties cannot be achieved by completely giving up the objectives of one party in favor of the interests of the other parties.

Rather, a fair balance of the interests of all participants in consideration of the respective application or scenario seems desirable. We denote technologies that balance conflicting security objectives in a given application or that at least establish transparency regarding the enforceable security objectives as technologies for *multilateral security* [180, 173].

For the case of multilaterally secure audit data analysis for misuse detection we advocate an approach based on pseudonyms. In the following, legal arguments from the literature are exploited for and translated to the technical concept of pseudonyms (see Sect. 6.1 and Sect. 6.1.1). Most importantly, it is clarified under what circumstances and subject to what assumptions pseudonyms can be legally disclosed (see Sect. 6.1.2 and Sect. 6.1.3). Based on these results a primarily technically inclined framework for pseudonyms is introduced in Chap. 7.

# 6.1 A Law-driven Approach Using Pseudonyms

A pseudonym-based approach to multilateral security was motivated and substantiated with legal arguments by Roßnagel and Scholz [191] and Jaeger [119]. The results that are relevant in the context of the German privacy law are summarized and interpreted by these authors. In the following Sections, the technical dimensions of this approach are examined.

When designing and selecting technologies for media- and tele-services, §3 Sect. 4 TDDSG [27] and §12 Sect. 5 MDStV [68] require to aim for collecting and processing only personal data that is really necessary. This requirement is substantiated in §4 Sect. 1 TDDSG [27] and §13 Sect. 1 MDStV [68] by the obligation of the service provider to facilitate the anonymous or pseudonymous access to and payment of the service, as far as technically possible and reasonable. Anonymity and Pseudonymity serve as means to implement system- and self-protection by realizing data avoidance or data reduction for informational self-determination [191].

In this context the term *personal identifiability* is meant to be relative, since the personal identifiability of given data depends on the actual external knowledge and on the actual time. Accordingly, the obligations of privacy law apply only to those data controllers, which can establish the relationship between the data and the data subject by means of the external knowledge available to them. Thus, the conflict between the objectives accountability and anonymity can be solved in a fair way by applying pseudonyms, such that the normal case (no accountability) can be distinguished from the exceptional case (accountability can be established) by controlling certain external knowledge [191].

### 6.1.1 Controlling the Disclosure of Pseudonyms

By means of pseudonyms, personal data can be modified in such a way that it can only with a disproportionate effort in time, cost and manpower be related to a certain person without the knowledge of the *pseudonym (to person) mapping*. In the exceptional case, the pseudonyms can be related to a certain person using the pseudonym mapping. For data controllers who know the pseudonym mapping, the pseudonymous data is personal data. For the data controllers who do not know the pseudonym mapping, the pseudonymous data is practically anonymous [191, 198].

Hence, for data controllers who do not know the pseudonym mapping, the pseudonymous data is not subject to the (German) privacy law. While they only collect, store and process the pseudonymous data, these data controllers are free from the default prohibition and obligations imposed by the (German) privacy law (see Chap. 5) [191, 198].

As a result, pseudonyms are a key concept for the multilaterally secure handling of audit data. In many scenarios pseudonyms actually enable the lawful collection and storage of audit data.

## 6.1.2 Legal Disclosure of Pseudonyms

For a given data controller, some given pseudonymized data is anonymous data in the normal case, until in the exceptional case the original data that was replaced by the pseudonyms is disclosed[1] to the data controller by means of the pseudonym mapping. Then, the data is personally identifiable again and is subject to privacy law. For this reason the purpose of pseudonym disclosure must be chosen such that it is permitted by privacy law, and such that purpose binding can be effectively enforced. In the following, we consider some legal arguments for legally permitted purposes for pseudonym disclosure and derive the fundamental concept and assumption for the proposed approaches in Sect. 6.1.3.

The German Federal Office for Information Security (Bundesamt für Sicherheit in der Informationstechnik/BSI in German) holds the view that according to §14(2) BDSG [29] audit data documenting misuse or security policy violations, with the character of an indictable or regulatory offense, can be used for prosecution [26]. Jaeger argues in some more detail that due to the exemption in §6(3) TDDSG [27] misuse traces may be accounted for using personal data, if during the service access it can already be anticipated that this data will be later required for criminal prosecution. Jaeger finds further support in §6 Sect. 8 TDDSGÄndG [27], which allows tele-service providers to collect and store personal data of users, who misuse the tele-service. As a pre-requisite the data controller must document the clues that corroborate the suspicion of a user misusing the service. For the purpose of litigation, the service provider is allowed to store and process the concerning personal data beyond the mandatory time limits.[2]

---

[1] In this text the term *pseudonym disclosure* means that the original data, which has been replaced by a pseudonym, is disclosed. It does not mean that the pseudonym itself is disclosed. Obviously, the pseudonym conceals some data and is itself always visible (see Sect. 7.1).

[2] Before its amendment, the TDDSG (apart from a few exemptions) generally prohibited the tele-service provider to collect and store personal data, such that the provider was not in the position even to reconstruct misuse of his service, let alone identify the responsible user by means of audit data [119, 120].

### 6.1.3 Conclusions and Main Assumption for the Legal Foundation of Audit Data Pseudonymization for Misuse Detection

From the legal arguments put forth in Sect. 6.1 to Sect. 6.1.2 we derive the fundamental concept and the underlying assumption of the approaches presented in this book. The natural wording used here is related to the more concise terms used for the more technically inclined elaboration in Part II and Part V.

First, we conclude from the statements of Roßnagel and Scholz (see Sect. 6.1.1) that during normal system operation it is permitted by privacy law to store clues (cf. Sect. 12.1: *observations of activity*) in pseudonymous form in the course of proceeding and a priori specified misuse activity (cf. Sect. 12.1: *disclosure context*). As long as the pseudonyms are not disclosed, restrictions of (German) privacy law do not apply, even if a misuse suspicion is not sufficiently corroborated over time (cf. Sect. 12.1: the *activity level* of the *disclosure context* does not satisfy the respective *disclosure condition*).

Second, based on the statements of the German BSI and Jaeger (see Sect. 6.1.2), we assume that it is permitted by (German) privacy law to make pseudonymous clues for a misuse accountable by disclosing the pseudonyms in the clues, as soon as the exceptional situation arises that the misuse activity proceeds to the point where the misuse suspicion is sufficiently corroborated (cf. Sect. 12.1: the *activity level* of the *disclosure context* meets the respective *disclosure condition*).

We use the term *technical purpose binding* (see Sect. 7.2) to denote the notion of technical enforcement of the conditions for pseudonym disclosure.

Even though this approach restricts pseudonym disclosure to situations where it is legal to handle personal data, the data controller still is subject to (limited) obligations of privacy law. Thus, for the case of pseudonym disclosure, precautions need to be taken, before that case occurs. Such precautions are selected in analogy to the obligations of the data controller. As an example, the data controller should inform the user that his pseudonym(s) can be disclosed, if the situation calls for it. Certainly, safeguards must be established to secure the pseudonym mapping, such that its use is limited to aforementioned situations (see Sect. 8.2). For more examples for necessary precautions refer to Rossnagel and Scholz [191].

# Pseudonyms – A Technical Point of View

Based on the legal framework for pseudonyms described in Chap. 6, in this Chapter the more technically inclined aspects of pseudonyms are examined. The terms and concepts associated with the notion of anonymity and pseudonymity used in this text are introduced in Sect. 7.1. Two properties of pseudonyms are most important for the approaches presented in this book: Pseudonym disclosure is examined in Sect. 7.2 and pseudonym linkability is focused in Sect. 7.3. For a slightly broader perspective, further pseudonym properties are mentioned in Sect. 7.4. Based on the pseudonym concepts described in this Chapter the architectural model for secure authorizations is extended for pseudonymity in Chap. 8.

## 7.1 Definition of Terms

The terms introduced in the following, are based on the definitions of Pfitzmann and Hansen for unlinkability and anonymity [174].

Two objects are *unlinkable* w.r.t. an attacker, if the probability that both objects are related does not change after any possible observation of the attacker; otherwise they are *linkable*. Two objects are related, if they correlate w.r.t. a feature, e.g. equal content, size or time stamp. Unless noted otherwise, when we talk about the linkability of two objects, in this text we mean that an attacker can observe that the objects have equal content. An *ID* is a principal that uniquely identifies an entity, e.g. a person. Then, an object is *anonymous*, if it is not linkable with any ID. Conversely, an object is *accountable*, if it is linkable with an ID, i.e. it is not anonymous. An example for an object is an audit record describing an event.

A *pseudonym* is a principal that, unlike an ID, cannot be used to identify the associated entity. An object can be *pseudonymized*, if it is anonymous after deleting all IDs from the object.[1] The term *pseudonymization* denotes the process of replacing the IDs in an object with pseudonyms, instead of deleting them. The respective *pseudonym mapping* uniquely[2] associates each pseudonym used during pseudonymization with the ID that was replaced by the pseudonym. Note, that several instances of a given ID can be replaced with distinct pseudonyms (see Sect. 7.3).

After pseudonymization, no feature of the object is linkable with some ID.[3] The *pseudonymized*, i.e. *pseudonymous*, object is practically *anonymous* w.r.t. entities which do not know the pseudonym mapping.[4] Entities that know the pseudonym mapping can *disclose* the pseudonyms. Pseudonym *disclosure* is the process of relating a given pseudonym to the pseudonym mapping. A pseudonymous object can be *reidentified* by replacing each of the contained pseudonyms with the IDs that are associated with the pseudonyms in the pseudonym mapping. After reidentification the object is accountable again.

In Sect. 6.1 an approach using pseudonyms was introduced to balance the conflicting security objectives pseudonymity and accountability. Both security objectives are directly connected to the controlled pseudonym disclosure (see Sect. 7.2). Another aspect of pseudonyms is the linkability of pseudonyms for a given objective, which is required for many services (see Sect. 7.3). Also, many methods for analyzing audit data do not work without the linkability of principals, i.e. IDs or pseudonyms. Considering the above definition of anonymity, it is obvious that the aspects disclosure and linkability of pseudonyms are not independent from each other.

## 7.2 Controlled Disclosure of Pseudonyms

The *controlled disclosure* of pseudonyms is the controlled ability to make pseudonymized objects accountable again. This ability is controlled by controlling who can use the pseudonymity mapping.

---

[1] Note, that an object is not necessarily anonymous after deleting all IDs from the object. The object could still be transitively linkable to an ID via other object features than content.

[2] When using *group pseudonyms*, the pseudonym mapping associates each pseudonym with all IDs that were replaced with the same pseudonym. Group pseudonyms are not considered in this text.

[3] Note, that the above definition of pseudonymization is rather strict. In practice it may be desirable to pseudonymize objects only partially. The pseudonymization approaches proposed in this book allow for pseudonymizing audit data partially. The text in the following also denotes partially pseudonymized objects as pseudonymized objects.

[4] Note, that in this text the terms of anonymity and pseudonymity sometimes are used interchangeably w.r.t. entities that do not know the pseudonym mapping.

In the following, the entity with the predominant security objective of anonymity or pseudonymity is denoted as $IA$ or *subject*. Likewise, the entity with the predominant security objective of accountability is denoted as $IC$ or *attacker* (w.r.t. the anonymity or pseudonymity of $IA$). An entity which $IA$ can trust to protect $IA$'s anonymity or pseudonymity is denoted as $TA$ or *agent*. Analogously, we introduce $TC$ for accountability. Finally, $TAC$ is an entity which $IA$ and $IC$ can trust to balance their interests in a fair way.

The disclosure of pseudonyms should be bound to a priori specified purposes. Purpose binding of pseudonym disclosure can be achieved in an organizational or in a technical way (see Sect. 7.2.1 and Sect. 7.2.2, respectively). For robustness, both approaches can be combined (see Sect. 7.2.3) to handle possible error cases (see Sect. 7.2.4). Section 7.2.5 provides some examples showing how pseudonym mappings can be implemented, and Sect. 7.2.6 investigates, which entities may control the pseudonym mapping.

### 7.2.1 Organizational Purpose Binding

The entity which manages the pseudonym mapping is responsible for performing reidentification for legal purposes of authorized entities only. If the responsible handling is conferred to a person, the reidentification is subject to *organizational purpose binding*. A correct purpose binding then provides for a fair balance of the security objectives pseudonymity and accountability in terms of multilateral security.

A correct organizational purpose binding can only be achieved reliably, if the reidentifying entity has no predominant interest in merely one of the security objectives. Hence, $IA$ and $IC$ are not eligible for this function. Instead, $IA$ and $IC$ can decide to trust the entity $TAC$ to balance their conflict of interests in a fair way. Alternatively, their trust can be distributed among two entities $TA$ and $TC$, e.g. using a threshold cryptosystem [67]. It must be ensured organizationally, that $IC$'s ability to reidentify pseudonymized data is restricted, such that $IC$ needs to involve $TAC$, or $TA$ and $TC$ for reidentification. As a result, pseudonym disclosure subject to organizational purpose binding is delayed if $TA$ or $TC$ do not cooperate in a timely fashion.

### 7.2.2 Technical Purpose Binding

The purpose of pseudonym disclosure can already be incorporated during pseudonym generation. The pseudonym mapping then is made available to $IC$ in a protected form, such that $IC$ normally cannot use it to reidentify pseudonymized audit data. Additionally, the pseudonymized audit data is supplemented with certain information that neutralizes the protection of the pseudonym mapping under certain conditions. The purpose of pseudonym disclosure determines under what conditions the protection becomes ineffective, and the pseudonym mapping can be used for reidentification. The pseudonyms can be disclosed only if these conditions are met. If the protection of the pseudonym mapping is customized for the disclosure conditions, such that it cannot be circumvented, the pseudonyms are subject to disclosure with *technical purpose binding*.

In contrast to organizational purpose binding, the purpose is incorporated in technically implemented conditions, i.e., the disclosure conditions are specific to the given purpose and application. Given that the disclosure conditions control the technical purpose binding, the conditions must only be controlled by an entity which is trusted by $IA$ and $IC$ to balance the conflicting interests according to the purpose and in a fair way (here $TAC$). When technical purpose binding of pseudonym disclosure is employed, $IC$ can reidentify pseudonymized data promptly and without the cooperation of $TAC$, as soon as the disclosure conditions are satisfied.

### 7.2.3 Combining Organizational and Technical Purpose Binding

A situation, which cannot be properly handled using technical purpose binding alone, arises when the disclosure conditions do not completely model the intended purpose. To be able to disclose already generated pseudonyms after revising the disclosure conditions, these pseudonyms would have to be re-generated using the revised parameters. In general, this is not a viable option.

If it is required to be able to disclose already generated pseudonyms in accordance with revised disclosure conditions, the technical purpose binding should be complemented with organizational purpose binding. Then, in the usual case the technical purpose binding allows for a timely reidentification, and in the seldomly occurring situation described above, the slower organizational purpose binding can be used.

### 7.2.4 Handling Disclosure-occurrences that are Incompatible with the Purpose

The complementary use of organizational purpose binding compensates for the problem of technical purpose binding that pseudonymized data cannot be reidentified, if the disclosure conditions have not been completely modeled (error class 1).[5] However, a flawed model of disclosure conditions may also result in the controlled disclosure of pseudonyms, which actually do not sufficiently corroborate a misuse suspicion (error class 2).[6] To mitigate the latter problem, the

---

[5] In terms of misuse detection, error class 1 corresponds to false negatives, i.e., no alarm is generated in spite of the existence of a sufficiently corroborated misuse suspicion.

[6] In terms of misuse detection error, class 2 corresponds to false positives, i.e., an alarm is generated, though no sufficiently corroborated misuse suspicion exists.

following approach is proposed for the disclosure of pseudonyms that are subject to technical purpose binding.

Each pseudonym disclosure conducted by $IC$ is recorded, together with a purpose-oriented justification and together with the data that is required to judge the legitimacy of the disclosure. The data subject $IA$ should be informed of the respective disclosure. This could be implemented in such a way that $IC$ must give clearance for each recorded disclosure to be brought to the attention of either $IA$ or $TA$. If the detailed inspection of the recorded disclosure yields the occurrence of a class 2 error, $IA$ can be informed immediately and directly. However, if the inspection yields a sufficiently corroborated suspicion that $IA$ misused the service, it could be counterproductive to inform $IA$ immediately. Instead, $IC$ could defer informing $IA$ for the duration of the investigation and give proper justification. In return, $TA$, who advocates the pseudonymity interest of $IA$, can read all recorded reidentifications that $IC$ has deferred, together with the justification. As such, $TA$ can officiate his control function (organizational purpose binding).

### 7.2.5 Example Implementations of the Pseudonym Mapping

There exist several alternatives to implement the pseudonym mapping. If it is implemented as a table, the table must be protected appropriately. To disclose a pseudonym, it is located in the table, where it is associated with the respective ID.

If the pseudonym mapping is implemented as a cryptographic function, the function can be made public, but the secret parameters must be protected. The function can be a cryptographic decryption function, such that a pseudonym can be disclosed by decrypting the pseudonym using the secret parameters. Conversely, pseudonyms are generated by encrypting an ID using the corresponding encryption function and the corresponding parameters. In this setting, technical purpose binding can be implemented by means of cryptographically sharing the decryption key, which is the approach followed in Part II and Part V.

An alternative approach uses a cryptographic and collision-resistant (parameterizable) hash function instead of an encryption function (see Jaeger pseudonymizer in Sect. 9.2). In this case, the hash function is one-way, such that according to the definitions in this text, there is no pseudonym mapping for controlled pseudonym disclosure. Note, that this approach is adopted in Part V for technically bound pseudonym linkability (see Sect. 7.3).

However, if the parameters and candidate IDs are known, the pseudonyms still can be disclosed using a dictionary attack. The hash values, i.e. pseudonyms, for all candidate IDs are computed and compared to the pseudonyms to be disclosed. In the same way the ID of a suspicious user can be found in a set of pseudonyms by generating the respective pseudonym and comparing it to the set of pseudonyms. Note, that these attacks also work for the other implementation alternatives.

In Part V a combination of hashing and encryption is used, where the hash-values are the pseudonyms seen by the application and which provide suitable linkability, and the cryptograms can be used for pseudonym disclosure.

### 7.2.6 Controlling the Pseudonym Mapping

The pseudonym mapping and the pseudonymized data, which is stored with a data controller who can use the pseudonym mapping, are personal data w.r.t. this data controller and thus are subject to privacy law [191]. Therefore, such data controllers must arrange for the protection of the personal data. In the following is specified, who may control/store the pseudonym mapping [174, 191].

For each case, additional information is given: Is the data considered to be personal data for the data controller $IC$, such that it is subject to privacy law? Can we achieve multilateral security w.r.t. pseudonymity and accountability, or only unilateral security w.r.t. to one of the security objectives? Will $IC$ have to interact with the party who controls the pseudonym mapping for reidentification, or can $IC$ reidentify the data autonomously? If organizational purpose binding is used, $IC$ needs to cooperate with the entity who controls the pseudonym mapping. In the case of technical purpose binding $IC$ needs the pseudonymized data including the information to neutralize the protection of the pseudonym mapping in order to perform reidentification.

Public: personally identifiable; unilateral security (accountability); autonomous disclosure

Data controller ($IC$): personally identifiable (not personally identifiable for third parties); unilateral security (accountability); autonomous disclosure

Agent ($TAC$, or $TA$ and $TC$): not personally identifiable; multilateral security, if the agent(s) are trustworthy, otherwise unilateral security; disclosure requires cooperation of the agent(s)

Data: not personally identifiable; multilateral security, if the pseudonymizing agent $TAC$ is trustworthy, otherwise unilateral security; autonomous disclosure

Subject ($IA$): not personally identifiable; unilateral security (anonymity); disclosure requires cooperation of the subject

A pseudonym mapping that is known to the public or controlled by the data controller $IC$ cannot afford anonymity of $IA$ w.r.t. $IC$. At the other end of the spectrum we find pseudonym mappings which are merely controlled by the subject $IA$. If $IA$ decides not to disclose his pseudonym(s), the pseudonymized data remains anonymous. As a result, for pseudonym disclosure subject to technical and/or organizational purpose binding, the pseudonym mapping should be controlled by trustworthy agents. The function of the pseudonymization agent $TAC$ may be carried out by a trustworthy privacy protection official (PPO). See also Sect. 8.1.1.

## 7.3 Linkability and Uncontrolled Disclosure of Pseudonyms

From the definition of anonymity used in this text follows the influence of linkability on the anonymity of a given object. For more concise definitions refer to Steinbrecher and Köpsell [210]. The more often and in the more different contexts a given pseudonym is used, the more other objects are directly or transitively linkable with that pseudonym. This increases the probability that in the set of objects, which are linkable to a given pseudonym, there is an accountable object, such that an *uncontrolled disclosure* of the pseudonym w.r.t. this set of objects is feasible.

Therefore, a given pseudonym should be used as scarcely and in as few contexts as possible, i.e., it is recommended to frequently change the pseudonym for a given entity, such that the pseudonyms of the entity are unlinkable. Accordingly, pseudonyms can be classified w.r.t. the contexts where they are used. Pfitzmann and Hansen [174] propose certain contexts in which a given pseudonym is used exclusively. In the order of increasing resistance against uncontrolled disclosure the pseudonyms are denoted as:

subject pseudonym: used in all contexts

role pseudonym: used in the context of a specific role

relationship pseudonym: used in the context of a specific communication relationship

role-relationship pseudonym: used in the context of a specific role in the context of a specific communication relationship

transaction pseudonym: used in the context of a specific transaction

Also the purpose of processing pseudonymized data can be incorporated in the process of pseudonym generation, which is comparable to the technical purpose binding of pseudonym disclosure. The purpose of processing determines the parameters of the algorithm used for the data processing, and therewith in which contexts the pseudonyms need to be linkable. In contrast to the purpose binding of pseudonym disclosure, for the *purpose binding of pseudonym linkability* the pseudonyms are usually not supplemented with additional protected information.

If the processing of the pseudonymous data requires that the pseudonyms are linkable in a specific context, the pseudonyms for a given subject are generated such that they are directly linkable (by content). Otherwise the pseudonyms of the subject are generated to be unlinkable. This is the approach for pseudonym linkability followed in Part V.

The processing of the pseudonymized data by the service usually is in the interest of the data subject as well as of the data controller, such that no direct conflict of interest exists. However, the degree of pseudonym linkability influences the possibility of uncontrolled pseudonym disclosure, and as such, indirectly affects the interests of $IA$ and $IC$. Hence, the pseudonym generation must be controlled, in analogy to the purpose binding of disclosure, by $TAC$, so that the trade-off between linkability and uncontrolled disclosure, which is required for the processing of the pseudonymous data in the mutual interest, is not extended to the disadvantage of $IA$.

## 7.4 Further Properties of Pseudonyms

The scientific community has published various approaches to provide for additional features of pseudonyms and property statements [174, 135], which are addressed in detail elsewhere. Useful examples are:

- mandatory cooperation of specific responsible agents during the certification of property statements and/or the generation of pseudonyms;
- transferable pseudonyms, with or without the requirement for disclosure of valuable secret information during the authentication of the presenting party;
- pseudonym transformation while maintaining the validity of the carrying property statement;
- limiting the number of available pseudonyms per subject;
- limiting the number of uses of a pseudonym or a property statement;
- limiting the period of validity of a property statement;
- allowing certain parties to revoke the validity of or to block a property statement at any time.

# 8

## An Architectural Model
## for Pseudonymous and Secure Authorizations

Based on the framework for pseudonyms given in Chap. 7 the model introduced in Chap. 3 is extended by the concept of pseudonymity in this Chapter. The property statements from Sect. 3.3 are interpreted in terms of pseudonyms in Sect. 8.1. The architecture introduced in Sect. 3.4 is extended by reidentification, audit data collection, and audit data processing in Sect. 8.2. Also, the control requirements are extended in Sect. 8.2. The application domain of the architectural model and the attacker model are described in Sect. 8.3. Finally, different architectures and the specific control requirements are given in Sect. 8.4. Most notably, the simplified control requirements for technical purpose binding over organizational purpose binding are explained in Sect. 8.4.1. The various architectures presented in this Chapter are compared in Chap. 9.

## 8.1 Pseudonymous Property Statements

In many cases person-identifying IDs are not necessary to verify certified property statements and to provide a service [217]. Mostly, it is sufficient that the included attributes are correctly associated with the presenting entity, that the property statement is valid and that it was certified by an agent, whom the verifier or the service trust. As an example, an admission ticket to the zoo (see Sect. 2.2) does not contain the name of the ticket owner, but a unique ticket number, which can be interpreted as a pseudonym of the ticket owner in the context of the zoo service.

If for a given application IDs are not necessary, property statements and their references can be pseudonymized by replacing the subject principal with a pseudonym that has suitable properties (see Sect. 8.1.1). The German signature act already allows for pseudonymous certificates (§7 Sect. 1-3 SigG [30]) [191]. It must be ensured, that the other components of the property statement do not contain IDs of the subject entity or allow inferences by virtue of uniqueness. Additionally, in the model it is assumed that the recipients of a property statement do not make any observations after which the pseudonym is linkable with an ID of the subject entity. Aside from the controlled pseudonym disclosure by the agent, the property statement is practically anonymous for the recipient.

That way it is not necessary for the zoo ticket booth employee to learn the name of the student. Rather, it is important that the property *student* is properly associated with the person which presents a valid student ID,[1] and that the certifying university is known to and trusted by the zoo management.[2] To that effect, the student ID could be designed to be pseudonymous, by using the registration number of the student for the subject component, instead of the student's name.

On the one hand, the agent is additionally responsible to the interest of accountability of the recipients of the property statement, for disclosing pseudonyms in accord with his pre-engaged policy to specific entities for specific purposes only. On the other hand, the agent is also responsible to the interest of the subject entity in pseudonymity, for protecting the pseudonym mapping and adhering to the declared policy w.r.t. pseudonym disclosure and linkability.

### 8.1.1 Suitable Pseudonyms

In order to choose pseudonyms that are suitable for pseudonymous property statements, the desired properties must be determined for both aspects of pseudonyms – (controlled) disclosure and linkability.

Pseudonym mappings that are known to the public or controlled by the data controller of the pseudonymized data are not useful for pseudonymous property statements, because only unilateral security can be achieved in favor of accountability, but to the disadvantage of pseudonymity. Conversely, also pseudonym mappings that are controlled by the subject entity are not useful for pseudonymous property statements, because only unilateral security can be achieved in favor of pseudonymity, but accountability cannot be dependably established (see Sect. 7.2.6). To that effect, the useful alternative are pseudonym mappings that are controlled by agents.

An agent can bind pseudonym disclosure technically and/or organizationally to the purpose declared in his policy (see Sect. 7.2). An agent also can limit the use of pseudonyms to specific contexts (see Sect. 7.3). In principle, the complete spectrum from subject to transaction pseudonyms is possible. However, transaction pseudonyms are not useful, if references to certified property statements are used. After each transaction the pseudonym of the property statement and of the reference would have to be renewed synchronously, i.e., in the statement repository and at the user. To employ transaction pseudonyms, it is advised to refrain from the use of references to property statements.

---

[1] In this case the term student ID does not refer to the ID in the subject component of the property statement, but to the property statement itself.

[2] Note, that in the real world it is rarely the case that student IDs from remote universities are recognized as being invalid, even in the case they actually are.

## 8.2 Role of the Attacker Model for Control Requirements

The degree of anonymity achieved by the use of pseudonyms should be proportional to the risk of collection and processing of the given personal data and to the effort required for a successful attack on the pseudonymity. Determining the degree of anonymity that a system for anonymous property statements provides, requires a system-specific analysis of the potential working points of an attacker w.r.t. linkability and disclosure [210]. A precise assertion of the degree of anonymity that is achievable with a given architecture requires a detailed analysis of the implemented system w.r.t. a given attacker model. Systems implementing different architectures for anonymous or pseudonymous property statements can then be compared w.r.t. a given attacker model.

However, even if we forbear from determining the degree of achievable anonymity, we can still identify certain properties of architectures for anonymous or pseudonymous property statements which give information about the working surface of an attacker, about the dependability of the property statements and about the practicability of the respective architecture (see Sect. 9.1).

For the following considerations, the *attacker model* specifies the possibly collaborating parties which can collect and correlate personal data (see Sect. 8.3). The architecture of a system for pseudonymous or anonymous property statements determines *when* and *where* personal data can be pseudonymized in the system, i.e., against what attacker models it can provide protection. The earlier in the data path the personal data is anonymized or pseudonymized, the more system components the attacker may control, without impairing the achievable anonymity. As a result, given an attacker model, a suitable architecture can be chosen (see Sect. 8.4). However, it must be kept in mind that the attacker may be able to access (personal) data on the different layers of the OSI reference model [188]. The semantics of property statements and services are not limited to the application layer and need to be interpreted for all OSI layers. A suitable architecture for anonymization or pseudonymization should be chosen for each layer where the attacker can access data.

For the design of architectures for anonymous or pseudonymous property statements several factors need to be considered w.r.t. the given attacker model. Considering pseudonymity in terms of multilateral security, i.e., not only anonymity, but also accountability, it is imperative that the pseudonym mapping is not controlled by an agent alone, who is predominantly interested in merely one of the security objectives, i.e. accountability or anonymity. Hence, the system components controlled by the involved parties need to be defined and isolated, preferably technically, otherwise organizationally (see Sect. 8.4). The method for pseudonymization and for the controlled pseudonym disclosure determines the number of mandatorily cooperating parties (see Sect. 7.2 and Sect. 8.4.1). If possible, pseudonym disclosure and linkability should be parameterized to allow for a fair balance of interests. The parameter values should be announced to the affected parties or to their representatives.

## 8.3 Domain of Application and Corresponding Attacker Model

Considering architectures for anonymization or pseudonymization, the given attacker model is significant, because it determines the control requirements and limits in which phase (see Sect. 3.4.3) IDs must be pseudonymized at the latest. The pseudonyms need to be introduced during a phase that is processed before the phases are processed that are within the observable scope of the attacker, so that the attacker cannot make any observations that allow him to link a pseudonym to a subject ID.

In the following, the basic model from Fig. 3.4 is extended by the *site security officer* (SSO) of the service provider, who, by means of audit data, observes and analyzes the behavior of the service users, and if necessary, conducts appropriate response (see Fig. 8.1). The audit data is collected by the *audit component* of the service and is conveyed to the *analysis* component of the SSO (see 'E1' in Fig. 8.1). According to the *purpose of analysis*, i.e. purpose of processing, the analysis component generates *event reports* and provides them to the *response* component (see 'E2' in Fig. 8.1). The response component reacts on the event reports, for example by informing the SSO and by suggesting appropriate action. An event report can comprise an *analysis context*, which is a sub-set of the audit data.

For this text we consider an intrusion detection system (IDS) as an instance of the described additional components, where the purpose of processing of the analysis component is the detection of misuse scenarios[3] that are caused by the service users. In IDS parlance, an event report is an *alarm*, which contains as analysis context the *clues* corroborating the misuse suspicion. The clues are included in the form of *audit records* documenting the progression of the misuse, in order to support further investigation (see Sect. 6.1.2).

In this architecture, the SSO can observe the behavior of the service user only by means of the audit data, which is provided by the service's audit component. The SSO's primary objective is sustained service security. Therefore, the users do not trust the SSO unconditionally w.r.t. a fair balance between anonymity and accountability. Consequently, and though it may appear harsh, the SSO is modeled to be part of the possible threat or attacker of anonymity or pseudonymity. Thus, in the following only architectures are inspected, which introduce pseudonyms before the audit data is provided to the SSO-controlled analysis component. In return, the SSO is not subject to legal restrictions and obligations w.r.t. the pseudonymous audit data (see Sect. 6.1.1).

---

[3] Models of misuse scenarios are activity patterns that are known to the IDS, i.e., here we consider so-called misuse detection, but not so-called anomaly detection.

## 8.4 Architectures and Control Requirements

After extending the basic model by components for audit data collection, analysis and alarm response (see Fig. 8.1), the model is modified to allow for pseudonymization of user IDs, before they can be observed by the SSO in the audit data. As contemplated in Sect. 8.3, pseudonymization can be integrated with one or more phases (see Sect. 3.4.3) occurring before the audit data is provided to the SSO, i.e., during certification, authorization or after audit data generation, but before the transmission of the audit data (see Fig. 8.2 to Fig. 8.5).[4]

The graphical elements in Fig. 8.1 to Fig. 8.6 call for some explanation. The *solid arrows* indicate the flow of accountable and certified or evidenced property statements or accountable references to property statements. The *dashed arrows* indicate the flow of anonymous or pseudonymous property statements or references thereof. The *dotted arrows* indicate the flow of the pseudonym mapping. Each *fat grey frame* indicates the control requirement of a certain entity w.r.t. the framed components. According to Sect. 2.3 an entity $B$ must not control the components implementing the interest $I_A$ of another entity $A$, which is in conflict with the interest $I_B$ of $B$. The *dark grey frames* represent the user's interest in pseudonymity, i.e., $A$=users, $I_A$=anonymity/pseudonymity, $B$=SSO, $I_B$=accountability. Conversely, the *light grey frames* represent the SSO's interest in accountability, i.e., $A$=SSO, $I_A$=accountability, $B$=users, $I_B$=anonymity/pseudonymity. Finally, the *black boxes* together implement a function of multilateral security. Note, that they are surrounded by a dark as well as by a light grey frame, i.e., the interests are clashing and need to be balanced. In the following, the control and trust requirements of the different architectures are investigated.

As motivated in Chap. 6, the easiest solution is to provide only unilateral security, i.e., to give up all security objectives that are in conflict with the security objectives of a given entity. According to Sect. 2.3, Fig. 8.1 shows how user anonymity is sacrificed in favor of the accountability requirements of the SSO. The SSO here needs to trust the certifier, the authorizer and the service w.r.t. accountability. Since the user's requirement for anonymity is in conflict with the SSO's requirement for accountability, the SSO could not trust the user to reidentify his property statements in a dependable way.

By virtue of the same argument, a unilaterally secure architecture can be built in favor of anonymity. In such an architecture the certifier does not verify that the subject component provided by the user contains an ID which actually identifies the user (see plausibility check in Fig. 8.2).[5] The user's management component can then choose arbitrary pseudonyms for the property statement and the

---

[4] Note, that the versions of the model in Fig. 3.9 to Fig. 3.12 can also be extended to support pseudonymity. Anyhow, the properties of the various possible versions and combinations are not examined in this text.

[5] Note, that this is actually the case for many web-based services on the Internet.

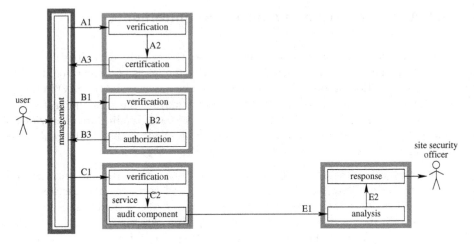

**Fig. 8.1.** Unilateral security: accountability

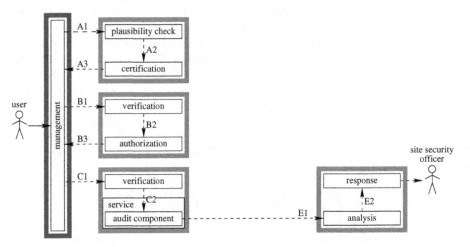

**Fig. 8.2.** Unilateral security: management anonymizes

corresponding pseudonym mapping is also controlled by the user's management component. Since the SSO would have to rely on the user to disclose his pseudonyms, which he actually does not trust him for, dependable accountability is not possible (see Fig. 8.2 and Sect. 8.1.1).

If an entity, which certifies property statements under pseudonyms, refuses to disclose the pseudonyms, also merely unilateral security can be achieved in favor of anonymity. The SSO cannot trust such an entity w.r.t. his security objective accountability. In Fig. 8.3 to Fig. 8.5 the light grey frame around the entity would be missing as well as the dotted arrow and the reidentification component. The verification and reidentification boxes would not be filled out.

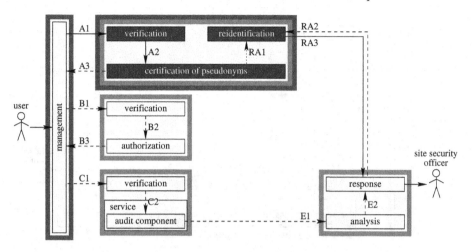

**Fig. 8.3.** Multilateral security: certification of pseudonyms

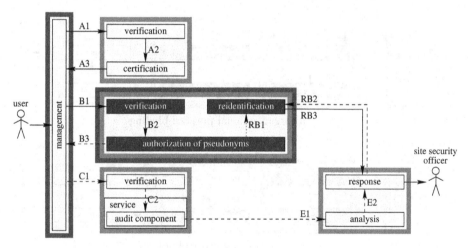

**Fig. 8.4.** Multilateral security: authorization of pseudonyms

The architectures for unilateral security can be easily realized, because the entity who benefits from the unfair situation merely needs to trust agents who enforce only his security objectives, which is an easier task than balancing conflicting interests.

Architectures providing multilateral security take conflicting interests into account. In Sect. 2.3 and Sect. 8.2 was derived that the entities who pursue the conflicting interests should not be able to control the objects of interest, i.e. the pseudonyms in the property statements. Instead, for multilateral security the pseudonym mapping should be controlled by one or more agents, which the users and the SSO need to trust (see Fig. 8.3 to Fig. 8.5). While the agent is responsible to balance pseudonymity and accountability, and controls the com-

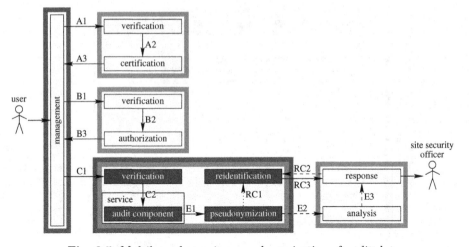

**Fig. 8.5.** Multilateral security: pseudonymization of audit data

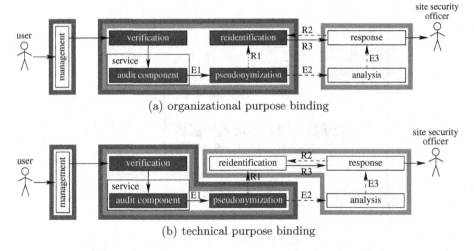

(a) organizational purpose binding

(b) technical purpose binding

**Fig. 8.6.** Purpose binding of controlled pseudonym disclosure

ponents that implement these functions, the users and the SSO must not have any control over the very same components.

The architectures for multilateral security are harder to implement, since for the operation agents are required, who both, users and SSO, can trust simultaneously to balance their interests in a fair way. In Sect. 9.1 the trust problem is investigated in some more detail for the different layers. One solution to solve this problem is to disperse the responsibility, such that the interests can only be satisfied, if several agents cooperate. This can be technically realized by multiple encryption, such as in the Mix approach [80], or by using threshold cryptosystems [212, 67]. These advanced options are out of the scope of this text.

Figure 8.3 to Fig. 8.5 depict only architectures and control requirements for the organizational purpose binding of controlled pseudonym disclosure. Section 8.4.1 describes how the control requirements can be relaxed by using technical purpose binding for pseudonym disclosure, instead of organizational purpose binding.

### 8.4.1 Influence of Purpose Binding on Control Requirements

Figure 8.6 shows for the architecture with audit data pseudonymization at the service layer (which is the architecture used for our approach in Part II), how the control requirements can be relaxed by using technical purpose binding for pseudonym disclosure, instead of organizational purpose binding.[6]

For technical purpose binding the pseudonym mapping is provided to the reidentifier in a protected form (see 'R1' in Fig. 8.6b).[7] However, the pseudonymous audit data is supplemented with information needed to neutralize the protection of the pseudonym mapping (see 'E2' in Fig. 8.6b). Due to the nature of the protection of the pseudonym mapping, reidentification is only possible in accordance with the a priori defined purpose of controlled pseudonym disclosure. As a result, the user does not need to trust the entity any more, which controls the reidentification component. Hence, the SSO may control the reidentification component and may disclose pseudonyms in a timely and autonomous fashion, as soon as the respective purpose permits.

Technical purpose binding is also possible in the certification and authorization layers of the model, but yields varying benefit (see Sect. 9.1).

---

[6] As proposed in Sect. 7.2.3, Sect. 16.6 and Sect. 28.4.2, organizational and technical purpose binding can be employed simultaneously to complement one another. Naturally, both methods use an individual pseudonym mapping, such that 'R1' in Fig. 8.6a and Fig. 8.6b must be considered individually, as well as the respective reidentification component. The control requirements for the distinct reidentification components remain as depicted in Fig. 8.6a and Fig. 8.6b.

[7] In Sect. 16.3 we propose providing the pseudonym mapping inlined with the pseudonymized audit data. In such a setting the arrow 'R1' in Fig. 8.6b is obsolete.

# Comparing Architectures

In Sect. 9.1 criteria are given to compare the individual phases of service utilization w.r.t. pseudonymization within the architectural model introduced in Chap. 8. Using numerous examples, in Sect. 9.2 it is shown how the architectural model can be used to classify existing privacy-enhancing technologies (PETs). Finally, in Sect. 9.3 the related work on PETs is separated into direct and indirect audit data pseudonymization. Direct audit data pseudonymization is examined in more detail in Chap. 10.

## 9.1 Criteria and Comparison

Figure 8.2 to Fig. 8.5 depict the different phases or layers where pseudonyms can be introduced in the model, such that the analysis component works only on pseudonymized audit data. Introducing pseudonyms in a given layer or phase has specific benefits and disadvantages, which are investigated in the following and summarized in Table 9.1.

**Table 9.1.** Summary of architecture properties, grouped by relation to the issues of trust, security and cost of deployment. Each criterion can be '$\sqrt{}$'=met, '−'=not met, or '%'=irrelevant in the given context

| property criteria | pseudonymizing entity | | | |
|---|---|---|---|---|
| | management | certifier | authorizer | service |
| multilateral security | − | $\sqrt{}$ | $\sqrt{}$ | $\sqrt{}$ |
| independence of service | $\sqrt{}$ | $\sqrt{}$ | − | − |
| dependable attributes | − | $\sqrt{}$ | $\sqrt{}$ | % |
| technical purpose binding | − | − | $\sqrt{}$ | $\sqrt{}$ |
| verifiability of pseudonyms b.a. | $\sqrt{}$ | $\sqrt{}$ | $\sqrt{}$ | − |
| independence of user | − | − | − | $\sqrt{}$ |
| independence of infrastructure | $\sqrt{}$ | − | − | $\sqrt{}$ |

**Multilateral Security**

In the model can multilateral security only be supported by entities which do not pursue one of the conflicting interests that they are supposed to balance. In other words, the pseudonymizing agents should take a neutral position w.r.t. the security objectives pseudonymity and accountability. In the model, such entities are the certifier, the authorizer and the service (cf. criterion *Independence of Service* for the service). Note, that these entities could still act unilaterally in favor of only one of the security objectives.

In contrast, entities pursuing merely one of the conflicting security objectives are expected to act only unilaterally in their own interest, such as the user management component.

**Independence of Service**

Even if an entity does not itself pursue a certain security objective, the organization it is affiliated with and which it depends on, still can pursue a certain security objective. Due to the dependence on an organization, the entity's activity could be biased in favor of the organization's interests.

When selecting a certifier as pseudonymizer this problem can be avoided. This is not necessarily the case, when an authorizer shall act as a pseudonymizer. Due to the fact that authorizations are tightly coupled to the service, the authorizer often also is associated with the service.

In the real world, one hopes to avoid the problem of biased decision-making by conceding an elected person a secure position within the organization, such that he can make decisions that are in conflict with the organization he depends on, without thereby threatening his own employment. Such a position has been created by the German labor law for the works council and by the German privacy law for the privacy commissioner.

However, the extent of dependence of a person on an organization may influence the probability that the person is tempted to act unilaterally in the interest of the organization, instead of balancing the interests. In terms of the model, this means that the service users are less willing to trust an authorizer, which is tightly coupled to the service provider, or the service provider itself, to protect the user's pseudonymity. Conversely, the users would straightforwardly trust an entity to protect their pseudonymity, if it is independent of the service, such as the certifier or the user's management component.

**Dependable Attributes**

Depending on which entity responsibly certifies a pseudonymous property statement, can the evaluating party rely on the statement, i.e. that the respective entity or person actually enjoys the certified properties. It is expected that an agent, which pursues the security objectives of the service provider, can be trusted to provide dependable attributes in property statements. Conversely, if the user's management component affirms that the user enjoys certain properties without providing proof, this statement is not necessarily dependable (see Sect. 2.3). Note, that in the case, where the service pseudonymizes audit data, no attributes are certified, such that this criterion is meaningless.

## Technical Purpose Binding

While in Sect. 8.4.1 technical purpose binding of pseudonym disclosure is described for audit data, in principle it can also be realized for the certifier or the authorizer.

Considering technical purpose binding for the certifier, one has to bear in mind that a given certificate is used to acquire authorizations for various services with various purposes for processing and for audit data analysis. The pseudonyms and the respective technical purpose binding would have to support all of these anticipated purposes for disclosure as well as linkability. This would come along with a massive erosion of the pseudonymity of the respective certificates, such that it seems inappropriate to realize technical purpose binding for pseudonymizing certifiers.

This problem does not apply to pseudonymizing authorizers. Technical purpose binding seems to be a useful concept to be implemented for pseudonymizing authorizers.

Finally, property statements made by the user's management component cannot be dependably accounted to the user, such that the effort for any purpose binding would be a waste.

## Verifiability of Pseudonyms before Service Access

As long as pseudonyms are introduced before the service access phase, the service can verify the pseudonymous authorization and the properties of the pseudonyms. Service requests with invalid pseudonyms can be detected by the service's verification component and can be rejected to avoid losses. But, if pseudonyms are introduced after the access decision is made, e.g. when pseudonymizing audit data, detecting invalid pseudonyms cannot help to avoid the commenced service access. Note, that this criterion is complementary to the criterion *Independence of User*.

## Independence of User

If the pseudonymization involves a software component that is controlled or operated by the user, the pseudonymization is said to be dependent on the user.

On the one hand, this leaves the user in control, such that he is responsible for a proper use. On the other hand, the service provider is anyway obliged to comply with the privacy law and cannot shift this obligation to the users (see Sect. 5.2 and Sect. 5.5). Moreover, a software component, which needs to be made available to the user, generates additional cost. From this perspective, independence of the user can be valued positively. Note, that this criterion is complementary to the criterion *Verifiability of Pseudonyms before Service Access*.

**Independence of Infrastructure**

The architectures based on certificates and authorizations require trustworthy agents for certification and authorization, respectively. The effort for establishing such an infrastructure must not be underestimated. Experiences with pilot projects for anonymous communications services and for electronic cash show that these are quite time-consuming and expensive endeavors, which only a few service providers could afford [104]. Moreover, similarly complex infrastructures such as PKI or Passport still are not in widespread use, despite the availability of mature technology [98]. Independence of infrastructure therefore is in the interest of a quick and cost-efficient deployment of anonymity or pseudonymity.

## 9.2 Example Architectures for Pseudonymous Authorizations

In the following, for each of the pseudonymizing entities in Table 9.1, exemplary privacy-enhancing technologies (PETs) are given. The selection does not claim to give a comprehensive or representative survey over PETs. The intention is rather, to give an impression how the model can be used to classify PETs. Also, the scope is limited to architectures for pseudonymous or anonymous authorizations. The text does not cover all possibilities for acting pseudonymously or anonymously, for example anonymous publishing [199, 104], anonymous elections [199], anonymous auctions [199], anonymous (peer-to-peer) file-sharing [70], Private Information Retrieval (PIR) [48] and its applications [124] are not considered.

In the literature currently three other approaches or models to describe anonymous or pseudonymous authorizations are known. In the following, these approaches are briefly outlined and later accounted for, where the respective entities and the corresponding components are discussed.

Alamäki et al. define various functional components (*Profile Broker, Identity Broker, Authenticator*) that are required for architectures for anonymous or pseudonymous authorizations [2], however without distinguishing the respective properties and specifying the control requirements.

The Dutch privacy authority *Registratiekamer* together with the information and privacy commissioner of Ontario, Canada, developed a model for information systems with a focus on privacy [217, 23]. Based on this model, the authorization process, including the respective audit data, is described in analogy to the architecture in Fig. 3.11, where the service holds the property statements, such that no further responsible agents are needed and the service needs not to verify the validity of the property statements. Accordingly, the users merely obtain references to the statements about their properties. A so-called *Identity Protector* can be placed at several locations in the model. The Identity Protector acts as a pseudonymizing entity which separates components where user IDs are known from components, where merely the respective pseudonyms are processed. For each proposed placement of the Identity Protector the resulting architecture is described, however without distinguishing the respective properties and specifying the control requirements. A later study about privacy in intelligent software agent systems gives alternatives for applying and implementing the Identity Protector [22].[1]

The third approach describes *Privacy-enhancing Identity Management* (PIM), where the user decides on his discretion, who can get which of his personal data, and where the user can separate his activity in different spheres, such that different addressees of his activity may have a different view of the partial identities (personae) of the user [111]. PIM comprises the applications, the middleware and the communication infrastructure [51, 52]. At the application layer the identity manager of the user (cf. 'management' in our model) and the service provider (cf. 'service' in our model) negotiate the requirements for partial identities (represented by property statements in our model). Beyond anonymous authorizations this approach also addresses e-commerce and e-government. Therefore, PIM leverages not only pseudonymizing certifiers and authorizers (see below) and an infrastructure for anonymous communication (see below, anonymity of sender and/or recipient), but also requires additional mediators or trustees for the digital exchange of goods, settling of liabilities, electronic payment (see below electronic cash), and finally, the delivery of physical goods in the real world.

In the following, the three described and rather general approaches to PETs, as well as stand-alone PETs are mapped to the terms and architectures of our model, i.e. to anonymization or pseudonymization at the management layer (see Sect. 9.2.1), at the certification layer (see Sect. 9.2.2), at the authorization layer (see Sect. 9.2.3) or at the service layer (see Sect. 9.2.4).

## 9.2.1 Architectures with Pseudonymizing Management

Identity Protector: In the model of Rossum, Borking et al. the Identity Protector corresponds to the management component, when implemented near the

---

[1] Interestingly, the study points out that strong privacy requirements rule out the following abilities of software agents: mobility, cloning, and the use of third-party agents.

user, i.e., in between of the user representation and the service [217, 23]. In agent systems this corresponds to the integration with or the wrapping of the user representation [22].

Identity Broker: Alamäki et al. define Identity Brokers as entities which introduce pseudonyms (cf. Trusted Mobile Terminal in Alamäki et al. [2]).

Profile Broker: Alamäki et al. define Profile Brokers as user profile access points, where user profiles correspond to the attributes of property statements [2]. Profile Brokers can be complemented with Contract Brokers, which verifyably negotiate the mutual requirements of users and services w.r.t. disclosure of user profiles (cf. Trusted Mobile Terminal in Alamäki et al. [2]).

Privacy-enhancing Identity Management: On the one hand, in the real world people repeatedly need to re-orient and self-organize, and therefore implicitly and naturally manage their partial identities or personae. However, explicitly managing their partial identities in the digital world may overtax the very same people [133]. Hence, it is useful to assist the user with the management of his partial identities and the linkability thereof [112]. Identity management components installed on the user's personal device (e.g. personal digital assistant, PDA) assists the user with creating and selecting his partial identities or identity profiles, which contain property statements [195, 59].

Instead of locating this functionality on the user device, it can also be located at one or more third parties, also denoted as *infomediaries*, which the user trusts [100, 99, 101]. Some implementations thereof are for example [55, 51]: Proxymate or Lucent Personalized Web Assistant (LPWA)[2], digitalme[3] by Novell, SuperProfile by Lumeria[4], iPrivacy[5], PrivacyBank[6], Persona by Privaseek[7], v-GO by Passlogix[8] and the Freedom[9] Security and Privacy Suite.

The user's management component can record each property statement that it has sent out [135, 25], in order to assists the user with judging his actual degree of anonymity in the digital world. Property statements to be sent out are selected, e.g. using P3P [54], by matching the security requirements and the privacy policy of the given recipient to the privacy requirements tied to the partial identities defined by the user, while considering the actual situation in which the user acts [51, 52, 135, 122, 102]. In analogy to the trust evaluation carried out by the recipients of property statements, the user's management component evaluates the trust w.r.t. the recipient's privacy policy, before selecting and sending a property statement.

---

[2] http://www.bell-labs.com/project/lpwa
[3] http://www.digitalme.com
[4] http://www.lumeria.com
[5] http://www.iprivacy.com
[6] http://www.privacybank.com
[7] http://www.privaseek.com
[8] http://www.passlogix.com
[9] http://www.freedom.net

## 9.2.2 Architectures with Pseudonymizing Certifier

Identity Protector: In the Model of Rossum, Borking et al. the Identity Protector corresponds to the certifier when implemented as a third party between the user representation and the service [217, 23]. In agent systems the certifier corresponds to the nearest trustworthy party that provides privacy safeguards for an agent [22].

Identity Broker: see Sect. 9.2.1, see also Physical Separation of Identity and Profile in Alamaki et al. [2].

Authenticator: Alamäki et al. define Authenticators as entities which provide for the authentication of users. In our model this is part of the verification boxes (see Fig. 3.3).

Privacy-enhancing Identity Management: PIM    leverages    anonymous    or pseudonymous credentials (see below).

Anonymity of Sender and/or Recipient: To effectively provide anonymous communication in distributed systems, personally identifying data must be avoided in all layers of the OSI reference model. Hence, anonymous services in the application layer require additional services that provide for anonymous communication. Secure anonymous communication services may also support conditional anonymity [136]. Usually they correspond to the architecture version in Fig. 3.12. As an example, Mix systems distribute the trust, which the user needs to invest, over several autonomous parties. There are various implementations of Mix systems: Onion Routing/TOR, Hordes, Freedom Network, JAP, Babel and Mixmaster-Remailer. Crowds and Cypherpunk-Remailer are based on similar concepts. Simpler systems, which do not distribute the necessary trust, are or were for example Anonymizer.com, Anonymouse and Anon.penet.fi. Surveys of these technologies have been published by several authors [73, 80, 10, 199, 104, 105]. Moreover, there are concepts for unconditional anonymity of the sender (DC networks) or the recipient (broadcasting) [80, 64], alas they cannot be implemented efficiently in most of the internetworked environments in practice.

Anonymous Credentials: Anonymous or pseudonymous credentials are introduced as anonymous or pseudonymous property statements in Sect. 8.1. Various approaches for implementation are published [43, 46, 44, 45, 216, 24, 103, 212, 34, 33, 145]. Pfitzmann et al. gave a simple construction based on an arbitrary signature system and a communication system providing sender anonymity [175]. Also a provably secure approach exists [58], alas, it is not sufficiently efficient for practical use. Anonymous or pseudonymous credentials can either be used as certificates or as authorizations.[10]

---

[10] Note, that when using references to such property statements, such as in Fig. 3.9, observations of all accesses to a given property statements can cumulate to a usage profile. A first approach to conceal the accesses using private information retrieval (PIR) has been proposed by Iliev and Smith [115].

Anonymous Authentication: Verifying anonymous or pseudonymous property statements comprises anonymously or pseudonymously authenticating the presenting party (see authentication component in Sect. 3.3). There are several publications on authentication technology subject to controlled identity disclosure [193, 109, 113], or at least with strong mechanisms to discourage the unauthorized sharing of pseudonyms with other users [110]. Anonymous authentication is frequently realized using group signatures [36, 130, 129, 20].

Electronic Cash: Fair electronic offline cash usually provides for controlled identity disclosure subject to technical purpose binding in the case that someone spends a given electronic coin more than once (commonly denoted as *double spending*) [162, 199, 171, 61, 35, 50, 176, 161]. For several systems this is realized using group signatures [62, 215, 146], magic ink signatures [121] or fair blind signatures [209]. However, also anonymous credentials could be used, encoding the monetary value in the attributes and being valid for being shown only once (*one-show* credentials).

ANIDA-Kerberos (1): For the privacy-enhanced intrusion detection system ANIDA the *Kerberos Authentication Server* was conceptually[11] extended to use pseudonyms with controlled disclosure subject to organizational purpose binding [32].

### 9.2.3 Architectures with Pseudonymizing Authorizer

Identity Protector: see Sect. 9.2.2.

Identity Broker: see Sect. 9.2.2.

Privacy-enhanced Identity Management: see Sect. 9.2.2.

Anonymous Credentials: see Sect. 9.2.2.

Anonymous Authentication: see Sect. 9.2.2.

ANIDA-Kerberos (2): Büschkes and Kesdogan proposed a second approach to privacy-enhanced intrusion detection, where the *Kerberos ticket granting server* is complemented with a multilaterally secure Mix [32]. The resulting architecture corresponds to the version in Fig. 3.10.

Unlinkable Serial Transactions: Serial transactions can be authorized in a completely unlinkable fashion by extending the validity of one-show credentials at each use for the following transaction only [213].

Anonymous Log-in to Internet Access Points: Based on the fair electronic coins of Chaum et al. [47] Internet dial-in users can anonymously log-in to dial-in access points of their Internet providers [40].

Pseudonymous User Accounts: The identifiers of user accounts can be used like role pseudonyms, if appropriate organizational provisions are made [80, 217] (see the architecture version in Fig. 3.11, see also Sect. 3.5).

---

[11] The concepts have not been implemented.

### 9.2.4 Architectures with Pseudonymizing Service

The confidentiality of (personal) data processed by a service can be protected in two ways: controlling access to the data itself (access control approach) or concealing the data and controlling access to the information that is needed to neutralize the "cloak" (e.g. encryption or pseudonymization).

The access to and processing of collected personal data can be regulated using access control with a policy extension to express allowed processing purposes. According to this idea Fischer-Hübner proposed, formalized and implemented an access control model, which takes into account the tasks and functions of the data controller [80]. As a complement to, or instead of access control, personal data can be protected by means of anonymization or pseudonymization, whereby the purpose binding of pseudonym disclosure can be enforced cryptographically. Since this work focuses on pseudonymization, the access control approach is not considered.

In the following is only personal data considered that has already been collected by a service in the form of audit data for misuse detection. When considering service-side anonymization or pseudonymization, it is useful to keep the criteria summarized in Table 9.1 in mind. To be able to react timely on detected misuse, a timely pseudonym disclosure is desirable, preferably without the need to involve third parties. This can be realized using technical purpose binding of pseudonym disclosure. Also, the solution should be practical und independent from users and expensive infrastructures. As shown in Table 9.1 these requirements can be met at the service layer in a cost-efficient way. In the following, approaches for anonymization or pseudonymization of audit data at the service layer are given. In Chap. 10, criteria are developed to compare these approaches, and selected approaches are presented in some more detail.

Identity Protector: In the Model of Rossum, Borking et al. the Identity Protector corresponds to an audit data pseudonymizer, when implemented between the service representation and the audit data [217, 23].

Pseudonymizing Audit Data for Intrusion Detection: In her seminal work on *Intrusion Detection and Avoidance* (IDA) Fischer-Hübner proposed in 1993 the concept of misuse detection using pseudonymized audit data. The developed architecture was only partially implemented [79, 80, 205, 81].

The concept of pseudonymized audit data for misuse detection is used by Sobirey, showing that the concept is workable with operational intrusion detection systems. The IDA concepts have been integrated with the fully working IDS *Adaptive Intrusion Detection* (AID), thereby heavily modifying the underlying architecture [151, 204, 80, 205, 206, 203].

Lundin developed and implemented a simple pseudonymizer for the audit data of an operational firewall, to be able to legally use the pseudonymized audit data for anomaly detection experiments [143, 142, 141].

As Lundin, also Rieck was motivated by privacy law to pseudonymize Solaris BSM audit data [117], which was set aside for anomaly detection experiments (*bsmpseu*). *Bsmpseu* does not support controlled pseudonym disclosure [185].

The approach developed in this book can be used to pseudonymize audit data for misuse detection in a multilaterally secure way, where the controlled pseudonym disclosure and pseudonym linkability are subject to technical purpose binding [88, 15, 92, 91, 90, 87, 86, 85, 84, 83, 13, 14, 12].

Pseudonymizing Web Server Audit Data: Pircher's *Anonymouse* web server log file pseudonymizer retains only top level domain names of web server client addresses in the web server's audit data [73]. The most significant parts of the user address is deleted, such that each top level domain constitutes a group pseudonym for all user addresses from this domain. Anonymouse does not support controlled pseudonym disclosure.

The commercial web content filtering system *WebWasher* can optionally pseudonymize the generated audit data/reports. The vendor's marketing publications merely reveal that organizational purpose binding can be used for pseudonym disclosure, distributing the required trust on two persons [221].

The lawyer Jaeger roughly proposed an audit data pseudonymization concept based on cryptographic one-way hash functions for IP addresses contained in log files of Internet access points or service providers [119].

Pseudonymizing Internet Traffic Traces: Pang et al. developed and implemented the pseudonymizer *BROanonymize* for network audit data (*tcpdump* packet traces) to prevent privacy problems when publishing packet traces to the research community [169]. *BROanonymize* is integrated with the IDS *BRO*, which serves as an advanced parser for locating and rewriting syntactical elements [170]. Note, that the pseudonymization, alas, is not integral part of the regular misuse detection function of *BRO*.

Similar but simpler tools have been implemented by Mishall [156], Peuhkuri [172] and Xu et al. [223].

None of the described tools support the controlled disclosure of pseudonyms.

## 9.3 Distinguishing Direct and Indirect Audit Data Pseudonymization

This book addresses the problem of (1) pseudonymizing audit data (2) for privacy respecting misuse detection. Pseudonymous audit data (1) can be achieved by implementing pseudonymization at any of the described layers (management, certifier, authorizer, service), resulting in different architectures as shown in Sect. 8.3 and Sect. 8.4. For each of these architectures, a number of example systems has been given in Sect. 9.2.

Considering all existing systems that are implementing any of these architectures, we find a large amount of relevant literature. In this book we focus on direct audit data pseudonymization at the service layer (cf. Sect. 9.2.4). In the following we therefore distinguish between direct and indirect audit data pseudonymization.

Many architectures can be used to indirectly achieve pseudonymous audit data by pseudonymizing property statements before they are translated into authorized access of the service (see Sect. 9.2.1, Sect. 9.2.2 and Sect. 9.2.3). These approaches are denoted as *indirect audit data pseudonymization*, because personal data is already pseudonymized before the audit data is generated. The audit data itself is not modified to provide pseudonymous audit data. These architectures achieve pseudonymity on a wider scale, where audit data pseudonymization is a mere by-product. Each of these architectures has its strengths and weaknesses, but if pseudonymity is required only specifically for audit data, none of these approaches can take on with direct audit data pseudonymization (see Table 9.1).

Alone for pseudonymous audit data, the cost for establishing an infrastructure for pseudonymous property statements is disproportionately high. In addition, for misuse detection purposes (2) the solution should technically enforce purpose binding of pseudonym disclosure. These requirements are only met by audit data pseudonymizers at the service layer (see Sect. 10.1). Direct audit data pseudonymization or anonymization (see Sect. 9.2.4) is inspected in more detail in Chap. 10, also w.r.t. the specific requirements of misuse detection.

# 10

# Audit Data Pseudonymization

In Chap. 9 architectures for anonymous and pseudonymous authorizations have been reviewed. In this Chapter, approaches for direct audit data pseudonymization are examined and compared (cf. Sect. 9.3). The task of directly anonymizing or pseudonymizing audit data makes some specific demands, which are described in Sect. 10.1. In Sect. 10.2 criteria are given, which allow to compare existing approaches. Selected approaches are described in Sect. 10.3. Finally, the distinction between the presented approaches and the approaches developed in this book is emphasized in Sect. 10.4. In the remainder of this book we denote *direct audit data pseudonymization* simply as audit data pseudonymization.

## 10.1 Specific Requirements of Audit Data Pseudonymization

While pseudonymizing already collected audit data achieves a comparable effect in the legal domain as authorizing service users with pseudonymous property statements [191], for pseudonymization of audit data for misuse detection different requirements need to be accounted for, for the concept, architecture and implementation. Possible attacks on the interests of both, the user and the SSO result in specific requirements for the performance and the throughput of audit data pseudonymization.

In order to avoid the uncontrolled disclosure of identifying information of the user, the path taken by newly generated audit records should be as short as possible to be easily protectable. Therefore, audit records should ideally be pseudonymized on the same device where they are generated, i.e. the device delivering the service.[1] The response time of the service should not be degraded unreasonably by pseudonymization.

---
[1] When relying on audit data, we are always confronted with the risk of integrity loss in case an attacker achieves sufficient privilege to manipulate the audit data or the

Hence, if audit data is generated on the device that an attacker is trying to gain control of, to avoid loss of accountability, the pseudonymized audit data should be transported as quickly as possible to a remote location that securely stores audit data from possibly various audit components. Therefore, before transportation, audit data should ideally be locally pseudonymized on the fly. Pseudonymization should not introduce a significant delay between the generation of an audit record and its transportation. Specifically, pseudonymization should be able to keep up with the audit data volume generated on the device. For some kinds of audit data the volume generated may be huge, e.g. if the audit data documents the sequence of system calls. As a result, the techniques for audit data pseudonymization should be chosen such that the performance requirements can be satisfied, i.e., the involved computational complexity and delay must be sufficiently low. This can be achieved as demonstrated in Part IV for the approach developed in Part II and implemented in Part III.

The above-mentioned performance and security issues need to be considered after audit data is generated and before it is analyzed w.r.t. misuses. Additionally, it must be considered, whether misuses detected by analyzing the pseudonymous audit data call for a timely response, and whether pseudonyms need to be disclosed for an appropriate response. When pseudonym disclosure is subject to technical purpose binding, it can be performed in a timely fashion. The reason is that due to the simplified control requirements the site security administrator can disclose pseudonyms as soon as granted by the technical purpose binding (see Sect. 8.4.1). Organizational purpose binding in contrast involves two or more persons to ensure proper adherence to the defined purpose. The purpose checking then usually is performed manually, such that pseudonym disclosure is delayed, if one or more of the involved persons are not immediately available.

## 10.2 Criteria and Comparison

The approaches for audit data pseudonymization introduced in Sect. 9.2.4 are in the following compared w.r.t. the pseudonym properties (see Chap. 7) and the control requirements (see Sect. 8.4). The performance requirements described in Sect. 10.1 need to be considered for the approaches where audit data is pseudonymized on the fly to be analyzed for misuse detection (see IDA in Sect. 10.3.1, AID in Sect. 10.3.2, and Pseudo/CoRe in Chap. 20). Note, that the

---

process of its generation. Though countermeasures have already been proposed [197] they are not yet in wide-spread use. Even in the face of these problems, weakly protected audit data today is still one very important source of information that is used to resolve attack situations or to gather early indications thereof. In the same way in which an attacker can manipulate audit data or its generation, he may also corrupt the integrity of pseudonyms in pseudonymized audit data to evade later identification. We argue that we can rely on the pseudonyms generated on a host under attack as long as we can rely on the audit data generated on that host.

reviewed approaches readily satisfy the performance requirements. More details on selected approaches are given in Sect. 10.3.

The approaches are summarized and compared in Table 10.1 w.r.t. to the following criteria:

disclosure support: Does the approach support pseudonym disclosure (see Sect. 7.2)?

  pseudonym mapping: How is the pseudonym mapping implemented (see Sect. 7.2.5)?

  purpose binding: How is the purpose binding of pseudonym disclosure enforced (technically, organizationally) (see Sect. 7.2.1 to Sect. 7.2.3)? How is technical purpose binding safeguarded?

  controller of purpose binding: Which entity controls the pseudonym mapping (see Sect. 7.2.6)? This entity ensures the purpose binding for pseudonym disclosure (for technical purpose binding during pseudonymization, and for organizational purpose binding during disclosure).

linkability support: Are the generated pseudonyms linkable? In which contexts are pseudonyms linkable (see Sect. 7.3)?

  additional pseudonym renewals: Are pseudonyms additionally renewed in contexts other than specified in the field "linkability support"? For example, in some approaches all pseudonyms are renewed periodically.

  technical purpose binding: Is pseudonym linkability technically bound to the purpose of processing (see Sect. 7.3)? How is technical purpose binding safeguarded?

  controller of linkability: Which entity controls the (technical purpose binding of) linkability of the generated pseudonyms (see Sect. 7.3)?

properties of architecture: Which properties exhibits the architecture of the approach, in particular the method for enforcing dual control for organizational purpose binding. Does the approach respect the control requirements discussed in Sect. 8.4?

In this area we identified problems for all previously known approaches that were originally designed for multilateral security. Either the requirements for trust and control were not accounted for completely, such that the SSO can bypass the purpose binding and directly access the pseudonym mapping. Or an inappropriate method was selected for enforcing dual control for organizational purpose binding, such that a shared and confidentially distributed decryption key is known after pseudonym disclosure to at least one of the involved entities.[2]

---

[2] An appropriate method for multi-party decryption while keeping the decryption key confidential is threshold cryptography [67].

**Table 10.1.** Summary of the properties of selected approaches for anonymization or pseudonymization of audit data. '$\sqrt{}$'=criterion met, '–'=criterion not met, '%'=unknown/missing information, '(?...?)'=presumption.

| approach (implementation) | disclosure support (7.2) | linkability support (7.3) |
|---|---|---|
| | pseudonym mapping (7.2.5) | additional ps.-nym renewals |
| | purpose binding (7.2.1-7.2.3) | techn. purpose binding (7.3) |
| | controller of purpose binding | controller of linkability |
| | properties of architecture: root cause | |
| Anonymouse [73] (web server) log file pseudonymizer (research prototype) | – | $\sqrt{}$ · group pseudonyms |
| | coarsening | – |
| | – | – |
| | – | PPO |
| | unilateral, pseudonymity: pseudonym disclosure not supported | |
| Jaeger [119] audit data pseudonymizer (concept) | – | $\sqrt{}$ · subject pseudonyms |
| | one-way hash function | – |
| | – | – |
| | – | PPO |
| | unilateral, pseudonymity: pseudonym disclosure not supported | |
| TCPDpriv [156] network trace pseudonymizer (available) | – | $\sqrt{}$ · subject pseudonyms |
| | table | – |
| | – | – |
| | – | PPO |
| | unilateral, pseudonymity: pseudonym disclosure not supported | |
| Peuhkuri [172] network trace pseudonymizer (research prototype) | – | $\sqrt{}$ · subject pseudonyms |
| | symmetric encryption | – |
| | – | – |
| | – | PPO |
| | unilateral, pseudonymity: pseudonym disclosure not supported | |
| Xu, Fan, Ammar [223] network trace pseudonymizer (concept) | – | $\sqrt{}$ · subject pseudonyms |
| | prefix-preserving encryption | – |
| | – | – |
| | – | PPO |
| | unilateral, pseudonymity: pseudonym disclosure not supported | |
| BROanonymize [169] network trace pseudonymizer (research prototype available) | – | $\sqrt{}$ · subject pseudonyms |
| | table, one-way hash function | – |
| | – | – |
| | – | PPO |
| | unilateral, pseudonymity: pseudonym disclosure not supported | |

Table 10.1 continued from page 80

| approach (implementation) | disclosure support (7.2) | linkability support (7.3) |
|---|---|---|
| | pseudonym mapping (7.2.5) | additional ps.-nym renewals |
| | purpose binding (7.2.1-7.2.3) | techn. purpose binding (7.3) |
| | controller of purpose binding | controller of linkability |
| | properties of architecture: root cause | |
| **BSMpseu [185]** anomaly detection audit data pseudo-nymizer (research prototype available) | – | √ · subject pseudonyms |
| | table, pseudo-random | – |
| | – | – |
| | – | PPO |
| | unilateral, pseudonymity: pseudonym disclosure not supported | |
| **Lundin (10.3.3)** anomaly detection audit data pseudonymizer (research prototype) | √ | √ · subject pseudonyms |
| | table, coarsening | regularly discard mapping |
| | – | – |
| | SSO | PPO |
| | unilateral, accountability: SSO controls pseudonym mapping | |
| **WebWasher [221]** web content filter log file pseudonymizer (commercial product available) | √ | % (?√ · subject pseudonyms?) |
| | % (?encryption?) | % (?–?) |
| | organizational (?only once?) | % (?–?) |
| | % (?PPO?) | % (?PPO?) |
| | % (?unilateral, accountability: dual control can be bypassed?) | |
| **IDA (10.3.1)** misuse and anomaly detection audit data pseudonymizer (concept) | √ | √ · subject pseudonyms |
| | symmetric encryption | regularly change encr. key |
| | organizational (only once) | – |
| | PPO | PPO |
| | unilateral, accountability: dual control can be bypassed | |
| **AID (10.3.2)** misuse detection audit data pseudonymizer (research prototype) | √ | √ · subject pseudonyms |
| | symmetric encryption | regularly change encr. key |
| | – / organizational | – |
| | – / PPO | PPO |
| | unilateral, accountability: SSO controls pseudonym mapping | |
| **Pseudo/CoRe (20)** misuse detection audit data pseudo-nymizer (research prototype available) | √ | √ · role pseudonyms |
| | symmetric encryption | time out/insufficient suspicion |
| | techn. + org. · secret sharing | – |
| | PPO | PPO |
| | **multilateral, pseudonymity and accountability** | |
| **Signature-net-based approach (26) (concept)** | √ | √ · transaction pseudonyms |
| | symmetric encryption | misuse scenario incomplete |
| | techn. + org. · secret sharing | techn. · one-way hash |
| | PPO | PPO |
| | **multilateral, pseudonymity and accountability** | |

## 10.3 Exemplary Approaches to Audit Data Pseudonymization

Some of the related approaches compared in Sect. 10.2 are closer to the focus of this book than others. In the following, the approaches that directly pseudonymize audit data for intrusion detection and which also support pseudonym disclosure are described in more detail. As an interesting contrast, also one approach for indirect audit data pseudonymization is described in Sect. 10.3.4.

### 10.3.1 IDA Misuse and Anomaly Detection Audit Data Pseudonymizer

The *Intrusion Detection and Avoidance* system (IDA) and its fundamental privacy concepts were developed by Fischer-Hübner [81, 79, 205].

IDA monitors certain system calls concerned with user sessions and clearance levels as well as object creation, deletion, access and respective permission modifications. Apart from protecting personal data by conventional mechanisms, IDA introduced the notion of pseudonymous audit analysis. The kernel reference monitor generates subject pseudonyms before audit data is passed to the kernel-integrated analysis component (comprising anomaly detection as well as misuse detection). The IDA concept incorporates the introduction of pseudonyms wherever subject identifiers are used, particularly for access control. To restrict pseudonym linkability, i.e. the risk of uncontrolled pseudonym disclosure, relationship pseudonyms derived from combinations of subject and object identifiers are proposed. These relationship pseudonyms are proposed for access control only, but not for audit analysis, which in IDA requires linkability across subjects, i.e. subject pseudonyms. Analysis proceeds on pseudonymized audit data. The close coupling of the analysis and decision components to the reference monitor allows enforcement of decisions without the need for automated reidentification. Obviously, in the IDA approach pseudonymization is deeply entangled with the innards of the operating system, limiting its applicability.

The IDA concept uses symmetric encryption as pseudonym mapping for subject identifiers in audit data. To limit the linkability of the subject pseudonyms, pseudonym changes by rekeying after certain time intervals are proposed. Since IDA can react without requiring automatic pseudonym disclosure, organizational purpose binding is sufficient, and was designed to be enforced by sharing the symmetric key between the SSO and the PPO. Prerequisite to this proceeding is that the symmetric key used in monitored systems is safe against attackers, i.e. the SSOs must not be able to control the responsible subsystems. Unfortunately, after the first pseudonym disclosure either the SSO, or the PPO knows the symmetric decryption key, such that organizational purpose binding can be subverted.

## 10.3.2 AID Misuse Detection Audit Data Pseudonymizer

The privacy-related aspects concerning the *Adaptive Intrusion Detection* system (AID) are described by Sobirey et al. [203, 206, 205, 204, 151]. In case of conflicting information in these publications we base our summary on the most recent information.

The AID implementation comprises distributed event monitoring agents and a central misuse detection analysis station based on an RTworks expert system. The Solaris-based analysis station controls and adaptively polls the agents for Solaris BSM audit data and Windows NT audit data.[3]

AID uses the Solaris BSM audit component to monitor system calls and selected applications concerned with user sessions, file creation, deletion, accesses and respective permission modifications, as well as processes and administrative activity, some of which is non-attributable to any user. The fundamental concepts of pseudonymous audit analysis of IDA and AID are fairly similar, but the realizations differ in detail. AID introduces subject pseudonyms on monitored hosts after audit records have been emitted by the Solaris user level process `auditd`. Owing to the implementation of AID being based on an off-the-shelf platform, there is no holistic concept for pseudonyms as in IDA. Monitoring agents pseudonymize audit records, add supplementary information needed for misuse analysis and convert the records into an AID-specific format. Misuse analysis proceeds on pseudonymous audit data in the central station.

Pseudonym disclosure occurs automatically, when the expert system generates an alarm, or when alarm reports are generated, and before audit trails are archived in encrypted form. All AID monitoring agents reporting to the same central analysis station use the same symmetric key to encrypt, i.e. pseudonymize, person-identifying features. It follows that, if an adversary monitors the key on any AID host, the adversary is able to reidentify any audit records he monitors. Since AID uses a confidential channel for audit data transport (SecureRPC), an adversary is limited to AID host access, the central station being the most desirable target. Even if the control requirements from Sect. 8.4 for the audit components and pseudonymizers are met, the architecture of AID violates the control requirements for reidentification, which is, but should not be, controlled by the SSO (cf. Fig. 8.5). Hence, the SSO can disclose pseudonyms irrespective of any good cause.

Reviewing archived audit records is subject to organizational purpose binding and requires the SSO to cooperate with the PPO, because the archive encryption key is shared between the SSO and the PPO. Unfortunately, the organizational purpose binding of AID is conceptually identical to the one of IDA, such that

---

[3] Note, that the Windows NT processing capabilities of AID were developed under a grant for the German Army and are therefore classified. Hence, the available publications do not describe the Windows NT issues.

it is also ineffective. However, AID records reidentifications, but there are no provisions forcing the SSOs to make these records available to the PPOs.

To limit the linkability of the subject pseudonyms, as in IDA, pseudonym changes by rekeying after irregular time intervals are proposed.

### 10.3.3 Lundin Anomaly Detection Audit Data Pseudonymizer

Lundin and Jonsson describe an anomaly detection tool that uses statistical methods to analyze pseudonymous audit data [141, 142, 143].

The tool analyzes log-in event audit records generated by a firewall. Pseudonyms are introduced in large batches of audit records before exporting the batches together with the pseudonym mappings for anomaly analysis. This violates the on-the-fly requirement from Sect. 10.1. Note, that the pseudonymizer, however, is technically prepared to pseudonymize audit data on the fly.

Some identifying features are pseudonymized: user names, server host names, client host names as well as free text fields containing user and host names. Other potentially identifying features not being used as profile discriminators, but statistically analyzed, such as user activity and time stamps, are not pseudonymized. The pseudonym mapping is implemented as a table containing sequentially numbered place holders denoting the respective feature type (e.g. user0, user1, ...). Host names and each domain name part are mapped separately. IP addresses are mapped to an address in the same address class, allowing to determine the IP address class of a given pseudonym. Anomaly analysis proceeds on the pseudonymized audit records.

There are no documented precautions taken protecting the confidentiality of the pseudonym mapping, neither while in transit nor during analysis. Pseudonym disclosure is not supported in an automatic way and must be established manually by the SSO. No purpose binding is enforced for pseudonym disclosure, i.e., w.r.t. the SSO the pseudonymization is practically useless.

Several improvements are proposed by Lundin an Jonsson [141, 142]. Based on the ideas of Fischer-Hübner et al. [205] subject pseudonym linkability could be limited by re-generating the pseudonym mapping from scratch. Similar to the idea of Büschkes and Kesdogan [32] (see GRPs in Sect. 10.3.4), it is proposed to aggregate users into groups to support the SSO's intuitive manual anomaly detection capabilities, but also losing the ability to account events to individual users.

### 10.3.4 ANIDA Anomaly Detection Audit Data Pseudonymizer

The work on the *Aachener Network Intrusion Detection Architecture* (ANIDA) belongs to the category of indirect audit data pseudonymization (see Sect. 9.3).

However, it is interesting to consider the implications of such an approach for the IDS and for the service environment. The privacy aspects concerning the Windows NT-based ANIDA are described by Büschkes and Kesdogan [32].

In contrast to the other examined systems, ANIDA's architecture is geared towards analyzing network-based audit data from client-server applications and underlying protocol stacks. The concept comprises components monitoring all traffic on the network and the traffic exchanged with selected networked services. Hence, it is not sufficient merely to pseudonymize the audit data. The user's service accesses must be pseudonymized by the certifier or by the authorizer. Thus, ANIDA fundamentally relies on a generic distributed authentication and access control infrastructure. As a result, the monitored services need to support this framework, too. For the purpose of concealing identifying information related to a connection, Kerberos was chosen and modified concerning the tickets, the initial authentication and some protocol steps. An approach to concealing even the fact of a connection taking place is realized by integrating Mixes with Kerberos [41, 128].

ANIDA introduces pseudonyms either in the authentication service after user authentication (see certifier in our model for Kerberos in Sect. 3.5), or by one (or more) trusted Mix(es) that are coupled with the *ticket granting server* (TGS) (see authorizer in our model for Kerberos in Sect. 3.5). The pseudonyms are supplemented with group identifiers, confirming group memberships for the purpose of access control. Kerberos tickets were modified to use these augmented pseudonyms, referred to in ANIDA parlance as group reference pseudonyms[4] (GRP), instead of a client principal name. Furthermore, the client's host network address is omitted from tickets. GRPs are valid and can be used for several transactions until the bearing ticket expires. Thus, GRPs can be classified somewhere in between relationship pseudonyms and transaction pseudonyms. The choice of appropriate timeouts allows balancing pseudonym linkability, i.e. the risk of uncontrolled pseudonym disclosure, against the overhead involved in making out new tickets. The ANIDA approach implies group-based and thus coarse-grained access control[5] and entity profiling for intrusion detection.[6]

Pseudonym disclosure requires the cooperation of the GRP introducer (the Kerberos authentication server, i.e. certifier, or the TGS Mix, i.e. authorizer), which must be independent of SSOs and could be controlled by the PPO. There are

---

[4] This kind of pseudonyms including group associations should not to be mistaken for group pseudonyms, because individual users can still be distinguished by individual pseudonyms.

[5] While group-based access control is widely in use for the authorization of network service accesses, it may be too coarse-grained for many system internal authorizations such as file accesses.

[6] Note, that group-based profiling for anomaly detection offers several advantages, such as requiring cooperation of the group majority to achieve unnoticed profile drift defining malicious behavior as acceptable. This concept emerged with the IDS NIDES [144].

no monitoring components internal to client hosts and the GRP introducer, and SSOs should not be able to observe activity on client hosts and on the GRP introducer.

## 10.4 Distinction from Existing Approaches

In the following, the results from the comparison in Sect. 10.2 and from the more detailed descriptions in Sect. 10.3 are summarized and related to the approach developed in this book.

In this book we provide a secure and practical approach for audit data pseudonymization for misuse detection, such that:

1. person identifying data is concealed by pseudonyms in the audit data,

2. the linkability of pseudonyms respects the requirements of audit data analysis, such that

   a) the pseudonymized audit data can still be analyzed for misuse activity, such that legal restrictions w.r.t. person-identifying data in audit data do not apply or are relaxed,

   b) either as many pseudonyms are linkable as original features, or

   c) pseudonym linkability is subject to technical purpose binding, such that pseudonyms are linkable only where required for audit data analysis,

3. misuse activity detected in the pseudonymized audit data can be made accountable by disclosing the respective pseudonyms,

4. pseudonym disclosure is subject to purpose binding, most preferably technical purpose binding, such that

   a) pseudonyms can be disclosed to the SSO in a timely fashion,

   b) only those pseudonyms can be disclosed, which are involved in a sufficient misuse suspicion, i.e., a fair balance of anonymity and accountability is achieved in terms of multilateral security,

5. organizational purpose binding, if used, is properly enforced using appropriate cryptographic primitives,

6. the pseudonym mapping is appropriately protected, also as a result of strict adherence to design criteria w.r.t. control requirements, and

7. additional cost for the deployment of a complex infrastructure is avoided.

Existing approaches for direct audit data pseudonymization already satisfy 1, 2a, 2b, 3 and 7 and commonly violate 2c, 4, 5 and/or 6. Existing approaches for indirect audit data pseudonymization, as the ANIDA approach, generally do not satisfy 4 and 7.

The most distinguishing advantages of the set-based approach, design and implementation described in Part II and Part III are:

- restricting pseudonym linkability to different misuse suspicions (2a and improving on 2b),

- enforcing technical purpose binding for pseudonym disclosure w.r.t. set-based models of misuse scenarios (4),

- integrating organizational purpose binding of pseudonym disclosure in a secure way (5), and

- consequently respecting the control requirements (6).

The set-based approach from Part II is further refined in Part V, yielding the following additional advantages:

- enforcing technical purpose binding for pseudonym linkability w.r.t. fine-grained models of misuse scenarios (2a and 2c), and

- enforcing technical purpose binding for pseudonym disclosure w.r.t. fine-grained models of misuse scenarios (4).

# Part II

# Set-based Approach

This Part presents an approach for pseudonymizing audit data, where the pseudonym disclosure is subject to technical purpose binding. In Chap. 11 the assumptions, requirements and the trust model of the approach are derived from Part I. Chapter 12 describes how conditions for the purpose binding of the controlled pseudonym disclosure can be modeled, whereas Chap. 13 shows how modeled disclosure conditions can be enforced by cryptographic means. A new problem emerging due to the way we apply a certain cryptographic primitive is described, analyzed and solved in Chap. 14. Chapter 15 ties together the solutions from the previous Chapters and informally gives an algorithm that implements the approach. Eventually, Chap. 16 presents extensions to the approach, some of which will be used in Part III. Part III shows how the approach from this Part can be applied in practice.

# 11

# Requirements, Assumptions and Trust Model

The objective of the various possible architectures in the model from Sect. 8.4 is achieving pseudonymity for the activity of users of a service towards the site security officer (SSO) of the service provider. Pseudonymization can be used to make inferences on the pseudonymized data difficult or even impractical. However, we cannot avoid inferences that take into account additional information outside the scope of pseudonymization. At the same time the SSO shall be able to detect certain scenarios of activity, and he shall be able to establish accountability for these scenarios, i.e. disclose the pseudonyms of users who are causing these scenarios.

In the architectural model the audit component of the service observes the user activity while the users access the service. The audit component generates audit records that describe the observed activity. The SSO can observe the user activity only by inspecting and analyzing the audit data that the audit component of the service generates. We assume that the audit data correctly and completely describes the activity that is relevant for the SSO. If it cannot be avoided that the SSO can observe the user activity also through other channels, a separate pseudonymization architecture needs to be considered for each of these channels (see Sect. 8.2). These are outside the scope of this book.

The analysis of the audit data is supposed to be automated and it results in a report, if a scenario has been detected. The report about the detected scenario contains the audit records describing the activity, which constitutes the relevant context of the scenario. The report is sent to the response unit, which can reidentify audit records in the report by disclosing the pseudonyms. After reidentification the response unit may inform the SSO (see Sect. 8.3).

In Sect. 8.4 three basic architectures are presented, which achieve user pseudonymity (see Fig. 8.3, Fig. 8.4 and Fig. 8.5). It is assumed that the SSO's main interest in accountability is conflicting with the users' interest in anonymity or pseudonymity, and vice versa. According to the rationale in Sect. 8.4 therefore both the SSO and the users are exempted from controlling components that

enforce the interests pseudonymity and accountability. Instead, a third party enjoys the trust of the users and of the SSO for the enforcement of a fair balance
of their conflicting interests. The third party may be the organization's privacy
protection official (PPO). The control and trust requirements for our approach
follow the same rationale.

In Sect. 8.4.1 is shown, how the technical purpose binding of pseudonym disclosure simplifies the control requirements. Since pseudonyms can only be disclosed,
if the conditions induced by the disclosure purpose are met, the reidentification
can safely be controlled by the SSO (see Fig. 8.6b). This enables the SSO to
disclose pseudonyms without any delay if it is necessary, i.e. independently from
any third parties.

Our solution shall satisfy the following requirements. We want to provide a practical solution that allows for multilateral security with technical purpose binding
of pseudonym disclosure. As the comparison of the architectures in Sect. 9.1 has
shown, these requirements can be met in a cost-efficient way by pseudonymizing the audit data right after its generation (see Table 9.1). Consequently, our
solution provides pseudonymization of audit data as well as disclosure of the
pseudonyms in audit data, subject to technical purpose binding.

With these basic models and requirements from Part I in mind, we describe the
basic structure of our solution in the following. The description follows the flow
of identifying features and pseudonyms in Fig. 11.1, while elaborating on certain
issues, where necessary.

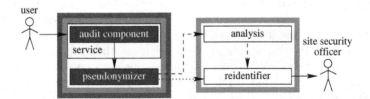

**Fig. 11.1.** Trust and control in the architectural model of our approach

In Fig. 11.1 we focus on the components that implement our approach as described in this Part. A user accesses a service that observes the user activity by
means of an *audit component*. The audit component generates audit records that
describe the observed activity. The audit data is pseudonymized by a *pseudonymizer*, which replaces identifying features in audit records with pseudonyms and
which generates the *pseudonym mapping* allowing pseudonym disclosure later
on.

Each fat grey frame illustrates an area where the security interest of an entity is
enforced and where entities with conflicting interests may not exert any control.
Both, the audit component and the pseudonymizer shall enforce the conflicting
interests of the user and the SSO in pseudonymity (see the dark grey frame in

Fig. 11.1) and accountability (see the left hand bright grey frame in Fig. 11.1), respectively. That is, the dark boxes in the multi-framed areas in Fig. 11.1 together enforce multilateral security. Consequently both, the user and the SSO may not control the audit component and the pseudonymizer. Instead, they are controlled by the PPO, who should be able to verify the proper functionality and configuration of the pseudonymizer and the audit component.[1] The SSO controls the application-specific analysis component and the reidentifier.

The pseudonymity of the audit data and the properties of the pseudonyms depend on the behavior of the audit component as well as of the pseudonymizer. Both components can be configured with a priori knowledge, which must express a fair consensus between the interest in pseudonymity and the interest in accountability. We roughly sketch a process that is carried out in the real world, and which is suitable to reach such a consensus.

First, the PPO – preferably in cooperation with further advocates of the user interests, e.g. the works or staff council – defines, which features in audit data need to be pseudonymized. Second, the SSO – possibly in cooperation with a lawyer – specifies, which of the pseudonyms of these features he needs to be able to disclose for what purposes. The SSO elaborates, which conditions (as induced by each purpose) must be met, such that pseudonym disclosure is justified. When the requirements reflecting the conflicting interests are defined, they should be openly discussed and refined, until a fair consensus is reached. Finally, the consensus is translated to the languages that the pseudonymizer and the audit component understand. The PPO ensures that the pseudonymizer and the audit components are configured accordingly. Then, the consensus is enforced in the digital world, given that the required control conditions are not violated.

After its pseudonymization, the audit data together with additional data needed for pseudonym disclosure is transmitted to the SSO to be analyzed. The solid arrows in Fig. 11.1 illustrate the flow of identifying features, whereas the dashed arrows in Fig. 11.1 show the flow of pseudonymized features. Additionally, updates to the pseudonym mapping are transmitted to the reidentifier, signified by the dotted arrows in Fig. 11.1. The generation of the additional data for pseudonym disclosure and of the pseudonym mapping is designed such that attacks on pseudonymity are resisted as soon as this data leaves the pseudonymizer. Note, that we introduce an extension in Sect. 16.3, such that the separate transmission of the pseudonym mapping is not necessary.

According to the given application, the pseudonymous audit data is analyzed for occurrences of certain scenarios of activity. We define our approach in a general way, such that it is usable for various applications. The examples, though, center around a specific application: the detection of misuse scenarios. However, this

---

[1] In practice, widely used operating systems do not support this kind of integrity requirement in a straightforward way. If the service runs on a Unix system, the PPO needs exclusive **root** and physical access to ensure that the pseudonymizer and the audit component work as desired.

should not lead the reader astray. The definitions nevertheless are of a general nature.

To detect a scenario we assume that in the given application the analysis uses some kind of rule-based system, e.g. an expert system. For more complex detection tasks the analysis requires the correlation of features from several events in audit records. The pseudonyms we generate shall still support that kind of correlation. For rule-based systems the correlation works by comparing features in events, that is the pseudonyms of these features need to be linkable by content. The linkability requirements of the analysis are specific to the given application. For a general approach that works for arbitrary applications we cannot a priori specify the linkability property for the pseudonyms to be generated.[2] Another assumption concerns the format of the events in the audit data. We assume that the format expected by the analysis is rigid, such that we cannot modify the syntactical format of the embedded features. Also, we assume that we cannot delete or insert features in events without interfering with the given analysis.

Consequently, the format and the content-linkability of the pseudonyms are not part of the set-based approach. In Part III we describe the design an implementation of the set-based approach for audit data, but still for general applications. There, the format and linkability can be freely adjusted by the users to fit the application at hand. In Part V we focus specifically on intrusion detection systems (IDS) as an application and give concise rules how content-linkability of pseudonyms can be tailored to the given misuse scenario models of an IDS.

If, and only if a scenario has been detected by the analysis, the pseudonyms in the audit data from the corresponding report can be disclosed by the reidentifier.[3] After reidentification, the report audit records contain events with the original identifying features and can be further processed by the SSO.

Additionally, we have to meet the specific requirements for audit data pseudonymization (see Sect. 10.1). First, audit records should be pseudonymized on the same device on which they are generated. Second, pseudonymization should also occur on the fly, such that the pseudonymized audit data can be transported as soon as possible to a secure remote location. Third, pseudonymization should not impair the performance and response time of the service. Therefore, pseudonymization should employ techniques with a low computational complexity and a low delay. The cryptographic schemes we choose in this Part and the design we develop in Part III satisfy these requirements, as validated in Part IV.

---

[2] To be able to determine the linkability requirements of an application one needs to know exactly what audit data processing the application performs (see Part V).

[3] In annex C the Common Criteria [53] provide for the application of the Privacy class (FPR) to FAU_GEN.2. The Privacy class FPR contains the families Anonymity FPR_ANO, Pseudonymity FPR_PSE, Unlinkability FPR_UNL and Unobservability FPR_UNO. The Pseudonymity family (FPR_PSE) provides accountability and FPR_PSE.2 offers reversible pseudonyms liable to specified reidentification conditions. Basically, our approach is implementing FPR_PSE.2 for FAU_GEN.2.

Given the described precautions, we may assume that the audit data and the embedded pseudonyms are still valid when being analyzed. Compensating for this assumption is in principle possible using more elaborate cryptographic primitives and protocols (see Sect. 22.2). Unfortunately, in practice such mechanisms do not satisfy the audit data pseudonymization requirements w.r.t. time and computational complexity (see Sect. 10.1 and Sect. 22.3).

# 12

## Modeling Conditions
## for Technical Purpose Binding
## of Controlled Pseudonym Disclosure

In Part I we introduced an approach to conditional anonymity based on pseudonyms (see Sect. 6.1). The disclosure of pseudonyms should be subject to organizational and technical purpose binding (see Sect. 7.2). In the following, an approach to technical purpose binding of pseudonym disclosure is developed. More specifically, pseudonym disclosure is subject to certain technically enforced conditions, where the technical enforcement of the conditions is implemented by cryptographic means.

Using this approach, activity of entities appears under pseudonyms in the audit data, until a legal purpose requires pseudonym disclosure (see Sect. 6.1.3). Precondition to the purpose coming into effect is that certain conditions are met, where the conditions are specific for the application under consideration and can be described as the transgression of an application-specific threshold.

In Sect. 12.1 a model for the disclosure conditions is developed. The model is based on events, which are defined in Sect. 12.1.1. Section 12.2 shows how the events and models can be described by certain a priori knowledge and Sect. 12.3 describes how this knowledge is effectively applied to events.

## 12.1 Set-based Model of Disclosure Conditions

Our approach assumes that in a given application the entities normally appear under pseudonyms in the audit data that the SSO can see. The exception from the normal situation occurs when the result(s) of certain activity of an entity warrant the disclosure of the entity's pseudonym(s). Such an exception is denoted as a *disclosure scenario*.

A disclosure scenario usually is detected based on the activity that is observable in the application. A *disclosure context* describes the set of *weighted observations of activity* that is potentially related to a disclosure scenario, where the observation weight represents the contribution of a given observation w.r.t. the disclosure context and of the corresponding activity w.r.t. the disclosure scenario. The sum of the weights of observations in a given disclosure context is a measure for the *activity level* of the disclosure context. Note, that we assume here that every (repeated) occurrence of a given observation raises the activity level by its observation weight. In Sect. 16.4 we give an extension that removes this assumption. Also note, that here the weight may for different observations be either positive or negative. Though we firstly restrict the approach to positive weights in Sect. 12.2, we relax this restriction in Sect. 16.5.

With each disclosure context is associated an application-specific threshold. The transgression of the threshold models the *disclosure condition* of the disclosure context. If in a given disclosure context the activity level is lower than the threshold, then the disclosure condition is not met. Conversely, if the activity level exceeds the threshold, i.e. activity level $\geq$ threshold, then the disclosure condition is met.

Summarizing, the disclosure of pseudonyms in observations contributing to a given disclosure context shall be feasible if and only if the respective application-specific disclosure condition is met. If this requirement holds and if the corresponding disclosure scenario has been correctly modeled by the disclosure context and condition, then pseudonym disclosure is bound to those purposes that are tied to the occurrence of the disclosure scenario as precondition to requiring accountability.

This set-based definition of disclosure context is not always sufficient to model disclosure scenarios in arbitrary applications. We give some extensions in Chap. 16 and refine the approach in Part V for specific applications based on Petri-Nets.

### 12.1.1 Observations

An activity observation in the sense of the above definition is a feature of an abstract event of a certain type which is symptomatic to be generated during the occurrence of a given disclosure scenario. Events generated in real applications have various formats, but they can be abstracted to the definition given below, capturing the properties that are relevant for our approach. In the remainder of Part II we mean abstract events when we talk about events. Events can be wrapped in *audit records*. If an audit record does not provide additional data, it is just the container of the event. An ordered set of audit records is denoted as *audit data*.

An *event* exhibits an *event designator* allowing event-discrimination (see frame 1 in Fig. 12.1), an *event type* specifying the number and types of the included features (see frame 2 in Fig. 12.1), and as many pairs of ⟨feature designator, feature⟩ as specified by the event type (see frames 3–8 in Fig. 12.1). A *feature designator* specifies the meaning and the format of the corresponding feature.

$$\boxed{\text{1066815145}}^1, \boxed{\textit{loginfail}}^2, \langle\, \boxed{\textit{usr}}^3, \boxed{\textbf{deedee}}^4 \rangle, \langle\, \boxed{\textit{acct}}^5, \boxed{\textbf{root}}^6 \rangle, \langle\, \boxed{\textit{term}}^7, \boxed{\textbf{pts/14}}^8 \rangle$$

**Fig. 12.1.** An example abstract event

The meaning usually is the role that an entity assumes in the activity described by the event, whereas the *feature* is the actual name or value of the entity. The loose concept of role here includes, but is not limited to subjects and objects of the activity.

The meaning of the example event in Fig. 12.1 could be described as follows. The event designator in frame 1 is the time stamp of the event in seconds since "00:00:00 1970-01-01 UTC", allowing discrimination of identical events that occurred at distinct times. The event type *loginfail* in frame 2 signifies that a certain user failed to log into a certain account from a certain terminal. This event type also specifies that three pairs of ⟨feature designator, feature⟩ describe the event using the feature designators *usr*, *acct* and *term*. The feature designator *usr* in frame 3 signifies that the format of the feature **deedee** in frame 4 is that of a user account name and that the role of the entity described by the feature **deedee** is that of the user account from which the log-in has been unsuccessfully attempted. The feature designator *acct* in frame 5 signifies that the format of the feature **root** in frame 6 is that of a user account name and that the role of the entity described by the feature **root** is that of the user account to which the log-in has been unsuccessfully attempted. The feature designator *term* in frame 7 signifies that the format of the feature **pts/14** in frame 8 is that of a terminal identifier and that the role of the entity described by the feature **pts/14** is that of the terminal being used by the entity described by *usr* to attempt the log-in.

We define a *feature type* as the combination of an event type and a feature designator, hence a *feature* can be considered to be an instance of a feature type. As a direct result, the feature type allows to differentiate features, even if they describe the same entity, but in the context of different events. This is important, because a given feature may identify a person in the context of some events, while it would not in others.

Hence, differentiated by feature type, we pseudonymize features that allow indirect identification of persons, but may ignore them in other events. Certainly we have to pseudonymize directly identifying features in all events. Finally, features that do not identify persons do not need to be pseudonymized and can be ignored. Therefore, in the following where using the term feature type we denote exclusively those, whose respective features identify persons, i.e. such a feature may in the following be consequently denoted as an *identity*.

## 12.2 A Priori Knowledge

For both, the pseudonymization and the pseudonym disclosure certain a priori knowledge is required. While processing events, the pseudonymizer shall be able to determine the feature type of each feature, associate a given feature type with the relevant disclosure contexts, and prioritize feature types within disclosure contexts. According to the given application, the a priori knowledge specifies, which feature types occur in which disclosure contexts and the weight of their contribution w.r.t. the activity level of the disclosure context. The same knowledge must be available to reidentifiers.

In a nutshell, the a priori knowledge provides:

- the features types that need to be pseudonymized, as initially defined by the PPO, particularly the corresponding event types and feature designators, and

- the disclosure contexts and conditions, as initially defined by the SSO, particularly the associations between feature types and disclosure contexts, as well as the respective weights of feature types and thresholds of disclosure contexts.

As described in Chap. 11 the a priori knowledge is the result of a constructive discourse between the PPO and the SSO. Based on our assumption from Chap. 11 the initial requirements of both sides have been considered and a fair and practical consensus has been negotiated. The fairness and practicability represented by the a priori knowledge are functions of this political process, which has been settled in the real world and which is beyond the control of technical solutions.

The basic idea of our approach is enabling pseudonym disclosure, if an entity has caused an activity level of a given disclosure context to exceed the corresponding threshold. Since an application may require pseudonym disclosure under several different disclosure contexts, we allow for the grouping of feature types, and for the assignment of a separate threshold $t_g$ to each $I_g$ representing a disclosure context. This association is expressed as pairs $\langle I_g, t_g \rangle$.

It may be the case that the feature types of a given event contribute to the activity level of different disclosure contexts with a distinct weight. Thus, we assign a weight[1] $w_{f,g} \in \mathbb{N} \setminus 0$ to each feature type $f$ associated with $I_g$, representing $f$'s contribution to the activity level of $I_g$. The knowledge about associations between feature types and disclosure contexts is represented by triplets $\langle f, I_g, w_{f,g} \rangle$. Each triplet expands to a quadruple:

$$\langle \text{event type, feature designator}, I_g, w_{f,g} \rangle$$

Note, that this representation has the following properties:

---

[1] The restriction to strictly positive weights is relaxed by an extension described in Sect. 16.5.

- A given feature type can be associated with more than one disclosure context, with a different weight for each, i.e. the corresponding quadruples contain the same event type and feature designator, but different disclosure contexts and possibly different weights.

- Different feature types may have an identical instance, representing an identity. In other words, there may be multiple occurrences of the identity of a given entity in different feature types of one or more events. We thus can associate a given entity with different disclosure contexts, even if the corresponding quadruples do not exhibit identical pairs of event type and feature designator.

In a nutshell, a given identity may be associated with several disclosure contexts. Nevertheless, due to the properties of the pseudonym generation described in the following Chapters, the contributions of the identity to the activity levels of the disclosure contexts are not transferable from one disclosure context $I_1$ to another disclosure context $I_2$ in order to prematurely satisfy the disclosure condition of $I_2$, or vice versa.[2]

## 12.3 Decision Structures

The tuples defined above form a decision tree such as in Fig. 12.2 with a virtual root connected to all specified event types. Each event type is connected to all feature designators contained in tuples with that event type. Likewise, all pairs of $\langle I_g, w_{f,g} \rangle$ are connected to the respective feature designator.

For an incoming event the pseudonymizer determines in the decision tree the matching event type. Then, the feature types are determined according to the feature designators in the subtree of the current event type.

For each feature designator the pseudonymizer determines the respective feature, i.e. identity. For each identity it iterates over all disclosure contexts represented by $I_g$ that are connected to the corresponding feature designator. It retrieves the respective data structure denoted by $I_g$ and checks, whether the identity is already a member of $I_g$. In case it is not, a pseudonym mapping entry for the identity is allocated and initialized in $I_g$.

Finally, for each $I_g$ and according to $w_{f,g}$, additional data is generated, which is required to disclose the pseudonym. The pseudonymizer replaces the identity in the event with an appropriate pseudonym and links the additional data to the pseudonym in the event.

---

[2] However note, that a given identity may with a negligible probability be associated with the same polynomial in different disclosure contexts. Moreover, the sample points of a given polynomial in one disclosure context may with a negligible probability be useful to interpolate a different polynomial in another disclosure context.

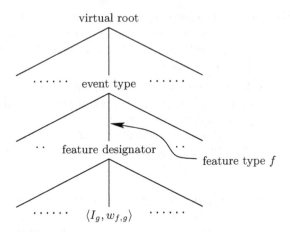

**Fig. 12.2.** Decision tree used for assigning disclosure contexts $I_g$ and weights $w_{f,g}$ to feature types $f$

Similarly proceeding, reidentifiers can relate incoming pseudonyms and additional data with their respective disclosure contexts. This, however, is not sufficient if a pseudonym is associated with more than one disclosure context, because for each disclosure context $I_g$ additional data has been generated by the pseudonymizer. The additional data needs to be associated properly with the corresponding $I_g$. Therefore, the identifier of $I_g$ is provided together with the additional data by the pseudonymizer. As a result, the reidentifier can directly locate $I_g$ and does not need to use the decision tree to relate pseudonyms and additional data with their respective disclosure contexts.

# 13

# Cryptographic Enforcement
# of Disclosure Conditions

The set-based approach is not concerned with the selection of appropriate pseudonyms, due to reasons given in Chap. 11. Rather, our approach is concerned with the protection of the pseudonym mapping, which enables the controlled disclosure of the pseudonyms. In this Chapter we show how we can use cryptographic primitives to technically enforce the disclosure conditions of disclosure contexts as defined in Sect. 12.1.

Section 13.1 describes how the choice of pseudonyms can be decoupled from the mechanism for controlled pseudonym disclosure. Section 13.2 explains how we cryptographically protect the pseudonym mapping against adversaries. Section 13.3 shows how the cryptographic protection of pseudonym mapping entries can be neutralized in a secure way by using threshold schemes for secret sharing. Also, a suitable scheme is selected and Sect. 13.4 describes how it is applied in our approach. Due to the parallel use of several secret sharing schemes a problem emerges, which is defined, studied and solved in Chap. 14.

As the assignment of identities to different disclosure contexts $I_g$ and respective weights $w_{f,g}$ is just a matter of using the decision structures (see Sect. 12.3), for the forthcoming Sections we focus on a given $I_g$ and omit the indexes of $I$ and $w$ wherever useful.

## 13.1 Pseudonymity-layer Data

According to the assumptions in Chap. 11, legacy applications may not tolerate modifications of the audit data format. Also, for each identity, i.e. feature, that needs to be replaced by a pseudonym, the corresponding feature designator signifies the format and the meaning (see Sect. 12.1.1). Any feature of a given event may be an input of the given application, which relies on the format and meaning of the feature. The meaning of the feature includes the linkability property of the feature. In order not to impair the given application, a pseudonym has to retain the original format and at least the linkability property of the identity it replaces.[1] Thus, on the one hand the choice of the bit strings that represent pseudonyms is constrained by the format and meaning of the identities. Cryptographic security of pseudonym disclosure on the other hand hinges on the pseudo-randomness of certain parameters. Consequently, here it is not a good idea to use cryptographic parameters directly as pseudonyms. Moreover, our approach for pseudonym disclosure should be independent of the given application and its linkability requirements. Since linkability requirements directly influence the pseudonyms that can be used in the audit data, we choose to decouple the pseudonyms from the mechanism for controlled pseudonym disclosure. As a result, pseudonyms can be chosen arbitrarily (see (2) in Sect. 20.3).

We introduce a further layer of data in addition to the audit data. This data layer in the following is denoted as the *pseudonymity-layer* and holds the additional data we need to provide for controlled pseudonym disclosure. The data stream in the pseudonymity-layer can be generated on demand and in parallel to the audit data stream, which resides in the *application-layer*. The pseudonyms reside in the application-layer, retaining format and meaning of the events. The linkage between a given pseudonym in the application-layer and the corresponding data in the pseudonymity-layer can be established syntactically (see Sect. 19.2.1).

The pseudonymity-layer and the application-layer conceptually are two separate streams of interrelated data. In practice, both streams will be multiplexed suitably, and the pseudonymity-layer data will be wrapped, such that it can be embedded in the application-layer data stream (see Sect. 19.2), i.e. the dashed arrows in Fig. 11.1 signify the flow of the application-layer data and of the pseudonymity-layer data.

## 13.2 Protecting Identities in the Pseudonym Mapping

The purpose of a pseudonym mapping is to enable the disclosure of pseudonyms in a controlled way. It is a structure that maps a given pseudonym to the identity that has been replaced by the pseudonym (see Sect. 7.2.5). We do not use this direct pseudonym-to-identity mapping in our approach due to the following rationale.

Since our approach provides technical purpose binding of the controlled pseudonym disclosure, the party performing the pseudonym disclosure is considered to be a potential adversary with regard to the pseudonymity of events. This party is also assumed to have complete control over the machine performing pseudonym disclosure (see Chap. 11). Therefore, we cannot rely on the operating system of

---

[1] Linkability is sufficiently retained when pseudonyms are linkable, where the original features are linkable. However, linkability can be further reduced when considering the actual requirements of the application for linkability. This issue is examined in detail in Part V.

this machine to protect the confidentiality of the pseudonym mapping, i.e. we cannot provide the identities in the clear.

Therefore, we pseudo-randomly choose a secret $s_i$ unique w.r.t. $I$ for each distinct identity $id_i$ associated with $I$. The secret $s_i$ cryptographically protects the corresponding identity $id_i$ in the pseudonym mapping. Naturally, also the secrets cannot be stored in the clear in the pseudonym mapping.

In the basic version each entry $e_i$ of the pseudonym mapping comprises a verifier-cryptogram pair $e_i = \langle v_i, c_i \rangle$. The verifiers $v_i = H(s_i)$ are just the value of a secure one-way hash function $H()$ applied to the secret $s_i$, i.e. a message digest.[2] The secrets are provided in the pseudonymity-layer in a protected form (see Sect. 13.3). The pseudonym corresponding to a secret can be located using the linkage between the pseudonymity-layer and the application-layer.

Given a tentative secret $s^*$, the corresponding pseudonym mapping entry can be located by matching $H(s^*)$ against the verifiers in the pseudonym mapping. If an entry $e_i$ with $H(s^*) = v_i$ has been located, the cryptogram $c_i = E(\tilde{k}_i, id_i)$ can be decrypted to yield the original identity $id_i$. This works, because we use the secret $s_i$ as the decryption key $k_i$, matching the encryption key $\tilde{k}_i$, pseudo-randomly chosen and unique w.r.t. $I$. The uniqueness requirement for the secrets discourages the decryption of $id_j, j \neq i$ for a given $s_i$. Note, that the keys are not chosen independently, which slightly reduces the search space for an attacker who already knows several secrets. This effect can be compensated for by using a larger $P$, which is the security parameter of the cryptographic primitives we use in Sect. 13.3. Also note, that our construction allows for the use of asymmetric as well as symmetric cryptosystems. In Part III we use a symmetric cryptosystem due to the lower computational complexity, in order to meet the performance requirement from Chap. 11.

If the pseudonymizer has added new entries to the pseudonym mapping, the mapping needs to be made available to the reidentifiers as soon as possible (see the dotted arrow in Fig. 11.1). Note, that the pseudonym mapping here is provided separately from the application-layer and pseudonymity-layer data. In Sect. 16.3 we present an extension that embeds the pseudonym mapping in the pseudonymity-layer.

Section 13.3 and Sect. 13.4 describe how the secrets are protected in the pseudonymity-layer while the disclosure condition is not satisfied.

## 13.3 Protecting Secrets in the Pseudonymity-layer

The fundamental idea of our approach to protect the secrets in the pseudonymity-layer, is to cryptographically split a given secret $s_i$ that protects the pseudonym

---

[2] Note, that we do not use pairs $\langle n_i, c_i \rangle$ of pseudonyms and cryptograms, because we intend to keep pseudonym disclosure, and hence also the pseudonym mapping, decoupled from the choice of pseudonyms.

mapping entry $e_i$ into as many shares as are needed to pseudonymize events containing the corresponding identity $id_i$, at maximum $P - 1$ shares (see Sect. A.1). The shares of $s_i$ shall have the property that given any $t$ shares, but not less, it is feasible to recover $s_i$. Having recovered $s_i$ from the shares in the pseudonymity-layer, the corresponding $c_i$ can be located and decrypted in the pseudonym mapping (see Sect. 13.2). In such a way the identity that has been replaced by the pseudonym(s) in the application-layer can be revealed. These requirements can be met using threshold schemes for cryptographic secret sharing (see Appx. A).

For these purposes we exploit Shamir's threshold scheme for secret sharing [200] (see Sect. A.1) with some modifications. This scheme has some desirable properties: it does not rely on any unproven assumptions, and it is ideal as well as perfect [153]. In our approach an ideal scheme generates shares of the same size as the secrets and is thus more efficient w.r.t. to time and space than non-ideal schemes. Arbitrary sets of $t - 1$ or less shares from perfect schemes do not provide any information about the protected secret. The shares generated by perfect schemes with the same threshold do not themselves indicate from which scheme they originate. As a result, in our approach two given shares do not reveal if they are related to the same identity or to two different identities. Shamir's scheme is particularly suitable for our approach due to the possibility to compute new shares independently from previously issued shares, and due to the possibility to prioritize entities by issuing an appropriate number of shares. Consequently, we can compute virtually as many shares and thus pseudonymize virtually as many events as we desire, provided $P$ is chosen appropriately. The possibility for prioritization supports the notion of weights we introduced in Sect. 12.2. Müller considered further secret sharing schemes as candidates for our approach [159]. From the schemes considered by Müller, only Shamir's threshold scheme exhibits all of the above properties.

## 13.4 Adapted Application of Shamir's Threshold Scheme

Owing to different conditions of deployment of Shamir's threshold scheme for secret sharing, we make some modifications with regard to its application. First, in our approach we don't have a group of participants, of which each confidentially receives and stores one or more shares, until $t$ of them pool their shares for secret recovery. Instead, we have one or more reidentifiers, each of them receiving *all* shares. A reidentifier is always in the position to recover the secret, which protects the pseudonym mapping entry for the identity $id_i$ associated with a polynomial $p_i(x)$, as soon as it received $t$ distinct shares from the pseudonymity-layer. Additionally, since from the point of view of the pseudonymizer all reidentifiers are potential pseudonymity adversaries, the confidentiality requirements regarding shares cease to apply.

While in conventional applications of secret sharing schemes it is feasible to determine the number of shares preliminarily to be issued, the same is impractical in our approach, since it is unknown which identities in the near future will require pseudonym generation. We thus take a stepwise approach to the choice of $x$-coordinates and to share generation, and we distribute $p_i(x)$ paired with its respective $x$. We have to preclude content-linkability w.r.t. the $x$-coordinates of shares within a disclosure context. If we chose the same $x$-coordinate for shares of different identities being members of the same disclosure context $I$, which is allowed by Shamir's scheme, it were obvious that the shares belonged to different identities. Accordingly, we choose unique $x$-coordinates for all shares w.r.t. a given $I$, e.g. by counting[3]. Since we choose the polynomials $p_{i_1}$ and $p_{i_2}$ independently for a given identity $id_{i_1} = id_{i_2}$ in two disclosure contexts $I_1$ and $I_2$, respectively, we can use arbitrary $x$-coordinates for a given identity in different disclosure contexts.

Normally, certain products of pairwise combinations of the $x$-coordinates of shares pooled for secret recovery can be pre-computed and issued to the participants in order to improve the performance of secret recovery using Lagrange interpolation (see $b_j$ in Sect. A.1). Since the number of shares going to be issued for a given identity is unknown beforehand, one would have to issue an increasing number of pre-computed intermediary results together with each share. In order to profit from these intermediary results, a reidentifier would have to store all of them, because it generally does not know a priori, of which shares it is going to make use of. We therefore refrain from this optimization. Table 13.1 summarizes the adaptations we introduce when applying Shamir's scheme.

**Table 13.1.** Application of Shamir's threshold scheme for secret sharing

| adaptation aspect | traditional application | our approach |
|---|---|---|
| shares per recipient | fixed weight | all generated shares |
| share distribution | during setup phase, $x$-coordinates (in the clear), $y$-coordinate (confidential) | stepwise, $x$- & $y$-coordinate (both in the clear) |
| $x$-coordinates | unique per polynomial | unique per discl. context $I$ |
| "$x$-products" | pre-computation during setup | on demand |

---

[3] Counting is more efficient w.r.t. time and space than choosing unique $x$-coordinates pseudo-randomly.

# 14

## The Mismatch Problem

The way we apply Shamir's threshold scheme for secret sharing was described in Sect. 13.4. Having several parallel schemes, one for each identity in a disclosure context, can lead to incorrect pseudonym disclosure, denoted as mismatches. The mismatch problem is defined in Sect. 14.1 and the probability of its occurrence is given in Sect. 14.2. Though for sensibly chosen parameters the probability of mismatches is negligible, mismatches may be strictly inacceptable in certain applications. Two complementary solutions are discussed in Sect. 14.3 as well as described in Sect. 14.3.1 and Sect. 14.3.2.

Chapter 15 ties together the concepts presented so far, including one solution for the mismatch problem, and informally gives algorithms for pseudonymization and pseudonym disclosure.

## 14.1 Definition of Mismatches

Provided the pseudonymizer issues the shares of a secret $s_i$ as unmarked pairs $\langle x, p_i(x) \rangle$ according to Shamir's scheme, due to the perfectness of the scheme a reidentifier cannot determine which shares within a disclosure context $I$ belong to the same $s_i$, unless it tries to recover an identity from each set of $t$ shares, where $t$ is the threshold of $I$.

When 'blindly' combining $t$ shares, a reidentifier will not always choose $t$ shares stemming from the same polynomial. In Fig. 14.1 the situation is studied on the basis of polynomials over $\mathbb{R}$ instead of the finite field $\mathbb{Z}_P$, which is more illustrative, but does not change the underlying problem. Consider a reidentifier, which, as depicted in Fig. 14.1, chooses three shares stemming from three different polynomials $p_2, p_3$ and $p_4$. The solution $p^*$ of the linear equations in this case matches in $s^* = p^*(0)$ the secret $s_1$ of polynomial $p_1$. If the reidentifier reveals the respective identity, accountability could not be established correctly.

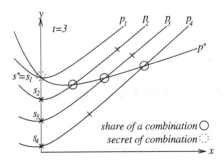

**Fig. 14.1.** A mismatch: the solution $s^*$ of a set of $t = 3$ incompatible shares matches a secret $s_1$, though it should not

Accordingly, if the solution of a set of $t$ shares matches a secret $s_i$ in $I$, it is denoted as a *valid match* if all shares are *compatible*, i.e. stem from the same polynomial $p_i$, otherwise it is called a *mismatch*.

## 14.2 Probability of Mismatches

Müller analyzed the mismatch problem for Shamir's scheme [159] and found that for $n_g$ polynomials over a finite field $\mathbb{Z}_P$ in a given disclosure context $I_g$ the probability that a mismatch occurs is $Pr(\text{Mismatch in } \{p_1, \ldots, p_{n_g}\}) = \frac{n_g}{P}$.

The number $n_g$ coincides with the number of identities stored in $I_g$. For the whole system we consider the upper bound of the probabilities for all disclosure contexts, i.e. the disclosure context with the largest $n_g$. Heuristically, this number can be approximated by the number of pseudonymous entities in the given application, e.g. the number of distinct identities. For a given application and the expected application-specific number $n$ of distinct pseudonymous entities the upper bound of the probability that a mismatch occurs is $Pr(\text{Mismatch}) = \frac{n}{P}$.

To give an impression of acceptable mismatch probabilities, we consider acceptable collision probabilities of cryptographic hash functions: $Pr(\text{Collision}) < 2^{-80} \approx 10^{-24}$ [196]. We propose to use a sufficiently large $P > n \cdot 2^{80}$ for a given application and an expected $n$. Based on this rule of thumb, conversely we can calculate the sensible upper bound for the number $n < P \cdot 2^{-80}$ of identities in an application for a given $P$.

As an example we consider the implementation of this approach (see Part III). We use 128 bits for the security parameters of the cryptographic primitives, i.e. $P \approx 2^{128}$. In this setting the mismatch probability is acceptable up to $2^{128} \cdot 2^{-80} = 2^{48} \approx 2.8 \cdot 10^{14}$ pseudonymous entities. This number of supported identities should be sufficient even for very large user populations. If more entities are expected in the given application, the security parameter $P$ needs to be adjusted appropriately.

## 14.3 Tackling the Mismatch Problem

As shown in Sect. 14.2 the occurrence of mismatches can be reduced to an acceptable probability by appropriate choice of $P$. Nevertheless, in certain applications it may not be acceptable that mismatches and thus wrong accusations can occur, no matter how low the respective probability is.

A general observation we made with anonymity technologies is that the strongest possible anonymity often comes at the price of an impractically high computational complexity and/or delay. Practical or fielded solutions typically are characterized by slightly relaxed anonymity requirements. In the same spirit we propose two solutions to mismatch handling. Their properties are summarized in Table 14.1.

**Table 14.1.** Properties of the proposed mismatch handling approaches

| property | mismatch handling approach | |
|---|---|---|
| | detection (verifiers) | avoidance (linkability labels) |
| achievable anonymity | + not affected | − reduced |
| computational complexity | − impractical | + practical |

The mismatch detection approach shown in Sect. 14.3.1 does not affect the unlinkability of shares. Since this approach retains the perfectness of Shamir's scheme it does not impair the achievable anonymity.

The other side of the coin is that for unlinkable shares searching for sets of compatible shares has a high computational complexity. The mismatch avoidance approach described in Sect. 14.3.2 sacrifices the unlinkability of shares in favor of a lower computational complexity in order to achieve a practical solution.

In Part III we follow the mismatch avoidance approach using linkability labels. In addition we (ab)use verifiers to detect data corruption in the pseudonymity-layer.

### 14.3.1 Mismatch Detection Using Verifiers

Section 13.2 described how for a given secret $s_i$ the corresponding entry $e_i$ in the pseudonym mapping can be identified using the verifiers $v_i = H(s_i)$ without storing $s_i$ in the clear in $e_i$. The same idea can be used to detect mismatches.

For each share $r_{i,m_i} = \langle x, p_i(x) \rangle$ the pseudonymizer can provide a pseudo-random verifier $d_{i,m_i} = \langle drand, H(drand, s_i) \rangle$ in the pseudonymity-layer. A fresh pseudo-random value $drand$ is used for each verifier, such that each share of $s_i$ is paired with a distinct verifier. The verifiers provided with shares are not content-linkable due to the pseudo-randomness of *drand* and they do not reveal information about the secrets. As a result, the perfectness of Shamir's scheme is not reduced by introducing the verifiers.

In order to detect mismatches, for each share used for recovering a tentative secret $s^*$ the reidentifier hashes $s^*$ together with *drand* from the corresponding verifier and compares the result to the hash value in the verifier. If both values match, the share stems from the same polynomial as $s^*$. If this is the case for all shares used to recover $s^*$, they all are compatible.

Otherwise, $s^*$ is not the same secret as the one of the polynomial from which a share stems. This means that some of the shares chosen are not compatible. The resulting $s^*$ is invalid and must not be used to reveal an identity and a different set of shares may be tried. If an entry in the pseudonym mapping exists which matches an invalid $s^*$, a mismatch has been detected (see Sect. 14.1).

Since the shares and verifiers are not content-linkable, in order to find compatible shares, a reidentifier must test all sets of $t$ shares by means of the verifiers. The computational complexity of this is impractically high.

### 14.3.2 Mismatch Avoidance Using Linkability Labels

The mismatch detection approach described in Sect. 14.3.1 does not adversely affect the unlinkability of the shares. Unfortunately, the use of unlinkable shares imposes such a high computational cost on reidentifiers that this venue is impractical.

A straightforward approach solves the discussed disadvantage of having unlinkable shares and simultaneously avoids the mismatch problem. Instead of pairing shares with verifiers in the pseudonymity-layer, shares are paired with linkability labels that enable reidentifiers to determine, whether two shares stem from the same polynomial. That is, all shares $r_{i,m_i}$ stemming from the same polynomial $p_i$, and thus from the same identity $id_i$ within $I$ are marked with identical labels $l_{i,m_i} = l_i$.

Then, events caused by a given identity in a disclosure context $I$, are linkable w.r.t. the labels, even before $t$ shares have been issued[1]. According to the terminology of Pfitzmann and Hansen [174] (see Sect. 7.3), the linkability labels of the shares grade the corresponding pseudonyms from transaction pseudonyms down to role pseudonyms, where the role is the disclosure context $I$ to which the shares are associated. This implies a reduction of the anonymity achievable for the pseudonymous entities.

Also, linkability labels may be used in the pseudonym mapping instead of verifiers, i.e. for an entry instead of $e_i = \langle v_i, c_i \rangle$ is used $e_i = \langle l_i, c_i \rangle$. The correct entry for a tentative secret can be located by directly matching the label of

---

[1] It would therefore be sufficient to choose $x$-coordinates unique w.r.t. each $p_i(x)$.

the shares used for recovering the secret against the labels in the entries. Note, that it is then only a small step to integrate the pseudonym mapping with the pseudonymity-layer by using $l_i = c_i$. Such an extension is proposed in Sect. 16.3.

# 15

# Operational Pseudonymization and Pseudonym Disclosure

In the following, we tie together the solutions presented in the previous Chapters of this Part and describe how to generate the pseudonym mapping and the data in the pseudonymity-layer as well as how pseudonym disclosure works. The associations and dependencies between the elements in the application-layer, in the decision tree, in the pseudonymity-layer, and in the pseudonym mapping are depicted in Fig. 15.1, already respecting the extensions in Sect. 16.3 and Sect. 16.6. Figure 15.2 depicts an abstraction of the respective data flow, showing for a given triplet of identity, disclosure context and weight the cryptographic operations for data in the pseudonymity-layer and in the pseudonym mapping, as well as the mismatch avoidance/detection and the selection of the pseudonym mapping entry corresponding to a recovered secret. In the gap between the pseudonymizer and the reidentifier in Fig. 15.2 the data is shown, which is actually transmitted from the pseudonymizer to the reidentifier. Considering this data, the encrypted features $c_i$ and the entry verifiers $v_i$ are components of the pseudonym mapping, whereas the remaining data resides in the pseudonymity-layer. Note, that Fig. 15.2 omits operations in the application-layer, the linkage to the application-layer, the initialization, the use of the decision tree and some further details.

In Part III we use the practical approach for mismatch avoidance using linkability labels (see Fig. 15.2a) instead of verifiers for misuse detection (see Fig. 15.2b). The solution presented in this Chapter therefore incorporates the approach for mismatch avoidance. An extension to the mismatch detection approach that even conceals the number of entities in the application is given in Sect. 16.2.

For each incoming event the pseudonymizer uses the decision structure described in Sect. 12.3 to locate the features or identities $id$, and to determine for each $id$ the respective disclosure context(s) $I_g$ and the pertinent weight(s) $w_{f,g}$. For each triplet $\langle id, I, w \rangle$[1] the pseudonymizer once initializes a pseudonym mapping

---

[1] Again, in the following description we focus on a given disclosure context $I_g$ and the respective weight $w_{f,g}$ of $id$. We therefore omit the indexes of $I$ and $w$.

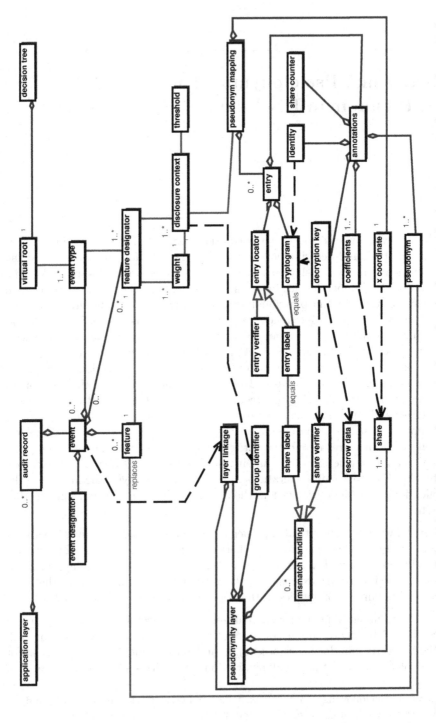

**Fig. 15.1.** Associations and dependencies between elements in the application-layer, in the decision tree, in the pseudonymity-layer, and in the pseudonym mapping

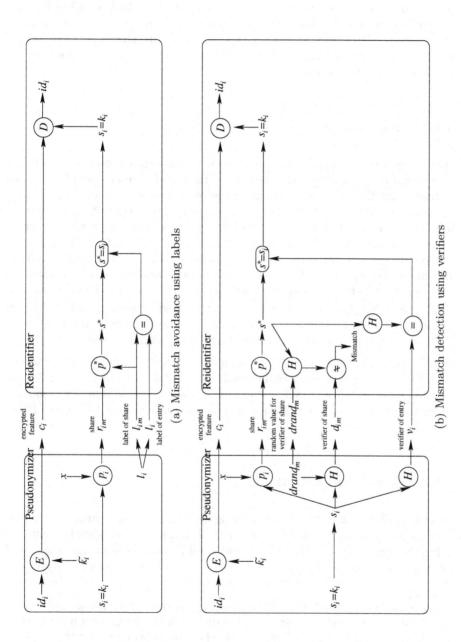

(a) Mismatch avoidance using labels

(b) Mismatch detection using verifiers

**Fig. 15.2.** Data flow between the pseudonymizer and the reidentifier

entry (see Sect. 15.1) and for each occurrence of the triplet it uses the initialized pseudonym mapping entry to provide the data in the pseudonymity-layer needed for pseudonym disclosure (see Sect. 15.2). Finally, Sect. 15.3 describes how the reidentifier can use the data in the pseudonymity-layer together with the pseudonym mapping to disclose pseudonyms. Two different modes of operation are outlined for the reidentifier in Sect. 15.3.1 and Sect. 15.3.2. Several extensions are described in Chap. 16.

## 15.1 Initialization

After isolating an identity $id$ and determining an associated disclosure context $I$ and weight $w$, check if the data structure of the pseudonym mapping for $I$ exists. If that is not the case, create it and initialize its $x$-coordinate counter $x$.[2] If $id$ is not yet a member of $I$, create a pseudonym mapping entry $e_i$ in $I$, choose a label $l_i$ and a pseudo-random encryption key $\tilde{k}_i$, both unique w.r.t. $I$, encrypt $id$ as $c_i := E(\tilde{k}_i, id)$ and store $l_i$ and $c_i$ in $e_i := \langle l_i, c_i \rangle$. In the following treat the respective decryption key $k_i$ as the secret $s_i = k_i$ to be shared. Annotate the new entry $e_i$ with: $id_i := id$, $s_i := k_i$, an initialized share counter $m_i$, and $t - 1$ pseudo-randomly chosen coefficients $a_{i,1}, \ldots, a_{i,t-1}$ for the polynomial $p_i(x) = s_i + \sum_{j=1}^{t-1} a_{i,j} \cdot x^j$, where $t$ is the threshold associated with $I$. Finally, choose a pseudonym $n_i$ and annotate $e_i$ with $n_i$. Make merely $e_i$ or the complete pseudonym mapping $I$, but not the annotations, available to the reidentifiers.

Note, that the pseudonyms can be chosen independently from the other parameters of $e_i$, but they need to meet the requirements of the application w.r.t. format and content-linkability as well as the pseudonymity requirements of the entities. Since the choice of $n_i$ is application-specific, it is not discussed here (see (2) in Sect. 20.3).

## 15.2 Pseudonymization

After isolating an identity $id$, determining an $I$ and $w$, and locating the initialized pseudonym mapping data structure for $I$, locate the corresponding entry $e_i$ using the annotation $id_i$. Write the identifier of $I$ to the pseudonymity-layer and determine the label $l_i$ from $e_i$, then write $l_{i,m_i} := l_i$ to the pseudonymity-layer.[3] Then, perform the following steps $w$ times: increment the $x$-coordinate counter

---

[2] Since the shares from different polynomials are marked with different labels, there is no need to conceal, whether the $x$-coordinates of the shares stem from different polynomials. We could as well use an individual counter $x_i$ for each entry $e_i$ instead of a global counter $x$ for each disclosure context.

[3] Since the labels $l_{i,m_i} = l_i$ for all shares $r_{i,m_i}$ of $s_i$ are identical, it is sufficient to mark collectively distributed shares with just one label.

$x$ of $I$ and the share counter $m_i$ in $e_i$'s annotations; compute the next share for $s_i$ as $r_{i,m_i} := \langle x, p_i(x) \rangle$, and write $r_{i,m_i}$ to the pseudonymity-layer.

When all $w$ shares have been been written to the pseudonymity-layer for all $I$ associated with $id$, $id$ can be replaced by a pseudonym. For the pseudonym $n_i$, check the pseudonymity and linkability requirements and decide, if $n_i$ could be renewed according to the requirements (see (2) in Sect. 20.3).[4] Then, (possibly after renewing $n_i$) replace $id$ in the event (in the application-layer) with $n_i$ and establish the linkage from the pseudonymity-layer to $n_i$ in the event. The linkage should be established without additions to the event, such that its format is sustained.[5]

Finally, make the rewritten event (application-layer) as well as the disclosure context identifier, the label and the shares (pseudonymity-layer) available to the reidentifiers.

## 15.3 Pseudonym Disclosure

We propose two modes of operation for the reidentifier: the batch mode in Sect. 15.3.1 and the on-the-fly mode in Sect. 15.3.2. In the batch mode, the reidentifier processes a given block of application-layer and pseudonymity-layer data, discloses all pseudonyms satisfying the disclosure condition and finishes. In contrast to this block-wise processing, in the on-the-fly mode the reidentifier as soon as possible discloses the pseudonyms in audit records coming in from an audit data stream. In the on-the-fly mode the reidentifier finishes if the stream ends. Due to the higher computational complexity and the higher complexity of the implementation of the on-the-fly mode, we chose to implement only the batch mode (see Part III). Note, that the pseudonymizer as described in Sect. 15.2 provides an on-the-fly mode and, as a result, can also be used for batch mode processing.

In both modes the reidentifier uses the same algorithm to reconstruct the pseudonym mapping from the pseudonymity-layer data and to recover secrets from the shares available from the reconstructed pseudonym mapping. The reidentifier collects all updates of the pseudonym mapping of $I$ and associates the labeled shares from the pseudonymity-layer with their corresponding pseudonym mapping entry $e_i$. The entry is located using the identifier of $I$ provided by the pseudonymizer and matching the collected label against the labels of the entries in $I$ (see Sect. 12.3 and Sect. 14.3.2). For each $e_i$, the reidentifier also keeps track

---

[4] Ensure that $n_i$ does not equal any other pseudonym for the current event, such that the linkage described in Footnote 5 is a unique search criterion.

[5] For the implementation we use the following solution (see Sect. 19.2). To link a given $n_i$ in a given event in the application-layer with the corresponding disclosure context(s), label(s) and share(s) in the pseudonymity-layer, the latter are complemented with $n_i$ and a message digest of the pseudonymized event H(event).

of the linkage (to the corresponding application-layer pseudonym) provided in the pseudonymity-layer by the pseudonymizer (see Sect. 19.2).

If the number of shares collected for a given $e_i$ exceeds the threshold $t$ associated with $I$, the reidentifier can recover the secret $s_i$ and use it to neutralize the protection of $e_i$.

To do this, choose a set of $t$ shares $\langle x_{i_1}, y_{i_1} \rangle, \ldots, \langle x_{i_t}, y_{i_t} \rangle$, all exhibiting the same label and thus being compatible. Then, compute $s^* := p^*(0) = \sum_{j=1}^{t} y_{i_j} \prod_{1 \leq o \leq t, o \neq j} \frac{x_{i_o}}{x_{i_o} - x_{i_j}}$ (Lagrange Interpolation) to recover the secret. Subsequently use $s^* = s_i = k_i$ to yield $id_i := D(k_i, c_i)$ from $e_i$.


### 15.3.1 Batch Mode

In the *batch mode* the reidentifier processes the pseudonymous audit data in two passes. In the first pass the reidentifier reconstructs the pseudonym mapping to the completeness degree possible given the available pseudonymity-layer data. While reconstructing the pseudonym mapping, the reidentifier recovers secrets as soon as the respective disclosure condition is satisfied, i.e. a sufficient number of shares has been collected for the corresponding label.[6] In the second pass, the reidentifier locates all pseudonyms in the application-layer audit data and replaces them with the corresponding identity, if it is found in the pseudonym mapping using the linkage (see Sect. 19.2.1).

In the batch mode the data in the pseudonymity-layer and in the application-layer is only processed once. For each pseudonym in the application-layer is a lookup performed in the pseudonym mapping. Lookups are performed by building a linkage for the current application-layer audit record and the current pseudonym and searching this linkage in the pseudonym mapping.

For a more detailed algorithm see Sect. 20.4, where i.a. the implementation of the batch mode is described.


### 15.3.2 On-the-fly Mode

In the *on-the-fly mode* the reidentifier reconstructs the pseudonym mapping from the pseudonymity-layer data like in the first pass of the batch mode (see Sect. 15.3.1). If some secrets are recovered, the reidentifier replaces the corresponding pseudonyms in the simultaneously incoming application-layer data with the respective identities like in the second pass of the batch mode (see Sect. 15.3.1). Differently from the batch mode in the on-the-fly mode, each time

---

[6] In the implementation the secret recovery is performed in the second pass, if the disclosure condition is satisfied for the pseudonym mapping entry for the current pseudonym (see Sect. 20.4).

a secret is recovered the reidentifier must re-consider all of the previously processed application-layer audit records that might still contain pseudonyms which could now be disclosed.

Compared to the batch mode, in the on-the-fly mode the reidentifier needs to perform an additional search in the already processed application-layer audit data for each pseudonym that is newly disclosed. For searching, the linkage for each application-layer audit record needs to be computed and compared to the target linkage from the pseudonym mapping entry of the disclosed pseudonym. To avoid the cost of the frequent re-computation of the linkage, the linkage should be cached by the reidentifier for the application-layer data. However, even if caching is used, the on-the-fly mode is computationally more demanding than the batch mode.

# 16

## Extensions

In this Chapter some extensions to the basic algorithms from Chap. 15 are proposed. The extension in Sect. 16.1 considers a finer-grained attacker model. In Sect. 16.2 an extension is given that allows to conceal the number of entities in a disclosure context. This extension does not work for shares marked with linkability labels. Conversely, the extension in Sect. 16.3 is suitable to implement the mismatch avoidance approach in practice. Two further extensions that allow to specify more concise models of disclosure scenarios are given in Sect. 16.4 and in Sect. 16.5. Finally, Sect. 16.6 outlines, how our approach for technical purpose binding of pseudonym disclosure can be combined with organizational purpose binding.

The extensions from Sect. 16.1 and from Sect. 16.2 are depicted in Fig. 16.1. Note, that the extensions from Sect. 16.3, Sect. 16.4, Sect. 16.5 and Sect. 16.6 have been implemented (see Part III).

## 16.1 Attacker Model

Hitherto we regarded reidentifiers as potential adversaries and equated them with any other attackers (see Chap. 11). In some applications it might be desirable to raise further obstacles for (external) attackers that cannot control any reidentifiers.

To do so, we initially perform a secure key exchange, such that both, the pseudonymizer and the reidentifiers, know an encryption key $\tilde{k}_e$. Only the reidentifiers know the respective decryption key $k_e$. The secret being shared then is not defined as the key $k_i$ needed for decrypting $c_i$. Instead, $k_i$ is encrypted under $\tilde{k}_e$ to form a secret $s_i := E(\tilde{k}_e, k_i)$ (see Fig. 16.1).

We also considered alternatively encrypting shares. For mismatch detection it is expensive to protect shares in the memory of reidentifiers against attackers,

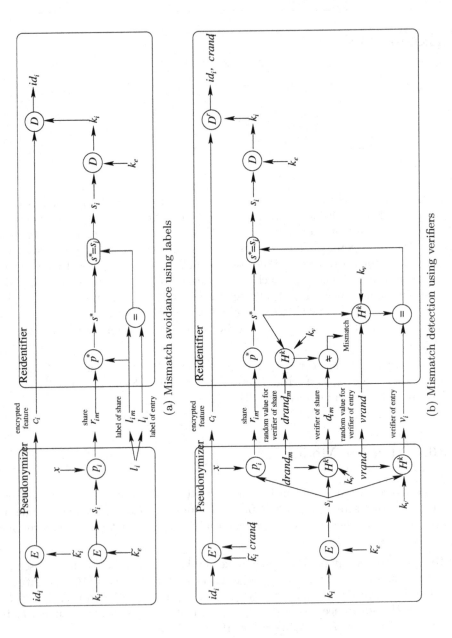

(a) Mismatch avoidance using labels

(b) Mismatch detection using verifiers

**Fig. 16.1.** Data flow between the pseudonymizer and the reidentifier, considering the extensions from Sect. 16.1 and from Sect. 16.2

because each share needs to be decrypted before interpolation. If we abandon in-memory protection of shares by decrypting them on reception, as an alternative we might protect the entire transmission channel using widely available standard solutions.

In the case that verifiers are used to detect mismatches, we could increase the efforts of an attacker also by using a keyed one-way hash-function $H^k()$ instead of $H()$ such that $v_i := H^k(k_v, s_i)$ (see Fig. 16.1), where the symmetric key $k_v$ has been securely exchanged between the pseudonymizer and the reidentifiers.

## 16.2 Coarsening the Number of Potential Actors

In the case that mismatch detection is used, we already use unlinkable shares. Additionally, it would be advantageous to conceal also the number of actually involved entities in order to make it harder for an adversary to apply external knowledge. For obvious reasons this cannot be achieved when using linkability labels for mismatch avoidance. Note, that due to the reasons given in Sect. 14.3.1 this extension has rather academic than practical merit.

We introduce dummy entities in $I$, which are treated like entries for real identities, except that they are annotated as dummies. The $id_i$ for dummies shall be pseudo-randomly selected from the identities possible for the current feature type for the given service, e.g. by using the local user account database. In case no mismatch handling is done, however we have to choose fictitious identities which do not match any real identities on the host. Otherwise, in the case of a mismatch we couldn't discern dummies from real identities. Fictitious identities shall also adhere to the operating system's rules concerning the syntax of identities.[1]

We can make real entries indistinguishable from dummy entries, as long as their secrets have not been recovered. We initialize $I$ with a number of dummy entries, and if a real identity needs to be stored in $I$, a dummy entry is replaced with a real entry. In order to make such replacements unobservable, we have to provide for the ability to completely change the appearance of all entries in $I$, without needing to change the information within the entries. Since all items used in our approach so far are invariant, we introduce some independently and pseudo-randomly chosen seed values $crand_i$, which can be varied over time. We use randomized encryption for the identity cryptograms $c_i := E^r(\tilde{k}_i, crand_i, id_i)$ using the pseudo-random seed $crand_i$ (see Fig. 16.1b). Also, we have to make sure that all $c_i$ exhibit the same size, e.g. by appropriate padding. We additionally choose for and distribute with each $I$ a pseudo-random value $vrand$ to randomize

---

[1] We also considered using dedicated dummy names, pseudo-random bit-strings for dummy naming and invalid verifiers $v_i$, but all of these are easier to spot as dummies in the case that a brute force attack on $k_i$ is tried.

the verifiers $v_i$ by hashing $vrand$ together with the secret $s_i$ (see Fig. 16.1b). If we change just $vrand$ and $crand_i$ for an $e_i$ in $I$, an observer cannot distinguish the effect on $c_i$ and $v_i$ from the effect of varying additional items such as the identity $(id_i)$ and keys $(\tilde{k}_i, \tilde{k}_e, k_v)$.

The maximum number of potential actors is bounded[2] by the number $rid_{max}$ of identities registered in the system's databases. If $rid_{max}$ is large and the expected maximum number of actors is $u \ll rid_{max}$, and the expected average number of shares generated per actor is $m$, then the maximum number of potential actors is bounded by $u \cdot m \leq rid_{max}$. Heuristically, we allocate $rid_{max}$ pseudonym mapping entries for $I$ if $u \approx rid_{max}$, otherwise we allocate $u \cdot m \leq rid_{max}$ entries. If the actual number of actors exceeds $u \cdot m \leq rid_{max}$, $I$ needs to be extended appropriately by $u \cdot m$ entries. Note, that the number of actors is known to be $(u \cdot m \cdot n) + 1, n = 1, 2, \ldots$ each time $I$ is extended. On initialization of an $I$, all entries are dummies, and we generate the cryptograms $c_i$ and verifiers $v_i$ as usual.

On pseudonym mapping entry initializations, we choose a dummy pseudonym mapping entry $e_i$ to be replaced, choose a new key pair $\tilde{k}_i, k_i$ and new pseudo-random values $crand_i$ and $vrand$, and compute $c_i$ and $v_i$. To conceal, which dummy $e_i$ was replaced, we also change the pseudo-random seeds $crand_j, j \neq i$ of all other entries, effectively re-computing all cryptograms (and verifiers). We also randomize the order of $I$'s entries. We make the modified $I$ available to the reidentifiers.

If an attacker observes the actual number $upd$ of updates of the pseudonym mapping of $I$, and the actual number $m'$ of shares issued from $I$ in the pseudonymity-layer, he can infer from $\frac{m'}{upd} > m$ that there are fewer than $u$ actors. Even worse, observing the number of pseudonym mapping updates provides the attacker with a good estimate of the number of actors. To prevent this, we generate apparently random dummy-traffic updates of $I$ such that $\frac{m'}{upd} \leq m$. For dummy-traffic updates, we change the pseudo-random values of $I$ ($vrand$) and of all its entries ($crand_i$). Accordingly, we also randomize the order of $I$'s entries, and subsequently make $I$ available to the reidentifiers.

## 16.3 Using Pseudonym Mapping Entries as Linkability Labels

Section 15.1 describes the initialization of a pseudonym mapping entry in a disclosure context and that the entry or the whole pseudonym mapping for all disclosure contexts needs to be made available to the reidentifiers after initialization. While the pseudonym mapping needs still to be managed by the pseudonymizer, we can slightly change the definition of the linkability labels, such

---

[2] In special cases we cannot conceal the number of actors, e.g. if several active identities sequentially trigger the issuing of a bulk of $t$ or more shares each.

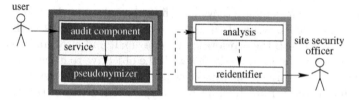

user

**Fig. 16.2.** Simplified architectural model due to the extension in Sect. 16.3

that the mapping needs not to be transferred separately to the reidentifiers (see Fig. 16.2, cf. Fig. 11.1).

We can define the linkability label of a pseudonym mapping entry to equal the encrypted identity $l_i := c_i$ (see the association between 'entry label' and 'cryptogram' in Fig. 15.1). Since the cryptograms $c_i$ are now directly provided in the pseudonymity-layer (see Sect. 15.2) and are associated with the corresponding shares, reidentifiers can collect them together in $e_i$. In other words, the pseudonym mapping is embedded and transmitted entry-wise, though redundantly, in the pseudonymity-layer. Hence, the dotted arrow from Fig. 11.1 is missing in Fig. 16.2. Labels are not used any more to locate the correct cryptogram in the pseudonym mapping, because they actually are that cryptogram.

## 16.4 Significance of Repeated Observations

In Sect. 12.1 we assumed for modeling disclosure scenarios that each distinct observation in a given disclosure context is significant and thus raises the activity level by its specific weight. This is a perfectly reasonable assumption for many disclosure scenarios.

For example, to model a password guessing misuse scenario, we assume that up to a certain number of observations in a row exhibiting the event type *loginfail*, we are seeing normal glitches in day to day operations. But, if that threshold is exceeded, we would like to disclose the account features that are involved (see Fig. 12.1). That is, if a given feature as an instance of a given feature type occurs several times in a row, the activity level of the disclosure context should increase for this feature. Another example for disclosure scenarios, where repeated observations are significant for the activity level, are resource exhaustion misuse scenarios.

Certainly there also are disclosure scenarios that we may need to model and where repeated observations shall not be significant. Rather, for these disclosure scenarios it shall be significant that an observation occurred at all or not at all.

Consider for example the class of worms attacking web servers to spread on the Internet. Attacking web servers involves requesting certain URLs in the hope to successfully exploit pertinent vulnerabilities. For a given worm, many of these

URLs can be very similar, they may differ in only one character in a specific position of the URL string. It is useful to classify these URLs as the same event type, firstly, to keep the a priori knowledge small and clear and secondly, to be able to detect variants. If we do this with the objective to disclose the IP address from where the worm attacked, we will observe the same feature type several times, due to the variant-tolerant event type defined above. But the number of observations may be of no interest or it may vary, such that it is difficult to define a fixed threshold. It may rather be of interest, which distinct event types, i.e. feature types, have been observed for a given IP address. This information tells us what kind of worm is performing the attack. Summarizing, we would first define the distinct event types over the URLs that let us determine the type of worm and then associate the corresponding source IP address feature types with a disclosure context that has for example a threshold equal to the number of distinct event types. The weights of the feature types could be defined equal to one and repeated observations would be defined as insignificant.

Treating the repeated occurrence of a feature type as insignificant means to increase the activity level only on the first occurrence of the feature type, but not for later occurrences. This can be done by remembering those features in the annotations of the pseudonym mapping, which have occurred at least once. If such a feature $f$ occurs the first time, the pseudonymizer stores $f$ in the annotations and generates $w$ shares as shown in Sect. 15.2. While doing this, the pseudonymizer additionally stores the used values of the $x$-coordinate counter together with $f$ in the annotations. The next time $f$ occurs, the pseudonymizer recollects that $f$ already has occurred and generates the exact same $w$ shares that were generated when $f$ occurred the first time. To do this, the pseudonymizer uses the $x$-coordinates stored in the annotations with $f$.

The reason for doing this is that the Lagrange interpolation will only for $t$ compatible shares for distinct $x$-coordinates recover the secret. Thus, the activity level can only increase if shares are generated for $x$-coordinates that differ from the $x$-coordinates of already provided shares.

Summarizing the results, this means: If $f$ never occurs, no shares are generated for $f$ and the activity level is not increased. If $f$ occurs the first time, a set $r_f$ of $w$ shares is generated and the activity level increases once by $w$. If $f$ occurs two or more times, the same set $r_f$ is generated as many times, but still the activity level increases merely once by $w$.

## 16.5 Reconciling Observations

In Sect. 12.2 we restricted the weights of feature types to strictly positive numbers from $\mathbb{N}$. A monotonically increasing activity level cannot model observations of activities that cancel each other out in the disclosure scenario.

This can be demonstrated using a password guessing misuse scenario as a disclosure scenario. We assume that up to a certain number of observations with the event type *loginfail*, we are seeing normal glitches in day to day operations. But, if a threshold is exceeded, we would like to disclose the account features that are involved (see Fig. 12.1). That is, if a given feature as an instance of a given feature type occurs, the activity level of the disclosure context for this feature should increase monotonically. But, if a legitimate user sometimes mistypes his password on the first try and logs in successfully on the second try, the failed login attempts already have increased the activity level of the disclosure context, even if they were only glitches. Eventually, the pseudonyms of the user will be disclosed in that disclosure context, even though the actual activity constitutes no password guessing misuse scenario.

Obviously, the model for the misuse scenario is inadequate, because it fails to capture successful log-in activity and to relate it to the failed log-in attempts. The problem disappears, if the model "knows" that a successful log-in cancels out previous failed log-in attempts, as long as the activity level has not yet exceeded the threshold.

The solution we propose is to allow for positive and negative weights $w \in \mathbb{Z}$ on the modeling level. As long as the activity level is lower than the threshold, it can increase for positive weights and it can decrease for negative weights.

Naturally, negative weights on the modeling level need to be implemented cryptographically somehow. The idea is to invalidate as many already provided distinct shares as specified by the negative weight. Invalidated shares cannot be used together with (still) valid shares to recover the secret. Since the valid shares and the shares that need to be invalidated have already been provided to the reidentifiers, they cannot be easily modified in hindsight. Instead, the polynomial is modified on the side of the pseudonymizer, such that the secret and the valid shares still are points on the modified polynomial, but the invalidated shares are not (see Sect. 16.5.1 for details). As a result, for a given secret, already provided shares still are accompanied with the same linkability labels in case mismatch avoidance is used, irrespective of being valid or invalidated. Finally, the $x$-coordinate counter $x$ is decreased as specified by the weight.

If mismatch avoidance is used, new valid shares are generated using the same linkability labels as the previously invalidated shares, such that the reidentifier can associate them with the same disclosure context entry. In case mismatch detection is used, new valid shares are generated using the same verifiers as the previously invalidated shares, such that the reidentifier can associate them with the invalidated shares. In both cases, new valid shares are generated re-using the $x$-coordinates of the invalidated shares, such that the new shares overwrite the previously collected shares with the same $x$-coordinates, which have been invalidated.

If all shares have been invalidated, the activity level in the model is zero. This is similar to a new start of the disclosure scenario. We therefore not only select a new polynomial, but we completely re-initialize the pseudonym mapping entry. Most importantly, in this disclosure context the old observations cannot be linked with forthcoming observations of the entity. Note, that this solves the possible problem that without this extension no more than $P$ shares can be generated. Also note, that due to the invalidation approach the lowest value for the activity level is zero and a negative value does not map directly to the approach.

Suppose that for a given secret $s$ already $t$ shares have been provided and $s$ has been recovered. If we afterwards invalidated some shares, they could not only still be used to recover $s$. Moreover, since any new shares are labeled with the same linkability label or verifiers as the previously provided shares, it would be obvious that they belong to the $s$ that already has been recovered. Therefore, if the activity level has already exceeded the threshold, a merely partial reduction of the activity level makes no sense. Instead, a complete reset of the activity level to zero would work. It may for example be desired that the activities of a given entity are not indefinitely accountable after some of its pseudonyms have been disclosed.

Note, that the complementary nature of observations is not a function of merely the usual semantics of the observations. Rather, the complementary nature of observations is a function of their semantics w.r.t. the given disclosure scenario. We give two examples. In many resource exhaustion misuse scenarios a certain observable activity $a$ that allocates a certain resource occurs so often that the resource cannot be allocated any further, resulting in denial of service. Usually, there is a complementary, observable activity $\tilde{a}$ that frees the resource. This activity is not part of the resource exhaustion misuse scenario, it rather occurs during normal operation. The complementary observations could be paired to cancel each other out. In a password guessing misuse scenario, an observed successful log-in $\tilde{a}$ shall render all previously observed failed log-in attempts $a$ void, if the activity level has not already exceeded the threshold of the disclosure context.

Note, that most operations in applications have a return value signifying the success of the operation. If the operation can be observed, usually also the return value is observable. Then, the observations of two attempted operations result in two distinct feature types if one attempt returns successfully and the other returns failed. It depends on the disclosure scenario at hand, how to use this knowledge profitably. For the resource exhaustion disclosure scenario it is useful to consider only the observations of successfully returning allocation and deallocation operations $a$ and $\tilde{a}$ as complementary activity. But, for the password guessing disclosure scenario the world is somehow reversed. There, a successful log-in $\tilde{a}$ shall cancel out failed log-in attempts $a$.

Hence, the pairing of given observations could vary for different disclosure scenarios. Therefore, we refrain from associating observations of complementary activity in a pairwise manner, such that the shares for the associated and earlier observation are invalidated. Instead, always the youngest $w$ shares are invalidated. The order of the shares is insignificant, anyway. The downside of this simpler approach is that a feature type $\tilde{f}$ with a negative weight will decrease the activity level, if possible, even if the complementary feature type $f$ with the positive weight has not yet occurred. In other words, $\tilde{f}$ will cancel the activity level contribution of any feature type, not only the one of $f$.

For some activity there exists no complementary activity that might eventually cancel out each other. In some disclosure scenarios it might nevertheless be useful to forget certain activity after a certain time interval or after a certain amount of overall activity. Using the idea of share invalidation, time-outs can be realized for arbitrary feature types. The pseudonymizer manages the time-outs in the annotations while remembering the weights of the concerned feature types. If a time-out actually occurs, the pseudonymizer invalidates the youngest $w$ shares as signified by the weight stored with the time-out.

## 16.5.1 Cryptographic Enforcement by Share Invalidation

To invalidate a share that has already been computed using a given threshold scheme and provided to the reidentifiers, the threshold scheme is modified, such that

- the secret and already provided and still valid shares remain unmodified,

- neither can invalidated shares be used exclusively to reconstruct the secret, nor can they be used in combination with valid shares that are provided after the threshold scheme modification,

- newly provided valid shares are distinct from already provided shares that have been invalidated.

For the adapted Shamir threshold scheme we can leverage its additivity property: If $s_1, \ldots, s_n$ are shares of a secret $s$ and $s'_1, \ldots, s'_n$ are shares of a secret $s'$, then $s_1 + s'_1, \ldots, s_n + s'_n$ are shares of a secret $s + s'$.

In order to invalidate a provided share $s_j = p(x_i), j \in \{1, \ldots, k\}$ after the shares $s_1, \ldots, s_k$ with $k < t$ have been provided, the polynomial $p(x) = \sum_{j=0}^{t-1} a_j \cdot x^j$ of the threshold scheme is modified by adding a carefully constructed polynomial $b(x)$ to $p(x)$. The polynomial $b(x)$ has the following properties:

1. $b(x_i) = 0$, if $i \in \{1, \ldots, k\} \backslash \{j\}$ to keep the provided valid shares unmodified,

2. $b(x_j) \neq 0$ to invalidate $s_j$,

3. $b(0) = 0$ to keep the secret unmodified, and

4. the degree of $b(x)$ is less or equal to $t - 1$, and

5. $b(x)$ is pseudo-random w.r.t. the previous properties.

Such a polynomial can be constructed by splitting $b(x)$ in two factors $c(x)$ and $d(x)$, where $b(x) = c(x) \cdot d(x)$. Properties (1) and (3) can be met by choosing $c(x) = x \cdot \prod_{i=1, i \neq j}^{k} (x - x_i)$.

To warrant that secret recovery is infeasible before the threshold is exceeded, in addition to demanding property (2), $d(x)$ must have no zeros. In order to satisfy properties (4) and (5), $d(x)$ must be a pseudo-random polynomial, $d(x)$ must not have zeros, and $d(x)$ has to be of degree at most $(t-1) - k$.

In order to invalidate share $s_j$, the polynomial $p(x)$ is modified to yield $p'(x) = p(x) + b(x) = p(x) + c(x) \cdot d(x)$ with $c(x)$ and $d(x)$ chosen as described above. Since all coefficients of $p(x)$, except for the linear term, are chosen uniformly and pseudo-randomly, this property holds for $p'(x)$ as well.

When $p(x)$ has been replaced with $p'(x)$ the invalidation can be repeated. Moreover, it is possible to invalidate two or more shares at the same time by appropriately adjusting $b(x)$.

Currently, work is underway to provide an appropriate definition of security for share invalidation and to prove that the construction given above is secure w.r.t. to this definition [160].

## 16.6 Organizational Purpose Binding

Our approach provides technical purpose binding for the disclosure of pseudonyms. As a complementary concept the organizational purpose binding of pseudonym disclosure has been introduced in Sect. 7.2.1. Here we give two examples for circumstances where it may be advantageous to use organizational purpose binding instead of or in addition to technical purpose binding (see also Sect. 7.2.3):

Example 1: In a given application some disclosure scenarios that are of a certain importance for the SSO may only be modeled with a disclosure context $I_g$ which is associated with some observation $f$ and with a threshold value $t_g \leq w_{f,g}$. That is, as soon as $f$ occurs, the disclosure condition for the pseudonyms of $f$ is met immediately. Hence, it would be futile to pseudonymize $f$ in the first place, if technical purpose binding is used. Instead, the PPO may use organizational purpose binding for the pseudonyms of $f$, such that the SSO can disclose the pseudonyms if and only if he cooperates with the PPO.

Example 2: In a given application some disclosure scenario might occur, which has not been anticipated and is not associated to the features involved in the scenario. Then, the relevant features cannot be disclosed by the SSO, because in general they do not meet a disclosure condition. Modeling the respective disclosure scenario in hindsight will not have any effect on the pseudonyms that have been generated in advance for the relevant features.

If it is important in the given application to be able to even disclose pseudonyms associated with disclosure scenarios that have not been anticipated, organizational purpose binding can be used in addition to technical purpose binding. In the more common case that a modeled disclosure scenario occurs, the associated pseudonyms can be disclosed by the SSO just in time. In the rare case that a disclosure scenario occurs, which has not been modeled in the a priori knowledge, the SSO must cooperate with the PPO to disclose the associated pseudonyms.

There are several possibilities to achieve organizational purpose binding. As examples we roughly outline two possible solutions in Sect. 16.6.1 and Sect. 16.6.2 without considering more intricate aspects, such as fairness and verifiability. In both solutions the PPO holds a secret decryption key $k_{o,PPO}$. The solutions do not require that the PPO discloses his secret decryption key to any of the SSOs. This ensures that the SSOs must cooperate with the PPO to be able to recover some secret. In the given solutions we assume that the SSOs trust the PPO to provide correct results. Moreover, the control requirements for pseudonym disclosure subject to organizational purpose binding must comply with Fig. 8.6a, irrespective of the control requirements for pseudonym disclosure subject to technical purpose binding depicted in Fig. 11.1 and Fig. 16.2.

### 16.6.1 Cryptographic Enforcement using Threshold Cryptography

Organizational purpose binding can be enforced using threshold cryptography [67], e.g. based on the El-Gamal cryptosystem and on Shamir's threshold scheme. In this solution certain sets of SSOs need to cooperate with the PPO to recover the secret $s_i$. The secret sharing scheme can be used to implement the desired access structure [211]. Each $SSO_j$ holds an individual decryption key $k_{o,j}$. The $k_{o,j}$ and $k_{o,PPO}$ are chosen such that they are cryptographic shares of a secret decryption key $k_o$ in a suitable secret sharing scheme.

When initializing a pseudonym mapping entry, the pseudonymizer encrypts the secret $s_i$ in the cryptosystem using the encryption key $\tilde{k}_o$ corresponding to $k_o$. When pseudonymizing, the pseudonymizer provides the resulting *escrow data* $c_{o,i} = E(\tilde{k}_o, s_i)$ instead of or in addition to the shares of $s_i$ in the pseudonymity-layer. From the escrow data the SSOs and the PPO can locally perform the decryption of $c_{o,i}$ yielding the partial results $s_{i,j} := D(k_{o,j}, c_{o,i})$ and $s_{i,PPO} := D(k_{o,PPO}, c_{o,i})$, respectively. Only cooperatively they can yield $s_i$ without revealing $k_o$, $k_{o,j}$ and $k_{o,PPO}$ by combining an eligible set of partial results $s_{i,j}$ and $s_{i,PPO}$ within the secret sharing scheme.

### 16.6.2 Cryptographic Enforcement using Symmetric Cryptography

Organizational purpose binding can also be enforced using symmetric cryptography. Here we assume stronger restrictions on the computational complexity of the cryptographic primitives that we may use. In return, we drop the requirement that only certain sets of SSOs are eligible to recover the secret $s_i$.

When initializing a pseudonym mapping entry, the pseudonymizer simply encrypts $s_i$ using $\tilde{k}_o = k_{o,PPO}$ in a symmetric cryptosystem. When pseudonymizing, the pseudonymizer provides the resulting *escrow data* $c_{o,i} = E(\tilde{k}_o, s_i)$ instead of or in addition to the shares of $s_i$ in the pseudonymity-layer. To reveal $s_i$ the SSOs need to cooperate with the PPO, who can decrypt $c_{o,i}$ and provide $s_i$.

# Part III

# Application to Unix Audit Data

In this Part we show how the set-based approach from Part II can be applied to audit data of operational systems in practice. We chose to use Unix systems for this purpose. Unix systems today are reliable and therefore wide-spread platforms for services offered via the Internet. Our approach can as well be shown to work in practice using different platforms.

Chapter 17 gives on overview of the relevant concepts of the audit architecture of and the audit data occurring in Unix systems. The predominantly used audit service *syslog* is described in the some detail in Chap. 18. In Chap. 19 is shown, how our set-based approach from Part II can be instantiated for *syslog*-style audit data. Finally, Chap. 20 describes the toolset *Pseudo/CoRe* that implements our approach for *syslog*-style audit data. Part IV indicates that the toolset *Pseudo/CoRe* is able to handle real-world audit data volumes in practice.

# 17

## Unix Audit Data

In this Chapter the relevant concepts of the audit architecture of Unix systems are introduced (see Sect. 17.1, Sect. 17.1.1 and Sect. 17.1.2). The different categories of audit data occurring in these systems are introduced in Sect. 17.1.3. In Sect. 17.2 is shown that all categories can be covered, if we implement our approach for ASCII format audit data, i.e. *syslog*-style audit data. In Chap. 18 *syslog* audit data is examined in more detail.

## 17.1 Unix Audit Architecture

Figure 17.1 depicts an abstraction of components relevant for auditing at the kernel level and at the user level. Basically, we find two situations. OS audit components and application processes either store their audit data in dedicated files or they deliver the audit data via an audit service.

Well known examples for implementations of audit services are `auditd` from Sun's Basic Security Module (see Sect. 17.1.1) and `syslogd` (see Sect. 17.1.2). *Audit services* provide standardized additional data for each audit record, such as a time stamp and an identifier representing the host on which the audit record was generated. They more or less unify audit data management by standardizing the audit record (header) format. Moreover, audit services in practice provide better manageability by merging or distributing audit data based on classifications.

### 17.1.1 Auditd

The audit service `auditd` is part of the SunSHIELD Basic Security Module (BSM) [117] which is included with Solaris starting with release 2.3. The BSM is intended to supplement Solaris for TCSEC C2 compliance (Trusted Computer System Evaluation Criteria [37, 38]).

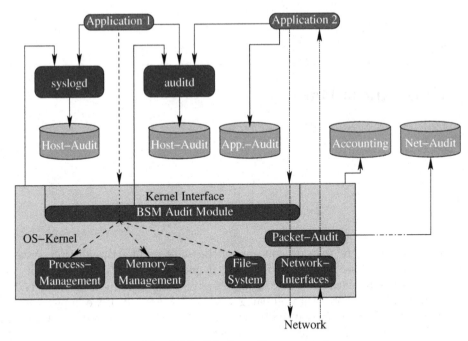

**Fig. 17.1.** Solaris audit components

Audit records may be delivered to **auditd** by the kernel and by user level applications. BSM kernel level events comprise system calls that allow for potentially
security sensitive activity. The dashed arrow in Fig. 17.1 from 'Application 1'
to the 'Kernel Interface' represents system calls of the application, whereas the
solid arrow from the 'BSM Audit Module' to '**auditd**' represents the flow of the
audit records for the corresponding system calls.

A few selected Solaris standard user level applications emit audit records via
**auditd**, such as some local and remote login services, **passwd**, **inetd**, **mountd**,
etc. In Fig. 17.1 this is signified by the solid arrows pointing from the applications
to **auditd**.

### 17.1.2 Syslogd

As **auditd**, also **syslogd** collects audit records from the kernel level and from
the user level. In Fig. 17.1 this is shown by the solid arrows pointing from 'Application 1' and from the 'OS-Kernel' to '**syslogd**'. Optionally **syslogd** also
accepts remotely generated audit records at UDP port number 514 (not shown
in Fig. 17.1). The *syslog* system is described in more detail in Chap. 18.

### 17.1.3 Audit Data Categories

We distinguish three categories of audit data:

Host-based audit data relates to activity taking place within a host system and it is also generated by audit components on that host system.

Network-based audit data is generated by audit components associated with network resources, where data is handled at abstraction levels below the application layer.

Out-of-band audit data refers to activity that is not monitored by the IT system.

While expanding on different data categories is helpful for classifying audit data analysis systems (e.g. intrusion detection systems [8, 63]), in this text we are mainly interested in covering with one design as many existing audit data categories as possible.

All mentioned audit data categories are represented in Fig. 17.1. Host-based data is collected in the storage components labeled 'Host-Audit', 'Accounting' and 'App.-Audit'. The respective audit components are part of the applications and of the kernel, e.g. the 'BSM Audit Module'. Network-based data also is extracted by a kernel module, in our case using *ip filter* [181] (see 'Packet-Audit' in Fig. 17.1).[1] The acquisition of out-of-band audit data is usually implemented by means of applications querying sources external to the IT system.

## 17.2 Selection of *Syslog*

When considering the pseudonymization of audit data, all relevant audit data categories mentioned above should be covered. Available audit components use various audit record formats. There have been proposed some common audit data formats [202, 11, 7] and many intrusion detection systems use their own canonical format, but in the past these formats have not been taken up on a wide scale.

With our design we aim at a non-invasive, easy to install toolset that covers as many categories of audit data as possible. We therefore decided to build a pseudonymizer for *syslog*-style audit data. Due to its uniformity and availability in most significant Unixes, many audit components in the Unix world leverage the *syslog* audit service for recording audit data. Also active network components such as routers provide for remote audit data recording using *syslog*. Finally,

---

[1] The packet audit data path in Fig. 17.1 actually is a simplified illustration. *Ip filter*, as commonly set up, sends audit data via `ipmon` to `syslogd`. The audit data path of other suitable products may vary.

there are several third party products available for Windows driven systems to integrate with an existing Unix *syslog* infrastructure.

By supporting *syslog* we can pseudonymize host-based, network-based and out-of-band audit data. *Syslog* supports host-based audit data generated by most network services and by the kernel. Network-based audit data as generated by many firewalls, routers and end systems protected by IP traffic filters, such as *ip filter*, can be directed to `syslogd`. Out-of-band data can be covered if applications are made aware of external activity and if these applications use *syslog* to record the corresponding audit records.

Actually, we do not limit our design to the *syslog* audit record format. The design supports arbitrary ASCII format audit data. Audit components not using *syslog*, but directing their audit data to dedicated files, can be covered directly or by means of a *redirector*, which directs audit data from arbitrary files to `syslogd` (see Sect. 19.4.2).

In practice, our design covers most of the audit data usually collected in Unix systems. In certain environments additional audit data is collected, which might need to be pseudonymized, but is not yet covered by our design. For example, many off-the-shelf Unix systems provide the ability to generate accounting data and TCSEC C2 audit data.

The Unix accounting monitors the utilization of shared system resources. Its record format is very similar on all Unixes, involving a low recording overhead. An audit record is emitted after the respective activity terminates. As a consequence, accounting records for daemon processes are normally being withheld. Thus, accounting will not generate privacy problems for networked service clients, but sensitive information regarding local users is recorded. Nowadays accounting is seldomly used. If at all, pseudonymizing accounting data makes the best sense for servers to which users log-in locally.

Audit record formats conforming to TCSEC C2 vary between implementations of diverse vendors. Tailoring our design to a specific format would limit its applicability. Anyhow, particularly Sun's BSM (see Sect. 17.1.1) is quite popular with host-based intrusion detection systems, which potentially can impair the privacy of users associated with a log-in session. In Part V we therefore refine and automate our approach w.r.t. misuse detection analysis.

# Syslog

In Chap. 17 has been shown that all categories of audit data can be covered by our approach, if it is applied to ASCII format audit data. A main source of ASCII format audit data is the *syslog* audit service, which is by default used by many audit components in Unix systems. Therefore, the *syslog* audit service is described in the necessary detail in this Chapter.

Sect. 18.1 summarizes which kinds of activity are documented in *syslog* audit data and Sect. 18.2 describes in some detail the processing of audit data by syslogd. Based on the knowledge about which input sources syslogd supports (see Sect. 18.2.1), how audit records can be selectively processed (see Sect. 18.2.2), and how the output format is defined (see Sect. 18.2.3), we propose several approaches in Sect. 18.3 for integrating our approach with the *syslog* audit service. In Chap. 19 is examined how the approach from Part II can be instantiated for *syslog*-style audit data.

## 18.1 Typical *Syslog* Audit Data

As described in Sect. 17.2, host-based, network-based and out-of-band audit data is consolidated via *syslog*. The audit data collected via *syslog* describes activity and conditions monitored by diverse audit components of the IT system. These audit components are categorized as *facilities* in *syslog* parlance. An audit component that monitors an activity or condition supplies a rating of its *severity* [214, 139]. The *priority* of an audit record is defined as the pairing of the corresponding facility and severity.

The severity ranges from *debugging* and *informational* over *error* conditions to *emergency* conditions. Primarily informational and diagnostics messages from the kernel and from network services are recorded via *syslog*. Some sample audit records are shown in Fig. 18.1. For the sake of presentation we numbered the audit records and omitted the priority, time stamp and host fields (PRI, TS and

```
1  ftpd[7427]: xferlog (send): 30 pony.puf 240369 0 240369 funstuff.tar.gz b _ o g dexter ftp 0 * c
2  ftpd[7427]: xferlog (send): 28 pony.puf 243943 0 243943 funstuff.tar.gz b _ o g dexter ftp 0 * c

3  pppoed[15459]: invalid state a7
4  pppoed[15459]: Failed to discover server!

5  Pluto[13321]: Starting Pluto (FreeS/WAN Version 1.9)
6  Pluto[13321]:     including X.509 patch (Version 0.8.1)
7  Pluto[13321]: X.509 certificate file '/etc/x509cert.der' not found
8  Pluto[13321]: OpenPGP certificate file '/etc/pgpcert.pgp' not found
9  Pluto[13321]: listening for IKE messages
10 Pluto[13321]: FATAL ERROR: bind() failed in find_raw_ifaces4(). Errno 13: Permission denied
12 sendmail[23248]: gethostbyaddr(192.168.3.1) failed: 1
13 wu.ftpd[4657]: warning: /etc/hosts.allow, line 12: can't verify hostname: gethostbyname(mport80.minerva.com.a...
14 wu.ftpd[4658]: warning: /etc/hosts.allow, line 12: can't verify hostname: gethostbyname(mport80.minerva.com.a...

15 kernel: LIDS: lidsadm (22 5 inode 28746) pid 14419 user (0/0) on ttyp181: try to open /etc/lids/lids.conf for...
16 portsentry[848]: attackalert: SYN/Normal scan from host: pony.puf/192.168.1.4 to TCP port: 21
17 tcplog[1040]:            SYN        RES2 : ftp from 192.168.1.4 port 45691
18 tcplog[1040]: FIN SYN    PSH   URG      : ftp from 192.168.1.4 port 45693
19 tcplog[1040]: FIN SYN    PSH   URG      : ftp from 192.168.1.4 port 45693
20 tcplog[1040]: FIN        PSH   URG      : port 34513 from 192.168.1.4 port 45697
21 tcplog[1040]: FIN        PSH   URG      : port 34513 from 192.168.1.4 port 45697
22 tcplog[1040]: QUESO: port 34513 from 192.168.1.4 port 45697
23 login[1510]: ROOT LOGIN on 'tty1'
24 login[12571]: ILLEGAL ROOT LOGIN on 'ttyS1'
```

Fig. 18.1. Sample *syslog* audit records

```
<36 |PRI|> Oct 31 03:13:37 |TS| pony |H| su |AC| 31337 |PID|: pam_authenticate: Authentication failure pts/14 deedee-root |MSG|
```

Fig. 18.2. Parts of a sample *syslog* audit record

H in Fig. 18.2). Figure 18.1 contains informational audit records (lines 1 and 2), diagnostic audit records (lines 3 and 4), diagnostic audit records related to security (lines 5 through 14) as well as possibly attack related audit records (lines 15 through 24).

Also serious activity of users associated with log-in sessions are recorded by *syslog*. Depending on the system configuration, a variety of other sorts of activity may be reported to *syslog*. As an example, the intrusion detection system *Snort* [186, 187] is capable of reporting alarms to *syslog*. Basically, *syslog* audit data is collected and used for troubleshooting and limited manual intrusion detection. Other intrusion detection systems also analyze *syslog* audit data, such as the *STAT Tool Suite* [219].

## 18.2 *Syslog* Audit Data Processing

Audit records that are intended to be recorded by the *syslog* audit service are received by the `syslogd` application process either from user level application processes, from kernel level code or optionally via the network from remote audit components. The ability to process audit data provided by remote audit components allows for the centralized consolidation of audit data from a variety of platforms, such as routers, firewalls, intrusion detection systems and end systems driven by widespread operating systems.

Unfortunately, the *syslog* application protocol is traditionally implemented over UDP (port number 514) without any security precautions. This opens several opportunities for attack [139]. Therefore, on most modern Unixes, the reception of *syslog* audit data from remote audit components is disabled by default or can be disabled by the system administrator. The IETF Syslog Working Group endeavors to develop a standard to secure the *syslog* protocol [158, 97]. In the mean time some alternative, purportedly more secure *syslog* replacements are available for Unix, such as `nsyslogd` [182]. Another option is to use IPSEC [127] to secure the *syslog* traffic.

### 18.2.1 Input

When delivering an audit record to *syslog*, the generating audit component provides the priority, i.e. the pairing of the according facility and severity, as well as the name of the respective audit component. At the discretion of the audit component and in addition to its name, a process ID is supplied, identifying the application process generating the audit record. Apart from this information the audit record comprises a description of noteworthy activity. The description is ASCII-encoded in a human-readable form, but there are no standards with regard to the format of the description. The description format thus is specific to a given audit component and may vary even between different versions of a given audit component.

### 18.2.2 Processing

The *syslog* processing of incoming audit records can be configured by the system administrator based on the record priority. Some implementations of `syslogd` allow finer grained selection criteria such as the name of the audit component. Basically, `syslogd` sequentially evaluates rules provided by the system administrator. The priority of each incoming audit record is matched against the rules. When a rule matches, the audit record is written out to the destination specified by the matching rule. Possible destinations are files, devices, named pipes, the console of one or more users being logged on, and `syslogd` processes on remote hosts. The details on rule specification are described elsewhere [214].

### 18.2.3 Output

Before writing an audit record out to the specified destination, `syslogd` prepends to the message content (see 'MSG' in Fig. 18.2) a local time stamp (date/time) (see 'TS' in Fig. 18.2), the (fully qualified domain) name or the IP address of the local host (see 'H' in Fig. 18.2) and the name of the audit component (see 'AC' in Fig. 18.2), optionally augmented by the respective process ID (see 'PID' in Fig. 18.2). Only when forwarding the audit record to a remote host, `syslogd` prepends the respective priority (see 'PRI' in Fig. 18.2) to the message, which encodes both, facility and severity, in one integer value.

## 18.3 Embedding Audit Data Pseudonymizers

There are several opportunities for pseudonymizing audit records along the path from the generating audit component to the consumer or sink. Figure 18.3 shows these possibilities. According to the reasoning in Sect. 17.2, we focus on ASCII format audit data in the following. The places where ASCII format audit data can be pseudonymized are marked with a dark disc in Fig. 18.3.

Some audit components write their audit data directly to files (see 'Application 2' writing to 'App.-Audit' and 'Packet-Audit' writing to 'Net-Audit' in Fig. 18.3). The straightforward solution to pseudonymize this audit data is to configure the system, such that the audit component writes the audit data to a named pipe, which a pseudonymizer reads simultaneously (see 'P' next to 'App.-Audit' and 'Net.-Audit' in Fig. 18.3). Also, archived audit data can be piped into pseudonymizers in order to be pseudonymized.

In some cases it might be useful to redirect the audit data of an audit component to an audit service, instead of writing it directly to a file. An example use is consolidating certain audit data in a single place. This can be achieved by configuring the system, such that the audit components write the audit data to a

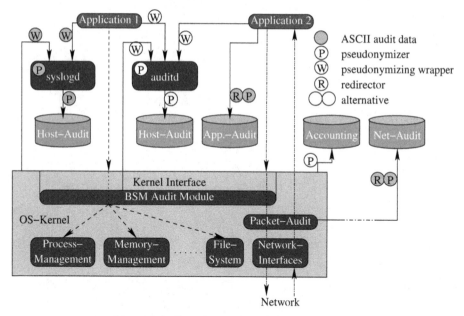

**Fig. 18.3.** Pseudonymizing Solaris audit data

named pipe, each. A *redirector* can pick up the audit data from the pipe[1] and deposit it e.g. at `syslogd` by means of the *syslog* API (see 'R' next to 'App.-Audit' and 'Net-Audit' in Fig. 18.3).

Finally, pseudonymizers can be integrated with the *syslog* audit service at three different levels. First, wrappers can intercept and pseudonymize the audit data before it is processed by `syslogd`, while `syslogd` is configured to receive the pseudonymized audit records from the wrapper (see 'W' above `syslogd` in Fig. 18.3). Second, pseudonymization can be embedded within `syslogd`, either by patching the source code of the native `syslogd` of the system, or by replacing the native `syslogd` of the system with another system's patched version of `syslogd` (see 'P' within `syslogd` in Fig. 18.3). Third, `syslogd` can be configured to write the processed audit data into named pipes that are simultaneously read by pseudonymizers (see 'P' below `syslogd` in Fig. 18.3). The three architectures implementing pseudonymization on the three levels are described and discussed in Sect. 19.4.

---

[1] In case an application executes accesses on its audit data files beyond appending audit records, the redirector could only be used by indirection via files. Those files shouldn't be pruned while the application might revisit old content.

**19**

# Instantiating the Set-based Approach
# for *Syslog*-style Audit Data

In this Chapter the set-based approach from Part II is instantiated for ASCII format audit data in Unix systems as proposed in Sect. 17.2. Sect. 19.1 shows how the treatment of abstract events can be instantiated for ASCII format audit records. Sect. 19.2 presents how the pseudonymity-layer data for pseudonym disclosure is embedded in application-layer ASCII format audit records. The trust model in use is described in Sect. 19.3. In Sect. 19.4 we briefly introduce the components of the architecture we design for the implementation of the pseudonymizer embeddings identified in Sect. 18.3. Chapter 20 describes the toolset *Pseudo/CoRe*, which implements the set-based approach for ASCII format audit data. Except for the specializations made for the application for ASCII format audit data, the approach works as described in Part II.

The set-based approach is formulated for the more general ASCII format audit records, and Sect. 19.4.2 describes how these audit records can be pseudonymized. As motivated in Chap. 18, *syslog-style* audit data is the most frequently occurring kind of ASCII format audit data. Hence, the design of the architecture is focused on the pseudonymization of *syslog*-style audit data. Sect. 19.4.1 describes in more detail, how the approach integrates with existing *syslog*-style audit data environments, while maintaining the trust model. Consequently, for the examples in this Chapter we use *syslog*-style audit records.

## 19.1 Locating Identifying Features in Application-layer Data

ASCII format audit records contain events, which can be regarded as a refinement of the abstract events defined in Sect. 12.1.1. In the following, we mean ASCII format audit records or *syslog*-style audit records when using the term *audit record*. We denote events contained in these audit records simply as *events*. When describing concepts on the conceptual level, we refer to *abstract events*.

In Part II the set-based approach has been described in terms of observations based on abstract events (see Sect. 12.1.1). To instantiate the approach for ASCII format audit records, the concepts tied syntactically to abstract events need to be mapped to the same concepts being expressed syntactically in ASCII format audit records.

Summarizing from Sect. 12.1.1, an abstract event comprises an event designator (see frame 1 in Fig. 12.1), an event type (see frame 2 in Fig. 12.1) and an arbitrary number of pairs of feature designators (see frames 3, 5 and 7 in Fig. 12.1) and features (see frames 4, 6 and 8 in Fig. 12.1). For events contained in *syslog*-style audit records the event designator is composed of an optional priority, a time stamp, a host and an optional process ID field (see 'PRI', 'TS', 'H' and 'PID' in Fig. 18.2). In these audit records the event type is encoded in the audit component field and in the message content (see 'AC' and 'MSG' in Fig. 18.2), whereas the feature designators and the features are encoded in the message content only (see 'MSG' in Fig. 18.2).

The syntactical concepts in (abstract) events that are actually used by the set-based approach from Part II are features of a certain feature type, where the feature type is composed of the event type and a feature designator (see Sect. 12.1.1). That is, an implementation of our approach needs to recognize the following syntactical concepts contained in audit records: event types, feature designators, features.

The abstract events defined in Sect. 12.1.1 are reasonably well-formed, such that the relevant syntactical concepts can be easily identified. This is not in general the case for ASCII format audit records, because the syntax of the audit records is primarily determined by the originating audit component (see Sect. 18.2.1). Thus, the recognition of event types, feature designators and features is based on the evaluation of contextual data, e.g. by means of regular expressions for pattern matching, as defined in the POSIX standard 1003.2 Sect. 2.8.

The audit record in Fig. 19.1 is used as an example to show how the recognition of the relevant syntactical concepts works for ASCII format audit records. For the sake of brevity we omitted the priority, time stamp and host fields in Fig. 19.1 (see 'PRI', 'TS' and 'H' in Fig. 18.2).

**Fig. 19.1.** Syntactical concepts in a sample *syslog* audit record

The event type is usually defined by the name of the audit component (see frame 1 in Fig. 19.1) and parts of the static content of the audit record (see frame 2 in Fig. 19.1). Thus, the event type corresponding to the string '*loginfail*' in frame 2 in Fig. 12.1 can be recognized using a regular expression matching both, frame 1 and frame 2 in Fig. 19.1. Often, the feature designators are not given explicitly in ASCII format audit records. In general, feature designators can be recognized by matching the static contextual content to the left and to the right of the respective features. Accordingly, the feature corresponding to a feature designator is defined as the data surrounded by the feature designator. For example, the feature designator corresponding to the string 'usr' in frame 3 in Fig. 12.1 can be recognized using one regular expression that matches frame 4 in Fig. 19.1 and one regular expression that matches frame 6 in Fig. 19.1. Then, the feature corresponding to the string '**deedee**' in frame 4 in Fig. 12.1 is found between frame 4 and frame 6, i.e. in frame 5 in Fig. 19.1. The complete mapping of the relevant syntactical concepts in the example events in Fig. 12.1 and in Fig. 19.1 is given in Table 19.1.

**Table 19.1.** Mapping of the syntactical concepts of observations from the abstract event in Fig. 12.1 to the same concepts contained in the *syslog*-style event in Fig. 19.1

| syntactical concept | concept instance in Fig. 12.1 | frame numbers abstract event in Fig. 12.1 | event in Fig. 19.1 |
|---|---|---|---|
| event type | *loginfail* | 2 | 1, 2 |
| feature designator | *usr* | 3 | 4, 6 |
| feature | **deedee** | 4 | 5 |
| feature designator | *acct* | 5 | 6, 8 |
| feature | **root** | 6 | 7 |
| feature designator | *term* | 7 | 2, 4 |
| feature | **pts/14** | 8 | 3 |

The decision tree described in Sect. 12.3 can be adapted to store the regular expressions needed to recognize event types and feature designators. As described in Sect. 12.3, features are located in an audit record firstly by matching the event type and then by matching the feature designators. For each matched feature designator the corresponding feature is the string between the data matched by the two regular expressions of the feature designator.

## 19.2 Generating Pseudonymity-layer Data for Pseudonym Disclosure

In Chap. 11 we assumed that the format of the application-layer audit records is application-specific and rigid. Therefore, additional data that we need to provide with each pseudonym, e.g. data needed for pseudonym disclosure, cannot be embedded in the pseudonymized application-layer audit records. For providing additional data with the pseudonyms embedded in the application-layer, the pseudonymity-layer was introduced as a solution in Sect. 13.1. Conceptually, the pseudonymity-layer and the application-layer are two separate streams of inter-related data. For practical reasons both streams shall be multiplexed suitably and the pseudonymity-layer data shall be wrapped appropriately, such that it can be embedded in the application-layer data stream. Accordingly, the dashed arrows in Fig. 19.4 signify the flow of the application-layer data and of the pseudonymity-layer data in one multiplexed stream, where the pseudonymity-layer audit records are located close to the corresponding application-layer audit records. Note, that due to the extension in Sect. 16.3 the pseudonymity-layer data includes the pseudonym mapping.

Figure 19.3 shows the pseudonymized audit record from Fig. 19.2 together with the respective pseudonymity-layer data. For the sake of presentation we numbered the audit records and omitted the priority field (see 'PRI' in Fig. 18.2).

In order to embed the pseudonymity-layer data in the application-layer, it is wrapped and encoded, such that it syntactically conforms to the current ASCII format audit data in the application-layer. The format to be used for the audit record header (see frame 1 in Fig. 19.3) can be configured to mimic the format of the application-layer audit record headers (see Sect. 20.3). The facility, severity and additional options processed by syslogd can also be adjusted, such that the pseudonymity-layer data is ignored by the application (see (4) in Sect. 20.3). The actual pseudonymity-layer data is encoded in ASCII format and appended to the audit record header.

The sample audit record in Fig. 19.2 contains several identifying features, but for the example only the feature deedee shall be pseudonymized (see frame 1 in Fig. 19.2). Generally, application-layer audit records may contain several identifying features that need to be replaced by pseudonyms, such that after pseudonymization, an application-layer audit record contains one or more pseudonyms. The pseudonymity-layer data for each pseudonym in a given disclosure context is stored in a separate audit record. As an example, consider an application-layer audit record containing three pseudonyms of which one is associated with two disclosure contexts. Then, four audit records are generated, containing the respective pseudonymity-layer data required for pseudonym disclosure.

The pseudonymity-layer data stored in an audit record for a given pseudonym in the pseudonymized application-layer audit record contains the following fields. For the linkage between the pseudonymity-layer data and the application-layer data an identifier $z$ (see frame 2 in Fig. 19.3) is introduced, which is the same for all pseudonymity-layer audit records for the pseudonyms of a given application-layer audit record (see Sect. 19.2.1). Also for the linkage, the identifier $z$ is followed by the pseudonym $n_i$ that is associated with the following fields (cf. frame 3 and frame 14 in Fig. 19.3). The identifier of the disclosure context associates the information in the following fields with a disclosure context $I$ (see frame 4 Fig. 19.3, cf. Sect. 12.3). For the reconstruction of the pseudonym mapping and eventually for the disclosure of the encrypted identifying feature is the linkability

`Oct 31 03:13:37 pony su[31337]: pam_authenticate: Authentication failure pts/14 ` `deedee`[1]`-root`

**Fig. 19.2.** A sample *syslog* audit record

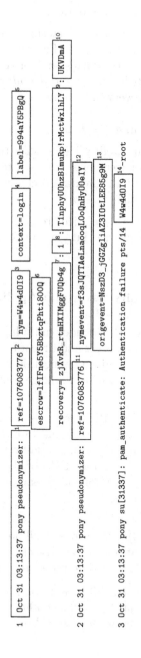

1 `Oct 31 03:13:37 pony pseudonymizer:`[1] `ref=1076083776`[2] `nym=W4w4dOI9`[3] `context=login`[4] `label=994aY5PBgQ`[5]
`escrow=lfIFne5Y5BbztqPhti8OOQ`[6]
`recovery=zjXvkR_rtmHXIMggFUQb4g`[7] : `1`[8] : `T1nphyUOhzBImuRp!rMctWxlhLY`[9] : `UKVDmA`[10]

2 `Oct 31 03:13:37 pony pseudonymizer:` `ref=1076083776`[11]
`nymevent=f3sJQTIAeLnaooqLOoQnHyOOeIY`[12]
`origevent=NszD3_jGGZg1iAZ3IOtLEE85g9M`[13]

3 `Oct 31 03:13:37 pony su[31337]: pam_authenticate: Authentication failure pts/14` `W4w4dOI9`[14]`-root`

**Fig. 19.3.** Sample pseudonymized *syslog* audit record with pseudonymity-layer data

label $l_i$ included (see frame 5 Fig. 19.3, Sect. 15.3 and Sect. 16.3).[1] The pseudonym disclosure subject to organizational purpose binding is enabled by the field containing the escrow data $c_{o,i}$ (see frame 6 in Fig. 19.3 and Sect. 16.6.2).[2] The pseudonym disclosure subject to technical purpose binding is supported by the following recovery data. Summarized, the pseudonymity-layer data for pseudonym disclosure comprises:

$$\langle z, n_i, I, l_i, c_{o,i}, \text{recovery data} \rangle$$

The recovery data for pseudonym disclosure subject to technical purpose binding contains the shares $r_{i,m_i}$ (see frame 7 and frame 8 in Fig. 19.3 for $p_i(x)$ and $x$, respectively; see also Sect. 15.2) as well as the corresponding verifiers $d_{i,m_i}$ (see frame 9 and frame 10 in Fig. 19.3 for $H(drand, s_i)$ and $drand$, respectively; see also Sect. 14.3.1).[3] Summarized, the recovery data comprises one or more pairs of:

$$\langle \langle p_i(x), x \rangle, \langle H(drand, s_i), drand \rangle \rangle$$

Note, that we avoid mismatches using linkability labels, such that the verifiers actually are not necessary. The verifiers nevertheless are used to verify that the implementation works as expected. Our implementation checks the verifier for each share to detect faulty recoveries of the secret $s_i$.

The pseudonymity-layer records need to be tied to the pseudonyms in application-layer records for which they provide information. Section 19.2.1 describes, how this can be done.

### 19.2.1 Linkage between Pseudonymity-Layer and Application-Layer

The audit records described above contain the pseudonymity-layer data required for pseudonym disclosure. All pseudonymity-layer audit records, providing information for the disclosure of pseudonyms in a given application-layer audit record are linked to this application-layer audit record by a linkage contained in an additional pseudonymity-layer audit record.

The linkage audit record (see line 2 in Fig. 19.3) contains the identifier $z$ (see frame 11 in Fig. 19.3), a message digest $H(b)$ (see frame 13 in Fig. 19.3) of the original application-layer audit record $b$ (e.g. the sample audit record in Fig. 19.2) and a message digest $H(b^p)$ (see frame 12 in Fig. 19.3) of the pseudonymized application-layer audit record $b^p$ (e.g. the pseudonymized sample audit record in line 3 in Fig. 19.3):

$$\langle z, H(b^p), H(b) \rangle$$

The identifier $z$ (see frame 11 in Fig. 19.3) is used to bind all pseudonymity-layer records together, which provide information for the disclosure of pseudonyms in the application-layer audit record $b^p$, and that therefore contain the same

---

[1] The linkability label is encoded using an adapted Base64 algorithm.

[2] The escrow data is encoded using an adapted Base64 algorithm.

[3] The shares and the verifiers are encoded using an adapted Base64 algorithm.

identifier $z$ (see frame 2 in Fig. 19.3). The message digest $H(b)$ (see frame 13 in Fig. 19.3) of the original application-layer audit record is not strictly necessary, but it can be used to verify that the implementation works as expected. Our implementation compares $H(b)$ against the message digest of the audit record after complete reidentification in order to detect faulty reidentifications.

Finally, $H(b^p)$ (see frame 12 in Fig. 19.3) is used to bind the pseudonymity-layer audit records to the pseudonymized application-layer audit record $b^p$. Together with a given pseudonym $n_i$ from the application-layer audit record $b^p$ (see frame 14 in Fig. 19.3) is $H(b^p)$ a unique search criterion to locate the corresponding entry in the (partially) reconstructed pseudonym mapping in the disclosure context $I$.[4] Note, that it is important that the pseudonyms for different pseudonym mapping entries in a given audit record differ. This is ensured by the pseudonymizer. Also note, that the linkability labels from the pseudonymity-layer data are used to reconstruct the pseudonym mapping, but the entries in $I$ corresponding to the pseudonyms to be disclosed are located using only information available in the pseudonymized application-layer audit records, i.e. the pseudonyms and the message digest $H(b^p)$ (see Sect. 15.3).

## 19.3 Trust Model and Related Aspects

The architectures for embedding pseudonymizers that are developed in Sect. 19.4 support the trust model described in Chap. 11. Additionally, the extension from Sect. 16.3 is used, such that we have a trust model as depicted in Fig. 19.4.

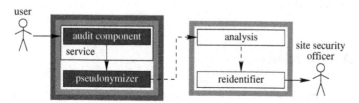

**Fig. 19.4.** Trust and control in the architectural model of the approach applied to Unix audit data (see Fig. 16.2)

Here, the more practically inclined trust aspects of audit data pseudonymization need to be considered. According to the specific audit data pseudonymization

---

[4] The message digest alone is not a sufficient search criterion, because a given audit record may contain several pseudonyms in $I$. Also the pseudonym alone is not a sufficient search criterion, because the same pseudonym may be used for different entries in the pseudonym mapping of $I$, then occurring in different audit records. This might happen, if the configuration only allows strongly restricted name spaces for these pseudonyms (see Sect. 20.3).

requirements, audit records should be pseudonymized on the fly on the physical component where they are generated, and they should be securely transferred as soon as possible to the audit data analysis component (see Sect. 10.1). This may not be possible in some situations, e.g. when consolidating audit data generated by routers or Windows driven systems as is proposed in Sect. 17.2. In such cases additional measures must be taken to provide a secure channel between the audit component and the pseudonymizer (see Sect. 18.2).

The performance requirements from Sect. 10.1 also imply the use of cryptographic primitives with a low computational complexity and delay. While our approach already considers these requirements (see Chap. 11), the cryptographic primitives used for the implementation of the architectures shall be suitable to keep up with the audit data volume in practice. Hence, for encryption and decryption we use a symmetric cryptosystem, such that $k_i = \tilde{k}_i$. Accordingly, for organizational purpose binding we use the solution from Sect. 16.6.2, which also uses a symmetric cryptosystem. Note, that Fig. 19.4 depicts only the control requirements for pseudonym disclosure subject to technical purpose binding. While the implementation presented in Chap. 20 is prepared for pseudonym disclosure subject to organizational purpose binding, the respective reidentifier has not been implemented. The control requirements of such a reidentifier must comply with Fig. 8.6a, irrespective of the control requirements for pseudonym disclosure subject to technical purpose binding depicted in Fig. 19.4.

The choice of the pseudonymization techniques and the performance of the implementation of the cryptographic primitives used are evaluated in Part IV.

Also for performance reasons, the more practical approach for mismatch avoidance using linkability labels is favored over the approach for mismatch detection using verifiers (see Sect. 14.3).

## 19.4 Architecture

The architectures proposed in the following are based on several software components. In a nutshell, the `redirector` can be used to redirect local audit data to the local `syslogd`, the `rlogger` transfers local audit data to a remote `syslogd` and the `wrapper` intercepts audit data before it is read by the local `syslogd`. Using these tools, audit data can be redirected or fed into the `pseudonymizer` to be pseudonymized. Conversely, the `reidentifier` can be used to disclose the pseudonyms in pseudonymized audit data, subject to purpose binding.

The `shared` and the `combined` provide the cryptographic primitives for the `pseudonymizer` and the `reidentifier`, respectively. The `shared` may run on the same machine as the `pseudonymizer`, or it may run remotely. This allows several distributed `pseudonymizers` to use a central `shared` with the result that the linkability labels for a given identifying feature are linkable across the corresponding distributed audit components. The protocol used for communication between the **pseudonymizer** and **shared** transfers identifiable features. Since the privacy protection official (PPO) might not control the network between the **pseudonymizer** and the **shared**, the channel is protected by means of encryption, if **shared** runs remotely.

The **combined** may run on the same machine as the **reidentifier**, or it may run remotely. The protocol used for communication between the **reidentifier** and **combined** transfers identifiable features. Since identifiable features are transferred only if a disclosure condition is satisfied, i.e. the site security officer (SSO) is allowed to see the features, there is no need for a channel providing confidentiality.[5]

The software components of the architecture were only briefly mentioned above. For more details on the functionality of the various components refer to Sect. 20.4.

### 19.4.1 Pseudonymizing *Syslog* Audit Data

Pseudonymizers can be integrated with the *syslog* audit service at three different levels (see 'W' above **syslogd**, 'P' within **syslogd** and 'P' below **syslogd** in Fig. 18.3). The three corresponding system architectures are depicted in Fig. 19.5.

While the domain controlled by the privacy protection official ('PPO domain') in Fig. 19.5 corresponds to the left hand part of Fig. 19.4, the domain controlled by the site security officer ('SSO domain') in Fig. 19.5 corresponds to the right hand part of Fig. 19.4. More specifically, the audit data is collected by the audit component in the PPO domain and after pseudonymization it is transferred to a **syslogd** on a remote machine in the SSO domain, where it is written to a file ('pseudonymized audit data'). That is, the audit components, the **redirector**, the **wrapper**, the **rlogger**, the local **syslogd**, the **pseudonymizer** and the **shared** are controlled by the PPO. Conversely, the remote **syslogd** receiving the pseudonymized audit records as well as the **reidentifier** and the **combined** are controlled by the SSO.

It is noteworthy that, using the architectures in Fig. 19.5, audit data is written to files only after it has been pseudonymized. As a consequence of using the extension from Sect. 16.3 and of embedding the pseudonymity-layer data in the application-layer the pseudonymized audit data comprises the application-layer as well as the pseudonymity-layer, including the protected pseudonym mapping (see Sect. 19.2). The pseudonymous audit data can be analyzed and, if necessary, reidentified (see the **reidentifier** in Fig. 19.5). Note, that the service and the analysis component from Fig. 19.4 are not shown in Fig. 19.5.

---

[5] If the SSO does not control the network between the **combined** and the **reidentifier** a confidential channel should be provided.

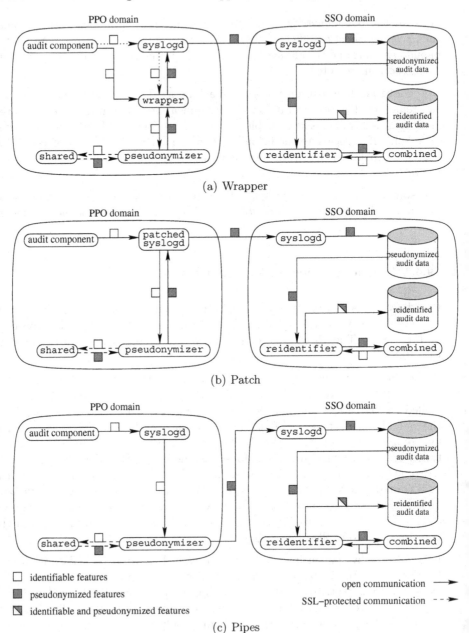

**Fig. 19.5.** Architectures integrating pseudonymization with *syslog*

On the first level, the `syslogd` in the PPO domain can be configured to write the collected audit data into named pipes, which simultaneously are being read by pseudonymizers (see 'P' below `syslogd` in Fig. 18.3). The respective system architecture is shown in Fig. 19.5c. In this architecture the pseudonymized audit data is not handed back to `syslogd`. The pseudonymized audit data can be transferred to the remote `syslogd` in the SSO domain by means of an additional program named `rlogger` (not shown in Fig. 19.5). This architecture has two drawbacks. First, since the audit data is read from a named pipe, the priority field is not available in the audit records (see Sect. 18.2.3). Instead, `rlogger` prepends a configurable fixed priority to each audit record, before transferring it to the remote `syslogd`. In order to retain the original priorities, a respective number of named pipes, **pseudonymizers** and rloggers need to be used. Second, `syslogd` merges subsequent identical audit records into a summarizing audit record, such that the original audit records cannot be pseudonymized individually. It is therefore recommended to embed pseudonymizers in a way that they can access the individual audit records and their priority fields, as in the next two architectures.

On the second level, `syslogd` may directly call the **pseudonymizer** for each audit record it processes (see 'P' within `syslogd` in Fig. 18.3 and the corresponding architecture in Fig. 19.5b). The native `syslogd` of the system can be patched or replaced by a patched version of another system's `syslogd`. The downside of this architecture is the required availability of either the source code of the system, or of a patched `syslogd` with the same functionality and interfaces like the native `syslogd`.

On the third level, a `wrapper` can be used to intercept and pseudonymize audit records before they are read by `syslogd` (see 'W' above `syslogd` in Fig. 18.3 and the respective architecture in Fig. 19.5a). Locally generated audit records can be read from `/dev/log` by the `wrapper`. Audit data generated by remote `syslogd`s and coming in on UDP port 514 can be intercepted and redirected locally to a UDP port read by the `wrapper`.[6] Audit data which the `wrapper` cannot intercept, is received via `syslogd` from a named pipe (see the dotted arrows in Fig. 19.5a).[7] The `wrapper` calls the **pseudonymizer** to pseudonymize each audit record and directs the pseudonymous audit records to `syslogd`.

### 19.4.2 Pseudonymizing Non-*Syslog* ASCII format Audit Data

Some audit components write their audit data directly to files (see 'Application 2' writing to 'App.-Audit' and 'Packet-Audit' writing to 'Net-Audit' in Fig. 18.3).

---

[6] This can be implemented by means of UDP port forwarding, redirecting packets that were originally sent to port 514 to the port where the `wrapper` listens.

[7] For example OpenBSD kernel audit data is written to `/dev/klog` and cannot be intercepted, because the native OpenBSD `syslogd` is hard-coded to read kernel audit data from `/dev/klog` and cannot be reconfigured to use another source.

A straightforward solution to pseudonymize this audit data is to configure the system, such that the audit component writes the audit data to a named pipe, which the **pseudonymizer** reads simultaneously (see 'P' next to 'App.-Audit' and 'Net.-Audit' in Fig. 18.3). Also archived audit data can be piped into the **pseudonymizer** in order to be pseudonymized. In both cases, the pseudonymized audit data is written to a new file by the **pseudonymizer**.

In some cases it might be useful to redirect the audit data of an audit component to an audit service, instead of writing it directly to a file. An example use is consolidating certain audit data in one place. This can be achieved by configuring the system, such that the audit component writes the audit data to a named pipe. A **redirector** can pick up the audit data from the named pipe[8] and store it, e.g. using **syslogd** by means of the *syslog* API (see 'R' near to 'App.-Audit' and 'Net-Audit' in Fig. 18.3).

When embedding pseudonymizers, it is important to comply with the trust model shown in Fig. 19.4. In the following is described how this can be achieved for the aforementioned cases.

If a given audit component directly feeds the **pseudonymizer** via a named pipe, the **pseudonymizer** can write the pseudonymized audit data into a named pipe being read by the **rlogger**. The **rlogger** transfers the pseudonymized audit data to a remote **syslogd**. This set-up is nearly identical to the architecture in Fig. 19.5c, but the audit component directly sends the audit data to the **pseudonymizer** without using the **syslogd**. When the **redirector** is used to consolidate audit data via *syslog*, an arbitrary architecture from Sect. 19.4.1 can be used.

---

[8] In case an application executes accesses on its audit data files beyond appending audit records, the redirector could only be used by indirection via files. Those files shouldn't be pruned while the application might revisit old content.

# 20

## Implementation: *Pseudo/CoRe*

The most commonly occurring and used audit data in Unix systems is ASCII format audit data, e.g. *syslog*-style audit data and audit data generated by web servers (see Sect. 17.2). Our pseudonymization approach can be instantiated for ASCII format audit data as shown in Chap. 19. By specifically supporting *syslog*-style audit data, audit data generated by many sorts of systems can be pseudonymized in addition to the audit data generated by Unix systems (see Sect. 17.2).

The architectures proposed in Sect. 19.4 are composed of several software components. These components have been implemented and are available as a toolset for audit data pseudonymization, named *Pseudo/CoRe*. Using the toolset, we can convince ourselves that the approach presented in Part II is workable in practice.

The compatibility of the software and the third-party software used is summarized in Sect. 20.1. Sect. 20.2 describes how the software components can be embedded in production Unix systems. How the pseudonymization can be configured to meet individual needs is explained in Sect. 20.3. The functionality and interplay of the main components is outlined in Sect. 20.4.

## 20.1 Software

The software toolset *Pseudo/CoRe* (*Pseudo*nymization with *C*onditional *Re*identification) comprises several software components: The **pseudonymizer** together with the **shared** perform the pseudonymization of audit data. The **reidentifier** together with the **combined** can be used to reidentify pseudonymous audit data. Finally, the **wrapper**, the **redirector** and the **rlogger** are used to weave the **pseudonymizer** into the audit data stream.

The **shared** and the **combined** provide the cryptographic primitives for the **pseudonymizer** and the **reidentifier**, respectively. For symmetric encryption and decryption the Blowfish algorithm is used and for cryptographic message digesting the SHA1 scheme is used, both from the OpenSSL crypto library [166].[1] Shamir's threshold scheme for secret sharing (see Sect. 15.2) and the Lagrange interpolation (see Sect. 15.3) are implemented using the GNU Multiple Precision arithmetic library (GMP) [108]. The extension in Sect. 16.5 is implemented using Shoup's Number Theory Library (NTL) [201]. The channel between the **pseudonymizer** and the **shared** is protected using the OpenSSL SSL/TLS library [167] when **shared** runs remotely (see Sect. 19.4).

*Pseudo/CoRe* implements the extensions from Sect. 16.3, Sect. 16.4, Sect. 16.5 and Sect. 16.6[2]. The **pseudonymizer** can be used on the fly and for batch processing, whereas the **reidentifier** can only be used for batch processing (see Sect. 15.3.1).

The source code of *Pseudo/CoRe* is written in portable C. The toolset has been used successfully on Solaris, OpenBSD and Linux operating systems. Hardware platforms tested were customary Intel Pentium personal computers and Laptops, Sun Ultra-SPARC workstations, as well as a Compaq iPAQ 3800 personal digital assistant (PDA) handheld computer running Linux. Note, that the resource requirements of *Pseudo/CoRe* in CPU time and memory were sufficiently low, such that it is usable on an off-the-shelf PDA.

The software toolset *Pseudo/CoRe* is available under the terms of the GNU General Public License (version 2) as published by the Free Software Foundation. *Pseudo/CoRe* can be downloaded from the Internet:
http://ls6-www.cs.uni-dortmund.de/pseudocore/
or
http://pseudocore.sourceforge.net/

## 20.2 Deployment

The deployment of *Pseudo/CoRe* is briefly described here for the three architectures described in Sect. 19.4.1 and depicted in Fig. 19.5. These architectures require the separation of the domains that are controlled by either the PPO or the SSO. This separation of control domains originates from the trust model from Sect. 19.3 and shown in Fig. 19.4. For the validity of the approach it is important to enforce the separation of control domains. In practice this is done by

---

[1] Blowfish and SHA1 were chosen historically and may not be appropriate choices in the future. Note, that the implementation can be easily adapted to use algorithms such as the Advanced Encryption Standard (AES) instead of Blowfish and other hash functions instead of SHA1, as soon as they are implemented in the OpenSSL crypto library.

[2] The **pseudonymizer** provides the escrow data in the pseudonymity-layer as described in Sect. 19.2. Tools that make use of the escrow data, in order to disclose pseudonyms subject to organizational purpose binding, have not yet been implemented.

using distinct machines in domains controlled by different parties and by making proper use of the access control and authentication facilities of these machines.

The machines in the SSO domain should be configured such that the SSOs have full control over the machines. The machines in the PPO domain must be configured such that exclusively the PPO can control the audit components, the *Pseudo/CoRe* components and the audit data being generated. The PPO must configure the audit components and the *Pseudo/CoRe* components, such that the agreed balance of user requirements for pseudonymity and the SSO requirements for disclosure are met. That is, the PPO controls, which kinds of audit data will be generated by the audit components, which types of features will be pseudonymized and under which disclosure conditions the pseudonyms can be disclosed. The PPO additionally uses the access control facilities of the machine to ensure that no audit data is visible to other parties on the machine or is transferred to remote machines, before it has been processed by the pseudonymizer. In fact, when properly implementing the architectures from Sect. 19.4.1, audit data is not written to any disk file, before it is pseudonymized and transferred to the SSO domain.

Before setting up any components of *Pseudo/CoRe*, the PPO chooses a suitable pseudonymization architecture for each of the machines in his control domain (see Sect. 19.4.1). Depending on the chosen architecture, the pseudonymizer is embedded in the audit data stream either by wrapping the input channels of syslogd using the wrapper (see Fig. 19.5a), by replacing the native syslogd with a patched version (see Fig. 19.5b) or by configuring the syslogd to write into named pipes being read by the pseudonymizer and by forwarding the pseudonymized audit data to the SSO domain by means of the rlogger (see Fig. 19.5c).

The PPO ensures that the wrapper, the pseudonymizer, the shared and the rlogger start up at system boot time such that they can communicate as required and can process the *syslog*-style audit data in background.

There are two alternatives to pseudonymize ASCII format audit data, which would not be processed by syslogd (see Sect. 19.4.2). First, using the redirector any ASCII format audit data can be redirected, if it is normally written to a disk file. The redirector is able to read from a named pipe or to monitor a log file for recently appended audit records and deposits them using the *syslog* API with a fixed priority field specified by the PPO. The result is that these audit records can be pseudonymized with an arbitrary architecture as described above. Second, the PPO can configure audit components to write ASCII format audit data into named pipes being simultaneously read by pseudonymizers. After pseudonymizing the audit data, the pseudonymized audit data can be forwarded to a remote syslogd using the rlogger.

When implementing these architectures, the syslogd and/or the rlogger(s) in the PPO domain are configured by the PPO to send the pseudonymized audit data to one or more remote syslogd(s) in the SSO domain. The remote syslogd(s) in the SSO domain receive(s) the pseudonymized audit data and process(es) it as configured by the SSO(s). If the SSO(s) wish(es) to be able to disclose pseudonyms in the pseudonymized audit data some time later, the syslogd(s) need(s) to be configured to write the pseudonymized audit data to disk files (see 'pseudonymized audit data' in Fig. 19.5).

Under the control of the SSO(s), the reidentifier can be invoked manually on demand or automatically, if a given event occurs. It is used like a filter to disclose as many pseudonyms from the pseudonymized audit data as possible. For the reidentifier to work, a running combined that is controlled by the SSO(s) needs to be reachable.

## 20.3 Configuration

After the deployment (see Sect. 20.2) the PPO configures *Pseudo/CoRe* with a priori knowledge that is tailored to the given application and which specifies:

1. the syntactical recognition of the feature types in the original application-layer data that shall be pseudonymized,

2. the application-specific requirements w.r.t. the format and content-linkability of the pseudonyms to be embedded in the application-layer data,

3. the requirements for pseudonymity-layer data enabling the pseudonym disclosure subject to technical and organizational purpose binding, and

4. the application-specific requirements w.r.t. the format of the audit records for the pseudonymity-layer data.

While 2) and 4) adapt *Pseudo/CoRe* to the requirements of the given application, 1) and 3) shall express a fair consensus between the interest in pseudonymity and the interest in accountability. Chapter 11 roughly sketched a process that is carried out in the real world, and which is suitable to reach such a consensus.

In the following is described, how the a priori knowledge can be expressed by the PPO using the syntax of the configuration file of *Pseudo/CoRe*. The various keywords are merely mentioned in the text.

*Ad 1:*

To be able to pseudonymize identifying features in ASCII format audit records, the pseudonymizer requires a specification of the respective feature types, which are defined by the event types and by the respective feature designators. Such a specification comprises a syntactical description for the recognition of event types and features designators. As explained in Sect. 19.1, event types (EVENT) and features designators (**LEFT**, **RIGHT**) are recognized by means of regular expressions for pattern matching.

Using the decision tree at run-time for a given audit record, the **pseudonymizer** determines the event type, possibly comprising the name of the audit component (see Sect. 19.1). For the current event type the **pseudonymizer** locates the feature designators. The feature is extracted from in between the patterns matched by both regular expressions of the current feature designator. After extracting a feature, the **pseudonymizer** replaces it by a pseudonym. Similarly, the **reidentifier** locates these pseudonyms in pseudonymized audit records (see Sect. 12.3).

*Ad 2:*

To satisfy application-specific requirements, the pseudonyms generated for a given feature type should retain the format and the content-linkability of the corresponding features (see Sect. 13.1). The PPO can define a suitable format for the pseudonyms of a given feature type (**TYPE**):

- IP address (**IP**)
- DNS name (**DNS**)
- positive integer number (**INT**)
- arbitrary string (**STRING**)

For pseudonyms in an address format the number of address levels being pseudonymized can be adjusted by the PPO (**IP BITS**, **DNS LEVELS**). Retaining some address levels of the identifying feature allows for a coarse-grained evaluation of addresses without disclosing the more significant address levels. In order to avoid the linkability of pseudonyms for numbers or strings w.r.t. their length, a fixed length can be specified for these pseudonyms (**LEN**). If the linkability of these pseudonyms w.r.t. their length is not a problem, the original length of the identifying features can be retained (**KEEPSIZE**).

The pseudonyms replacing a given feature in a given disclosure context, but in different places in the application-layer, can be generated such that they are either linkable or unlinkable w.r.t. their content (**LINK**, **UNLINK**). That is, for a given feature in a given disclosure context the **pseudonymizer** uses the same pseudonym to retain content-linkability, which may be required by the given application. If the application does not require content-linkability of the pseudonyms, the **pseudonymizer** uses strings chosen independently and pseudo-randomly within the constraints of the specified format. Note, that the content-linkability of the pseudonyms is specified for the application-layer only. The pseudonyms in the application-layer are linked to the pseudonymity-layer data by means of the linkage. Since *Pseudo/CoRe* implements the mismatch avoidance approach from Sect. 14.3.2, the pseudonymity-layer contains linkability labels (see Sect. 19.2), which link all pseudonymity-layer data of a given feature in a given disclosure context. Hence, considering the linkability labels and the linkage in the pseudonymity-layer, also the pseudonyms in the application layer are (transitively) linkable for a given feature in a given disclosure context, irrespective of the manually provided settings for application-layer pseudonym linkability.

*Ad 3:*

Finally is specified, whether the pseudonyms generated for the current feature type can be disclosed later on (RECOVER, NORECOVER). If pseudonym disclosure is not desired for the pseudonyms of a feature type, no pseudonymity-layer data is generated for these pseudonyms. Hence, there is no controlled way to disclose these pseudonyms. If pseudonym disclosure is desired, the supported kinds of purpose binding are specified independently.

See Sect. 16.6 for examples motivating the use of organizational purpose binding. Enabling or disabling organizational purpose binding controls whether escrow data is generated in the pseudonymity-layer (ESCROW, NOESCROW).

To enable the disclosure of pseudonyms of the current feature type subject to technical purpose binding, the feature type is associated with one or more disclosure contexts (CONTEXT). For each disclosure context the disclosure condition is defined (GROUP, THRESHOLD) (see Sect. 12.2).

Also, for each of the disclosure contexts associated with the current feature type, the contribution of the occurrence of the feature type to the activity level of the disclosure context is specified in detail. The contribution is influenced by the significance of repeated occurrences of the current feature for the disclosure scenario (see Sect. 16.4). If each occurrence of the feature is significant, the activity level of the corresponding disclosure context should be changed each time the feature occurs (GROW). If it is only relevant that the feature occurred at least once, the activity level of the corresponding disclosure context should be changed only the first time the feature occurs (ONCE). The contribution of different feature types can be differentiated by changing the activity level of the associated disclosure contexts using different weights (see Sect. 12.2). The occurrence of observations of activity, i.e. feature types, that corroborate the suspicion that a certain disclosure scenario is taking place, should increase the activity level of the corresponding disclosure context (ADDWEIGHT). Conversely, the occurrence of observations of activity that clear the suspicion that a certain disclosure scenario is taking place, should decrease the activity level of the corresponding disclosure context (DELWEIGHT) (see Sect. 16.5). For modeling certain disclosure scenarios it is useful to lower the activity level of the respective disclosure context not only if certain observations occur, but also also after a specified time interval after the occurrence of a given event that increased the activity level (TIMEOUT) (see Sect. 16.5).

*Ad 4:*

To retain the application-specific requirements with respect to the format of the audit records, the pseudonymity-layer data is embedded in the application-layer, such that the pseudonymity-layer audit records mimic the format of the application-layer audit records. The embedded pseudonymity-layer data is ignored by the given application, but used during reidentification. Each relevant kind of application-layer audit record is defined separately (STYLEDEF). The format of the audit record header to be generated by the **pseudonymizer** for the pseudonymity-layer audit records must be specified (FORMAT). Conversely, for the **reidentifier** to be able to identify and locate the pseudonymity-layer audit records, a regular expression is specified, which matches the generated header format (SEARCH). Each event type definition is complemented with a reference to an audit record header format to be used for the pseudonymity-layer data generated for events of the given type (STYLE).

If the **pseudonymizer** is deployed as shown in Fig. 19.5a or Fig. 19.5b, the pseudonymity-layer audit records are handed back to the (patched) syslogd together with the pseudonymized application-layer audit records. While the priority field of the application-layer audit records is retained by the **pseudonymizer**, the newly generated pseudonymity-layer audit records need to be supplied with an own priority by the **pseudonymizer**. Accordingly, the facility and the severity must be specified for the pseudonymity-layer audit records along with additional optional *syslog* options (LOGFACILITY, LOGLEVEL, LOGOPTION). The header format and the priority should be specified such that the pseudonymity-layer records are ignored by the given application.

## 20.4 Functionality

The processes of pseudonymization and of reidentification are described here in some detail, assuming that the **pseudonymizer** and the **reidentifier** are properly weaved into the audit data stream. For details on how the audit data is intercepted and fed into the **pseudonymizer** and into the **reidentifier**, and on how it is forwarded after processing, refer to Sect. 19.4 and Sect. 20.2.

After the deployment of *Pseudo/CoRe*, the **pseudonymizer** is weaved into the audit data stream, such that it is sequentially fed with audit records. It examines each incoming audit record according to the configured a priori knowledge about (see Sect. 20.3):

• feature types that need to be pseudonymized (see Sect. 12.2),

- application-specific requirements w.r.t. the format and the content-linkability of the features as well as the pseudonyms (see Sect. 13.1),

- the possibility for pseudonym disclosure, subject to:

  technical purpose binding
  with set-based models of disclosure scenarios, which comprise:

    - disclosure contexts and disclosure conditions (see Sect. 12.2),

    - the significance of repeated occurrences of observations (see Sect. 16.4), and

    - the weights of feature types (see Sect. 12.2), using negative weights to model the effect of activities canceling out each other (see Sect. 16.5).

  organizational purpose binding
  cryptographically enforcing the organizational cooperation of the PPO and the SSOs (see Sect. 16.6),

- the application-specific requirements w.r.t. the format of the audit records for the pseudonymity-layer data generated to enable pseudonym disclosure (see Sect. 19.2).

According to the a priori knowledge the **pseudonymizer** replaces identifying features in the application-layer audit data with suitable pseudonyms. It leverages the a priori knowledge basically provided in the decision tree (see Sect. 12.3). The syntactical recognition of feature types and the extraction of features are based on regular expressions for pattern matching that are stored in the decision tree (see Sect. 19.1). Having extracted a feature that needs to be replaced by a pseudonym, the **pseudonymizer** decides on the format and content-linkability of the feature and replaces it with a suitable pseudonym. Subsequently, the possibilities to disclose this pseudonym are determined. The **pseudonymizer** supports pseudonym disclosure subject to technical and organizational purpose binding. For purpose binding, the **pseudonymizer** determines the disclosure context of the current feature type (see Sect. 12.3) and asks the **shared** to provide appropriate data in the pseudonymity-layer for the current feature in the disclosure context.

The **shared** manages the pseudonym mapping and it generates the pseudonymity-layer data required for pseudonym disclosure. From the pseudonym mapping the **shared** cryptographically generates shares and some additional data for technical purpose binding (see Sect. 15.2) and/or escrow data for organizational purpose binding (see Sect. 16.6.2). Then, the **shared** delivers the pseudonymity-layer data to the **pseudonymizer**.

Subsequently, the **pseudonymizer** provides the linkage of the pseudonymity-layer data to the current pseudonym in the application-layer (see Sect. 19.2) and complements the pseudonymity-layer data such that it conforms to the audit record format, i.e. the pseudonymity-layer data is firstly linked to the pseudonymized audit record and is then embedded in the application-layer. Then, the **pseudonymizer** writes the pseudonymized application-layer audit record together with the corresponding pseudonymity-layer audit records out to the configured output channel. According to the deployment of *Pseudo/CoRe* in the PPO domain, these audit records are fed back into the audit data stream, just behind the point of interception.

At some later point, the pseudonymized audit data is stored in a disk file. According to the deployment of *Pseudo/CoRe* in the SSO domain, the complete file or selected pseudonymized audit record can be fed on demand into the **reidentifier**. The **reidentifier** discloses all pseudonyms that are embedded in the input application-layer audit records and that satisfy their respective disclosure condition (see Sect. 15.3.1).

In the first pass, the **reidentifier** reconstructs the pseudonym mapping using all available pseudonymity-layer audit records. More specifically, the **reidentifier** uses the linkability labels to associate the labels as well as the corresponding shares and linkages with pseudonym mapping entries in the current disclosure context (see Sect. 15.3).

In the second pass, the **reidentifier** uses the regular expressions for pattern matching in the decision tree to locate the pseudonyms embedded in each application-layer audit record (see Sect. 19.1). For each pseudonym, the corresponding pseudonym mapping entry is located in the current disclosure context by searching for the message digest of the current audit record together with the pseudonym in the associated linkages (see Sect. 19.2.1). The **reidentifier** examines the current pseudonym mapping entry and checks the disclosure condition for technical purpose binding.[3] If the disclosure condition is met, and if the identifying feature corresponding to the pseudonym has not yet been disclosed, the **reidentifier** asks the **combined** to disclose the identifying feature in the pseudonym mapping entry.

Given a sufficient amount of compatible shares, the **combined** cryptographically discloses the identifying feature from the cryptogram in the corresponding linkability label (see Sect. 15.3) and delivers the identifying feature to the **reidentifier**.

The **reidentifier** stores the identifying feature in the current pseudonym mapping entry. Then, the identifying feature in the current pseudonym mapping entry is used to replace the pseudonym in the application-layer audit record. Finally, the **reidentifier** writes the (possibly reidentified) application-layer audit records out to the configured output channel.

---

[3] The pseudonym disclosure subject to organizational purpose binding has not yet been implemented. It can be implemented, such that it makes use of the escrow data provided in the pseudonymity-layer audit records (see Sect. 16.6.2 and Sect. 19.2).

# Part IV

# Evaluation

In this Part, we informally evaluate the theoretical design of the set-based approach and of the implementation *Pseudo/CoRe* from Part II and Part III, respectively. For the evaluation of the designs we use the basic building blocks for anonymity defined in the APES project. In Chap. 21 we introduce the APES project and motivate the use of basic building blocks for anonymity. In Chap. 22 we decompose our designs into basic building blocks for anonymity and consider the remaining building blocks for further improvement. The informal evaluation indicates that the designs are sound with respect to the given requirements and that they contain no deficiencies.

We also evaluate the performance of the implemented toolset *Pseudo/CoRe*. The performance evaluation in Chap. 23 demonstrates that the implementation is able to handle real-world audit data volumes in practice.

# APES:
# Anonymity and Privacy in Electronic Services

Section 21.1 provides a brief overview of the related work in the APES project. In Sect. 21.2 we motivate the APES approach of basic building blocks for anonymity in general and in particular as a vehicle for the evaluation of the designs from Part II and Part III. The APES approach is described in the necessary detail in Sect. 21.3 for connection-level and application-level building blocks (see Sect. 21.3.1 and Sect. 21.3.2, respectively) and for a strategy to compose anonymity systems out of building blocks (see Sect. 21.3.3). The basic building blocks are used in Chap. 22 to informally evaluate our designs from Part II and Part III.

## 21.1 APES Project Overview

In the APES project (Anonymity and Privacy in Electronic Services) the state of the art of anonymity systems has been surveyed and studied [199]. Anonymity systems for various applications are described: anonymous connections, email, web publishing, web browsing, electronic payment, electronic elections and electronic auctions. For each application a short overview of its functionality is given and the entities participating in the application are identified and mapped to roles as defined by the application independent terminology based on [174]. The anonymity requirements and properties of each of the applications are described.

For several of the applications exists more than one anonymity system based on different anonymity techniques. The anonymity techniques themselves are often composed of several subcomponents that are each responsible for a particular aspect of anonymity. In the APES project the anonymity systems have been decomposed into basic building blocks that can be reused for different systems, with a focus on *unconditional anonymity*, i.e. the anonymity cannot be revoked, e.g. by pseudonym disclosure. The basic building blocks are identified, their properties and requirements are described and their security and correctness are evaluated in an informal way [62]. These aspects will be described in more detail in Sect. 21.2.

An ad-hoc methodology for building block composition is proposed and used to provide anonymity for two selected applications, which have also been implemented [70]. A more detailed overview of the project is given by Diaz, Claessens and Preneel [71] and in the project deliverables [199, 62, 70].

## 21.2 APES Basic Building Blocks for Anonymity

Anonymity systems are often designed with a specific application in mind. Various parts of these systems, however, often have similar functionality that can be reused for other applications. As a part of the APES project De Win et al. [62] define reusable anonymity building blocks with minimal, yet useful functionality. This approach has several advantages:

1. Similar building blocks can be compared more easily than the more complex systems they originate from.
2. Given a list of building blocks with their properties, deficiencies in existing systems can be identified systematically.
3. Anonymity systems can be designed by systematically composing appropriate building blocks.

We present the APES anonymity building blocks approach in Sect. 21.3 in more detail. In Chap. 22 we use the APES approach to evaluate the designs from Part II and Part III by decomposing them into building blocks. In doing so we pursue the following objectives in accordance to the above advantages:

1. The building blocks used in our design are compared to different building blocks with similar functionality with the two possible results: The system design is already composed of building blocks that are optimal for the given application, or we obtain specific indications how we can improve the design by replacing some building block with some other building block, yielding stronger properties.
2. Given the attacker and trust model from Chap. 11 we may identify deficiencies in our design in an informal way by considering all building blocks in the list given by De Win et al. [62].
3. As a side-product, we obtain indications about the completeness of the list and classifications of APES building blocks with respect to our design.

## 21.3 APES Design Approach

APES basic building blocks are classified as being specific to the application-level or the connection-level: *Connection-level* basic building blocks are used to provide anonymous communication connections (see Sect. 21.3.1), whereas *application-level* basic building blocks are responsible for anonymity aspects of a given application (see Sect. 21.3.2). To obtain a completely anonymous system, application-level anonymity often needs to be complemented by connection-level anonymity.[1] Note, that several connection-level building blocks can also be employed at the application-level. The APES approach comprises a strategy for composing anonymity systems from basic building blocks (see Sect. 21.3.3).

### 21.3.1 Connection-level basic building blocks

Basic building blocks at the connection-level hide or remove identifying information that is available at that level. Identifying information can occur *explicitly* like IP-Addresses in IP packet headers. Connections can also be traced along the communication path using *implicit* features of the appearance or of the flow of the communication. Network packets can be linked by *appearance* using e.g. content, format or size. Also, the *flow* of network packets can be traced using knowledge about the packet processing regarding e.g. order and timing. Accordingly, APES basic building blocks at the connection-level either change the appearance or the flow (see the second column of Table 21.1).

For each basic building block the properties are given informally, such that building blocks with similar functionality can be compared (cf. the properties of application-level building blocks in Sect. 21.3.2):

- existential and/or operative requirements,

- attacks that are resisted and those that are still possible,

- performance, i.e. communication overhead, computational and space complexity, as well as message delay,

- parameters influencing the security,

- algorithmic sophistication required for processing, and

- behavior at operational limits.

---

[1] In Chap. 8 we introduced an architectural model for pseudonymous authorizations and surveillance in order to compare anonymity technologies w.r.t. an attacker restricted to audit data generated by a service. Nevertheless, the model can be used to describe architectures for pseudonymous authorizations under the assumption of other attacker models. As an example, consider an attacker that is able to listen to the communication between a client and a server. Then, for each layer in the OSI model which provides identifying information (e.g. MAC addresses, IP addresses) an architecture is required to anonymize authorizations. According to the OSI layers the respective architectures can be classified as being specific to the application-level or the connection-level.

**Table 21.1.** Basic anonymity building blocks as given and classified by De Win et al. [62]

| building block | connection-level appearance | flow | application-level |
|---|---|---|---|
| encryption | ✓ | | ✓ |
| padding | ✓ | | |
| substitution | ✓ | | |
| compression | ✓ | | |
| reordering | | ✓ | |
| latency | | ✓ | |
| dummy activity | | ✓ | |
| no replay | | ✓ | |
| filtering | | ✓ | |
| caching | | ✓ | |
| (untraceable) broadcast | | ✓ | ✓ |
| multiplexing | | ✓ | |
| bulletin board | | ✓ | ✓ |
| (fair) blind signature | | | ✓ |
| group signature | | | ✓ |
| threshold cryptosystem | | | ✓ |
| multi-party computation | | | ✓ |
| homomorphic encryption | | | ✓ |
| deniable encryption | | | ✓ |
| secret sharing schemes | | | ✓ |
| zero-knowledge | | | ✓ |
| pseudonyms | | | ✓ |
| trusted third party | | | ✓ |

A complete comparison regarding performance is provided by De Win et al. [62].

To provide anonymous connections, explicitly as well as implicitly identifying information must be hidden. Therefore basic building blocks need to be composed to change the appearance as well as the flow of the messages.

The following compositions of basic building blocks to so-called *local setups* are proposed:

serial: Building blocks are executed after each other, where the input of a block is the output of the preceding block.

parallel: Functionally unrelated building blocks can be executed simultaneously, given that at most one building block changes the appearance of the message.

nested: The execution of the outer building block is suspended for the execution of the inner block. This may be required for advanced message transformations or block dependencies [62].

A local setup is controlled by one entity of the anonymity system. The single point of trust failure problem may be solved by serially composing an anonymity system, also called a *global setup*, of several identical local setups, which are each controlled by different entities.

## 21.3.2 Application-level basic building blocks

Basic building blocks at the application-level conceal or remove identifying information that is available at this level. They implement techniques that have been developed to provide anonymity in a particular type of application (see the third column in Table 21.1).

For each basic building block the properties are given informally (see also the properties of connection-level building blocks in Sect. 21.3.1):

- existential and/or operative requirements and cryptographic assumptions,
- attacks that are resisted and those that are still possible,
- performance, i.e. computational complexity,
- security,
- verifiability of results,
- trust requirements,
- (un-)conditional anonymity, i.e. ability for controlled anonymity revocation.

De Win et al. found that several building blocks at this level are no basic building blocks, they rather solve an application-specific anonymity problem by combining several more elementary building blocks, which do not offer anonymity by themselves [62]. These more elementary building blocks have not been described. Also, the functionality of the building blocks at this level is rather different, i.e. we cannot choose between several alternative building blocks to achieve a specific functionality. As a result, some building blocks already are complete local setups and can hardly be locally combined with other building blocks. Nevertheless, anonymity systems can be composed as global setups of such building blocks, if they are used between different entities or during different phases of the application.

## 21.3.3 Composition strategy

In APES the following factors need to be considered for the composition of an anonymity system out of building blocks:

application: anonymity requirements, attacker model, overall application structure building blocks: properties, dependencies, trade-off of security vs. performance

APES does not provide an algorithm composing anonymity systems from building blocks, given the above information as input. Instead, in APES a pragmatic ad-hoc approach is used to compose two example applications, starting out with a simple attacker model and sketching the composition of the anonymity system. In each further iteration a slightly stronger attacker is assumed and the composed anonymity system is complemented with building blocks that remove the enhanced possibilities for attack [70].

# Evaluating the Design
# Using Basic Building Blocks for Anonymity

In this Chapter we use the basic building blocks for anonymity from the APES project, as introduced in Chap. 21, to evaluate the designs from Part II and Part III.

In Sect. 22.1 we decompose our designs and map the functionality that is relevant for certain anonymity aspects to appropriate building blocks from the APES approach. Having decomposed our designs into building blocks for anonymity, in Sect. 22.2 we firstly describe the use of each building block in our design, and we secondly consider the unused building blocks for further improvement of our design. The findings of this analysis are summarized in Sect. 22.3.

The rather theoretical results from this Chapter are corroborated in Chap. 23 by an empirical performance evaluation of the implementation from Part III.

## 22.1 Mapping the Design to Building Blocks

In our approach the SSO can observe the behavior of service users merely by inspecting pseudonymized audit data. That is, we assume that the SSO cannot monitor the user's service accesses over the network, i.e., the SSO can only see where the pseudonymized audit data originates. Since this information needs not to be protected, there are no connection-level anonymity requirements in our approach.[1]

Summarizing the relevant requirements of audit data pseudonymization from Sect. 10.1, pseudonymization should not use building blocks with a high computational complexity and that introduce a significant delay. As described in

---

[1] If we relax the latter assumption such that the SSO is able to monitor the user's service accesses over the network, the SSO can correlate monitored accesses with pseudonymous audit records. This situation raises the need for connection-level anonymity, which can be implemented independently from our approach, using existing standard solutions for anonymous connections (see Seys et al. [199]).

Chap. 11 and Sect. 19.3, we have respected this requirement when designing our approach in Part II and when choosing cryptographic primitives for the implementation in Part III.

Figure 22.1 shows how our set-based approach can be decomposed into APES building blocks: Fig. 22.1a shows the conceptual system as described in Part II and Fig. 22.1b shows the current implementation developed in Part III. In the following, the description of the pseudonymization process focuses on the basic building blocks used.

The audit components are configured to generate only audit data required for the given application (see Sect. 20.2 and the building block 'filtering' as well as the input 'application-layer audit data' in Fig. 22.1a/b). The audit data is delivered to the *pseudonymizer*, which inspects each incoming audit record for identifying features that, according to the a priori knowledge, shall be pseudonymized (see Sect. 12.3 and Sect. 19.1).

Each of these features is replaced by an optionally padded pseudo-random string that conforms to the application-specific requirements with regard to format and content-linkability of the feature (see (2) in Sect. 20.3 and the building blocks 'padding 1' and 'substitution' as well as the input 'pseudo-random string' in Fig. 22.1a/b). These strings are the pseudonyms which are embedded into the original application-layer audit data.

In the a priori knowledge the ability to disclose these pseudonyms is defined for each feature type (see (3) in Sect. 20.3). If the ability for disclosure is supported for a given pseudonym, then the corresponding identifying feature is encrypted, i.e. disclosure is the process of recovering the correct decryption key (see Sect. 15.2 and the building block 'encryption 1' as well as the input 'pseudo-random key' in Fig. 22.1a/b).

The pairing of the cryptograms of a given identifying feature together with the message digest of the corresponding decryption key (verifier), forms a pseudonym mapping entry (see Sect. 13.2 and the building blocks 'encryption 1' and 'one-way function 1' as well as the output 'pseudonym mapping' in Fig. 22.1a). Only a positively verified decryption key can be used to correctly decrypt cryptograms of the respective identifying feature.

To coarsen the number of actors in the given application, dummy entries are added to the pseudonym mapping. To avoid the linkability of the pseudonym mapping entries over time, they are padded and reordered (see Sect. 16.2 and the building blocks 'dummy generation', 'padding 2' and 'reordering' in Fig. 22.1a). To avoid the inference of the number of real pseudonym mapping entries based on the number of pseudonym mapping updates, dummy updates are used, even if no new entries have been inserted into the pseudonym mapping (see Sect. 16.2 and the building block 'dummy updates' in Fig. 22.1a).

Note, that the description of the pseudonym mapping and the respective dummy activity applies to the conceptual system depicted in Fig. 22.1a, only. The imple-

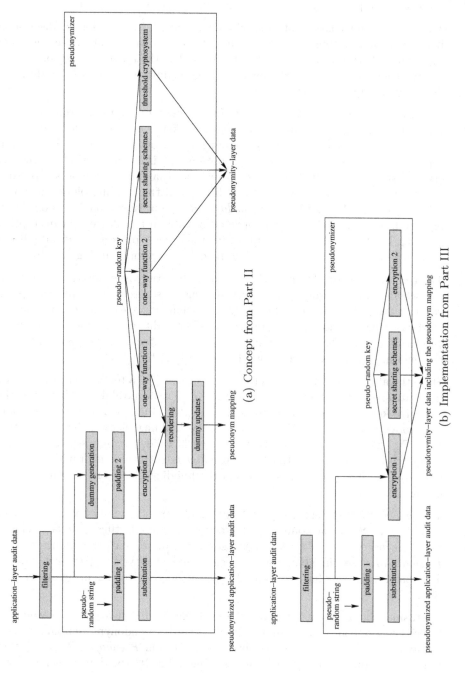

(a) Concept from Part II

(b) Implementation from Part III

**Fig. 22.1.** Decomposing our approach into building blocks according to De Win et al. [62]

mented system *Pseudo/CoRe* illustrated in Fig. 22.1b differs substantially with respect to the pseudonym mapping and dummy activity (see below).

The pseudonymity-layer data contains information for pseudonym disclosure. It is embedded in application-layer audit records with a configurable identifier signifying a fictitious audit component, such that the application ignores these records (see Sect. 19.2 and the output 'pseudonymity-layer data (including the pseudonym mapping)' in Fig. 22.1a/b).

To be able to use the pseudonym mapping for pseudonym disclosure, a valid decryption key is required. The recovery of such a key from the pseudonymity-layer data is subject to technical and/or organizational purpose binding. In the conceptual system the organizational purpose binding is enforced using a threshold cryptosystem to encrypt the decryption key, such that only eligible sets of persons can recover it cooperatively (see Sect. 16.6.1 and the building block 'threshold cryptosystem' in Fig. 22.1a). In *Pseudo/CoRe* the organizational purpose binding is implemented using a symmetric cryptosystem to enforce that decryption keys can be recovered in cooperation with the privacy protection official (PPO), only (see Sect. 16.6.2 and the building block 'encryption 2' in Fig. 22.1b).

The technical purpose binding of pseudonym disclosure is enforced using threshold schemes for cryptographic secret sharing to securely split the decryption key in shares that are provided in the pseudonymity-layer in addition to the corresponding pseudonymized application-layer audit records, containing observations of activity that are relevant for pseudonym disclosure (see Sect. 13.3 and the building block 'secret sharing schemes' in Fig. 22.1a/b).

Since the above described shares per se are unlinkable, a tentative key recovered from an arbitrary set of these shares could just be invalid. In that case the tentative key does not match any verifier in the pseudonym mapping mapping (see above and see Sect. 13.2 as well as the building block 'one-way function 1' in Fig. 22.1a). Even if the tentative key is valid, it could still represent a mismatch (see Sect. 14.1). To detect mismatches, each share is provided with an individual verifier (see Sect. 14.3.1 and the building block 'one-way function 2' in Fig. 22.1a).

The conceptual system supports unlinkable pseudonymity-layer data (see Sect. 14.3.1). Since the computational complexity of selecting unlinkable shares for the recovery of a valid key discourages practical use, for performance reasons *Pseudo/CoRe* uses linkability labels in the pseudonymity-layer (see Sect. 14.3.2). This basic difference has substantial consequences for the resulting system design.

First, since the pseudonymity-layer data is linkable in *Pseudo/CoRe*, it would be futile trying to conceal the number of actors in the pseudonym mapping. Hence, the extension from Sect. 16.2 is not implemented in *Pseudo/CoRe* (note, that the corresponding building blocks are missing in Fig. 22.1b: 'dummy generation', 'padding 2', 'reordering' and 'dummy updates').

Second, in *Pseudo/CoRe* the linkability labels are used to avoid mismatches during the recovery of decryption keys. Therefore it is unnecessary to provide a verifier with each share to detect mismatches (note, that the building block 'one-way function 2' is missing in Fig. 22.1b).[2]

Third, in *Pseudo/CoRe* the pseudonym mapping is embedded in the pseudonymity-layer, using the cryptograms of identifying features as linkability labels (see Sect. 16.3 and the output 'pseudonymity-layer data including the pseudonym mapping' in Fig. 22.1b). As a result, the cryptograms are directly associated with the shares of the corresponding decryption key. Hence, accessing the cryptograms requires no search in the pseudonym mapping, such that there is no need for the verifiers in the pseudonym mapping (note, that the corresponding 'one-way function 1' building block is missing in Fig. 22.1b).

Our approach provides conditional anonymity, i.e. pseudonym disclosure is enabled subject to certain conditions. Thus, the pseudonymization component is complemented by a reidentification component. While a given application needs only to take the application-layer data, i.e. the pseudonymized audit data, into account, the reidentification additionally requires the pseudonymity-layer data and in the conceptual system also the pseudonym mapping. Our proposed solution and implementation for the reidentification can be decomposed into building blocks with analogous results, but does not give any additional insights. We therefore do not provide the details here.

## 22.2 Considering Building Blocks for Improved Design

The fourth column of Table 22.1 summarizes the building blocks used in our designs, as identified in Sect. 22.1. Interestingly, though our approach does not aim at providing connection-level anonymity, it uses many connection-level building blocks that have not been considered for application-level anonymity in APES (see the '!' in the third column of Table 22.1). Note, that the building blocks 'pseudonyms' and 'trusted third party' are not shown in Fig. 22.1. However, the pseudo-random strings in Fig. 22.1 are the generated pseudonyms and the PPO controls the pseudonymizer in his function as a trusted third party.

APES primarily aimed at providing building blocks for unconditional anonymity. Exceptions are the following building blocks that can be used to provide conditional anonymity: 'fair blind signature', 'group signature', 'threshold cryptosystem', 'secret sharing schemes', 'pseudonyms', and 'trusted third party' (see the emphasized building blocks in the first column of Table 22.1). Our approach provides conditional anonymity and any given building block on this list is either used by our approach or it could be investigated for further improvement. Note, that our approach does not use any building blocks for conditional anonymity that were not defined for APES.

---

[2] *Pseudo/CoRe* nevertheless implements the share verifiers to detect malfunction.

But, our approach uses a more elementary building block named *one-way function* enabling to compare features for equality, while the features are concealed. A collision-resistant one-way function, e.g. as in our implementation a cryptographic hash function, is used to conceal the features, such that for two given features $f_i$ and $f_j$ if $h(f_i) = h(f_j)$ then with high probability $f_i = f_j$ [154]. This functionality has formerly not been identified as a separate APES building block, yet it is useful in various scenarios for conditional and unconditional anonymity at the application-level (see the building block 'one-way function' in Table 22.1).

**Table 22.1.** Basic anonymity building blocks used in our approach, '*building block*' = conditional anonymity, '!' = classification missing, '—' = building block missing, '?' = candidate building block for improvement

| building block | connection-level appearance | flow | application-level | our approach |
|---|---|---|---|---|
| encryption | √ | | √ | √ |
| padding | √ | | ! | √ |
| substitution | √ | | ! | √ |
| compression | √ | | | |
| reordering | | √ | ! | √ |
| latency | | √ | | ? |
| dummy activity | | √ | ! | √ |
| no replay | | √ | | |
| filtering | | √ | ! | √ |
| caching | | √ | | |
| (untraceable) broadcast | | √ | √ | |
| multiplexing | | √ | | |
| bulletin board | | √ | √ | |
| one-way function | — | — | — | √ |
| *(fair) blind signature* | | | √ | ? |
| *group signature* | | | √ | ? |
| *threshold cryptosystem* | | | √ | √ |
| multi-party computation | | | √ | ? |
| homomorphic encryption | | | √ | ? |
| deniable encryption | | | √ | |
| *secret sharing schemes* | | | √ | √ |
| zero-knowledge | | | √ | ? |
| *pseudonyms* | | | √ | ? / √ |
| *trusted third party* | | | √ | √ |

For each building block used in our approach we give the anonymity objective to which it contributes, the aspect (appearance or flow) considered by the building block (for connection-level building blocks only), as well as the effect of the building block that contributes to the anonymity objective. The basic building blocks are considered in the order of appearance in Table 22.1; for details on each building block refer to De Win et al. [62]:

encryption: conceal identifying features (appearance) (see 'encryption 1' in Fig. 22.1a/b): avoid linkability by means of the content of identifying features;

> organizational purpose binding of pseudonym disclosure (appearance) (see 'encryption 2' in Fig. 22.1b): allow use of the recovered decryption key only in cooperation with the PPO

padding: conceal identifying features (appearance) (see 'padding 1' in Fig. 22.1a/b): avoid linkability by means of the size of identifying features;

> coarsen the number of actors (appearance) (see 'padding 2' in Fig. 22.1a): avoid linkability by means of the size of the mapping entries

substitution: conceal identifying features (appearance) (see 'substitution' in Fig. 22.1a/b): replace identifying features by persistent, i.e. linkable, or one-time, i.e. unlinkable, pseudonyms[3]

reordering: coarsen the number of actors (flow) (see 'reordering' in Fig. 22.1a): avoid linkability by means of the order of the pseudonym mapping entries

dummy activity: coarsen the number of actors (flow) (see 'dummy generation' and 'dummy updates' in Fig. 22.1a): avoid linkability by means of the number of pseudonym mapping entries and pseudonym mapping updates

filtering: remove identifying features (flow) (see 'filtering' Fig. 22.1a/b): discard audit records that are not needed by the given application

one-way function: conceal identifying features (appearance) (see 'one-way function 1' and 'one-way function 2' in Fig. 22.1a): enable the comparison of decryption keys with tentative recovered keys while concealing the content of the decryption keys

threshold cryptosystem: organizational purpose binding of pseudonym disclosure (see 'threshold cryptosystem' in Fig. 22.1a): allow eligible sets of individuals to use the recovered decryption key only cooperatively

secret sharing schemes: technical purpose binding of pseudonym disclosure (see 'secret sharing schemes' in Fig. 22.1a/b): allow anyone to recover only decryption keys involved in the transgression of a scheme's threshold

pseudonyms: conceal identifying features (see 'pseudo-random string' in Fig. 22.1a/b): the pseudonyms replacing the identifying features have the following properties: unauthenticated, sharing is possible, linkable within the context of an attack, forgeable

---

[3] Note, that blanking of identifying features is in general not useful, because it may interfere with legacy applications that rely on the existence of specific features.

trusted third party: conditional anonymity (see the double fat grey frames in Fig. 8.6a/b, not shown in Fig. 22.1a/b): the PPO can be trusted to properly configure the system components in the PPO domain (see Fig. 19.5)

In the following, each APES building block that is not used in our approach is considered for possible improvements of the current solution. A number of building blocks is identified that could not be applied to the current system:[4]

compression: items to be concealed either are too small or have too high an entropy to be compressed

no replay: since the channels between the audit components and the pseudony-mizer are trusted, there is no need for the detection of audit record replay

caching: since the channels between the audit components and the pseudonymi-zer are uni-directional there is no responder that would need to be concealed

broadcast: there is no need to conceal the identity of the recipient of the audit records (given application)

untraceable broadcast: there is no need to conceal the identity of the senders of the audit records (audit-components)

multiplexing: there is no need to conceal the path of the audit records

bulletin board: see the broadcast building block

blind signature: does not allow for conditional anonymity with technical purpose binding

deniable encryption: for the current approach there seems to be no application

In the following, a number of building blocks is identified that could be explored for possible improvement of the current system (see the '?' in the fourth column of Table 22.1). Note, that except for the 'latency' building block these build-ing blocks are computationally expensive and may not meet the performance requirements of our application. Also, the 'latency' building block may conflict with stringent time requirements.

latency: could be used instead of dummy pseudonym mapping updates, if many new pseudonym mapping entries are created in a short time interval

fair blind signature: could be examined to provide technical purpose binding while reducing the power of the trusted third party

group signature: could be investigated to be used for conditional anonymity with organizational purpose binding; though, its computational complexity is much higher than that of threshold cryptosystems [62]

---

[4] For the reasoning to be understood, it is advisable to consult De Win et al. [62]. A more detailed description would duplicate text from De Win et al. [62] without producing any new results.

multi-party computation, homomorphic encryption: for certain applications not only the application-layer audit data may be processed, but also certain properties of the pseudonymity-layer data may be exploited by the application, independently of pseudonym disclosure; cryptographic primitives for multi-party computation and for homomorphic encryption could be examined for the generation of pseudonymity-layer data that has the desired properties

zero-knowledge: could be explored to provide a proof of validity for pseudonyms to reduce the power of the trusted third party

pseudonyms: other pseudonym systems could be examined to reduce the power of the trusted third party while gaining the following additional pseudonym properties: authenticated, sharing is impossible, unforgeable

## 22.3 Design Evaluation Results

We evaluated our designs using the APES approach of basic anonymity building blocks with two objectives: informally identifying room for improvement and informally identifying deficiencies in our design.

Regarding the first objective, we identified the 'latency' connection-level building block that could be used as an alternative to 'dummy activity' under specific circumstances. We identified six further application-level building blocks that could be explored to further reduce the power of the trusted third party in our approach in order to obtain more useful properties of the pseudonyms or to replace the 'threshold cryptosystem' or to support the exploitation of pseudonymity-layer data by the application. Though, probably none of the candidate building blocks will satisfy the requirements of our application regarding computational complexity or delay. As a result, given the APES building blocks list, the current design may only be improved if some of the current requirements are relaxed, trading stronger mechanisms off against time or computational complexity. With respect to the second objective, and given the APES building blocks list and composition methodology, we could not identify any deficiencies in our design.

Our experience in the exercise of decomposing a given system into basic building blocks confirms the APES approach: It is possible to analyze a given system design using APES basic building blocks. The analysis may stimulate improvement of the design and may point out weaknesses in the design.

The statements regarding both of the above objectives are the stronger, the more complete the list of considered building blocks is. Though De Win et al. intended to present an exhaustive list of building blocks for unconditional anonymity [62], it seems rather unlikely that future developments will not contribute new building blocks for unconditional anonymity. In fact, in our approach and for various purposes we found the necessity to compare features that need to be concealed. This can be achieved using one-way functions. Surely, one-way functions are already part of several APES building blocks. Anyway, they are also very useful as such for various applications without the functionality of the building blocks in which they are contained. We thus postulate the application-level building block named 'one-way function'. This is an indication that the current list of APES building blocks is probably not exhaustive.

As a result, we cannot even informally exclude that there exist better designs or that the design may have deficiencies. The above statements about the soundness of our design merely express strong indications based on the current state of the art.

In addition to the incompleteness of the list of building blocks, we found that the classification of building blocks is incomplete w.r.t. the level of their use, i.e. five connection-level building blocks were used at the application-level, regardless of the APES classification. Further investigation might reveal that (nearly) all connection-level building blocks can also be used at the application-level.

As a last note, we found that the given building blocks for conditional anonymity were sufficient to build our solution, though APES so far focused on building blocks for unconditional anonymity, i.e., the given building blocks may be perfectly sufficient to build various systems for conditional anonymity.

# Evaluating the Performance
# of the Implementation

The rather theoretical results from Chap. 22 are complemented in this Chapter by an empirical performance evaluation of the implementation from Part III.

To meet the specific requirements of audit data pseudonymization (see Sect. 10.1) the *pseudonymizer* must process the audit data on the fly. It is imperative to pseudonymize audit records sufficiently fast to avoid a bottleneck, which might impair the overall system performance. In contrast, the *reidentifier* is seldomly used and does not need to satisfy real-time requirements. Hence, the `reidentifier` of *Pseudo/CoRe* only supports batch processing, whereas the `pseudonymizer` supports processing on the fly, as well as batch processing. We therefore only evaluate the performance of the `pseudonymizer`.

The performance measurements were conducted on a customary single processor Intel Pentium III 650MHz machine with 256MB RAM and a 100Mbps Fast-Ethernet NIC, running OpenBSD 2.7.

To be able to better understand the performance behavior of the `pseudonymizer` together with the `shared`, the performance of the cryptographic primitives used by the `shared` are measured in Sect. 23.1. The measurements show that the thresholds used for the secret sharing schemes are a critical parameter. In Sect. 23.2 the performance of the `pseudonymizer` together with the `shared` is measured using synthetic audit data. These measurements confirm the influence of the threshold parameter on the overall performance. It is also shown that the pattern matching using regular expressions is the other main factor influencing the performance of the `pseudonymizer`.

In Sect. 23.3 the audit data volume is measured in a real-world environment. Comparing the measured audit data volumes with the performance measurements of the `pseudonymizer` shows that the system is able to handle real-world data volumes, even in pathological situations and even under unfavorable parameter settings.

## 23.1 Performance of the Cryptographic Primitives

We measured the performance of the cryptographic primitives used in **shared** and **combined**. For secret sharing and Lagrange interpolation the primitives operate over a finite field $\mathbb{Z}_P$, where $P$ is a prime number of 128 bits. For encryption we also use symmetric 128 bit keys. Thresholds used in the measurements default to 5. The results are averaged over 5 measurements for **encrypt()** and **share()**, over $1 + 10/t^2$ measurements for **initialize()** and over $1 + 10000/t^2$ measurements for **combine()**, where $t$ is the current threshold.[1]

The first time the **shared** processes a given feature in a given disclosure context, it uses the **initialize()** routine, which generates a pseudo-random polynomial, encrypts the feature and inserts the results in an AVL tree (see also Sect. 15.1).

We found that the Blowfish encryption in the OpenSSL crypto library operates at about 15370 encryptions per second for features of eight characters. It slows down slightly to about 15150 encryptions per second for features of 32 characters (see Fig. 23.1a). We expect most features to be pretty short strings. Note, that the encryption performance is independent of the number of bits used for the symmetric keys.

Depending on the threshold of the disclosure context associated with a feature, **initialize()** generates a number of pseudo-random coefficients for the corresponding polynomial (see Sect. 15.1). The higher the threshold, the more pseudo-random numbers are generated (see **initialize()** in Fig. 23.1b).

**share()** basically evaluates the polynomial that **initialize()** provides (see Sect. 15.2). Hence, the higher the threshold, the more expensive are the exponentiations **share()** calculates using the GMP library call **mpz_powm()** (cf. **share()** with/without **mpz_powm()** in Fig. 23.1b).

It is no surprise that GMP library calls take longer if we calculate with larger numbers (see Fig. 23.1c).

When evaluating the performance of the **share()** routine, we found some unexpected run time behavior of the GMP library. The GMP library calls take longer, the more often integer objects are reused, though **mpz_clear()** has been called to free the space the integer objects occupy (see Fig. 23.1d).

Again, an expected result is that the Lagrange interpolation (see Sect. 15.3), which the **combined** uses, is an expensive calculation for large thresholds (see **combine()** in Fig. 23.1b).

---

[1] The adaptive number of measurements is necessitated by the coarse granularity of the timers available via the operating system.

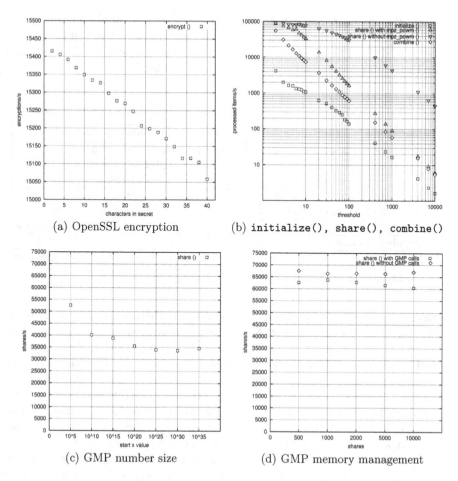

**Fig. 23.1.** Performance measurements of the cryptographic components

## 23.2 Performance of the Pseudonymizer

We measured the performance of the **pseudonymizer** for varying parameters using synthetic audit data and configurations. All the numbers reported are averaged over 5 measurements. The repetition of features was considered significant and no share invalidation was performed. When varying one parameter, all other parameters used fixed default values as shown in Table 23.1. The synthetic audit data we used for the measurements contained audit records, which all had the same number of identifying features, each with a size of three characters. All features in the audit data were required to be pseudonymized. Each feature in a given audit record was associated with a distinct disclosure context, assuming that the features in an audit record are different kinds of identifying data. The $i^{th}$ features in all audit records were associated with the same disclosure context.

Thus, the disclosure contexts could comprise events generated from several audit components. All disclosure contexts had the same threshold and all features were associated with the same weight. Audit records from different audit components and with different event types were generated cyclically.

**Table 23.1.** Default values for the parameters and how they were varied

| parameter | default value | varied by means of |
|---|---|---|
| communication with **shared** | Unix domain socket | command line |
| number of bits | 128 | source code |
| number of audit records | 1000 | audit data |
| disclosure context threshold | 5 | configuration |
| number of disclosure contexts | 1 | audit data & configuration |
| number of audit components | 1 | audit data & configuration |
| number of event types | 1 | audit data & configuration |
| number of features per record | 1 | audit data & configuration |
| weight | 1 | configuration |

**shared** handles features differently depending on whether they have already been seen in the audit data or not. If a feature is processed for the first time for a given disclosure context, `initialize()` generates a pseudo-random polynomial and stores it together with the encrypted feature (see Sect. 23.1 and Sect. 15.1). In any case, a polynomial is used to generate one or more fresh shares using `share()` (see Sect. 23.1 and Sect. 15.2). Owing to these different cases of feature handling we used two kinds of audit data to measure the best and the worst case performance. In the best case all features associated with a given disclosure context were *identical*. **shared** then calls `initialize()` only once per disclosure context. In the worst case we had *varying* distinct features associated with each disclosure context. As a result, **shared** calls `initialize()` for every feature in the audit data.

When increasing the number of processed audit records, we observe for varying features a mild performance penalty due to the growth of the AVL trees storing encrypted features and their corresponding polynomials (see Fig. 23.2a).

A growing number of audit components, event types and disclosure contexts has a linear influence on the performance, since these objects are managed using list structures (see Fig. 23.2b).

The more features per audit record are pseudonymized, the more often the **pseudonymizer** asks **shared** for pseudonymity-layer data. In addition to the communication overhead, also more feature designator patterns need to be matched by the **pseudonymizer** (see Fig. 23.2c). The pattern matching is the main cause for the performance loss, when many features need to be pseudonymized per audit record (see Fig. 23.2d).

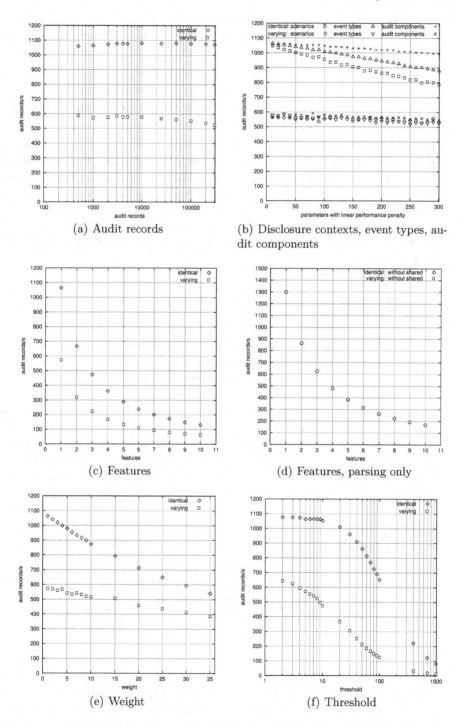

(a) Audit records

(b) Disclosure contexts, event types, audit components

(c) Features

(d) Features, parsing only

(e) Weight

(f) Threshold

**Fig. 23.2.** Performance measurements of the **pseudonymizer**

In contrast, the performance loss caused by generating more shares for larger weights is moderate (see Fig. 23.2e). There is no additional pattern matching or communication overhead involved.

Increasing the threshold does not only slow down the generation of shares using `share()`, but also the initial generation of pseudo-random numbers for each distinct feature in a disclosure context using `initialize()` (cf. `initialize()` and `share()` with `mpz_powm` in Fig. 23.1b and Fig. 23.2f).

Though the Blowfish encryption performance is independent from the number of bits used for the encryption key, we have to consider that the secret sharing slows down for larger numbers (see Fig. 23.1c). For reasonable key lengths we found only a negligible effect on the secret sharing performance (see the row for identical features in Table 23.2). In contrast, the impact on the initialization for secret sharing was significant, since larger pseudo-random numbers need to be generated and converted to mpz numbers for the GMP library calls (see the row for varying features in Table 23.2).

**Table 23.2.** Influence of the key length on encryption and secret sharing

| features | number of audit records/s for | | | |
|---|---|---|---|---|
| | 64 bits | 128 bits | 168 bits | 256 bits |
| identical | 1075 | 1064 | 1064 | 1062 |
| varying | 600 | 573 | 560 | 530 |

The `shared` can operate on the same or on a remote host as the `pseudonymizer` (see Table 23.3). Note, that there is a significant SSL overhead, if there is a lot of traffic between the `pseudonymizer` and a local `shared` connected to the loopback interface (cf. column 3 and column 4 in Table 23.3). We thus recommend to use Unix domain sockets in order to avoid the SSL overhead when communicating with a local `shared`.

**Table 23.3.** Influence of the communication technique used between the `pseudonymizer` and the `shared`

| features | number of audit records/s for | | | |
|---|---|---|---|---|
| | no shared | local Unix domain socket | SSL over loopback | SSL over Ethernet |
| identical | 1300 | 1064 | 444 | 400 |
| varying | 1300 | 573 | 328 | 377 |

In practice, the parameters will only in artificially unrealistic settings assume values as high as shown in Fig. 23.1 and Fig. 23.2. The critical threshold parameter will in practice usually assume values lower than 10 (see Fig. 23.2f). Hence, in practice the remaining critical parameter is the number of features pseudonymized per record, which should usually assume values lower than 5 (see Fig. 23.2c). In Sect. 23.3 we show that even for unrealistic settings and during rare pathological situations the performance of the **pseudonymizer** is sufficient to cope with the audit record volume of a large site.

## 23.3 An Example of Performance Requirements

To be able to judge whether our **pseudonymizer** performs sufficiently fast in a real-world server environment we evaluated *syslog* and *Apache* audit records from a central server at the Center for Communication and Information Processing at the University of Dortmund. The machine hardware consisted of a Sun Ultra Enterprise 4000 with 3GB RAM, six Ultra SPARC 168MHz CPUs, three disk arrays totaling 396GB and a 100Mbps full-duplex Fast-Ethernet up-link. For backup services the machine was also connected to an IBM 3494 storage tape robot. The server ran Solaris 7 and about 1050 users were registered (employees and students of the University of Dortmund). During working hours an average number of 25 users were logged in simultaneously. The main services provided by the machine were:

Web: 37 world accessible *Apache* web servers

FTP: about 112000 transfers per month with a volume of 12GB

Email: about 45000 emails per month (SMTP, IMAP, POP)

DBMS: one Oracle DBMS for several web applications and a Cambridge chemical structure DB

Education: education system ARCVIEW

Software: large software binary archive for several platforms, exported via NFS

Backup: about 4.5 Terabytes of data stored for 450 client machines

We evaluated all *Apache* access audit records collected over a period of 13 days for all 37 web servers (see Fig. 23.3a and Fig. 23.3c). We have also evaluated all *syslog* audit records collected over a period of four weeks (see Fig. 23.3b and Fig. 23.3d). The *syslog* audit records were collected at other days than the *Apache* audit records. The *syslog* audit records are generated by the following audit components: `sendmail`, `imapd`, `ipop3d`, `in.ftpd`, `in.lpd`, `in.telnetd`, `in.rlogind`, `in.rshd`, `in.rexecd` and `in.comsat`.

For both, *syslog* and *Apache* we counted the number of audit records written per hour $(ar/h)$. For each of the 24 hours of a day we determined the minimum, the maximum and the average $ar/h$ over all days for which we had audit data available (see Fig. 23.3a and Fig. 23.3b). For each of the days for which we had audit data available we also determined the minimum, the maximum and the average $ar/h$ over all hours of that day (see Fig. 23.3c and Fig. 23.3d).

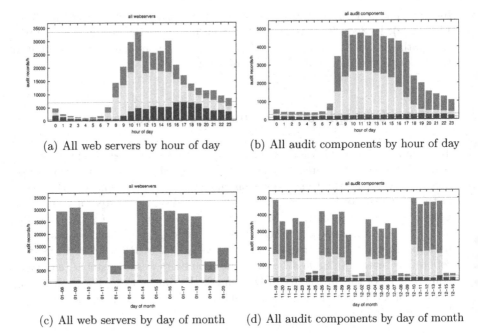

(a) All web servers by hour of day

(b) All audit components by hour of day

(c) All web servers by day of month

(d) All audit components by day of month

**Fig. 23.3.** Server statistics: number of audit records generated per hour

We noticed that in the later hours the maximum *syslog ar/h* deviates significantly from the average *syslog ar/h* (see Fig. 23.3b). This is due to an abnormally high number of `in.ftpd` audit records at the $10^{th}$ of December after 4pm (see Fig. 23.4). The root cause of this event is out of the scope of this text.

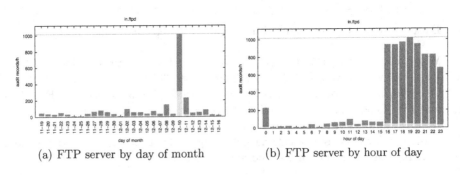

(a) FTP server by day of month

(b) FTP server by hour of day

**Fig. 23.4.** The day when FTP went wild

The crucial point here is that the **pseudonymizer** is able to keep up with the number of audit records generated even in situations where some audit component generates an abnormally high number of audit records and even under artificially unfavorable parameter settings. See Table 23.4 for the maximum numbers of audit records we measured.

**Table 23.4.** Maximum number of audit records generated per second

| audit component | number of audit records per hour | per second |
|---|---|---|
| *Apache* | 33506 | 9.31 |
| *syslog* | 4956 | 1.38 |
| $\sum$ | 38462 | 10.68 |

# Part V

# Refinement of Misuse Scenario Models

Two limitations of the set-based approach for pseudonymization developed in Part II and implemented in Part III are identified in Chap. 24. It is proposed to develop a superior approach for pseudonymization that is tightly bound to models of misuse scenarios used by intrusion detections systems (IDSs). An appropriate Petri-net-based framework for modeling misuse scenarios is presented in Chap. 25. Based on a carefully restricted version of the framework a superior approach to audit data pseudonymization is introduced in Chap. 26. The issues of pseudonym linkability and pseudonym disclosure are investigated in detail in Chap. 27 and Chap. 28, respectively. By exploiting knowledge in given models of misuse scenarios, pseudonym linkability and pseudonym disclosure are tightly tailored to the models and to the analysis algorithm of the IDS. Due to the general nature of the modeling framework the results are widely applicable to existing and future misuse scenarios and IDSs.

# Motivating Model Refinements

The approach for audit data pseudonymization introduced in Part II is useful for and compatible with many applications. However, due to two limitations the approach may not satisfy the requirements of certain other applications. The limitations are studied in Sect. 24.1 and Sect. 24.2, raising the need for a superior approach for pseudonymization to avoid the described limitations. It is proposed to bind pseudonymization more tightly to the models of misuse scenarios used by intrusion detection systems (IDS). An appropriate framework for modeling misuse scenarios is presented in Chap. 25. Based on a carefully restricted version of the framework a superior approach to audit data pseudonymization is introduced in Chap. 26.

## 24.1 Coarse-grained Disclosure Context

In Part II disclosure contexts are modeled as sets of weighted observations of activity (see Sect. 12.1). Such a definition does not meet the requirements of certain applications w.r.t. expressiveness of disclosure contexts. We thus proposed two extensions to the disclosure context model concerning the semantics of repeated observations (see Sect. 16.4) and complementary observations (see Sect. 16.5). The extended framework, however, may still not meet specific requirements of IDSs for misuse detection [131].

Such IDSs usually allow to specify detectable misuse scenarios as signatures using a specific language. The expressiveness of signature specification languages varies for different IDSs [152, 149]. More expressive signature specification languages allow for more concise models of misuse scenarios. Generally it is a good idea to model misuse scenarios as concisely as possible in order to avoid false alarms, i.e. false positives. Sometimes, a less concise model may be useful to match also variants of a misuse scenario. Note, however, that a less concise model should be motivated by the deliberate choice to match variants of a misuse scenario, and not by limitations of the specification language.

Advanced IDSs support very expressive signature specification languages, such as the Event Description Language (EDL) [194, 152]. Using such expressive languages it is possible to model misuse scenarios, which cannot be expressed equivalently using the extended set-based model from Part II. If we consider a misuse scenario modeled in a more expressive language, also other activity could meet the disclosure condition of the corresponding coarse-grained set-based model. With respect to the more concise model this constitutes a false positive (error class 2). Such a false positive results in pseudonym disclosure in situations that are similar to a given misuse scenario, but do not precisely match the definition of the misuse scenario. This may be acceptable for some applications, while it is not for others. In the latter case, the modeling framework for disclosure contexts needs to be extended to match the expressiveness of the signature specification language.

Note, that extended expressiveness comes at the price that the pseudonymizer must basically perform the same rather expensive audit data analysis as the IDS. The advantages and disadvantages of the set-based approach w.r.t. performance and false positives should be considered as a whole, before employing a more fine-grained approach.

## 24.2 Excess Pseudonym Linkability

In Part II the issue of pseudonym linkability is completely ignored. The implementation described in Part III allows the PPO to manually configure the linkability of pseudonyms for a given feature in a given disclosure context (see Sect. 20.3). Thus, the pseudonyms for a given feature in a disclosure context are either always or never linkable, as defined by the PPO. Unfortunately, pseudonym linkability can be (mis)configured independently from the actual requirements of the given application that uses the pseudonymized audit data.

However, requirements for linkability actually depend on the given application. Depending on the algorithm and the a priori knowledge of the application, certain pseudonyms need to linkable, while others do not. Considering these linkability requirements as our point of reference, the individual configuration of the pseudonymizer from Part III may not implement these requirements correctly. First, the PPO may have analyzed the algorithm and its a priori knowledge incorrectly. The PPO may configure the pseudonymizer to provide more linkability than actually necessary, such that the application still works correctly, but the excess linkability is undesirable from the point of view of privacy (see Sect. 7.3). Conversely, the PPO may configure the pseudonymizer to provide less linkability than required by the application. This is likely to result in false negatives in the application. That is, the application silently fails to recognize certain activity in the audit data. For IDSs this means that misuse scenarios are silently missed. This is considered extremely undesirable. Second, the static definition of pseudonyms to be always linkable or never linkable does not appreciate the fact that linkability requirements may dynamically depend on the current state of the application. Thus, while a feature/pseudonym may need to be linkable in a certain situation, it may not need to be linkable shortly thereafter. Hence, there is unused potential for dynamically reducing linkability in favor of privacy.

Considering misuse detection IDSs as a specific application, the signatures used for audit data analysis are known a priori, allowing to automatically infer a priori, where pseudonyms may need to be linkable. During run-time the state of the analysis algorithm can be considered to decide, whether the extracted knowledge about linkability requirements needs to be applied to a pseudonym, or if linkability is not an issue in the situation. Consequently, the linkability of pseudonyms can be tailored to a given set of IDS signatures, and it can even be further restricted considering the state of analysis during run-time, such that linkability is reduced to the amount necessary for audit data analysis. That is, linkability is technically bound to the purpose of audit data analysis, considering the algorithm of the application and its a priori knowledge.

Again, leveraging the a priori knowledge and state of the audit data analysis algorithm comes at the price that the pseudonymizer must basically perform the same analysis as the IDS. Thus, the cautionary note from Sect. 24.1 also applies here.

# Models of Misuse Scenarios

For the refinement of misuse scenario models we consider IDSs as the given application for analyzing (pseudonymized) audit data in order to detect misuse scenarios. *Misuse scenarios* are defined as *activity* considered to violate the service-specific security policy of the organization. The audit component of the given service observes the service activity. *Observations of activity* are manifested in the form of *events*, which are embedded in *audit records* (see Sect. 12.1.1). An ordered set of events is also denoted as the *manifestation* of certain activity, if these events are symptomatic to be observed when this activity takes place. Note, that a given activity can have several distinct manifestations. An ordered set of audit records is denoted as *audit data*.

*Misuse detection* is the process of detecting manifestations of misuse scenarios in audit data based on models of manifestations of misuse scenarios.[1] This is done under the assumptions that a manifestation is actually observed, when a misuse scenario takes place (*completeness*), and that a misuse scenario actually takes place, when its manifestation is observed (*correctness*). In the following, we assume that we have audit components that can observe misuse scenarios completely and correctly.[2]

This assumption simplifies the terms used for describing the concepts of misuse detection, because we do not need to strictly distinguish activity and observations or manifestations of activity. We can then talk about events, as if they are actual activity, instead of merely observations of activity. Also, it is then possible to talk about models of misuse scenarios that describe (misuse) activity, if we actually mean models that describe misuse scenario manifestations. Note, that a

---

[1] Note, that the model of a given misuse scenario does not describe the activity that is necessary to perform the misuse scenario (system input; exploit language according to Vigna et al. [218]), rather it describes the activity that is observable during the misuse scenario (output of the audit component of the system; detection language according to Vigna et al. [218]).

[2] If we do not have such audit components, we cannot expect to achieve complete and correct misuse detection.

given model of manifestations of a given misuse scenario should also *completely* describe the manifestations of misuse activity, such that the model does not miss a manifestation of the misuse scenario (false negative). Likewise, the model should describe the manifestations of the misuse scenario *correctly*, such that the model does not apply to manifestations of other activity (false positive).

Under the assumption of correct and complete audit components and correct and complete models (of manifestations) of misuse scenarios, one can conjecture from a model matching a manifestation in audit data that the corresponding misuse scenario activity took place. Also, if no model matches any manifestation in the audit data, one can conjecture that no misuse scenario activity is taking place.

A prerequisite to specifying complete and correct models of misuse scenarios is a sufficiently expressive modeling framework. The framework should also support human intuition during model specification in order to reduce the potential for human error.

To be processed by an IDS, the models of misuse scenarios usually are translated to or directly expressed in a purely textual language [148, 149], such as EDL [152, 149, 194]. The textual representation of models of misuse scenarios are commonly denoted as *misuse detection signatures, intrusion detection signatures* or just *signatures* in the literature about misuse detection or intrusion detection systems.[3]

In terms of pseudonymization, misuse scenarios are *disclosure scenarios*, i.e. it is desired to be able to disclose pseudonyms in a controlled way, if and only if a misuse scenario has been detected by the IDS. In our approach a disclosure scenario is modeled by an appropriate *disclosure context* over observations, i.e. events (cf. Sect. 12.1).

Clearly, disclosure contexts for IDS-specific audit data pseudonymization model the same concept as the models of misuse scenarios that are encoded in the signatures of the given IDS. Thus, to be able to tailor disclosure contexts and linkability of pseudonyms in audit data to the misuse scenarios of the IDS, we need to understand how misuse scenarios are modeled for the use by an IDS.

A brief overview about related work on misuse scenario modeling frameworks and signature languages is given in Sect. 25.1, motivating the need for a new modeling framework. The semantic requirements for misuse scenario modeling are summarized in Sect. 25.2. A suitable framework for modeling misuse scenarios is presented in Sect. 25.3. For the design of a pseudonymization approach based on models of misuse scenarios, the framework is artificially restricted in

---

[3] Vigna et al. distinguish several (attack) languages that are involved in the process of reproducing (exploit languages), documenting (event languages), detecting (detection/correlation languages), and responding to attacks (response/report languages) [218]. According to this classification, signature (specification) languages are detection languages.

Sect. 25.4, yielding a useful subset that still meets all important semantic requirements. Based on the limited framework a pseudonymization approach is developed in Chap. 26.

## 25.1 Related Work on Signature Languages

Several pertinent languages for specifying intrusion detection signatures have been proposed, such as RUSSEL for ASAX [157], P-BEST for EMERALD [138], LAMBDA [56], ADeLe [155], SHEDEL [150] and EDL [152].

Studying and engineering signatures requires a notation that allows for an intuitive understanding of the considered misuse scenarios. We argue that in contrast to a textual representation for complex signatures a graphical representation provides a more intuitive view on what misuse scenario(s) a signature describes. For some languages, a graphical representation has already been proposed: MuSigs for ARMD [137], STATL for the STAT Framework [74], SUTHEK [177] and IDIOT [132]. While MuSigs, STATL and SUTHEK use their own notions of Finite State Automata (FSA) to model misuse scenarios, IDIOT uses Colored Petri-nets (CPN). For a more comprehensive and detailed comparison of various signature languages refer to Meier [149].

Graphical misuse scenario modeling frameworks not only support an intuitive understanding of misuse scenarios, they are also largely independent from the actual syntax of the languages used to encode the signatures for an IDS. It has been shown by Pouzol et al. [177] that a signature specified using a sufficiently expressive graphical modeling framework can be translated to several existing signature specification languages.

For a deeper understanding of the required semantics and expressiveness of a general modeling framework for misuse scenarios, we analyzed existing signature languages and signatures. In the next step we identified a modeling approach that can be easily adapted to satisfy all of the requirements and which has already been used in the intrusion detection domain. We adopted the proposal of Kumar [132] to model signatures using CPNs and adapted and extended it w.r.t. modeling elements and semantics to accommodate the required expressiveness and semantics.[4]

---

[4] Note, that is was necessary to define our own notion of a modeling framework based on CPNs, because Kumar's model suffered from severe shortcomings [132]: Modeling the garbage collection of partial matches of misuse scenarios using invariants was error-prone and the implementation necessarily inefficient. The value of token variables could never change, such that different modes of repetition and step instance selection could not be expressed. Consumption of system state was modeled contraintuitively as a property of the places, limiting intuitive modeling and also required expressiveness (see Sect. 25.2 for definitions of the terms 'step instance selection' and 'consumptivity').

When compared to existing work on FSAs for misuse detection, CPNs provide three major advantages:

1. CPNs allow to specify partial orders in a compact way.

2. During signature engineering the CPN tokens can be used to illustrate partial detections of misuse scenarios along with their current variable bindings.

3. CPNs provide the required expressiveness to engineer signatures for the use with any IDS by translating the CPN models into the target signature language.[5]

Later, Meier approached the topic of semantics and expressiveness from a different angle, leveraging Zimmer's work on a meta-model for semantics of complex events in active DBMSs [148, 225, 224] (see Sect. 25.2). Our previous analysis of existing IDS signature languages and signatures together with Meier's analysis of Zimmer's meta-model provides strong indications that we came up with a complete set of requirements. Using a constructive approach, Meier has shown that CPNs satisfy all of these requirements [149]. Consequently, the CPNs we use provide the deterministic semantics required for misuse detection and can express all misuse scenarios that can be expressed in any currently existing signature language. Hence, the results about pseudonymization we develop in this Part apply to a large body of existing work on misuse detection.

## 25.2 Semantic Requirements

In the following, the semantic requirements for modeling misuse scenarios are shortly summarized (cf. Table 25.1). The presented requirements were obtained by analyzing domain knowledge (existing misuse detection signature languages and signature bases of IDSs) as well as by analyzing the semantics of events in a similar problem domain (triggers in active DBMSs) [148, 225, 224]. For details and examples refer to Meier [148, 149].

In the following, we denote a model of a given misuse scenario as a complex event.[6] A *complex event* consists of inter-related events, where each of the events is denoted as a *step* of the complex event. For a complex event to occur, matching events must have occurred and must be *bound* to each step of the complex event. Events that can be bound to a step are basic events and complex events. *Basic events* represent the basic observable unit, as provided by the audit component.[7]

---

[5] Note, however, that engineering signatures using CPNs is still limited by the expressiveness of the target signature language.

[6] Note, that here both, complex events and disclosure contexts, are models of misuse scenarios.

[7] Note, that the concept of complex events introduces a notion of abstraction, because also occurred complex events can be bound to steps. When a complex event occurs,

**Table 25.1.** Semantic requirements for models of misuse scenarios. The most commonly used mode of an aspect is *emphasized*

| dimension | aspect | instance |
|---|---|---|
| event pattern | type and order | *sequence* |
| | | disjunction |
| | | conjunction |
| | | simultaneous |
| | | negation |
| | repetition | exact |
| | | *at least* |
| | | at most |
| | continuity | *continuous* |
| | | non-continuous |
| | concurrency | *overlap* |
| | | non-overlap |
| | context conditions | intra-event conditions |
| | | inter-event conditions |
| step instance selection | | *first* |
| | | last |
| | | all |
| step instance consumption | | *consuming* |
| | | non-consuming |

When an event is bound to a step, the step is also said to be *instantiated*, and the instantiated steps are considered to be the (partial) *instance* of the complex event. If all steps of the complex event are instantiated, the (complete instance of the) complex event is said to *occur*.

Summarizing, a complex event models a misuse scenario by specifying how to identify the basic events that can be observed while the misuse scenario takes place. Since several misuse scenarios of the same type may be executed simultaneously, the modeling framework allows to model manifestation-specific state (e.g. bind features to variables, e.g. a file handle), to be able to distinguish distinct (partial) instances of a given (type of) complex event.

The semantics of complex events (for triggers in the domain of active DBMS) can be partitioned in three dimensions [224]:

Event pattern: Several criteria influence the decision whether a complex event is recognized in given audit data, e.g. the type and order of events. An event pattern defines the complex event to look for. Refer to Sect. 25.2.1 for details.

---

it must be represented by a "synthetic" manifestation, describing a more abstract occurrence. Such a manifestation is usually denoted as a misuse *alarm*. Sets of alarms can be analyzed just like basic events, such that our concepts of pseudonymization apply accordingly. However, such a scenario may involve distributed structures, which are not considered in this book. Therefore, in the following we assume that only basic events are bound to the steps of a complex event.

Step instance selection: For a given step of a given complex event, which is recognized to be contained in the audit data, there may exist several basic events in the audit data that can be bound to the step. Instance selection describes, which of the matching events should be bound to the steps of a complex event. This selection influences further inspection or correlation of the basic events bound to the steps of the recognized complex event. Refer to Sect. 25.2.2 for details.

Step instance consumption: A partial instance of a complex event represents also the partial system state that is relevant in the context of the complex event. Some basic events describe activity that changes (consumes) features of such system state. Step instance consumption specifies, whether the current partial instance of the relevant complex event can bind only the current instance of the basic event, or if it may also bind further instances of the basic event. Refer to Sect. 25.2.3 for details.

### 25.2.1 Event Pattern

An event pattern defines the complex event to look for. The frame of a complex event is formed by the steps (event *types*) and their *order*.

Many signatures describe simply consecutive events (*sequence*). Alternative activity can be modeled disjunctively, allowing to represent variants of misuse scenarios in a compact way (*disjunction*). Concurrent threads of activity can be modeled in a conjunctive way, such that all interleavings of the event sequences of the threads are accepted by the model (*conjunction*). Simultaneous events may occur in parallel systems and can be correlated using their time stamps (*simultaneous*). In the context of a complex event, certain basic events prohibit completion of the complex event. Such events can be modeled to be not allowed to occur within parts of the manifestation of a misuse scenario (*negation*).

It is useful to be able to specify the number of times a step must occur for a misuse scenario to complete (*repetition*), e.g. for dictionary attacks or denial of service attacks (*exactly*, *at least* or *at most n* times, or *at least n and at most m* times).

The *continuity* semantics of a misuse scenario model defines, whether between three consecutive steps of the event types $A$, $B$ and $C$ an event $c$ is allowed to occur between events $a$ and $b$, and if event $a$ may occur between $b$ and $c$. The *continuous* semantic allows for such occurrences and is most useful for the purposes of misuse detection.

When composing more complex patterns from a number of less complex patterns, it is necessary to decide about the *concurrency* of the less complex patterns. For concurrent composition the threads may *overlap*, i.e. interleave, and for sequential composition this is not the case (*non-overlap*). Note, that the concepts of conjunctive threads and of steps bound to complex events are similar, but not quite the same (see [148, 149] for details).

A very important aspect of the semantics is the ability to specify constraints on the context in which the steps of a complex event occur. Constraints that can be evaluated by merely inspecting the features of the current event are denoted as *intra-event conditions* and can be used for example to select events that affect a certain user, host or file. Note, that the event type selection criterion can be considered a special case of intra-event conditions. *Inter-event-conditions* can only be evaluated by inspecting at least two events, which implies to create state. For example, inter-event conditions can be used to correlate events that affect the same user, host or file.

### 25.2.2 Step Instance Selection

While a given event pattern specifies *when* a complex event occurs, the *step instance selection* defines, *which* of the possibly more than one matching events is bound to each step of the complex event. This is an important decision, if we are not only interested in the fact that a complex event occurred, but if we also need to document the events that lead to the complex event for further correlation and response. Meier adopts three of the instance selection modes proposed by Zimmer [148, 224]: selecting the *first* or the *last* event or *all* events that match the given step. These modes can be used for example to detect when a performance parameter exceeds a threshold, capturing the parameter value when the threshold was exceeded the first time, the current (last) value right before the next step occurred, or all values for further statistics.

### 25.2.3 Step Instance Consumption

The current system state that is relevant for a given complex event is reconstructed by binding events to the steps of the complex event, such that the partial instance of the complex event represents the reconstructed relevant system state. After an event has been bound to a given step of a complex event, the resulting partial instance of the complex event represents the occurrence of the event as well as the relevant system state that has been modified by the step.

Some events describe activity that changes features of system state, which are relevant in the context of the considered complex event, for example the destruction of system objects, e.g. process termination and file deletion, or the change of object features, e.g. renaming a file and changing access privileges. Such activity is said to *consume* the relevant system state, which has been created by previous activity, and which is represented by the matching partial instance of the complex event. Other (*non-consuming*) activity does not change relevant features of system state, e.g. reading from a file.

Step instance consumption defines, whether a given partial instance of a complex event can evolve into one or more partial instances by binding a consuming or a non-consuming event to a given step, respectively. Since a consuming event modifies the system state represented by the partial instance, the partial instance is evolved by binding the event to the step, effectively consuming the old partial instance. However, the partial instance is evolved for each occurrence of a given non-consuming event type, creating new partial instances representing each occurrence.

## 25.3 Modeling Framework

While the semantic requirements from Sect. 25.2 specify, *what* semantic aspects are relevant for the detection of manifestations of misuse scenarios, the modeling framework described here focuses on *how* the relevant aspects can be captured and modeled. The exposition restricts to summarizing the concepts needed to understand the pseudonymization approach described in Chap. 26. Please refer to Meier [149] for more details, many examples and a formalization. Meier also shows that the expressiveness of the framework meets all semantic requirements from Sect. 25.2 by providing equivalent signature-nets for each semantic aspect [149] (see Sect. 25.3.6).

Considering the semantic requirements from Sect. 25.2, modeling misuse scenarios is the process of characterizing complex events, i.e. specifically the relationships between observed events. We propose a modeling framework based on Petri-nets [9] with some extensions. Petri-nets allow the modeling of complex causal dependencies, and tokens can be used to simulate or analyze system dynamics [164, 165, 9].

In the following, models of misuse scenarios that are expressed in our modeling framework are denoted as *signature-nets*, accounting for the fact that we do not use standard Petri-nets and that the models also have a textual representation as signatures (see Sect. 25.3.6).

Signature-nets are comparable with non-autonomous Petri-nets [60], because the occurrence of transitions depends primarily on events, which occur externally to the model. In our modeling framework the basic building blocks of signature-nets are places and transitions that are connected by directed edges. The dynamics of signature-nets are simulated using tokens.

The *places* of a given signature-net represent reconstructed states of the observed system that are relevant for the misuse scenario modeled by the signature-net. System state is reconstructed by observing events. *Transitions* describe observable events of the misuse scenario, which are causing change of system state that is relevant in the context of the misuse scenario. The directed *edges* connecting places and transitions specify causal relationships between system states and events. Each token represents the system state so far caused by the activity thread of a single instance of the misuse scenario, i.e. a token represents an instance of a (partial) complex event. In addition to the state represented by the place, where the token currently resides, the token stores information about the current system state, which is specific to the (partial) complex event represented by the token. Specific information about system state is extracted during state changes from the observed events, which are bound to the steps of the complex event when a transition occurs.

If a given sequence of events causes transitions of a given signature-net to occur until a token reaches a defined final place of the signature-net, then this sequence of events represents a manifestation of the misuse scenario that is modeled by the signature-net. When the final place is reached, the complex event modeled by the signature-net occurs and can be further correlated or responded to using the information extracted from the sequence of events and stored in the token.

In the following, the basic building blocks of signature-nets are described in some more detail, i.e. places (Sect. 25.3.2), transitions (Sect. 25.3.3) and rules for transition occurrence (Sect. 25.3.5), edges (Sect. 25.3.1), as well as tokens (Sect. 25.3.4).

### 25.3.1 Edges

Directed edges are used to model which system state is a necessary precondition, such that a given event can occur, and which adjusted system state is the result if the event occurs. Hence, in a signature-net places and transitions are connected by directed edges to specify the order of the basic events to look for (cf. order in Sect. 25.2.1). We denote edges that are directed from places to transitions as *input edges* and edges that are directed from transitions to places as *output edges*.

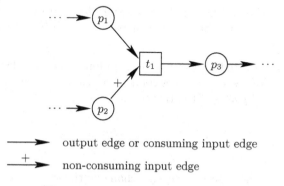

output edge or consuming input edge
non-consuming input edge

**Fig. 25.1.** Symbols for (non)-consuming edges

Additionally, input edges are characterized by the consumptivity (see Sect. 25.2.3) of the transition event type w.r.t. the state represented by the place connected to the transition (see Fig. 25.1). *Consuming edges* correspond to standard edges in Petri-nets, whereas *non-consuming edges* are similar to test edges in Petri-nets [49].

### 25.3.2 Places

The modeling framework distinguishes four types of places: initial, interior, escape and final places (see Fig. 25.2).

initial place          escape place

interior place         final place

**Fig. 25.2.** Symbols for types of places

Each signature-net contains one or more *initial places*. A signature-net describes one complex event and possibly also variants of the complex event. For the complex event and for its variants the signature-net contains one or more *final places*. If a token reaches a final place, then a manifestation of the corresponding (variant of the) complex event has been identified in the audit data, i.e. the respective (instance of the) (variant of the) complex event occurs.

*Escape places* characterize system state that a partial complex event instance has caused by means of the last transition, such that the complex event cannot be completed.[8] Consequently, tokens reaching an escape place are removed from the signature-net. Escape places have the important function of garbage collection by removing obsolete tokens.

Places that are neither initial, final nor escape places are denoted as *interior places*, which are visited by tokens on their path from an initial place to a final or escape place.

Moreover, places connected to a transition via input edges are denoted as *input places* of the transition, whereas places connected to a transition via output edges are denoted as *output places* of the transition.

### 25.3.3 Transitions

Transitions describe the observable events changing the system state along some path in the signature-net until some partial instance of some complex event

---

[8] In principle, for each signature-net at most one escape place is sufficient, but for more convenient modeling the framework allows for an arbitrary number of escape places per signature-net.

is completed or discarded. Transitions are characterized by an event type, by intra-event conditions, by inter-event conditions, by token bindings (cf. type, intra-event conditions, inter-event conditions and state in Sect. 25.2.1) and by actions. Moreover, a given transition is influenced by tokens in its *input places* and it influences tokens in its *output places*, representing the required system state such that the transition can occur and the adjusted system state after the transition has occurred, respectively (see Sect. 25.3.5). Each transition is associated with a transition label, which specifies the characteristics of the transition (see Fig. 25.3).

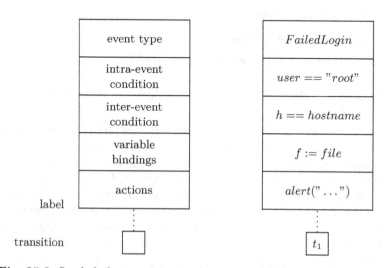

**Fig. 25.3.** Symbols for transitions and transition labels with an example

The *event type* of a transition identifies the type of event that the transition models as a step of the complex event (see event type 'FailedLogin' in Fig. 25.3).

*Intra-event conditions* specify additional restrictions w.r.t. the modeled event by requiring certain features of the event (see value 'root' required for the feature designated 'user' in Fig. 25.3).

*Inter-event conditions* relate the current event to events that were observed earlier. Atoms of inter-event conditions are features of the event or variable values of earlier token bindings (see the comparison of the value of the token variable named 'h' and the feature designated 'hostname' of the current event in Fig. 25.3).

*Token bindings* assign values to *token variables*, where the values are a function of constants, features of the event and values of token variables (see the assignment of the feature designated 'file' to the token variable named 'f'). As an example for the correlation of two distinct events $a$ and $b$, an inter-event condition may compare a feature of the current event $b$ with a feature of an earlier observed event $a$, which has been stored in a token variable (e.g. in Fig. 25.3 the token variable named '$h$' may contain the feature designated '*hostname*' of an event $a$ observed earlier).

*Actions* allow for the (early) response to (partial) complex events (see the action '*alert*(". . . ")' in Fig. 25.3). In actions the features of the current event, variable values or constant values can be used.

In accordance with the definitions in Sect. 12.1.1 the concepts specified in transition labels are mapped to events in audit data as follows:

- the event type is directly specified,
- features are referenced using feature designators, and
- variable values are referenced by the variable name.

Note, that a feature type is the combination of an event type and a feature designator.

Escape places are used for expressing that the current event makes it impossible for the complex event represented by the signature-net to occur. Consequently, the respective tokens are removed from the marking of the signature-net. In the following, we denote transitions that are connected to an escape place as *escape transitions*. An escape transition has the meaning that a complex event will not be completed and that no response will be necessary. In the following we assume that escape transitions do not need to execute actions. Note, that it is not useful to connect escape transitions to other output places, save the escape place. If escape transitions execute no actions and are merely connected to an escape place, it is useless if they perform token bindings, because the assigned token values could not be used by other non-escape-transitions. Escape transitions are used to remove tokens from the marking under certain conditions. Hence, it is not sensible to use non-consuming input edges for these transitions.

To be able to express conjunctively occurring events properly (see conjunction in Sect. 25.2.1), *spontaneous transitions* are introduced, which can occur independently from any events. They are therefore characterized by the fictitious event type $\epsilon$, and they always have empty intra-event conditions. The inter-event conditions of spontaneous events do not refer to event features, but only to variable values and constant values. Transitions that are not spontaneous, are denoted as *regular transitions*.

### 25.3.4 Tokens

A signature-net containing only places and transitions connected by edges can describe the causal relationships of events. To be able to describe instances of (partial) complex events, i.e. partially matched misuse scenarios, the marking of signature-nets needs to be defined, as well as the rules how a given marking can be transformed into a new marking.

The *marking* of a signature-net assigns a (positive and finite) number of tokens to each place of the signature-net. The *initial marking* is the state of the signature-net, where exactly one token is assigned to each initial place of the signature-net.

*Tokens* describe the system state w.r.t. the corresponding instance of a (partial) complex event, as it was reconstructed from the events observed so far. The system state is characterized by the place where a token resides as well as by the variable bindings of the token. Token variables are conceptually analogous to the color of tokens in Colored Petri-nets [123]. If a value is assigned to a token variable, the variable is said to be *initialized*, otherwise it is said to be *uninitialized*. Uninitialized variables are not depicted in the examples.

Figure 25.4 depicts a partial signature-net, its marking and a current event. The bindings of the token at the initial place are empty, i.e. all variables are uninitialized. Occurrences of transition $t_1$ have already generated three tokens in the output place of $t_1$. The token variable $v$ has been bound to different values for each instance of the partial complex event that is represented by each token. Note, that all features designated *oid* of the events that activated $t_1$ (see the token binding of '$t_1$' in Fig. 25.4) satisfied the intra-event condition of $t_1$.

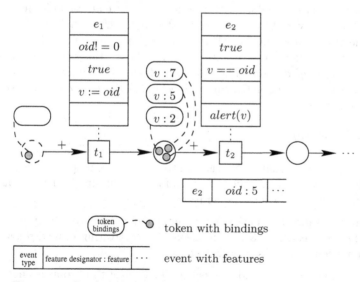

**Fig. 25.4.** Symbols for events and tokens as well as token bindings

Moreover, the current event with event type $e_2$ is depicted, where the feature designator *oid* corresponds to the feature 5. The inter-event condition of transition $t_2$ requires that the feature designated *oid* equals the value of the token variable named $v$. In Fig. 25.4 this condition is satisfied only for the input token, where the value 5 is assigned to the token variable named $v$, i.e. the partial complex event represented by this token will evolve.

In signature-nets a set of tokens is assigned to a place, i.e. if a marking would have identical tokens in the same place, the identical tokens are unified (merged) to a single token. This is being done because identical tokens represent the same instance of a misuse scenario. The identical tokens would simultaneously take the same path through the signature-net, i.e. trigger redundant responses.

### 25.3.5 Transition Activation and Occurrence

For misuse detection purposes it is useful that transitions in signature-nets occur in a deterministic way. In the following, rules are presented, which result in all activated transitions to occur for all activating unified tokens (see below).

To describe the rules for transition occurrence, some terms are defined. An *activating token set* of a given transition $t$ contains exactly one token from each input place of $t$. A set of tokens is *unifiable*, if for all initialized variables of all tokens in the set holds: the value assigned to an initialized variable named $v$ from token $t_i$ equals the assigned value of all variables named $v$ from all other tokens $t_j, j \neq i$. Each activating token set $s$ that is unifiable can be represented by a unified token $u$. The *unified token* $u$ contains all variables of all tokens from $s$. That is, $u$ contains variables with the same names of all variables from all tokens in $s$, where the variables of $u$ receive the values from the initialized variables from the tokens in $s$ and the other variables of $u$ remain uninitialized. A unified token that satisfies all inter-event conditions of $t$ w.r.t. a given event $e$ is denoted as *activating unified token*. The union of all activating unifiable token sets that are represented by the activating unified tokens is denoted as the set of *input tokens* of $t$ w.r.t. $e$.

*Transition activation:*

The marking of a signature-net is said to be *unstable* if spontaneous transitions are activated. Conversely, the marking of a signature-net is denoted as *stable*, if no spontaneous transitions are activated.

A given spontaneous transition $t$ is activated independently from any events occurring (see Sect. 25.3.3), i.e. if at least one activating unified token exists for $t$ in the marking of the signature-net.

For the current event $e$ and a given marking $m$ of the signature-net, a regular transition $t$ is activated if $m$ is stable, the event type of $e$ equals the event type of $t$, $e$ satisfies the intra-event condition of $t$, and at least one activating unifiable token exists for $t$ w.r.t. $m$ and $e$.

As a result of these activation rules, as long as the marking of the signature-net is unstable, only the activated spontaneous transitions may occur until the new marking is stable. Then, regular transitions may be activated.

*Transition occurrence:*

In the following, the rules for the occurrence of transitions are described. After the initialization of a given signature-net with the initial marking $m_0$, spontaneous transitions may occur if $m_0$ is unstable. After the spontaneous transitions have occurred according to the rules, the resulting marking $m$ is stable.

Owing to the rules, it can be assumed that the current marking $m$ of the signature-net is stable, whenever a current event $e$ is provided to the signature-net.

Scope:  All activated transitions occur virtually simultaneously for a given marking. Each activated transition $t$ occurs for all activating unified tokens.[9]

When a transition occurs, one or more tokens are generated in its output places (see below: token generation) and tokens may be removed from some of its input places (see below: token removal). Within the scope of the current event $e$ the resulting new marking $m'$ is allowed to activate spontaneous transitions, but no regular transitions.

As long as the virtually simultaneous occurrence of transitions results in an unstable marking, spontaneous transitions occur. When a stable marking is reached, all transitions have occurred within the scope of $e$ and the next event may be processed.

Token generation:  The token bindings of a given occurring transition $t$ are applied to each activating unified token $u$, i.e. values can be assigned to uninitialized variables of $u$ and new values can be assigned to initialized variables of $u$. A copy of $u$ (including the new token bindings) is placed in all output places of $t$.

Token removal:  Each token that is an element of the set of input tokens of a given occurring transition $t$ and that resides in an input place that is connected to $t$ with a consuming edge, is removed from the signature-net.

Response:  When a transition occurs, its associated actions are executed.

A more concise and formal definition of transition activation and occurrence is given by Meier [149]. The above informal definition is illustrated with the following example, which covers interesting cases of token generation and removal.

Figure 25.5 depicts a partial signature-net with a stable marking just before the event $e_1$ occurs. When $e_1$ occurs, there are four activating token sets for transition $t_1$: $s_1 = \{1,3\}, s_2 = \{1,4\}, s_3 = \{2,3\}$ and $s_4 = \{2,4\}$, where $s_1$

---

[9] Note, that conflicts in classical Petri-nets, where the intersection of the input token sets of two different transitions is non-empty, usually introduce non-determinism. Non-determinism is not useful for the application of signature-nets. Consequently, non-determinism is avoided in signature-nets, such that both transitions occur simultaneously, sharing a common subset of input tokens.

and $s_3$ are unifiable. The token sets $s_2$ and $s_4$ are not unifiable, because the contained tokens assign different values to the variable named $a$. Moreover, for transition $t_4$ exist two unifiable activating token sets: $s_5 = \{3\}$ and $s_6 = \{4\}$. The unifiable activating token set $s_1$ is represented by the unified token $u_1$, where the variables of $u_1$ are assigned with the following values: $a : 1, b : 3, c : 1$. Likewise, $s_3$ is represented by the unified token $u_2$, where $a : 2, b : 2, c : 1$. For $t_4$ the activating token sets $s_5$ and $s_6$ are represented by the unified tokens $u_3$ and $u_4$, respectively, where $u_3$ equals token 3 and $u_4$ equals token 4.

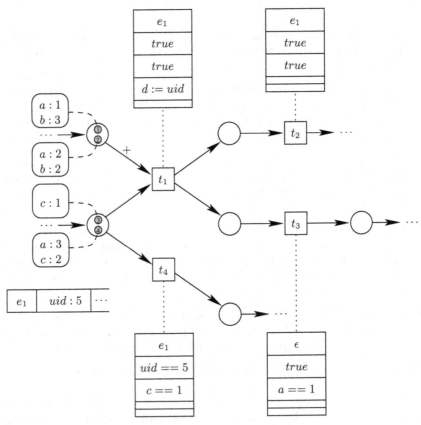

**Fig. 25.5.** Marking before any transitions occur for an event of type $e_1$

For the given marking in Fig. 25.5 and for the occurred current event $e_1$ the unified token $u_1$ and $u_2$ satisfy the conditions of $t_1$ and therefore both are activating unified tokens of $t_1$. For $t_4$ only $u_3$, but not $u_4$, satisfies the transition conditions, such that only $u_3$ is an activating unified token of $t_4$. Hence, $s_1 \cup s_3 = \{1, 2, 3\}$ is the set of input tokens of $t_1$, which are represented by $u_1$ and $u_2$, whereas $s_5 = \{3\}$ is the set of input tokens of $t_4$, as represented by $u_3$. Note, that the sets of input tokens of $t_1$ and $t_4$ have a common subset of $\{3\}$.

Moreover, $t_1$ and $t_4$ are labeled with the same event type $e_1$, and the marking is stable, i.e. no spontaneous transitions are activated, such that both $t_1$ and $t_4$ are activated. Due to the deterministic nature of transition occurrence in signature-nets, $t_1$ occurs for $u_1$ and for $u_2$, and $t_4$ occurs for $u_3$ virtually simultaneously.

When $t_1$ occurs, its token binding assigns the feature designated $uid$ to a variable named $d$ and extends $u_1$ and $u_2$ accordingly (see '$d$ : 5' in Fig. 25.6). A copy of the extended activating unified tokens $u_1$ and $u_2$ is generated in all output places of $t_1$ (see the tokens 5, 7, and 6, 8 in Fig. 25.6). Likewise, a copy of $u_3$ is generated in the output place of $t_4$, when $t_4$ occurs (see token 9 in Fig. 25.6). Note, that the transition labels are not shown in Fig. 25.6 (cf. Fig. 25.5).

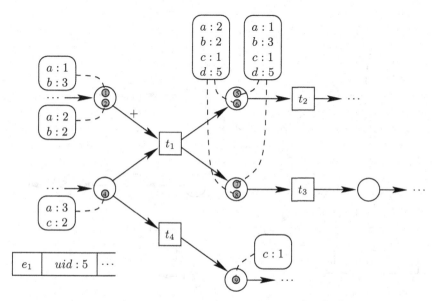

**Fig. 25.6.** Marking after $t_1$ and $t_4$ occurred for an event of type $e_1$

The set of input tokens is $\{1, 2, 3\}$ for $t_1$ and $\{3\}$ for $t_4$. The input tokens 1 and 2 are not removed, because the input place is connected to $t_1$ via a non-consuming edge. However, token 3 is removed, because the input place is connect to $t_1$ as well as to $t_4$ via consuming edges. Note, that token 3 would also be removed if the input place were connected with at least one consuming edge to one of the transitions, even if there were non-consuming input edges connected to the input place.

The new marking resulting from regular transitions occurring is not considered to activate regular transitions. Hence, transition $t_2$ is not activated and cannot occur. However, the new marking may activate spontaneous transitions, here $t_3$.

The newly generated tokens 7 and 8 in the input place of the spontaneous transition $t_3$ are considered as activating and unifiable token sets $s_7 = \{7\}$ and

$s_8 = \{8\}$ for $t_3$ (see Fig. 25.6). The unified token $u_4$ represents $s_7$ and satisfies the transition conditions of $t_3$, but the unified token $u_5$ – representing $s_8$ – does not. As a result, $t_3$ occurs for $u_4$, performs no token bindings and generates a copy of $u_4$ in the output place (see token 10 in Fig. 25.7). Since the input place, where the input token 7 resides, is connect via a consuming input edge to $t_3$, token 7 is removed. Figure 25.7 depicts the partial signature-net and its marking after the transition occurrence triggered by the event $e_1$. Figure 25.7 does not show the transition labels (cf. Fig. 25.5).

Note, that the transitions in the example were not labeled with any actions, such that no actions have been executed when the transitions occurred.

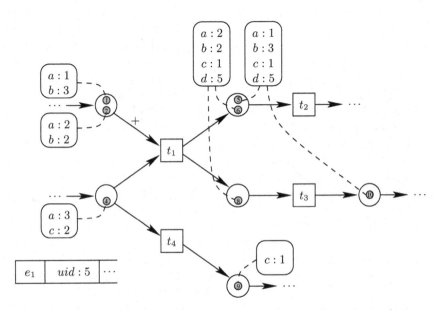

**Fig. 25.7.** Marking after all activated transitions have occurred

### 25.3.6 Semantic Requirements Met By Signature-nets

Meier shows that the expressiveness of the modeling framework satisfies the semantic requirements from Sect. 25.2 by giving equivalent signature-nets for each semantic aspect [149]. The results are briefly summarized in the following.

For many semantic requirements exist directly corresponding constructs in the modeling framework, such as place-transition sequences (*sequence*), input places connected to several transitions (*disjunction*), transitions connected to several output places (*conjunction*), *intra-event conditions* and *inter-event conditions* in transition labels, as well as *consuming* and *non-consuming* input edges. Also the most commonly used modes of *continuity* (*continuous*) and *step instance consumption* (*first*) are properties of the default behavior of signature-nets. Moreover, more complex signature-nets can be composed from more basic signature-nets by connecting the basic signature-nets sequentially (*non-overlap*) or conjunctively (*overlap*).

Other semantic aspects can be expressed by composing various elements of signature-nets. *Simultaneous* events can be modeled as conjunctive events with inter-event conditions on the time stamp.[10] *Negation* and *non-continuous* semantics are modeled as a disjunction connected to an escape place.[11] *Repetitions* are modeled as cycles in the signature-net, where token bindings and inter-event conditions are used to express conditions for termination. Cycles can also be used to express the *step instance selection* modes *last* and *all*. Note, that the mode *all* requires an extension to token variables and token bindings: Token variables may contain lists of values and token bindings may append values to such lists.

**Table 25.2.** Semantic requirements met by signature-nets. The most commonly used mode of an aspect is *emphasized*

| semantic requirement | signature-net construct |
|---|---|
| *sequence* | sequence |
| disjunction | disjunction |
| conjunction | conjunction |
| simultaneous | conjunction, token binding using time stamp |
| negation | disjunction, escape place |
| exact repetition | disjunction, token binding, escape place |
| *at least* repetition | disjunction, token binding |
| at most repetition | disjunction, token binding, escape place |
| *continuous* | default behavior |
| non-continuous | disjunction, escape place |
| *overlapping* concurrency | conjunction |
| non-overlapping concurrency | sequence |
| intra-event condition | intra-event condition |
| inter-event condition | inter-event condition |
| *first* step instance | default behavior |
| last step instance | unbounded repetition |
| all step instances | list type token variable |
| *consuming* step | consuming input edge |
| non-consuming step | non-consuming input edge |

---

[10] Simultaneous events can already be expressed via semantics for conjunctive events and inter-event conditions on time stamps. Hence, the semantic requirements as proposed by Zimmer [224] and as adapted to misuse detection by Meier [148] are not minimal.

[11] The non-continuous semantics can already be expressed using negation semantics.

Table 25.2 summarizes how the semantic requirements for misuse scenario modeling are met by signature-nets. For the detailed constructions refer to Meier [149]. Meier et al. also developed a signature language named Event Description Language (EDL) to encode signature-nets. Using the Signature Analysis Module (SAM), a prototypical implementation of a correlation algorithm using EDL, Meier et al. have shown empirically that the complexity of identifying misuse scenarios specified in an expressive language such as EDL, i.e. signature-nets, can be handled very well in practice. Actually, signature-nets allow for several general optimizations of the runtime evaluation, such that SAM outperforms other implemented misuse detection approaches [152].

## 25.4 Limiting the Framework for Pseudonymization

In Sect. 25.2 we have summarized the semantic requirements for models of misuse scenarios to be useful in the context of misuse detection. Subsequently, in Sect. 25.3 we have introduced a framework for modeling misuse scenarios using signature-nets, which satisfies the requirements summarized in Sect. 25.2 (see Table 25.2). Signature-nets have been introduced here in order to understand the problem of pseudonymization of audit data for misuse detection. The concepts for pseudonymization are developed in Chap. 26 and a pseudonymization approach is described, where pseudonym disclosure contexts are derived from given signature-nets and where pseudonym linkability is limited to the amount that is necessary for audit data analysis.

To reduce the design complexity of an appropriate pseudonymization approach, we do not consider arbitrary signature-nets. Rather, a limited subset of all possible signature-nets can be used as input for the knowledge extraction for pseudonym linkability and disclosure. For a given signature-net there is a set of signature-nets in a restricted form, which – with the exception of unbounded repetitions – retain the semantics of the original signature-net (see Sect. 25.4.1).

Note, that limiting the framework has three major impacts: First, for a given signature-net there is a set of a possibly large number of signature-nets in the limited form. As a result, the processing of the many signature-nets may turn out to be inefficient in practice. Second, the semantics cannot be retained for all possible signature-nets that can be formulated in the general framework, but only minor restrictions apply. Third, and motivating the limitations of the framework, a straightforward design for efficient pseudonymization is possible.

### 25.4.1 Serial Signature-nets

We define serial signature-nets as a restricted subset of all possible signature-nets. In Chap. 26 pseudonymization will be demonstrated for serial signature-nets, only.

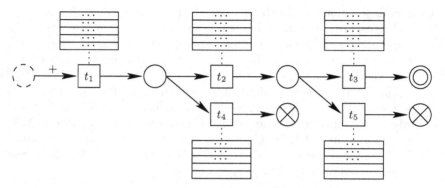

**Fig. 25.8.** An example serial signature-net

*Serial signature-nets* are signature-nets with the following restrictions (see Fig. 25.8):

- Only sequences are allowed with the following exception:
- Disjunctions that are connected to escape transitions are allowed.[12]
- All transitions are regular transitions.

These restrictions have several consequences that are considered useful for the pseudonymization approach developed in Chap. 26:

- There is only one initial place and only one final place.
- Each transition has only one input place and one output place.
- The marking is always stable.
- An activating token set of a transition $t$ contains exactly one token from the input place of $t$. It is not necessary to unify activating token sets. Hence, a token from the input place of $t$ is an activating (unified) token, if it satisfies the inter-event conditions of $t$ w.r.t. the current event. The activating token also is the input token.
- If a transition $t$ occurs for a given activating (unified) token $u$ from the input place of $t$, $u$ is a copy of the input token. The activating (unified) token $u$ may be modified by the token bindings of $t$ before a copy of $u$ (including the new token bindings) is placed in the output place of $t$. If the input edge of $t$ is consuming, the input token is removed.

More explicitly, the following semantic aspects are not directly supported by signature-nets:

---

[12] All escape transitions use virtually the same escape output place. For usability reasons it is allowed to model an arbitrary number of (virtually identical) escape places (see $t_4$ and $t_5$ in Fig. 25.8).

General disjunction (emulatable): General disjunctions can be emulated in serial signature-nets. Emulation is necessary, to retain the semantics of token
removal, if a disjunction contains at least one consuming edge. For each
outgoing edge of a place there is at least a serial signature-net containing
this edge and the transition connected to a non-escape place (for transition
'$t_1$' in Fig. 25.9a see serial signature-net (1) in Fig. 25.9b, and for '$t_2$' see serial
signature-net (2)). For such a given serial signature-net all other alternative
edges are connected to escape transitions (for transition '$t_1$' in Fig. 25.9a see
serial signature-net (2) in Fig. 25.9b, and for '$t_2$' see the serial signature-net
(1)). Escape transitions are retained (see transition '$t_3$' in Fig. 25.9a and the
serial signature-nets (1) and (2) in Fig. 25.9b).

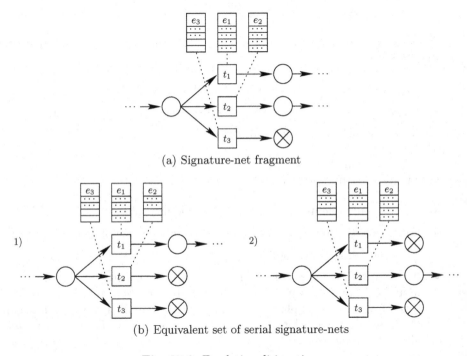

(a) Signature-net fragment

(b) Equivalent set of serial signature-nets

**Fig. 25.9.** Emulating disjunctions

Conjunction and spontaneous transitions (emulatable): Conjunctions can be
emulated using a set of serial signature-nets that enumerate all interleavings of the concurrent threads of the conjunction (see Fig. 25.10). Note, that
concurrent threads are in practice modeled in a well-formed way, where the
threads are introduced by a *fork* transition and are synchronized by a *join*
transition (see '$t_1$' and '$t_4$' in Fig. 25.10a) [149].

Spontaneous transitions are in signature-nets only used for modeling the
joining of concurrent threads [149]. Serial signature-nets do not directly sup-

port spontaneous transitions. However, they can be emulated by merging the inter-event condition, the bindings and the actions of the spontaneous transition with those of the preceding regular transition of each serial signature-net representing one of the interleavings of the conjunction (see how the labels of transitions '$t_3$' and '$t_4$' from Fig. 25.10a are merged to form the label of '$t_3$' in serial signature-net (1) in Fig. 25.10b, and how the labels of '$t_2$' and '$t_4$' are merged for '$t_2$' in signature-net (2)).

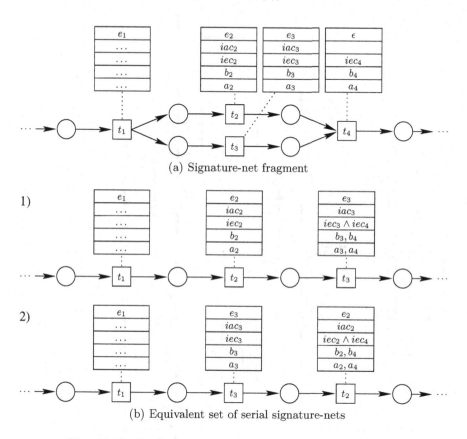

(a) Signature-net fragment

(b) Equivalent set of serial signature-nets

**Fig. 25.10.** Emulating conjunctions and spontaneous transitions

Simultaneous (emulatable): In signature-nets this semantic aspect is expressed using conjunctions and escape places [149]. Therefore, this aspect can be emulated as suggested above for conjunctions.

Repetition (partially emulatable): Only bounded repetitions, where the static number of repetitions can be computed in advance, can be represented by unfolding cycles of the signature-net (see how transition '$t_2$' from Fig. 25.11a is replicated $n$ times in the serial signature-net in Fig. 25.11b). In Fig. 25.11 the emulation for the *at least* semantics of repetitions is depicted. The se-

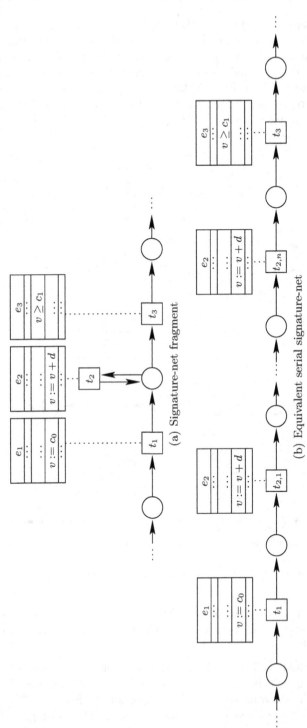

**Fig. 25.11.** Emulating repetitions with *at least* $n$ times semantics, where $c_1 = c_0 + n \cdot d, n \in \mathbb{N}$

mantics for *exact* repetitions and *at most* semantics can also be emulated in serial signature-nets, also emulating the additional disjunctions. Refer to Meier for the respective signature-nets [149].

Concurrency (emulatable): In signature-nets this semantic aspect can be expressed using sequences and conjunctions [149]. Therefore, this aspect can be emulated as proposed above for conjunctions.

Instance selection: While selecting the first instance is the standard selection mode for signature-nets, the modes *last* and *all* are expressed using unbounded repetitions [149]. Unbounded repetitions cannot be represented using serial signature-nets.

Summarizing, except for repetitions where the number of repetitions cannot be computed in advance, which are also used to express the instance selection modes *last* and *all*, all semantic requirements are satisfied by serial signature-nets. Fortunately, the unsupported aspects are expected to be rarely used in practice, if at all. Some semantic aspects are not directly supported, but they can be emulated using disjunctive escape paths, enumerating all interleavings, merging inter-event-conditions and unfolding cycles. Table 25.3 summarizes the semantic aspects supported by serial signature-nets.

**Table 25.3.** Semantic requirements met by serial signature-nets. The most commonly used mode of an aspect is *emphasized*

| semantic requirement | serial signature-net construct |
|---|---|
| *sequence* | sequence |
| disjunction | enumerate disjunctive pathes |
| conjunction | enumerate interleaving pathes |
| simultaneous | enumerate interleaving pathes, escape place |
| negation | disjunction, escape place |
| exact repetition | unfold cycle (only for static repetitions) |
| *at least* repetition | unfold cycle (only for static repetitions) |
| at most repetition | unfold cycle (only for static repetitions) |
| *continuous* | default behavior |
| non-continuous | disjunction, escape place |
| *overlapping* concurrency | enumerate interleaving pathes |
| non-overlapping concurrency | sequence |
| intra-event condition | intra-event condition |
| inter-event condition | inter-event condition |
| *first* step instance | default behavior |
| last step instance | — (unbounded repetition) |
| all step instances | — (unbounded repetition) |
| *consuming* step | consuming input edge |
| non-consuming step | non-consuming input edge |

Note, that the emulations given above require that the original signature-net is well-formed. Meier arguments that misuse scenarios that are actually useful for misuse detection can be modeled by well-formed signature-nets. Meier also introduces a notion of well-formedness of signature-nets [149].

Finally note, that serial signature-nets, as a sub-set of the more general signature-nets, can already be encoded in EDL for misuse detection using SAM.

# Pseudonymization Based on Serial Signature-Nets

As motivated in Chap. 24, in this Chapter we introduce a refined approach for pseudonymization based on the expressive serial signature-nets defined in Chap. 25. The requirements, assumptions and trust model presented in Chap. 11 also apply to the refined approach. The trust model still is based on the architecture depicted in Fig. 8.6b with the additional modification that the pseudonym mapping is provided in the pseudonymity-layer (cf. Sect. 16.3), which is provided simultaneously with the pseudonymized application-layer audit data (see Sect. 13.1). In contrast to Fig. 19.4 the response unit of the SSO-controlled IDS is explicitly depicted in Fig. 26.1. Analysis reports are immediately reidentified and made available to the response unit, which executes an appropriate response, specified as an action in the corresponding serial signature-net.[1]

The pseudonymizer depicted in Fig. 26.1 uses the same models of misuse scenarios as the analysis, which are specified as serial signature-nets. The pseudonymizer extracts requirements for pseudonym linkability and pseudonym disclosure from the serial signature-nets. Using the extracted knowledge the pseudonymizer can anticipate which pseudonyms need to be linkable and under what conditions pseudonyms need to be disclosed. For pseudonymization the pseudonymizer basically performs the same analysis on the audit data as the IDS, with some modifications for pseudonymization. The increase in computational complexity involved in performing basically the same analysis as the IDS is the price we have to pay for generating pseudonyms that are tailored to the more expressive serial signature-nets.

The IDS analysis engine needs to be made aware of where pseudonymized features in the audit data are compared to clear-text values in intra-event conditions of the given serial signature-nets. The analysis engine employs a minimal companion pseudonym generator (see 'p' in Fig. 26.1) in order to pseudonymize clear-text values on the fly while leveraging data in the pseudonymity-layer, such

---

[1] Note, that the response unit could also be depicted in Fig. 19.4, but has been omitted, because it is not necessarily part of an individual set-up of *Pseudo/CoRe*.

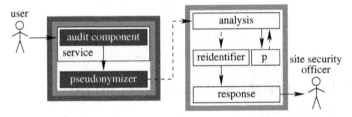

**Fig. 26.1.** Trust and control in the architectural model of the fine-grained approach

that the resulting pseudonyms can be compared to pseudonyms in the audit data. Note, that the pseudonyms we propose do not interfere with the evaluation of inter-event conditions. During analysis the engine collects disclosure information from the pseudonymity-layer data. Before an action is executed, the pseudonymized parameters of the action are disclosed using the collected disclosure information. The action can then be executed using the disclosed clear-text parameters.

Both, the pseudonymizer and the analysis engine are configured to know a priori, which features in the audit data are (to be) pseudonymized and which are not. Features that are left in the clear are not pseudonymized by the pseudonymizer and are processed by the analysis engine as if there was no pseudonymization taking place. We therefore focus on the processing of pseudonymized features in the following text.

In Chap. 27 and Chap. 28 pseudonym linkability and pseudonym disclosure are separately examined in the context of serial signature-nets. The approach for pseudonym generation is developed to carefully respect the requirements given by the syntactical structure of audit records, by the given serial signature-nets and by the analysis engine. Leveraging the knowledge in the serial signature-nets both, pseudonym linkability and pseudonym disclosure can be tailored tightly to the given serial signature-nets, such that pseudonyms are linkable only as required for the purpose of audit data analysis, and pseudonyms can only be disclosed, when the analysis engine executes an action for the purpose of an appropriate response. Employing appropriate cryptographic primitives, pseudonym linkability and pseudonym disclosure can be securely bound to the aforementioned purposes, such that an attacker cannot link pseudonyms, if the analysis engine does not need to link the pseudonyms, and the attacker cannot disclose pseudonyms, as long as the analysis engine does not need to execute an action.

Summarizing, this Part presents novel approaches for fine-grained and rigorous technical purpose binding of pseudonym linkability (see Sect. 7.3) and controlled pseudonym disclosure (see Sect. 7.2.2), leveraging knowledge in misuse scenario models specified in an expressive modeling framework. Additionally, controlled pseudonym disclosure subject to organizational purpose binding (see Sect. 7.2.1) is securely integrated with technical purpose binding.

The approaches presented in Chap. 27 and Chap. 28 for pseudonym linkability and pseudonym disclosure require some further restrictions, such that pseudonymized features can be evaluated by serial signature-nets:

- Token bindings are restricted to merely assign pseudonymized features to token variables. Pseudonymized features cannot be aggregated, e.g. $v := v \circ f$.[2] Note, that this restriction does not limit the repetition semantics in serial signature-nets, because the repetition counter variable value does not need to be pseudonymized. Moreover, repetitions are unfolded, such that counting repetitions is unnecessary (see Sect. 25.4.1).

- It is not allowed to rename variables to which pseudonymized features have been assigned, e.g. $v_1 := v_2$. Despite this restriction, it should be possible to express all useful models of misuse scenarios. Moreover, this restriction can be relaxed by extending the algorithm for linkability extraction given in Sect. 27.1, such that variable-to-variable assignments are represented in the linkability graph.

In addition to these restrictions, the approach presented in Chap. 27 for pseudonym linkability requires some limitations for features that need to be pseudonymized in serial signature-nets:

- Intra-event condition comparators are restricted to testing if some pseudonymized feature equals some constant value, and if two pseudonymized features equal in the current event.

- Inter-event condition comparators are restricted to testing if some pseudonymized feature equals the pseudonymized value of some token variable, and if the pseudonymized values of two token variables are equal.

That is, pseudonymized features or variable values cannot be compared to clear-text features or variable values. Hence, when specifying, which features need to be compared, one has to decide whether both or none of them shall be pseudonymized. This restriction can be removed by extending the linkability extraction algorithm given in Sect. 27.1, treating features and variable values that are compared with clear-text features or variable values as proposed for clear-text comparisons of intra-event conditions.

The summarized restrictions are motivated in some detail in Chap. 27 and Chap. 28.

---

[2] It seems possible that pseudonyms can be generated by homomorphically encrypting the features to be concealed, such that several operations can be performed on the pseudonyms, and the results apply also to the decrypted pseudonyms, i.e. the original features. This approach could be investigated to overcome the described limitation. However, in this book homomorphic encryption is not considered.

# Pseudonym Linkability

Section 7.3 motivates the objective of minimizing the use of a given pseudonym in order to reduce the working surface of an attacker for uncontrolled pseudonym disclosure. Moreover, the magnitude of the transitive closure of pseudonymized features that are linkable to a given pseudonym has a proportional impact, if this pseudonym is disclosed, irrespective of the fact that disclosure occurred in a controlled or in an uncontrolled way. That is, the smaller the magnitude of the transitive closure of pseudonymized features is, which are linkable to the disclosed pseudonym, the lower is the undesirable impact of its disclosure. Hence, it is desirable to reduce the linkability of pseudonymized features in audit data for misuse detection.

A rigorous solution to the challenge of reducing linkability is technically binding the linkability of pseudonyms to the purpose of audit data analysis for misuse detection (cf. Sect. 7.3). To formulate such a solution it is necessary to investigate the aspects of audit data analysis that inter-relate with the linkability of features in audit data.

Considering serial signature-nets as the model of choice for expressing misuse scenarios, it can be seen that the content of audit records is processed when transitions are considered for activation and when transitions occur (see Sect. 25.3.5).

When a transition occurs, its token bindings are performed by assigning features to token variables (see Sect. 25.3.3 and Sect. 25.3.4). It can be assumed that token bindings are used for three reasons, only. First, the feature bound to the variable is a parameter of the decision what transitions are activated later on. Second, the feature is a parameter of a transition action. Third, the feature value needs to be aggregated with some other values and the aggregate value is important for the first or the second case.

In the latter two cases, not merely the linkability of the feature is of interest, rather the value of the feature is the important factor. In the context of pseudonymization the value of a pseudonymized feature is generally not usable for mathematical operations except for testing two pseudonymized features for equality.[1] More precisely, the value of a pseudonymized feature is opaque until the original feature concealed by the pseudonym is disclosed. These considerations are examined in Chap. 28. Naturally, it is not useful to directly compare pseudonymized features with clear-text features.

If the inter-event condition of some transition compares the pseudonymized feature stored in a token variable with some pseudonymized feature in the current event or stored in another token variable, pseudonymization must respect that the same pseudonym is assigned to the same feature in both events. In that case, the pseudonyms are linkable and inter-event conditions work irrespective of pseudonymization. This also applies, if an intra-event condition compares two pseudonymized features in the current event. The features that need to remain linkable after pseudonymization, because they are subject to token bindings or transition conditions, are denoted as *pseudonym-linkable features* or *PL-features*.

A straightforward solution is to exploit the knowledge about transition conditions and token bindings in the given serial signature-nets in order to determine, which PL-features need to be linkable (see Sect. 27.1). During the pseudonymization of features that need to be linkable, the (pseudo-randomly chosen) pseudonym is committed to memory, when a feature is subject to the first token binding. From then on this pseudonym is used, if the same feature occurs in later events as a feature that needs to be linkable (see Sect. 27.3).

When transitions are considered for activation, also intra-event conditions are evaluated, such that features in the current event are compared to constant values defined in the condition (see Sect. 25.3.3). These features are denoted as *clear-text-linkable features* or *CL-features*. To CL-features applies a different rationale than to PL-features. The pseudonym of a CL-feature may be chosen arbitrarily, if it is feasible to pseudonymize the corresponding constant value during audit data analysis immediately before it is compared to the pseudonym. Hence, if CL-features are pseudonymized, the misuse detection engine must be enabled to pseudonymize constant values during audit data analysis (see 'p' in Fig. 26.1).

As described above, in order to allow pseudonymized audit data to be analyzed for misuse scenarios, some linkability needs to be retained. Even if linkability is reduced to the amount necessary for analysis purposes, it still represents a working surface for an attacker, albeit a much smaller one. The following linkability remains as an artefact of technical purpose binding of linkability:

PL-features: The linkability of PL-features may allow an attacker to exploit the transitivity of linkability in order to disclose pseudonyms. However, pseudonyms of PL-features are generated by the pseudonymizer to be linkable to pseudonyms of certain PL-features only (see Sect. 27.1). Hence, dictionary attacks can be avoided for PL-features (see Sect. 7.2.5).

---

[1] If the pseudonyms are generated by homomorphically encrypting the features to be concealed, several operations can be performed on the pseudonyms, such that the results apply also to the decrypted pseudonyms, i.e. the original features. However, in this book homomorphic encryption is not considered.

CL-features: This is not the case for CL-features, because the IDS needs to be able to compare clear-text values to arbitrary pseudonyms of CL-features. Hence, CL-features inherently provide the attacker with the ability to perform dictionary attacks.[2]

Note, that a feature may simultaneously be a PL- and a CL-feature, such that the possibility for a dictionary attack extends to the transitive closure of the feature. Apart from the linkability sustained for audit data analysis, knowledge about the semantics of audit data induces additional linkability:

Event semantics: Some events describe operations that semantically link their operands. For example the BSM event type AUE_RENAME links the old name of a file to its new name. If we can disclose the file's pseudonyms for its new name we can also link the undisclosed pseudonyms of the old name to the same file.

Section 27.1 describes how requirements for pseudonym linkability can be extracted from a given set of serial signature-nets, such that the capability to analyze the audit data is sustained despite pseudonymization. Primitives that can be used to operationalize pseudonym generation are proposed in Sect. 27.2. Section 27.3 describes how the extracted linkability requirements and pseudonym generation are coordinated to pseudonymize application-layer audit data. Finally, Sect. 27.4 shows how pseudonymized audit data can be analyzed for misuse detection.

## 27.1 Extracting Linkability Requirements

While it is possible to generate two or more distinct pseudonyms for a given feature, these pseudonyms are linkable in the case they are all used to replace the feature in the same audit record. Obviously, all of these distinct pseudonyms still represent one and the same feature in the audit record and are thus inherently linkable by exploiting knowledge about the syntactical structure of audit records.

Based on the argument that multiple pseudonyms for a given feature in a given audit record do not decrease the overall linkability of the feature, it is sensible

---

[2] Note, that it is not possible to pseudonymize the constants in intra-event conditions a priori, because in our attacker model the attacker knows the original constant values, too, and can then disclose the corresponding pseudonyms immediately. If we assume that the attacker knows only the pseudonymized signatures, for CL-features merely subject-pseudonyms could be used. This is highly undesirable, because then all pseudonyms for a given CL-feature are always linkable. The best achievable solution is that the pseudonyms of CL-features become only linkable in the case that a matching clear-text value has been found. A clear-text value may be found during the evaluation of an intra-event condition, or by means of a dictionary attack.

to replace a given feature with only one pseudonym in a given audit record. Additionally, when a pseudonym is chosen for a PL-feature in a given audit record, the choice must be carefully coordinated with the choice of the pseudonym for the same feature in other audit records. Otherwise the linkability required for audit data analysis may not be retained completely, resulting in false negatives during the analysis of the audit data. Conversely, if two different PL-features are replaced with the same pseudonym, false positives may occur during audit data analysis.

This problem can be solved by tracing linkability requirements from the point where they are specified, back to the origin where pseudonyms are initially chosen. Linkability requirements are specified by transition conditions testing features for equality. For a given feature that is tested for equality always the same pseudonym must be used in all events where the feature is extracted. The linkability requirements can be extracted based on the knowledge about the semantics of token bindings and transition conditions and the syntactical equality of variable names and feature types. Additionally, based on syntactical knowledge about the structure of audit records, linkability is constrained, such that a given feature is not replaced with more than one pseudonym in a given audit record.

In the following, the transitions and feature types used in the finite set $N$ of given serial signature-nets are represented as vertices of an undirected graph $G = (T, C)$, where $T$ and $C$ are finite. Two vertices $\tau_1 \in T$ and $\tau_2 \in T$ are connected by an edge $(\tau_1, \tau_2) \in C$ where the pseudonyms need to be generated consistently, when the transition(s) represented by $\tau_1$ and $\tau_2$ occur(s). Two pseudonyms $p_1$ and $p_2$ are consistent, if $f_1 = f_2 \Rightarrow p_1 = p_2$, where $f_1$ and $f_2$ are the original features that are replaced by $p_1$ and $p_2$, respectively. The connected components of $G$ represent the classes of transitions where pseudonyms for certain feature types need to be generated consistently. Identifying all connected components of $G$ can be implemented efficiently [168]. In the following, the definition of vertices and the rules for connecting vertices by edges are described in detail.

Vertices $\tau \in T$ are defined as tuples $(I, S, O, O)$, where $I$ is the finite set of transition identifiers used in $N$, $S = \{bvf, cvf, cff, cvv\}$ describes the semantics of the respective transitions (see below), and $O = F \cup V$ names the feature type(s) and token variable(s) that are subject to the semantics in $S$. $V$ is the finite set of token variable names used in $N$, and $F$ is the finite set of feature types used in $N$. Note, that a feature type is a combination of an event type and a feature designator (see Sect. 12.1.1) and that $F$ therefore represents a global name space w.r.t. $N$. Token variable names usually are chosen locally for each serial signature-net, such that they are extended with a signature identifier to form a global name space w.r.t. $N$. The transition identifiers in $I$ that refer to transitions in the same serial signature-net are ordered in the sense that if $i_1 < i_2$ then the position of the transition for $i_1$ is left to the position of the transition for $i_2$ in the serial signature-net. $I$ is a global name space w.r.t. $N$.

As described in Chap. 27 we can assume that pseudonymized features cannot be aggregated. To simplify the further considerations, it is assumed that it is not necessary assigning the value of one variable to another variable to be able to model useful serial signature-nets. With this restriction, it is sufficient to consider the following transition semantics in order to determine the linkability requirements and constraints:

$bvf$: A token binding of transition $i$ reads a feature type $f$ directly from an audit record and assigns the feature to the token variable $v$: $\tau = (i, bvf, v, f)$.

$cvf$: An inter-event condition of transition $i$ reads a feature type $f$ directly from an audit record and tests if the feature equals the value of the token variable $v$: $\tau = (i, cvf, v, f)$.

$cff$: An intra-event condition of transition $i$ reads two feature types $f_1$ and $f_2$ directly from an audit record and tests if the features are equal: $\tau = (i, cff, f_1, f_2)$.

$cvv$: An inter-event condition of transition $i$ tests if the values of the two variables $v_1$ and $v_2$ are equal: $\tau = (i, cvv, v_1, v_2)$.

Note, that a given transition may be represented by one or more vertices, e.g. if the transition uses inter-event conditions as well as token bindings.

There are two necessary conditions that need to be met, such that two vertices $\tau_1$ and $\tau_2$ can be connected by an edge $(\tau_1, \tau_2)$:

NL1) At least one of the vertices represents a transition that directly reads a feature type from an audit record, e.g. $\tau = (\cdot, bvf, \cdot, \cdot)$.[3] If no feature type is accessed in an audit record, also no pseudonym will be generated, i.e. considering linkability of pseudonyms is obsolete.

NL2) The vertices $\tau_1$ and $\tau_2$ represent (a) transition(s) that use(s) a common operand, e.g. $\tau_1 = (\cdot, bvf, v, \cdot)$ and $\tau_2 = (\cdot, cvf, v, \cdot)$. If there is no common operand, no direct dependence w.r.t. linkability can be derived by considering the two vertices.

If at least one of the necessary conditions is not satisfied, $\tau_1$ and $\tau_2$ will not be directly connected by an edge. However, they still may be part of the same connected component of $G$, i.e. transitive linkability dependencies may exist.

There are two sufficient conditions, such that two vertices $\tau_1$ and $\tau_2$ are connected by an edge $(\tau_1, \tau_2)$:

SL1) Both vertices represent (a) transition(s) that directly read(s) the same feature type, e.g. $\tau_1 = (\cdot, bvf, \cdot, f)$ and $\tau_2 = (\cdot, cvf, \cdot, f)$.

The reason that the pseudonym for this feature type must be consistent is that the vertices may represent the same transition or transitions that occur

---

[3] The symbol '$\cdot$' is used like a wild-card symbol acting as a placeholder for arbitrary appropriate symbols.

virtually simultaneously. Hence, they may read from the same audit record, such that the linkability constraint described above holds.

SL2) The vertices represent two transitions in the same serial signature-net, where the one transition indirectly reads a feature type with the help of the other transition, i.e. where the first transition directly reads a feature type and assigns the feature to a common variable, before the second transition uses the variable value.

Expressed more concisely, if there are three vertices $\tau_a = (i_a, bvf, v, f_a)$, $\tau_b = (i_b, bvf, v, f_b)$ and $\tau_c = (i_c, cv\cdot, v, \cdot)$, then $\tau_c$ is connected to $\tau_j \in \{\tau_a, \tau_b\}$, if the distance $d(i_j, i_c) = i_c - i_j$ is minimal and $d(i_j, i_c) > 0$. The transition represented by $\tau_c$ depends on the linkability of the pseudonym chosen for the feature when the transition represented by $\tau_j$ occurred.

For example, if $i_a = 2, i_b = 4, i_c = 7$, then $d_a = d(i_a, i_c) = 5 > 0$ and $d_b = d(i_b, i_c) = 3 > 0$ and $d_a > d_b$. In this example $\tau_c$ is connected to $\tau_b$. Another example: $i_a = 2, i_b = 9, i_c = 7$, then $d_a = d(i_a, i_c) = 5 > 0$ and $d_b = d(i_b, i_c) = -2 < 0$ and $d_a > d_b$. In this example $\tau_c$ is connected to $\tau_a$, since $d_b < 0$.

Note, that due to the naming convention for variable names defined above, a common variable name referenced by two vertices implies that the vertices represent (a) transition(s) in the same serial signature-net.

Concerning the above four conditions some remarks can be made. SL1 as well as SL2 implicitly satisfy NL1 and NL2. When listing all combinations of semantics of vertices that satisfy NL1 and NL2, the following pairs of vertices will not be connected, as defined by SL1 and SL2:

- Two vertices with inter-event condition semantics are not connected, if they use a common variable but do not access the same feature type. Considering the inter-event conditions alone it cannot be decided, if the variable(s) is/are actually bound by earlier vertices. If they are bound, a connection of the two vertices were redundant together with the connections to the variable binding vertices. If the variables are not bound, there are no linkability requirements for the variable values.

- If the token binding of a variable is performed after the variable is used ($d < 0$), the use of the variable represents no indirect access of the feature, which is bound later on. Hence, no linkability requirements exists for the common variable. Note, that for $d = 0$ both vertices represent the same transition. That is, the token binding is performed after the inter-event condition is evaluated, such that no linkability requirements exist for the common variable.

Consider the example serial signature-net $n_1$ in Fig. 25.4 without a marking. The token binding of $t_1$ in Fig. 25.4 is represented by $\tau_1 = (1, bvf, (n_1, v), (e_1, oid))$

in Fig. 27.1 and the inter-event condition of $t_2$ is represented by $\tau_2 = (2, cvf, (n_1, v), (e_2, oid))$. Note, that the transition identifiers have been chosen arbitrarily, but respecting the order of the transitions. Moreover, the variable names have been extended with the signature identifier $n_1$ and the feature types are combinations of event types and feature designators. The vertices $\tau_1$ and $\tau_2$ satisfy the sufficient condition SL2 and therefore are connected. Note, that the vertices do not satisfy SL1 due to distinct feature types. All pseudonyms for feature types in a connected component of the graph need to be generated consistently, i.e. the pseudonyms for $(e_1, oid)$ and for $(e_2, oid)$ must be generated such that they are linkable, if they represent the same feature.

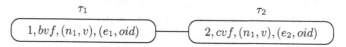

$\tau_1$ : $1, bvf, (n_1, v), (e_1, oid)$ — $\tau_2$ : $2, cvf, (n_1, v), (e_2, oid)$

**Fig. 27.1.** A linkability graph for the serial signature-net in Fig. 25.4

## 27.2 Primitives for Technical Purpose Binding of Linkability

We propose to use a cryptographic collision-resistant hash-function $h()$, and a pseudo-random number generator $r()$ to generate pseudonyms for features.

For a given PL-feature $F$ that needs to be concealed, the pseudonym $p := h(s|F)$ is generated. For PL-features the salt $s$ is used to control the linkability of the pseudonyms. If the linkability of several occurrences of a given feature in different events is necessary, the same salt $s$ is chosen in order to generate compatible, i.e. content-linkable, pseudonyms. Conversely, if a given feature needs not to be linkable to any of its occurrences in other events, a different salt is chosen. This can be done pseudo-randomly, such that $s := r()$, as long as the value range for $s$ is sufficiently large, i.e. the probability that the resulting pseudonyms are compatible is negligible.[4] Finally, the pseudonyms for two distinct features will automatically be generated to be different, except for the case that a collision of $h()$ occurs. Then, for distinct features and for distinct salts identical pseudonyms may be generated, which may cause a false positive during audit data analysis. However, due to the nature of $h()$ the probability of collision occurrences is negligible, too.[5]

---

[4] The occurrence of duplicate salts can be avoided entirely by committing all used salts to memory and by checking for duplicates.

[5] If the value range for a pseudonym is restricted due to the format requirements of the audit data, duplicate pseudonyms can be avoided by holding all used pseudonyms in memory and by checking for duplicates.

For PL-features only the pseudonymizer knows the salts that it used to generate the corresponding pseudonyms. Any other observer who does not know the salts, i.e. the IDS or an attacker, can gain only the following information when observing the generated pseudonyms (assuming that no collisions occur for $h()$): If two given pseudonyms are content-linkable, they represent the same concealed feature. If two given pseudonyms are different, either the corresponding features are different, or distinct salts were used to generate the pseudonyms. That is, for distinct pseudonyms it cannot be decided if they represent the same feature or distinct features. This property together with the one-way property of $h()$ enforce the purpose binding of pseudonym linkability in a secure way, i.e. it cannot be circumvented by an attacker.

For a given CL-feature $F$ that needs to be concealed, the pseudonym $p := h(s|F)$ is generated just like for a PL-feature, but the salt $s$ is made available, such that it can be used to pseudonymize any clear-text value $c$ to be compared with $p$: $h(s|c) == p$. If the CL-feature is also a PL-feature, $s$ is chosen as described for PL-features. Otherwise the salt is chosen pseudo-randomly $s := r()$. Note, that providing the $s$ enables an attacker to mount a dictionary attack.

A feature can simultaneously be a PL-feature and a CL-feature. In that case $s$ is chosen like for a PL-feature and is made available like for a CL-feature.

The pseudonym $p$ for a given feature $F$, where $F$ is not a CL-feature and not a PL-feature, is chosen pseudo-randomly, such that $p := r()$. Due to the nature of $r()$ the probability that $p$ matches an already existing pseudonym (possibly causing a false positive during audit data analysis) is negligible.[6]

Linkability in audit data is usually required to perform various kinds of tests in inter- and intra-event conditions. Due to the proposed approach to pseudonymization merely PL- and CL-features can be tested only for equality/difference where required by inter- and intra-event conditions. Other tests are not supported by the proposed approach for pseudonymization.

## 27.3 Operation of the Pseudonymizer

In the following the operation of the pseudonymizer is described, focusing on the aspects of pseudonym linkability only. The pseudonymizer requires a priori knowledge specifying, which features need to be pseudonymized in the audit data. Also, the pseudonymizer needs to know the format of the features in order to appropriately encode pseudonyms. Moreover, the format of pseudonymity-layer data needs to be specified, such that it can be embedded in the application-layer audit data. Note, that this a priori knowledge is the same as used for the pseudonymization approach presented in Part III.

---

[6] If the value range for a pseudonym is restricted due to the format requirements of the audit data, duplicate pseudonyms can be avoided by holding all used pseudonyms in memory and by checking for duplicates.

Unlike that approach, here the pseudonymizer uses the same serial signature-nets as the IDS to determine, where linkability is necessary for pseudonyms. While this knowledge is manually provided in the approach in Part III, here it is automatically derived from the models of misuse scenarios during initialization. To do this, the pseudonymizer constructs the graph $G$ and identifies its connected components as described in Sect. 27.1.

For each connected component the pseudonymizer initializes a pseudonym mapping table, where an entry of the table has the form $\langle F, s, h(s|F) \rangle$. A mapping entry associates a clear-text feature $F$ with the salt $s$ chosen to compute the pseudonym $h(s|F)$. A given pseudonym mapping comprises all features that need to be pseudonymized in a consistent way. For a given feature the salts and pseudonyms stored in different pseudonym mappings of different connected components of $G$ differ with high probability. As a result, pseudonym linkability is reduced where no compatibility is required for pseudonyms.

The pseudonymizer takes the original audit data as its input and outputs the pseudonymized audit data as well as the pseudonymity-layer data. During operation the pseudonymizer processes the next audit record from the queue of incoming audit records, just like the IDS. The processing differs only slightly from the processing of the analysis engine of the IDS. The pseudonymizer additionally locates features that need to be pseudonymized and carefully generates appropriate pseudonyms. After replacing the original features with the corresponding pseudonyms and providing salts for CL-feature tests in the pseudonymity-layer, the pseudonymizer forwards the pseudonymized audit data and the pseudonymity-layer data to the IDS. That is, the pseudonymizer does not execute actions when (partial) complex events occur.

For a given current audit record the pseudonymizer executes the process of transition activation for all serial signature-nets. Before the activated transitions may occur, the pseudonymizer identifies the features that need to be pseudonymized and generates appropriate pseudonyms as follows.

For a given feature $F$ that needs to be pseudonymized, the pseudonymizer determines if $F$ is a PL-feature and/or a CL-feature w.r.t. the set of activated transitions. The salt and the pseudonym for $F$ are initially undefined.

- If $F$ is a PL-feature, the pseudonymizer chooses any activated transition $t$ in the context of which $F$ is a PL-feature and then chooses any vertex $\tau$ that represents $t$ with the feature type $f$ of $F$. Note, that it does not matter which transition and which representing vertex is chosen, because all possible resulting vertices are connected (due to SL1). Hence, for both searches the first matching result can be used. The pseudonymizer then locates $F$ in the pseudonym mapping that is associated with the connected component containing $\tau$. If $F$ is found, the pseudonymizer uses the salt $s$ and the pseudonym $p$ that are associated with $F$ in its pseudonym mapping entry. If there is no entry for $F$, the pseudonymizer computes $s := r()$ and $p := h(s|F)$, while respecting the specified format of the feature type and of the pseudonymity-layer data, and inserts $\langle F, s, p \rangle$ in the pseudonym mapping.

- If $F$ is (also) a CL-feature, the pseudonymizer checks if the salt is defined. If it is, $F$ is also a PL-feature and $s$ and $p$ have already been chosen appropriately. If not so, the pseudonymizer computes $s := r()$ and $p := h(s|F)$ while respecting the specified format of $f$ and of the pseudonymity-layer data. Subsequently, the pseudonymizer inserts $\langle p, s \rangle$ in the pseudonymity-layer data.[7]

- If $F$ is neither a PL-feature nor a CL-feature, the pseudonymizer computes $p := r()$, while respecting the specified format of the feature type. Note, that even if no transitions are activated, this case ensures that features are still pseudonymized.

Note, that the choice of $p$ here depends on the set of activated transitions. As a result, pseudonym linkability is only established where required by the current state of the analysis. That is, the static analysis of the signature-nets restricts pseudonym linkability to the amount necessary in principle for all possible states of audit data analysis. This amount of pseudonym linkability is further restricted during run-time to the actually required amount at any given moment.

After choosing an appropriate pseudonym, the pseudonymizer pushes the pair $\langle f, p \rangle$ on a stack and examines the next feature that needs to be pseudonymized. After pseudonyms have been chosen for all these features, the pseudonymizer lets all activated transitions occur. After transition occurrence, the pseudonymizer pops the pairs from the stack and replaces each clear-text feature – as identified by its feature type $f$ and specified to be pseudonymized – by the corresponding pseudonym. When the current event has been processed completely, the pseudonymized audit record and the pseudonymity-layer data is provided to the IDS, and the next event from the queue is processed.

Note, that the pseudonymizer does not modify the operation of the serial signature-nets, and the serial signature-nets operate on the unpseudonymized audit data. Only after an event has been completely processed by the serial signature-nets, it is pseudonymized.

The process of application-layer audit data pseudonymization is illustrated in Sect. 27.3.1.

### 27.3.1 Example Operation of the Pseudonymizer

In Fig. 27.2 we recapitulate the example serial signature-net from Fig. 25.4 and the corresponding linkability graph from Fig. 27.1 and demonstrate the operation of the pseudonymizer using this simple example. During initialization the

---

[7] For implementation there needs to be a mechanism that establishes the linkage between the current pseudonymized event and the salt values for this event (cf. Sect. 19.2.1).

pseudonymizer loads the a priori knowledge including the serial signature-nets. Then, the pseudonymizer constructs the linkability requirements graph $G$ and associates the connected component of the graph with an empty pseudonym mapping. After initialization the pseudonymizer is ready to process incoming audit records. Each audit record is processed separately and at first the embedded event is extracted from the current audit record. Fig. 27.2 depicts two events with the event type $e_1$ and $e_2$. When the first event is processed, transition $t_1$ is activated. The pseudonymizer is configured to pseudonymize the feature types $(e_1, oid)$ and $(e_2, oid)$. The feature 5 in the current event $e_1$ is a PL/CL-feature w.r.t. $t_1$. The vertex $\tau_1$ represents $t_1$ and the feature type $(e_1, oid)$ in $G$. The pseudonymizer chooses $\tau_1$ and locates the empty pseudonym mapping that is associated with the connected component containing $\tau_1$. Then, the salt $s = 3$ is pseudo-randomly chosen by the pseudonymizer and the pseudonym $h(3|5)$ is computed. The triple $\langle 5, 3, h(3|5) \rangle$ is stored in the pseudonym mapping. The salt $s$ is labeled with $p$ and inserted in the pseudonymity-layer data: $\langle h(3|5), 3 \rangle$. The pseudonymizer also provides appropriate linkage between the salt and the corresponding pseudonym in the current application-layer audit record (not shown in Fig. 27.2). After pushing the pseudonym on the stack, $t_1$ occurs and assigns the clear-text feature 5 to the token variable $v$. Then, the pseudonymizer pops the pseudonym $h(3|5)$ from the stack and replaces the feature 5 in the original event with $h(3|5)$. This finishes the processing of the first event and the second event is processed. Since the token variable value $v : 5$ satisfies the inter-event condition of transition $t_2$, $t_2$ is activated. The pseudonymizer determines that the feature type $(e_2, oid)$ needs to be pseudonymized, and that the feature $oid : 5$ is a PL-feature w.r.t. $t_2$. Using $\tau_2$ the pseudonymizer locates the pseudonym mapping entry for the feature 5, and pushes the corresponding pseudonym $h(3|5)$ on the stack. After $t_2$ occurred, the pseudonym is popped from the stack and replaces the original feature in $e_2$. Figure 27.2 depicts the linkability requirements graph $G$ for the serial signature-net $n_1$ and the connected component of $G$, as well as the state of the pseudonym mapping after the processing of the two events. Also $n_1$ and its marking are depicted in addition to the two events in their original form and in the pseudonymized form, as well as the corresponding pseudonymity-layer data.

## 27.4 Operation of the Analysis Engine

In the following, the operation of audit data analysis is described, focusing on the aspects of pseudonym linkability, only. Only the necessary extensions are pointed out, such that pseudonymized audit data can be analyzed. The analysis engine merely needs to know, which CL-features are pseudonymized and what the format of the pseudonymity-layer data is. If during the process of transition activation for an event $e$ (see Sect. 25.3.5) an intra-event condition evaluates the value of a pseudonymized CL-feature $p = h(s|F)$, the engine locates the

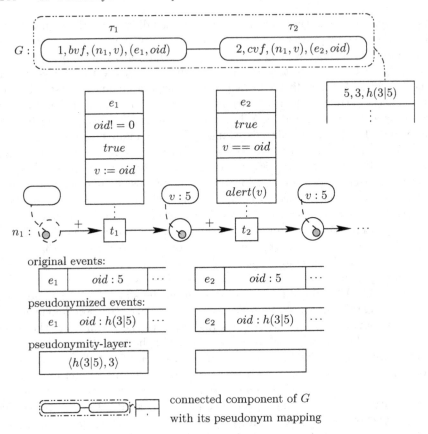

**Fig. 27.2.** Example operation of the pseudonymizer (only linkability)

salt $s$ corresponding to $p$ in the pseudonymity-layer data. Using $s$, the analysis engine can pseudonymize the clear-text value $c$ in the intra-event condition as $p_c = h(s|c)$ and test whether $p_c = p$. Due to the nature of $h()$ holds that $c = F \Leftrightarrow h(s|c) = h(s|F)$ and $c \neq F \Leftrightarrow h(s|c) \neq h(s|F)$.[8] Ignoring the aspect of pseudonym disclosure, there are no further extensions necessary to the analysis engine to cope with pseudonymized audit data. Note, that without pseudonym disclosure the transition actions will use the pseudonyms instead of the original features.

The process of analyzing pseudonymized audit data is illustrated in Sect. 27.4.1.

---

[8] The undesirable case that $c \neq F$ while $p_c = h(s|c) = h(s|F) = p$ constitutes a collision of $h()$ and may lead to a false positive. However, the probability of this case is negligible, if the value range of $p$ and $p_c$ is sufficiently large. If this is not the case, collisions can be avoided by testing each generated CL-feature pseudonym $p = h(s|F)$ against the pseudonymized clear-text value $p_c = h(s|c)$. If $F \neq c$, but $h(s|F) = h(s|c)$, then a new salt $s$ is chosen and $p$ is recomputed.

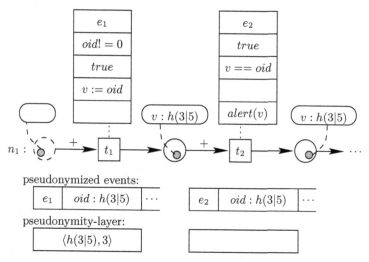

**Fig. 27.3.** Example operation of the analysis engine (only linkability)

## 27.4.1 Example Operation of the Analysis Engine

Continuing the example from Sect. 27.3, we consider that the pseudonymized audit data and the pseudonymity-layer data has been made available to the analysis engine of the IDS for misuse detection. The basic functionality of the analysis engine is described by the given serial signature-nets. For the example we focus on the serial signature-net $n_1$ in Fig. 27.3. When the first pseudonymized event is processed, the analysis engine detects that the event type $e_1$ is relevant for transition $t_1$ and that $t_1$ evaluates an intra-event condition using the pseudonymized CL-feature $h(3|5)$. Thus, the analysis engine uses $h(3|5)$ and the linkage between the pseudonym in the current application-layer audit record and the pseudonymity-layer data (not shown in Fig. 27.3) to locate the salt $s = 3$. Then, the clear-text value 0 is pseudonymized as $p_0 = h(3|0)$. The test $h(3|0) \neq h(3|5)$ returns *true*, i.e. the intra-event condition is satisfied and $t_1$ can occur. When $t_1$ occurs, the pseudonym $h(3|5)$ is assigned to the token variable $v$. After processing the first event, the second event is considered for transition activation. Since the event type $e_2$ is relevant for transition $t_2$, the inter-event condition of $t_2$ is evaluated. During the evaluation, the value of $v$ and of the pseudonymized feature $h(3|5)$ are compared. The test $h(3|5) = h(3|5)$ returns *true*, such that $t_2$ can occur. Since pseudonym $h(3|5)$ cannot be disclosed, the *alert()* action is executed using the pseudonym as parameter. Figure 27.3 depicts the serial signature-net $n_1$ and its marking after the processing of the two pseudonymized events.

# Pseudonym Disclosure

The approach for pseudonym generation described in Chap. 27 is designed such that it does not interfere with the analysis of audit data using serial signature-nets. The aspect of linkability of pseudonyms is focused on the given audit data alone, while respecting the state of serial signature-nets. However, it is not necessary to extend the state of the serial signature-nets. Though the pseudonyms are carefully chosen, such that the analysis of pseudonymized audit data is still feasible, the aspect of accountability or controlled pseudonym disclosure is missing.

Technical purpose binding of the controlled disclosure of pseudonyms in audit data has been introduced in Sect. 7.2.2 and a coarse-grained approach has been presented in Chap. 13. In contrast to the linkability aspect the disclosure aspect can be designed independently from the audit data by introducing the pseudonymity-layer (cf. Sect. 13.1). Moreover, disclosure contexts are coupled to the process of misuse scenario detection, i.e. the state of the analysis process.

Under optimal conditions the disclosure contexts are models of misuse scenarios, such that pseudonyms are only disclosed, if a misuse scenario is detected. However, the set-based model proposed in Part II cannot describe misuse scenarios as fine-grained as (serial) signature-nets. Hence, the more coarse-grained set-based disclosure contexts allow pseudonym disclosure also in situations, where a more fine-grained (serial) signature-net would not have triggered an action. In the following, the basic ideas from the approach developed in Part II are refined to achieve a tight coupling between disclosure contexts and misuse scenario models. As it turns out, the tighter coupling requires some extensions to the state of serial signature-nets, which are specifically necessary for pseudonym disclosure.

As demonstrated in Chap. 27, the process of audit data analysis can be carried out without arranging for pseudonym disclosure. The need for pseudonym disclosure arises where an appropriate response to analysis results must be generated. A response may create a feedback to the observed system, either directly, or via the decision and action of the site security officer (SSO). A feedback to the observed system necessarily references principals or objects in that system, which in the given approach cannot be referenced in a pseudonymous way.[1] Therefore, pseudonyms in analysis results must be disclosed, before the results can be used for a response.

In the framework of (serial) signature-nets, analysis results are interfaced to response components by means of transition actions (see Sect. 25.3.3 and Sect. 25.3.5). Hence, pseudonyms in action parameters must be disclosed before the actions are executed. Actions may be parameterized using constant values, variable values and features from the current event. Constant values are already available as clear-text in the specification of the given serial signature-nets. Consequently, the investigation of pseudonym disclosure focuses on variable values and features.

In the following, a feature is denoted as a *disclosure feature* or *D-feature*, if it is a parameter of some transition action(s). This can be the case if (1) a feature of the current event is used as an action parameter, or if (2) the feature is assigned to a variable $v$ during the token binding of a transition $t_1$, and if $v$ is a parameter of an action of a later transition $t_2$. The transition with the action in its label is denoted as a *disclosure transition*. Note, that a disclosure transition may disclose several D-features simultaneously, where the D-features may have been assigned to variables by several other transitions.

It could be argued that it makes not much sense to pseudonymize features that will be immediately disclosed during analysis (see case (1) above). Considering information for pseudonym disclosure to be separated from the audit data, it may be useful to pseudonymize such features. The pseudonymized audit data could be given to third parties without providing the disclosure information in the pseudonymity-layer. While the third parties can analyze the pseudonymized audit data, they cannot determine the original features, because only the missing (pseudonymity-layer) data provides information about the original features.

The approach for pseudonym disclosure proposed in the following allows to express disclosure conditions in the framework of serial signature-nets. When a token activates a disclosure transition, only those pseudonymized D-features that are used when the action of the current transition is executed, are disclosed. A token may contain further pseudonymized D-features that are not disclosed for the actions of the current transition, but when a later disclosure transition occurs. A token represents an event pattern, which has been detected as an instance of a (partial) complex event that may require some response, i.e. pseudonym disclosure. Only the D-features of this token and/or the current event are disclosed if they are required to execute an action of the current transition.

---

[1] In the approach followed here, pseudonymity is established within the audit data, only. As described in Sect. 8.4 and discussed in Chap. 9 more costly approaches can be used to establish pseudonymity, such that principals can be referenced pseudonymously. This, however, is not the focus of the solutions presented in this book.

Other pseudonymized D-features of the same or other token(s)/event(s) remain concealed.

However, a given disclosed D-Feature may also be evaluated in the context of another serial signature-net, where it needs not be disclosed. Due to the syntactical structure of the audit record from which the disclosed D-feature originates (see Sect. 27.1), it is in principle linkable to its copies in tokens of other serial signature-nets and may be considered disclosed w.r.t. all given signature-nets, even though the disclosure may be technically inhibited for the copies in the other tokens. Also, within a given serial signature-net, copies of pseudonyms of already disclosed D-features may linger in token copies as a consequence of non-consuming transitions. Such pseudonyms must be considered disclosed, even if the disclosure transition never occurs for these tokens. These situations result from the fact that a given D-feature in a given event may simultaneously be part of several instances of (partial) complex events. If at least one instance of the (partial) complex events requires a response, the D-feature is disclosed in the context of this instance with the effect that it cannot be kept confidential w.r.t. to the other instances.

With the assumptions made in Sect. 25.3.3 concerning escape transitions and escape places, they can be safely ignored for the aspect of pseudonym disclosure, as long as extra disclosure-specific state is discarded, when the corresponding token is removed.

Section 28.1 investigates the extraction of requirements for pseudonym disclosure from a set of given serial signature-nets. Appropriate cryptographic primitives for technical enforcement of purpose binding of pseudonym disclosure are developed in Sect. 28.2 using threshold schemes for cryptographic secret sharing. The proposed approach is compared to the approach from Part II and the applicability of extensions from Part II is examined. Leveraging the extracted knowledge about disclosure requirements, as well as about the structure of the given set of serial signature-nets, descriptions for the on-demand generation of threshold schemes are derived in Sect. 28.3. The disclosure information provided by the pseudonymizer for pseudonym disclosure is described in Sect. 28.4. Section 28.5 presents, how the pseudonymizer uses the knowledge about disclosure requirements and scheme descriptions to provide disclosure information for the analysis engine of the IDS. Finally, Sect. 28.6 describes how the analysis engine extracts disclosure information from the pseudonymity-layer in order to disclose pseudonyms subject to technical purpose binding.

## 28.1 Extracting Disclosure Requirements

Aside from the limitations arising inherently from the structure of audit data (see above), controlled pseudonym disclosure shall be considered separately for each instance of a given (partial) complex event. In the framework of serial signature-nets this means that pseudonym disclosure needs only to consider each individual token of a serial signature-net, while ignoring other tokens in the same serial signature-net and in other serial signature-nets.

However, as described above, disclosure must be sensitive to the D-feature token bindings of earlier transitions. To correctly disclose the D-features that are parameters of some actions and to keep other D-features securely pseudonymized, it is necessary to leverage the knowledge about token bindings and actions, which is specified in the given serial signature-nets. More specifically, it is necessary to determine, which features are bound by what transition and to what token variables, and by which disclosure transitions the corresponding pseudonyms are used as action parameters. The disclosure transitions can be used as a starting point, because they can be easily identified. A solution can be designed in a similar way as described in Sect. 27.1, exploiting the semantics of token bindings and the syntactical equality of variable names. There is no need to respect limitations from the structure of audit data, because information generated for pseudonym disclosure can be arbitrarily structured in the pseudonymity-layer.

Again, transitions are represented as vertices of an undirected graph $H = (U, D)$, where $U$ and $D$ are finite. Two vertices $\tau_1 \in U$ and $\tau_2 \in U$ need to be connected by an edge $(\tau_1, \tau_2) \in D$ where the pseudonyms generated during the occurrence of $\tau_1$ should be able to be disclosed when $\tau_2$ occurs. The connected components of $H$ represent the token binding and the disclosure of the D-features. This structure does not yet respect the fact that D-features need to be disclosed only once, even if they are used in the actions of subsequent transitions. Also, the approach for pseudonym disclosure proposed in Sect. 28.2 can take advantage of the fact that some D-features are disclosed simultaneously. The algorithm described below is designed to account for both of these facts.

Vertices $\tau \in U = X \cup Y$ are defined as tuples $(I, bvf, O, O) \in X$ or $(I, W, O) \in Y$, where $I$ is the finite set of transition identifiers, $W = \{dv, df\}$ describes the semantics of the disclosure transitions (see below), and $O = F \cup V$ names the feature type(s) and token variable(s) (see Sect. 27.1 for the definition of $I, F$ and $V$). We also assume here that useful serial signature-nets can be modeled without assigning the pseudonymized value of one variable to another variable. With this assumption, it is sufficient to consider the following transition semantics in order to determine the requirements for pseudonym disclosure:

*bvf*: A token binding of transition $i$ reads a feature type $f$ directly from an audit record and assigns the feature to the token variable $v$: $\tau = (i, bvf, v, f)$.

*dv*: An action of transition $i$ uses the value of the token variable $v$ as a parameter: $\tau = (i, dv, v)$.

*df*: An action of transition $i$ reads a feature type $f$ directly from an audit record and uses the feature as a parameter: $\tau = (i, df, f)$.

Note, that a given transition may be represented by one or more vertices, e.g. if the action of a transition has several parameters or if a transition assigns values to two or more variables.

There are three necessary conditions that need to be met, such that two vertices $\tau_1$ and $\tau_2$ can be connected by an edge $(\tau_1, \tau_2)$:

ND1) At least one of the vertices represents a transition that directly reads a feature type from an audit record, e.g. $\tau = (\cdot, bvf, \cdot, \cdot)$. If no feature type is directly accessed in an audit record, also no pseudonym will be generated which could be disclosed, i.e. considering disclosure of pseudonyms is obsolete.

ND2) At least one of the vertices represents a transition that discloses a feature, i.e. $\tau = (\cdot, d\cdot, \cdot)$. If no feature is disclosed, it is obsolete to consider pseudonym disclosure.

ND3) The vertices $\tau_1$ and $\tau_2$ represent (a) transition(s) that use(s) a common operand, e.g. $\tau_1 = (\cdot, bvf, v, \cdot)$ and $\tau_2 = (\cdot, dv, v)$. If there is no common operand, no direct dependence w.r.t. disclosure can be derived by considering the two vertices alone.

If at least one of the necessary conditions is not satisfied, $\tau_1$ and $\tau_2$ will not be directly connected by an edge. There are two sufficient conditions, such that two vertices $\tau_1$ and $\tau_2$ are connected by an edge $(\tau_1, \tau_2)$:

SD1) The vertices represent two transitions, where the one transition indirectly reads a feature type with the help of the other transition, i.e. where the first transition directly reads a feature type and binds the feature to a common variable, before the second transition uses the variable value as an action parameter.

Expressed more concisely, if there are three vertices $\tau_a = (i_a, bvf, v, f_a)$, $\tau_b = (i_b, bvf, v, f_b)$ and $\tau_c = (i_c, dv, v)$, then $\tau_c$ is connected to $\tau_j \in \{\tau_a, \tau_b\}$, if the distance $d(i_j, i_c) = i_c - i_j$ is minimal and $d(i_j, i_c) > 0$. The transition represented by $\tau_c$ depends on the disclosure information for the pseudonym that is chosen for the feature when the transition represented by $\tau_j$ occurred. Note, that any vertex $(\cdot, dv, v)$ is connected to at most one vertex $(\cdot, bvf, v)$.

SD2) The vertices represent the same transition, where the one vertex directly reads a feature type and the other vertex uses the feature as a parameter for an action. Two combinations of vertices meet this condition: $\tau_1 = (i, bvf, v, \cdot), \tau_2 = (i, dv, v)$ and $\tau_1 = (i, bvf, \cdot, f), \tau_2 = (i, df, f)$. Note, that in both cases the pseudonym is directly disclosed by the IDS when transition $i$ occurs.

Concerning the above five conditions some remarks can be made. SD1 as well as SD2 implicitly satisfy ND1, ND2 and ND3. When listing all combinations of semantics of vertices that satisfy ND1, ND2 and ND3, the following pairs of vertices are not connected, as defined by SD1 and SD2:

- Two disclosure vertices $\tau_1 = (i, dv, v_1)$ and $\tau_2 = (i, dv, v_2)$ are not connected, because the variable values can be disclosed independently. However, both variables are disclosed simultaneously during the occurrence of the same transition $i$. The solution for disclosure proposed in Sect. 28.2 can take advantage of this fact.

  Owing to this property of the solution, the two vertices $\tau_1$ and $\tau_2$ are connected.

- Two disclosure vertices $\tau_2 = (i_2, dv, v)$ and $\tau_4 = (i_4, dv, v)$ with $i_2 < i_4$ are not connected, because it cannot be decided by considering only $\tau_2$ and $\tau_4$, whether the same value is assigned to $v$ for both vertices. We assume that there exists a vertex $\tau_1 = (i_1, bvf, v, \cdot)$ with $i_1 \leq i_2$. If there exists also a vertex $\tau_3 = (i_3, bvf, v, \cdot)$ with $i_2 < i_3 \leq i_4$, then the values assigned to $v$ must be disclosed independently for $\tau_2$ and $\tau_4$ and the vertices $\tau_2$ and $\tau_4$ must not be connected.

  If there exists no such $\tau_3$, the edge $(\tau_2, \tau_4)$ were redundant with the edges $(\tau_1, \tau_2)$ and $(\tau_1, \tau_4)$. Hence, no such connection is inserted in $H$. Even more importantly, in this case the pseudonym is disclosed at first by the transition represented by $\tau_2$. After its disclosure, there is no need to disclose the D-feature again for $\tau_4$, because the analysis engine can cache it. The algorithm described below accounts for this fact and removes the edge $(\tau_1, \tau_4)$. Note, that inserting an edge $(\tau_2, \tau_4)$ would sabotage the effect of removing $(\tau_1, \tau_4)$.

- If the token binding of a variable is performed after the variable is used in an action ($d < 0$), the use of the variable represents no indirect access of the feature, which is bound later on. Hence, no disclosure requirements exist for the common variable. Note, that for $d = 0$ both vertices represent the same transition. That is, the token binding is performed directly before the action is executed (see SD2).

Note, that all connected vertices in $H$ either use a common variable name or represent the same transition. Hence, all vertices of a given connected component of $H$ belong to the same serial signature-net.

Since $H$, as defined above, does not reflect the fact that the approach for pseudonym disclosure proposed in Sect. 28.2 can take advantage of already disclosed D-features, some further processing of $H$ is required. The goal is that vertices $\tau_1 = (i_1, bvf, v, \cdot)$, where exist $\tau_2 = (i_2, dv, v), \tau_3 = (i_3, dv, v)$, etc. with $i_1 \leq i_2 < i_3$, but no further $\tau_0 = (i_0, bvf, v, \cdot)$ with $i_2 < i_0 \leq i_3$ exists, are only considered in the connected component containing $\tau_2$ ($d(i_1, i_2) < d(i_1, i_3) <$ etc.), i.e. the edges $(\tau_1, \tau_3)$, etc. are removed from $H$. Then, the disclosure of $v$ is only performed for $\tau_2$ and the result is cached for $\tau_3$, etc.

This can be achieved by visiting all vertices $\tau_j = (i, d\cdot, \cdot)$ in ascending order for $i$, and by checking if there is a directly connected $\tau_k = (\cdot, bvf, \cdot, \cdot)$ and then removing all edges $(\tau_k, \tau_l), l \neq j$. Finally, all unconnected (spurious) vertices $(\cdot, dv, \cdot)$ and $(\cdot, bvf, \cdot, \cdot)$ are removed from $H$. As a result, the components of $H$ describe the D-features that need to be disclosed simultaneously when a certain disclosure transition occurs. Note, that $H$ may still contain unconnected vertices $(\cdot, df, \cdot)$.

Consider the example serial signature-net $n_1$ in Fig. 25.4 without a marking. The token binding of $t_1$ in Fig. 25.4 is represented by $\tau_3 = (1, bvf, (n_1, v), (e_1, oid))$ in Fig. 28.1 and the action of $t_2$ is represented by $\tau_4 = (2, dv, (n_1, v))$. Note, that the transition identifiers have been chosen in accordance with Fig. 27.1. Moreover, the variable names have been extended with the signature identifier and the feature types are combinations of event types and feature names. The vertices $\tau_3$ and $\tau_4$ satisfy the sufficient condition SD1 and therefore are connected. Note, that the vertices do not satisfy SD2. For all pseudonyms for feature types in a connected component of the graph $H$ the information for their simultaneous disclosure must be provided when the transition occurs, where the feature is pseudonymized, i.e. when transition $t_1$ represented by $\tau_3$ occurs.

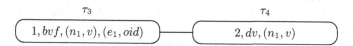

$\tau_3$                                         $\tau_4$

$1, bvf, (n_1, v), (e_1, oid)$           $2, dv, (n_1, v)$

**Fig. 28.1.** A disclosure graph for the serial signature-net in Fig. 25.4

## 28.2 Primitives for Technical Purpose Binding of Disclosure

We shortly recapitulate the definitions of the terms that are relevant for technical purpose binding of pseudonym disclosure from the set-based approach in Part II in order to point out the differences of the approach proposed here. Section 12.1 defines a *disclosure scenario* as activity that warrants pseudonym disclosure. A disclosure scenario is modeled as a *disclosure context*, which is a set of weighted observations of activity from the respective disclosure scenario. The *activity level* of a disclosure context is the sum of the weights of the observations that are relevant for the disclosure context. The activity level is determined for each distinct feature in a disclosure context. Finally, the *disclosure condition* is defined as the transgression of a threshold on the activity level of a feature in the disclosure context. If the disclosure condition is met for a given feature in a given disclosure context, then only the pseudonym of that feature can be disclosed. Note, that a disclosure scenario does not necessarily match a misuse scenario, if the misuse detection approach supports more elaborate models of misuse scenarios, such as signature-nets.

The above model of disclosure scenarios is refined and redefined, such that a *disclosure scenario* exactly matches a misuse scenario. Here, the *disclosure context* is defined as a (partial) complex event that can be detected using a serial signature-net, which evaluates observations of activity from the respective misuse scenario (the definitions for observations in Sect. 12.1.1 still apply). The *activity level* of a disclosure context is the number of non-escape transitions that have occurred in the serial signature-net due to the token that represents the (partial) complex event, i.e. the number of steps of the (partial) complex event that have been bound to observed events. The *disclosure condition* is defined as the occurrence of a disclosure transition due to the token that represents the (partial) complex event. A serial signature-net may contain one or more disclosure transitions. With respect to pseudonym disclosure each distinct path from the initial place to a disclosure transition is considered as a separate disclosure context that is associated with the token. Hence, a token is associated with one ore more disclosure contexts, if there are one or more disclosure transitions in the serial signature-net. Each disclosure condition can be regarded as the transgression of a threshold on the activity level of a token in an associated disclosure context. If a given token activates a disclosure transition, and if the transition occurs, all pseudonyms of D-features that are parameters of the action of this transition shall be disclosed simultaneously. That is, only those pseudonyms shall be disclosed that are associated with the disclosure context that corresponds to the disclosure transition. Pseudonyms of D-features that are associated with other disclosure contexts of that token shall not be disclosed. Moreover, pseudonyms in other tokens also shall not be disclosed.

### 28.2.1 Simulating Set-based Disclosure Context with Serial Signature-nets

Any disclosure context defined according to the set-based approach from Part II (all weights equal 1, repetition of events is significant, events cannot be reconciled) with $N$ distinct feature types $f_i, i = 1, \ldots, N$ and a threshold $t$ can be expressed as $N^t$ disclosure contexts based on distinct serial signature-nets with $t$ transitions each. Note, that all $f_i$ refer to the same concept, e.g. user name, IP address. If repetition of events is considered insignificant, there are only $\frac{N!}{(N-t)!}$ distinct serial signature-nets. Each transition of these serial signature-nets is labeled with an $e_i$, where $e_i$ is the event type implied by $f_i = \langle e_i, d_i \rangle$ ($d_i$: feature designator). The first transition $t_1$ binds an $f_{i_1}$ to a variable $v$, which is used as a parameter of the action of the last transition $t_t$. The intra-event condition of all $t_j, j = 1, \ldots, t$ is *true*.[2] The inter-event condition of each $t_j, j = 2, \ldots, t$

---

[2] Note, that the implementation in Part III allows for expressing intra-event conditions as part of the regular expression matching the event type. For the simulation we assume that the intra-event condition is also expressed as part of the event type.

restricts transition activation such that the feature for $f_{i_j}$ equals the value of $v$. If the disclosure condition of the set-based disclosure context is met, also the disclosure condition of one of the serial signature-nets is met. Thereafter, the feature assigned to $v$ is considered disclosed. The set-based disclosure context is represented by the set of disclosure contexts of the serial signature-nets.

Given a set of serial signature-nets that simulates a set-based disclosure context, it is obvious that serial signature-nets allow for more fine-grained disclosure context than the set-based model. Intuitively, we can refine the granularity by removing arbitrary serial signature-nets from the simulation set. Yet, the basic idea for technical purpose binding of pseudonym disclosure described in Sect. 13.3 can be applied (see below).

### 28.2.2 Requirements for Threshold Schemes

For the approach in Part II the set-based definition of disclosure context allowed to apply pseudonym disclosure to subsets of the original audit data. This is a useful property, for example if it is not desired to make the whole audit data available or if it is too expensive to process the whole audit data. In these cases audit records are filtered out, and pseudonym disclosure can be applied to the remaining audit data. For this to work, it is necessary that for a given feature a virtually unlimited number of shares can be generated using the threshold scheme for secret sharing associated with the feature in a given disclosure context. Shamir's threshold scheme has been selected in Sect. 13.3 because it has this property in addition to other desirable properties [200].

However, the requirements are slightly different for the serial signature-net-based definition of disclosure contexts. Due to the semantic expressiveness of such disclosure contexts, pseudonym disclosure is not as robust against filtering of arbitrary audit records. Aside from this, a set-based definition of disclosure contexts allows for virtually unlimited observations for a given feature in a given disclosure context, while a definition based on serial signature-nets restricts the relevant observations to a known fixed number per token. However, the number of tokens is virtually unlimited. Hence, the number of threshold schemes associated with tokens is virtually unlimited. As a result, for the approach proposed here, it is not necessary that the threshold scheme allows to generate a virtually unlimited number of shares for a given secret.

### 28.2.3 Naïve Application of Threshold Schemes

Since there is no need to generate a virtually unlimited number of shares per threshold scheme, further options are available to choose candidate threshold schemes [159]. Aside from generating an arbitrary number of shares, the threshold scheme proposed by Karnin, Greene and Hellman (KGH) offers the same advantageous properties as Shamir's threshold scheme (ideal, perfect, cf. Sect. 13.3)[3] and can be implemented even more efficiently [126] (see Sect. A.2). The KGH threshold scheme can be implemented using a pseudo-random number generator and operators for addition and subtraction of big numbers. Managing, evaluating, manipulating and interpolating polynomials is not necessary in the KGH threshold scheme. As a result, in the KGH threshold scheme all important operations can be carried out very efficiently (share generation, share invalidation, secret recovery).

We briefly summarize how Shamir's threshold scheme is used in Part II to provide information for pseudonym disclosure, and then we describe how the KGH threshold scheme is used here. Note, that instead of the KGH threshold scheme here also the less efficient Shamir threshold scheme could be used. The way threshold schemes are used in the following, both schemes – KGH and Shamir – provide protection of secrets in an equally secure way.

In Part II for a given observed feature type $f$ the disclosure contexts $I_g$ are determined where $f$ is relevant, as well as the weights $w_{f,g}$ of the observation of $f$ in each of the disclosure contexts. For each of the determined disclosure contexts exists a separate threshold scheme for the observed feature, which is used to generate the next $w_{f,g}$ shares. There is virtually no limit to the number of shares generated from a given threshold scheme, if the feature is repeatedly observed.

Here, threshold schemes are tied to tokens in the marking of serial signature-nets. Assuming that all transitions in a serial signature-net are consuming transitions, a given token starts out at the initial place and each time a non-escape transition occurs the activity level w.r.t. to that token increases by 1, until a disclosure transition occurs, i.e. the disclosure condition is met. A straightforward approach is implementing each disclosure context as a KGH threshold scheme that is associated with a token. The secret protected by the scheme is the decryption key that is needed to decrypt the D-features for pseudonym disclosure. Each time a transition in the serial signature-net occurs for the token a share is generated and provided in the pseudonymity-layer. The scheme is chosen such that the threshold corresponds to the occurrence of the disclosure transition in the disclosure context. If D-features are directly accessed by the disclosure transition, the threshold would have to be chosen to be 1, which is pointless. In this case the affected original D-features are provided in the pseudonymity-layer instead of a share.

With this construction each disclosure context associated with a token is processed individually, i.e. the disclosure in one disclosure context does not affect other disclosure contexts. If a disclosure condition is satisfied, all D-features that are parameters to the action of the disclosure context can be disclosed simul-

---

[3] The KGH threshold scheme also supports the notion of weights. However, this property is not used by the definition of disclosure contexts based on serial signature-nets.

taneously using the recovered decryption key. If a token is removed due to the occurrence of an escape transition the associated threshold schemes are also removed. Since the threshold of the removed schemes will never be exceeded, the D-features will not be disclosed by means of these schemes.

## 28.2.4 Elaborate Application of Threshold Schemes

The assumption that all transitions of a serial signature-net are consuming transitions is a strong restriction. This restriction is removed in the following by appropriately extending the use of threshold schemes.

If a transition $t$ occurs that is connected with a non-consuming edge to the input place, the input token $o$ is not removed and can later still serve as input for the transition. Each time $t$ occurs, a copy of $o$ is generated in the output place. Because these copies might be extended by the token bindings of $t$ or later transitions, we denote them as *child tokens*, while $o$ is denoted as their *parent token*. Child tokens that originate from the same parent token are denoted as *sibling tokens*. The child tokens are associated with copies of the threshold schemes that are associated with the parent token $o$. Consequently, if one of the child tokens of $o$ activates a disclosure transition, all D-features associated with the threshold scheme for this transition are disclosed. This is not a problem as long as the child tokens have not bound newer D-features than the parent token. In that case the D-feature pseudonyms that are disclosed for a child token are linkable with the pseudonyms in the parent and sibling tokens. Hence, if the disclosure of one child token allows the disclosure of the same pseudonyms in the parent and sibling tokens no information is divulged that exceeds the information already provided via pseudonym linkability.

But, if the child tokens contain D-features that the parent token does not contain, these newer D-features can be disclosed simultaneously in all sibling tokens, even if only one child token activates a disclosure transition. This is clearly undesirable; the newer D-features in the other sibling tokens should remain confidential.

A straightforward solution to this problem is to modify the disclosure context that is associated with a child token, if the parent token is accessed via a non-consuming edge. In this solution each child token will be assigned an individual disclosure context, such that the disclosure contexts of all sibling tokens are different. This solution is optimal, if we ignore the information that pseudonym linkability provides (see above).

If we take the information provided by pseudonym linkability into account, the solution proposed above creates different disclosure contexts regardless of the fact that some of the pseudonyms for sibling tokens are linkable. Even if the disclosure of the pseudonyms for one token does not allow to disclose the pseudonyms of the sibling tokens, pseudonym linkability allows to infer, which of the disclosed D-features are also present in the sibling tokens. Considering these circumstances, a more efficient solution must take into account the location of non-consuming input edges as well as of subsequent token bindings of D-features.

The revised solution is based on the idea that disclosure contexts for tokens in a serial signature-net are partitioned where on the right hand side of a non-consuming edge the nearest D-feature bindings are located. Note, that the partitioning may be different for each disclosure context, because the relevant D-feature bindings may be located differently. Each partition is represented by an individual threshold scheme. For each partition a virtually unlimited number of such schemes can be generated on demand to be associated with copies of child tokens that exist due to the non-consuming edge. The schemes for neighboring partitions are inter-connected in a tree structure, where each path from the root of the tree to the leaves represents a distinct disclosure context for an individual token. New child nodes in the tree are generated each time a child token binds a D-feature for the first time. The new child node is a sibling of the threshold schemes of its sibling tokens. Some example trees are shown in Fig. 28.3.

The way the schemes are inter-connected warrants that for each distinct disclosure context the D-features, which were accessed on that path, can be disclosed, but no D-features that were not accessed on that path. The secrets for schemes in the first partition are chosen pseudo-randomly ($s^1 := r()$), such that all tokens start with a distinct scheme. This design decision reflects the fact that the first edge of all (serial) signature-nets is a non-consuming edge. Due to this initialization, the first edge does not need to be considered as a non-consuming edge in the following.

The schemes for the last partition are chosen such that the last share corresponds to the occurrence of the disclosure transition that is associated with the given disclosure context. If there are no non-consuming edges on the left-hand side of some D-feature bindings, then the first and the last partition are the same, i.e. the construction works as described in Sect. 28.2.3. The inter-connection of parent and child schemes is shown in Fig. 28.2.

If there is a D-feature binding on the right-hand side of a non-consuming edge, the current partition reaches up to the predecessor transition and the next partition starts with the transition that binds the D-feature(s). The current partition $i$ and the next partition $i + 1$ are represented by threshold schemes that are inter-connected as follows. The threshold $t^i$ of the current scheme is increased by 1, such that there is an additional share $s_{t^i}^i$.[4] The share $s_{t^i}^i$ is not associated with any transition and is never provided in the pseudonymity-layer during pseudonymization. Instead, $s_{t^i}^i$ serves as the secret $s^{i+1}$ of the child schemes. As a result, the secret $s^i$ of the current scheme can only be recovered if the shares $s_1^i, \ldots, s_{t^i-1}^i$ are extracted from the pseudonymity-layer and the share $s_{t^i}^i = s^{i+1}$ has been recovered from one of the child schemes. Thus, all child schemes can benefit from the same parent scheme, while all sibling schemes can be chosen

---

[4] Note, that superscript here denotes the partition index (not the exponentiation operation).

differently. Section 28.3 describes the details of disclosure context partitioning and appropriate threshold scheme generation.

The disclosure information $E(k^i, F)$ is provided when a given D-feature $F$ is pseudonymized in the $i^{th}$ partition. The encryption key is chosen such that $k^i = s^1 \oplus s^i_{t_i}$. Note, that even though all sibling schemes in partition $i$ use the same secret $s^i = s^{i-1}_{t_{i-1}}$, the sibling schemes are chosen differently, such that $s^i_{t_i}$ differs with high probability for all sibling schemes. The component $s^1$ ensures that the whole path of threshold schemes from a given leaf node to the root node of the tree must be available to be able to recover $k^i$, and the component $s^i_{t_i}$ warrants that there is with high probability an individual $k^i$ for each token in partition $i$.

## 28.2.5 Extensions

For the set-based approach in Part II several extensions have been developed in Chap. 16. In the following, each extension is briefly examined to determine whether it can still be applied or is already subsumed by the more elaborate approach.

The extension in Sect. 16.1 additionally protects the secrets of threshold schemes by encrypting them. Only the reidentifier knows the corresponding decryption keys, such that only he can use the recovered secrets. External observers can recover the encrypted secrets, but cannot decrypt and use the secrets. This extension can also be used here to encrypt the decryption key $k^i$. Alternatively, the pseudonymity-layer data could be transmitted over an encrypted channel from the pseudonymizer to the IDS.

Section 16.2 introduces dummy data in the pseudonym mapping to make it harder to determine the number of actors in an observed system. The extension in Sect. 16.2 is only effective, if the shares are unlinkable. It must be considered that there is a linkage between shares in the pseudonymity-layer and pseudonyms in the application-layer. For the implementation in Part III the pseudonymity-layer data is linkable within disclosure contexts, and the application-layer pseudonyms may be specified to be linkable. Also, for the more elaborate approach there is a linkage between the shares in the pseudonymity-layer data and the application layer pseudonyms. Hence, the precondition for the extension to work does also not hold for the refined approach.

The extension in Sect. 16.3 has been used for mismatch avoidance in the implementation of the set-based approach. The extension proposes to use the cryptograms of features as labels for shares from the same threshold scheme. This however does not work for the approach based on serial signature-nets, because disclosure contexts are not associated with the feature types, but with distinct tokens. An appropriate solution is described in Sect. 28.4.

To overcome the limitations of a set-based definition of disclosure contexts it has been proposed in Sect. 16.4 to make disclosure contexts (in-)sensitive to the repetition of certain events. This extension has also been implemented. The expressiveness of serial signature-nets subsumes this extension.

Another important extension concerns the expressiveness of set-based disclosure contexts and has also been implemented. The extension in Sect. 16.5 is based on the observation that the activity level of a disclosure context may degrade over time or when certain events occur. This notion of forgetting and garbage collection is modeled in serial signature-nets with the help of escape places and time stamp features for time-outs. Hence, if a token is removed, the associated threshold schemes are discarded, such that their secrets cannot be recovered. Hence, there is no need for share invalidation (cf. Sect. 16.5.1) in the serial signature-net-based approach.

Finally, the extension in Sect. 16.6 integrates organizational purpose binding for pseudonym disclosure with the set-based approach. The same solutions can be used here (see Sect. 16.6.1 and Sect. 16.6.2). The notion of escrow data is integrated in Sect. 28.4.2.

Wrapping up the results, the extensions to overcome limitations of the set-based model are obsolete in the approach based on serial signature-nets, the trick used to label shares is not applicable and the extensions that strengthen the system against external observers and that allow for organizational purpose binding of pseudonym disclosure are easily integrated. An extension for coarsening the number of actors is not directly applicable.

## 28.3 Extracting Threshold Scheme Descriptions

For each disclosure context the partitioning can be extracted efficiently from a given serial signature-net. First, the connected components of the disclosure requirements graph $H$ (see Sect. 28.1) are determined [168]. The connected components containing one or more $(\cdot, dv, \cdot)$-vertices represent the disclosure contexts for which partitions need to be determined. Each of these connected components is associated with a control block that is used to collect information about the structure of the serial signature-net. The *control block* comprises a partition counter that identifies the partition that is currently examined (initial value: 1), a transition counter that contains the number of transitions that have been examined in the current partition (initial value: 0), a boolean flag that signifies whether one of the transitions counted for the current partition is connected to a non-consuming edge (initial value: *false*), and the transition identifier where the currently examined partition starts. Finally, the control block contains a boolean flag signaling whether the disclosure context has been completely partitioned, such that no further inspection is necessary for this disclosure context (initial value: *false*).

After the initialization of the control blocks for the disclosure contexts the given serial signature-net is examined (in linear time), starting from the first transition up to the last transition. Before a transition is examined, it is checked if all disclosure contexts are already completely partitioned. If that is the case, the algorithm terminates.

When examining the current transition, firstly the transition counters in the control blocks for all not yet completely partitioned disclosure contexts are incremented to account for the current transition. Then, it is determined whether the current transition is connected to a non-consuming input edge and if so, the corresponding flag is set to the value *true* in all control blocks of all incomplete disclosure context partitionings. As described in Sect. 28.2.4 the non-consuming edge that is connected to the initial place is ignored, i.e. considered to be a consuming input edge, because it is specially considered when creating the scheme description for the first partition (see below).

If the current transition executes an action that uses variable parameters, any corresponding vertex in $H$ is determined. For the control block that is associated with the connected component that contains this vertex a scheme description for the current partition is created (see below). Since the current transition represents the disclosure of the disclosure context, its partitioning is complete. The corresponding flag is set to the value *true* in the control block.

If a non-consuming edge has been seen, it is determined if the current transition (also) performs (a) token binding(s) on D-features. First, in $H$ the $(\cdot, bvf, \cdot, \cdot)$-vertices representing the D-feature token binding(s) are located. Then, for each connected component that contains such a vertex the associated control block is determined. For each such control block of an incomplete disclosure context partitioning a scheme description is created (see below). Since the current transition starts a new partition, the partition counter is incremented, the transition counter is set to the value 1 accounting for the current transition in the new partition. The identifier of the current transition is stored in the control block as the starting point of the new partition, and the edge flag is reset to the value *false*. Note, that the current transition is considered in the scheme description of the former partition as the connecting share/secret inter-connecting both partitions (cf. Sect. 28.2.4).

Note, that for transitions that perform D-feature token bindings and that also execute actions with variable parameters both of the above cases apply. After the examination of the current transition, the next transition is examined.

A *scheme description* for a partition describes the structure of threshold schemes that are created on demand for a given partition of a given disclosure context. If for a given disclosure context and a given partition no scheme description has already been created, a scheme description is initialized and filled out using the data from the corresponding control block. The scheme description comprises the following information:

- The number of the partition $i$ of the disclosure context for which the description is valid. This number is taken from the current value of the partition counter.

- The threshold $t^i$ of the threshold schemes. This number is taken from the current value of the transition counter.

  If the current partition is the last partition of the disclosure context, the transition counter describes the number of shares that represent the transitions in this partition.

  If the current partition is not the last partition of the disclosure context, the transition counter includes the number of shares that represent the transitions in the current partition plus an additional share that connects this scheme to its child schemes. Note, that the first partition of a disclosure context may also be its last partition.

- A function that determines how the secret for the threshold scheme must be chosen.

  If the current partition is the first partition of the disclosure context, the secret is chosen pseudo-randomly: $s^1 := r()$. This accounts for the fact that the edge connected to the initial place of each serial signature-net is a non-consuming transition [149]. Hence, it is ensured that each token is associated with an individual set of distinct threshold schemes.

  If the current partition is not the first partition of the disclosure context, the secret is chosen to be the last share of the parent scheme that was generated for the previous partition: $s^i := s^{i-1}_{t^{i-1}}$.

- A function that determines how the shares must be chosen that represent the transitions of the current partition. All but the last share are chosen pseudo-randomly: $s^i_j := r(), j = 1, \ldots, t^i - 1$. Due to the nature of the KGH threshold scheme, the last share is chosen to be $s^i_{t^i} := s^i - \sum_{j=1}^{t^i-1} s^i_j$.

  If the current partition is the last partition of the disclosure context, all $t^i$ shares represent the transitions in the disclosure context.

  If the current partition is not the last partition of the disclosure context, the last share is never provided in the pseudonymity-layer, but is used as the secret $s^{i+1}$ of the child schemes. This share connects the generated scheme to its child schemes in a tree structure.

  Note, that this step can be adapted to fit Shamir's threshold scheme. The shares are chosen as usually, creating a pseudo-random polynomial that is evaluated at arbitrary, but distinct points.

For the example serial signature-net $n_2$ in Fig. 28.2 the disclosure requirements graph $H$ is depicted with its connected components for the disclosure transitions $t_4$ and $t_6$. The escape transitions and escape places of $n_2$ are not shown in Fig. 28.2. Each connected component represents a disclosure context. For the disclosure contexts for $t_4$ and $t_6$ the partitions are shown as well as the scheme description for each partition. It can be seen that the partitionings for the both disclosure contexts are different, due to the different locations of the relevant

D-feature bindings $(t_2, t_3)$. Note, that the binding of $f_2$ is associated only with the disclosure context of the nearest disclosure transition $(t_4)$. Moreover, non-D-feature token bindings are completely ignored ($v_1 := f_1, v_4 := f_4, v_5 := f_5$). Therefore, the non-consuming input edge of $t_5$ does not have any effect on the partitioning.

A scheme and its shares are generated on demand using the appropriate scheme description. The light-grey boxes in Fig. 28.2 comprise the elements of a scheme description for a partition. The parameters on grey background are used to determine the location of a scheme in the serial signature-net (see *start* in Fig. 28.2), to determine its threshold (see *threshold* in Fig. 28.2) and to generate its secret (see $s^i$ in Fig. 28.2). These parameters are never inserted in the pseudonymity-layer. In contrast, the white fields show the shares that are generated in correspondence to the transition occurrences. These shares are inserted in the pseudonymity-layer when the corresponding transitions occur. The secret of child schemes is chosen to be the last share of the parent scheme, such that all child schemes are interconnected with their parent schemes (see the dashed lines in Fig. 28.2). This share is also not provided in the pseudonymity-layer.

The black frames in Fig. 28.2 show the components for encryption key generation for disclosure information about D-feature token bindings. From each scheme the last share is used in conjunction with the secret of the first scheme. The last share ensures that the key for all schemes is different with high probability, while the secret of the first scheme ensures that all transitions on the path from the initial place to the disclosure transition have occurred for the token. Note, that due to the way the schemes are inter-connected, the secret of the first scheme can only be recovered if all shares for the transitions on the path are available.

The scheme descriptions for the partitions of the disclosure contexts of the serial signature-net $n_2$ from Fig. 28.2 are instantiated by the pseudonymizer, if there is a marking for $n_2$. Figure 28.3 depicts an example marking for $n_2$ (the transition labels, escape transitions and escape places are not shown). The marking comprises 8 tokens, where the tokens 2 and 3 are child tokens w.r.t. token 1 due to the non-consuming input edge of $t_1$. Furthermore, due to the non-consuming input edge of $t_2$ the tokens 4 and 5 are child tokens w.r.t. token 2, and the tokens 6 and 7 are child tokens w.r.t. token 3. Finally, due to the non-consuming input edge of $t_5$, token 8 is a child token w.r.t. token 7.

Each token – except for token 1 from the initial marking – is associated with its own threshold scheme (see the token symbols next to the threshold schemes in Fig. 28.3). For the instantiated schemes the meaning of the white fields is slightly different in Fig. 28.3. Here, they show the shares that have already been used, because the corresponding transition has already occurred for the token that is associated with the scheme. In the example the threshold schemes are calculated modulo $P = 100$.

For the marking in Fig. 28.3 several noteworthy remarks can be made. First, there is no one-to-one relationship between the schemes associated to parent

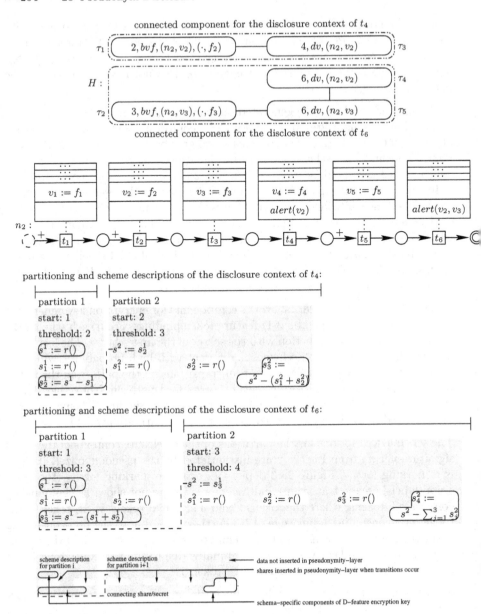

**Fig. 28.2.** Example disclosure contexts with partitioning and scheme descriptions

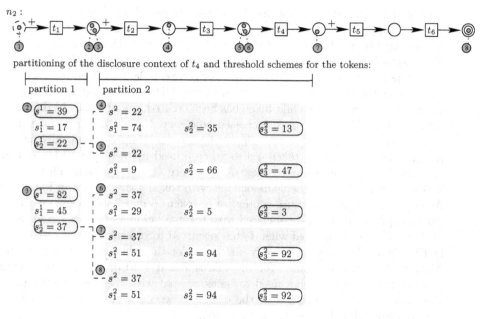

partitioning of the disclosure context of $t_4$ and threshold schemes for the tokens:

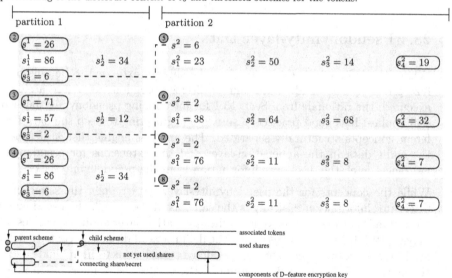

partitioning of the disclosure context of $t_6$ and threshold schemes for the tokens:

**Fig. 28.3.** Example disclosure contexts with instantiated threshold schemes

tokens and to their child tokens. For example, the child token 4 uses a copy of the scheme for its parent token 2 in the disclosure context of $t_6$. The same applies for the child token 8 of the parent token 7 in both disclosure contexts. The reason is that disclosure contexts are sensitive only to child tokens that may have different D-feature bindings, as justified in Sect. 28.2.4. Thus, child schemes are only generated from scratch where the first D-feature binding occurs in a disclosure context after a child token has been created, e.g. at $t_3$ for the disclosure context of $t_6$. The result is an increased efficiency, because fewer schemes need to be created from scratch and more schemes can simply be copied from the parent token. Second, as token 4 also token 5 used its own copy of the scheme of token 2 in the disclosure context of $t_6$ before $t_3$ has occurred. This scheme looked exactly like the scheme associated with token 4 (not shown in Fig. 28.3). Analogously, in the disclosure context of $t_6$ tokens 6 and 7 were each associated with a copy of the scheme associated with token 3 before $t_3$ occurred, and the $s_2^1$ of these schemes were used when $t_2$ has occurred for tokens 6 and 7 (not shown in Fig. 28.3). Third, since already all shares for the schemes for the disclosure context of $t_4$ have been used for the tokens 7 and 8, in order to save space in practice the schemes do not need to be associated with these tokens any more. The same applies to token 8 in the disclosure context of $t_6$. Token 8 will be removed immediately after $t_6$ has occurred.

## 28.4 Pseudonymity-layer Data

While the IDS analysis engine needs to be slightly extended to be able to analyze pseudonymous audit data and to disclose pseudonyms before actions are executed, the rationale from Sect. 13.1 for introducing pseudonymity-layer data still applies. It is good practice of software engineering to keep the data for different concepts structurally separated. The analysis engine then still processes the audit data in the application-layer and the extensions for pseudonymity-awareness fetch the disclosure information from the pseudonymity-layer.

While the concepts for the pseudonymity-layer data remain the same and the disclosure information basically is the same as in Sect. 19.2, the pseudonymity-layer data is not tied to the events in the application-layer audit data as described in Sect. 19.2.1. Instead, in Sect. 28.2 the definitions of disclosure context, activity level and disclosure condition tie pseudonym disclosure to individual tokens in the marking of the serial signature-nets. Hence, disclosure information must be tied to individual tokens in a way that can be computed by the pseudonymizer as well as by the analysis engine.

We firstly review the characterizing features of an individual token in the marking of a serial signature-net. In the second step we design a compact representation of these features, such that information about the tokens is concealed and such that it can be computed efficiently. A given token in the marking of a serial signature-net $n$ is characterized by the place where it resides in $n$ and by the values that are assigned to its variables. In serial signature-nets a given place where a token resides is equivalent with the sequence of transitions that have occurred, such that the token has been generated in that place. Albeit the history of token bindings for the token provides slightly more information than the current variable-value assignment, it can serve the same objective. Hence, a token can be characterized by the following features: the sequence of transitions that occurred for the token (or its parent tokens such that the token was generated) and the sequence of variable-value assignments due to token bindings. Note, that the sequence of transitions uses transition identifiers, which are a global name space w.r.t. all serial signature-nets.

While this information could be used as a token identifier, it certainly is sub-optimal in space and therefore cost for locating the identifier, as well as w.r.t. the confidentiality of the state of the serial signature-nets. Note, that the latter property here is considered undesirable, but it may as well be leveraged such that the IDS analysis engine can take advantage of the analysis state computed by the pseudonymizer, saving computation time on the side of the IDS. A more compact and concealing representation can be achieved by using a cryptographic collision-resistant hash-function $h()$ to digest the features of a token identifier into a single value. The size of the resulting value must be chosen appropriately, considering a reasonable upper bound for the number of tokens that are expected during day-to-day operation.[5]

Cryptographic hash-functions can be applied repeatedly to their own output $b_{i-1}$ while using additional input data $c_i$, such that $b_i = h(b_{i-1}|c_i), b_0 = \epsilon$. The result is that $c_1, \ldots, c_i$ are represented by $b_i$. As long as no collision occurs, this value can only be regenerated by using the same input in each round [154].

This property can be leveraged by the pseudonymizer to initialize the identifier $o$ for the tokens with a known fixed value, e.g. $o := NULL$. When a token is the input to an occurring transition, the hash-function can be applied to the token identifier $o_{in}$ of the input token together with the transition identifier $l$ as well as the variable-value assignments $v_1 : p_1, \ldots, v_k : p_k$, such that $o_{out} := h(o_{in}|l|v_1 : p_1|\ldots|v_k : p_k)$.

The values $p_i$ must be available to the pseudonymizer and the analysis engine. For pseudonymized features the $p_i$ are the corresponding pseudonyms. Consequently, if the pseudonymizer and the analysis engine use the same serial signature-nets and use the same pseudonymized audit data for token identifier generation, then the analysis engine can associate a token identifier (as provided by the pseudonymizer) with the corresponding token in the markings of its serial signature-nets.

---

[5] The occurrence of collisions of $h()$ could be exploited to incapacitate pseudonym disclosure. Hence, this issue warrants closer examination.

### 28.4.1 Organizational Purpose Binding of Pseudonym Disclosure

Some remarks need to be made with respect to organizational purpose binding of pseudonym disclosure. As motivated in Sect. 16.6, organizational purpose binding can be useful if

1. a feature would be disclosed immediately, or if

2. some misuse scenario might occur, which has not been modeled.

For the first case, D-features that would be disclosed immediately can be determined automatically using the graph $H$: A feature type is directly accessed and disclosed by the same transition. Instead of providing the disclosure information for such D-features in the clear, it can be protected by organizational purpose binding. However, the PPO needs to specify a priori that this shall happen.

In the second case, it is by definition impossible to extract the information, which features could warrant disclosure subject to organizational purpose binding, because the serial signature-net is missing, from which the information would be extracted. Thus, in this case the PPO (together with the SSO) manually specifies a priori, which of the pseudonymized features might warrant disclosure subject to organizational purpose binding.

Note, that the control requirements for pseudonym disclosure subject to organizational purpose binding must comply with Fig. 8.6a, irrespective of the control requirements for pseudonym disclosure subject to technical purpose binding depicted in Fig. 26.1.

### 28.4.2 Disclosure Information

Disclosure information is tied to a given token by labeling it with the token identifier. The disclosure information comprises the following elements:

$\langle v, p, E(k^i, F) \rangle$: For D-feature token bindings where the variable is used in a later disclosure transition, e.g. $\tau_1 = (i, bvf, v, f)$ connected to $\tau_2 = (j, dv, v)$ and $i < j$ (see condition SD1 in Sect. 28.1). The name of the token variable $v$ and the encrypted D-feature $F$ are provided. The encryption/decryption key $k^i$ is chosen as described in Sect. 28.2.4.

In addition to the token variable name, also the pseudonym $p$ of $F$ is provided. Using $p$, the cryptograms and shares can be easily associated with the application-layer audit data, such that pseudonym disclosure could be performed independently from audit data analysis, e.g. using a separate tool that does not analyze the audit data, but merely discloses as many pseudonyms as possible. Note, that this may have practical merit in certain environments, while in other environments it may be undesirable.

$\langle v, p, F \rangle$: For D-features that are directly read from the audit data and assigned to a variable that is disclosed by the same transition, such that the analysis engine would disclose the pseudonym immediately, e.g. $\tau_1 = (i, bvf, v, f)$ connected to $\tau_2 = (i, dv, v)$ or $\tau_2 = (i, df, f)$ (see condition SD2 in Sect. 28.1). The name of the token variable and the D-feature clear-text $F$ are provided.

Concerning the provision of $p$ the remark from above applies. If $F$ shall not be provided in the clear, it can be replaced by the escrow data as defined below.

$\langle p, F \rangle$: For D-features that are directly read from the audit data and are disclosed by the same transition without being assigned to a variable, e.g. $\tau_2 = (i, df, f)$ not connected to any $\tau_1 = (i, bvf, v, f)$ in $H$.

Note, that $p$ cannot be omitted here. If $F$ should not be provided in the clear, it can be replaced by the escrow data as defined below.

$\langle p, E(\tilde{k}_o, F) \rangle$: Organizational purpose binding for pseudonym disclosure can be easily added to the disclosure information. The respective feature $F$ is encrypted using an escrow key $\tilde{k}_o$. For the details on the cryptographic enforcement of organizational purpose binding refer to Sect. 16.6.1 and Sect. 16.6.2. Note, that $F$ takes the place of $s_i$ here.[6]

Pseudonym disclosure can be subject to organizational purpose binding, independently of the fact that it is already subject to technical purpose binding. In case (2) (see above) a pseudonym $p$ can be specified to be disclosed even in the absence of actions. Then, $\langle p, E(\tilde{k}_o, F) \rangle$ is provided in the pseudonymity-layer. Note, that $p$ cannot be omitted here.

Disclosure w.r.t. organizational purpose binding can also be used in addition to technical purpose binding, such that $\langle v, p, E(k^i, F), E(\tilde{k}_o, F) \rangle$ is provided. Also, instead of immediately disclosing certain D-features, disclosure can be subject to organizational purpose binding if we use $\langle v, p, E(\tilde{k}_o, F) \rangle$ or $\langle p, E(\tilde{k}_o, F) \rangle$ (see case (1) above).

$\langle m, s_j^i \rangle$: If a transition occurs, for each disclosure context the identifier $m$ of the respective disclosure transition is provided to identify the disclosure context, as well as the share $s_j^i$ from the threshold scheme currently associated with the disclosure context, where $s_j^i$ corresponds to the occurring transition.

Since the shares are labeled with the token identifier, the analysis engine can keep track of the shares belonging to the same threshold scheme of a disclosure context that is associated with the corresponding token. This mechanism implements the idea of mismatch avoidance (cf. Sect. 14.3.2), such that the mismatch problem described in Chap. 14 is not an issue.

Section 28.5 describes how the pseudonymizer actually generates the pseudonymity-layer data for given application-layer audit data.

---

[6] $E(\tilde{k}_o, k^i)$ cannot be used because $k^i$ protects all D-features within the disclosure context $i$. However, merely $F$ shall be disclosed.

## 28.5 Operation of the Pseudonymizer

In the following, the operation of the pseudonymizer is described. While it would be possible to consider pseudonym disclosure independently from pseudonymization, providing disclosure information for unpseudonymized audit data seems to be pointless. Thus, the operation of the pseudonymizer for pseudonymization with pseudonym linkability subject to technical purpose binding is considered to be an integral part of the following description. The generation of pseudonyms in the application-layer data and of salts in the pseudonymity-layer data are only briefly referenced here. The required a priori knowledge for pseudonymization and the details on choosing appropriate pseudonyms are described in Sect. 27.3.

The pseudonymizer requires a specification of the format of pseudonymity-layer data. More importantly, the pseudonymizer needs to know a priori, which pseudonyms of D-features need to be disclosed subject to technical purpose binding and which features need to be disclosed subject to organizational purpose binding. As described in Sect. 28.4 the specification of the possibility for pseudonym disclosure subject to organizational purpose binding is provided manually for each feature type.

Unlike the set-based approach in Part II and Part III, here the pseudonymizer uses the same serial signature-nets as the IDS to determine, where pseudonym disclosure subject to technical purpose binding is necessary. While this knowledge is manually provided in the set-based approach, here it is automatically derived from the given models of misuse scenarios during initialization. To do this, the pseudonymizer constructs the graph $H$ as described in Sect. 28.1 and generates corresponding threshold scheme descriptions (see Sect. 28.3).

The pseudonymizer takes the original audit data as its input and outputs the pseudonymized audit data as well as the pseudonymity-layer data. During operation the pseudonymizer processes the next audit record from the queue of incoming audit records, just like the IDS. The processing differs moderately from the processing of the analysis engine of the IDS. Using the a priori knowledge, the pseudonymizer additionally locates features that need to be pseudonymized and determines, which of the pseudonyms need to be disclosed. Then, the pseudonymizer carefully generates appropriate pseudonyms and provides the corresponding disclosure information. After inserting the disclosure information in the pseudonymity-layer data, and after replacing the original features with the corresponding pseudonyms, the pseudonymizer forwards the pseudonymized audit data and the pseudonymity-layer data to the IDS. That is, the pseudonymizer does not execute actions when (partial) complex events occur.

Pseudonym disclosure requires some additional state. Since pseudonym disclosure is tied to individual tokens, each token is associated with its own token extension. A token extension comprises the following elements:

- the token identifier (see Sect. 28.4),

- for each disclosure context (identified by its disclosure transition identifier $m$) (see Sect. 28.3):
  - the secret $s^1$ for the first partition
  - the scheme for the current partition

When a token is generated from scratch, also a token extension is generated. The fields of the extension are initialized with fixed $NULL$ values, and the extension is associated with the token. When a token is generated as a copy of a parent token, also the parent token's extension is copied and this copy is associated with the token copy.

For a given current audit record the pseudonymizer executes the process of transition activation for all signature-nets. For a given transition the (unified) tokens that are considered during activation are virtual copies of the tokens from the input place of the transition. When a (unified) token meets the inter-event conditions, an actual copy is made, including the associated token extensions. The transition occurrence is processed on this copy, including the associated copy of the token extensions.

After the transition activation phase the application-layer pseudonyms are chosen as described in Sect. 27.3 and pushed on a stack. Additionally, the salts $s$ for CL-feature pseudonyms $p$ are inserted in the pseudonymity-layer. Note, that the pseudonym-salt pairs $\langle p, s \rangle$ are considered to be token-independent, because they may be evaluated by several transitions in several serial signature-nets. Hence, no token identifier accompanies the salt information.

Subsequently, the transition occurrence phase is processed. For a given activating (unified) token for a given transition with identifier $l$ the provision of disclosure information comprises three phases:

1. determining the token identifier,
2. providing a share for each disclosure context, and
3. providing (encrypted) features.

The first phase of determining the token identifier can be hooked into the execution of token bindings. The string $a$ of token bindings is initialized as an empty string. When a feature is assigned to a token variable $v$, the corresponding $\langle f, p \rangle$ pair is looked up in the stack where the pseudonyms are stored for later use (see Sect. 27.3). Then, $\langle v : p \rangle$ is concatenated to the end of $a$. After all token bindings have been performed, the token identifier for the (unified) token is updated to $o_{out} := h(l|o_{in}|a)$ in the token extension, where $o_{in}$ is the former token identifier. Before any (encrypted) features or shares are provided in the pseudonymity-layer, the token identifier $o_{out}$ is provided.

In the second phase, the occurrence of the current transition is accounted for by providing the corresponding share for each disclosure context that contains the transition. For each disclosure context only the scheme for the last used partition is held in the token extension. For a given disclosure context the identifier $l$ of the current transition is used to determine the current partition $i$. If the disclosure context does not *contain* the transition ($l > m$, $m$: transition identifier of the disclosure transition of the disclosure context) no share is provided in the pseudonymity-layer. If no scheme is initialized in the token extension, a new scheme is instantiated for the first partition according to the corresponding scheme description of the disclosure context (see Sect. 28.3), and the scheme secret $s^1$ is copied to the respective field in the token extension. Note, that the secret $s^1$ is used for encryption key generation and is individually stored in the token extension before the scheme of the first partition gets replaced by the scheme of another partition. If an existing scheme belongs to the previous partition $i-1$, a new scheme is instantiated according to the corresponding scheme description, and the old scheme is replaced by the newly generated scheme.

Now exists a valid scheme for the current partition, and the share $s^i_j$ corresponding to the current transition is retrieved. The share is labeled with the identifier $m$ of the disclosure transition of the current disclosure context, such that $\langle m, s^i_j \rangle$ is provided in the pseudonymity-layer. Share provision and possibly scheme instantiation is performed for all disclosure contexts that contain the current transition. Note, that no shares are provided for escape transitions, because they are not associated with any disclosure context.

In the third phase, the features of the current event are determined, for which disclosure information must be provided. Features that are disclosed subject to technical purpose binding are identified using the graph $H$ (see Sect. 28.1). For the current transition identifier $l$ the vertices for D-features are identified and the following information is provided in the pseudonymity-layer:

$\tau_1 = (l, bvf, v, f)$: if an edge $(\tau_1, \tau_2)$ exists with

$\quad \tau_2 = (j, dv, v)$: with $l < j$,
$\qquad$ for technical purpose binding only: $\langle v, p, E(k^i, F) \rangle$

$\qquad$ for technical and organizational purpose binding:
$\qquad \langle v, p, E(k^i, F), E(\tilde{k}_o, F) \rangle$

$\quad \tau_2 = (j, dv, v) \vee \tau_2 = (j, df, f)$: with $l = j$, (see case (1) in Sect. 28.4.1)
$\qquad$ for technical purpose binding only: $\langle v, p, F \rangle$

$\qquad$ for organizational purpose binding only: $\langle v, p, E(\tilde{k}_o, F) \rangle$

$\tau_1 = (l, df, f)$: and no edge $(\tau_1, \tau_2)$ exists with $\tau_2 = (j, bvf, v, f)$, $l = j$, (see case (1) in Sect. 28.4.1)
$\quad$ for technical purpose binding only: $\langle p, F \rangle$

$\quad$ for organizational purpose binding only: $\langle p, E(\tilde{k}_o, F) \rangle$

The pseudonym $p$ for a feature type $f$ is retrieved from the stack where the pseudonyms are stored for later use (see Sect. 27.3).

The key $k^i$ is determined as follows: The connected component of $H$ that contains $\tau_1$ is associated with a disclosure context. Using the current transition identifier $l$, the current partition $i$ of the disclosure context can be determined. For partition $i$ exists the corresponding scheme in the token extension (see phase two above). From the scheme the share $s^i_{t_i}$ is retrieved and together with the secret $s^1$ from the token extension the key $k^i := s^1 \oplus s^i_{t_i}$ is calculated.

Some feature types are not found in $H$, but are specified for pseudonym disclosure subject to organizational purpose binding (see case (2) in Sect. 28.4.1). For these feature types $\langle p, E(\tilde{k}_o, F) \rangle$ is provided.

After generating the pseudonymity-layer data, the (unified) token including token bindings from phase one is placed in the output place of the current transition. In two cases no output token is generated and the token is removed: First, if the output place is an escape place. Second, if the token identifier equals the token identifier of another token that resides in the output place (duplicate token). Finally, if the input edge of the current transition is a consuming edge, the input token is removed from the input place. Removing a token implies also discarding the associated token extension.

This process is performed for all activating (unified) tokens for all activated transitions. After the transition occurrence phase, the application-layer pseudonyms are popped from the stack and used to pseudonymize the current audit record (see Sect. 27.3). When the current event has been completely processed, the pseudonymized audit record and the corresponding pseudonymity-layer data are provided to the IDS and the next event from the queue is processed.

## 28.5.1 Example Operation of the Pseudonymizer

In Fig. 28.4 we extend the example from Fig. 27.2 for pseudonym disclosure, also using the disclosure requirements graph $H$ from Fig. 28.1.

During initialization the pseudonymizer loads the a priori knowledge including the serial signature-nets. Then, the pseudonymizer constructs the linkability requirements graph $G$ (not shown in Fig. 28.4, see Fig. 27.2) and the disclosure requirements graph $H$. In $G$ the pseudonymizer associates the connected component with an empty pseudonym mapping. Using $H$, the pseudonymizer associates the connected component with the disclosure context of $t_2$, determines the partition of the disclosure context and generates the signature description for the partition. Then, token 1 in the initial place is associated with an initialized token extension.

After initialization, the pseudonymizer is ready to process incoming audit records. Each audit record is processed individually and at first the embedded event is extracted from the current audit record. Fig. 28.4 depicts two events with the event types $e_1$ and $e_2$.

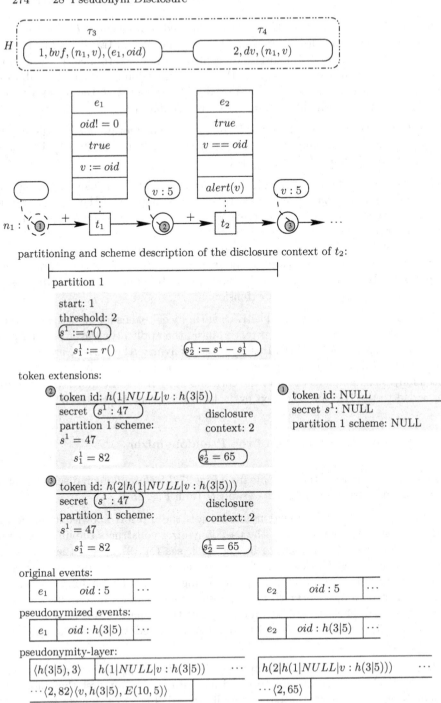

partitioning and scheme description of the disclosure context of $t_2$:

partition 1

start: 1
threshold: 2
$s^1 := r()$
$s_1^1 := r()$                    $s_2^1 := s^1 - s_1^1$

token extensions:

② token id: $h(1|NULL|v : h(3|5))$
secret $s^1 : 47$                    disclosure
partition 1 scheme:                  context: 2
$s^1 = 47$
$s_1^1 = 82$                    $s_2^1 = 65$

① token id: NULL
secret $s^1$: NULL
partition 1 scheme: NULL

③ token id: $h(2|h(1|NULL|v : h(3|5)))$
secret $s^1 : 47$                    disclosure
partition 1 scheme:                  context: 2
$s^1 = 47$
$s_1^1 = 82$                    $s_2^1 = 65$

original events:

| $e_1$ | $oid : 5$ | $\cdots$ |
|---|---|---|

| $e_2$ | $oid : 5$ | $\cdots$ |
|---|---|---|

pseudonymized events:

| $e_1$ | $oid : h(3|5)$ | $\cdots$ |
|---|---|---|

| $e_2$ | $oid : h(3|5)$ | $\cdots$ |
|---|---|---|

pseudonymity-layer:

| $\langle h(3|5), 3 \rangle$ | $h(1|NULL|v : h(3|5))$ | $\cdots$ |
|---|---|---|

$\cdots \langle 2, 82 \rangle \langle v, h(3|5), E(10, 5) \rangle$

$h(2|h(1|NULL|v : h(3|5)))$    $\cdots$

$\cdots \langle 2, 65 \rangle$

**Fig. 28.4.** Example operation of the pseudonymizer (linkability and disclosure)

When the first event is processed, transition $t_1$ is activated for token 1. The pseudonymizer is configured to pseudonymize the feature types $(e_1, oid)$ and $(e_2, oid)$. Using $H$, the pseudonymizer has determined that $(e_1, oid)$ is a D-feature, which needs to be disclosed subject to technical purpose binding when $t_2$ occurs. Moreover, no features have been specified to be disclosed subject to organizational purpose binding. The feature 5 in the current event $e_1$ is a PL/CL-feature w.r.t. $t_1$. The vertex $\tau_1$ represents $t_1$ and the feature type $(e_1, oid)$ in $G$ (see Fig. 27.2). As described in Sect. 27.3.1 the pseudonymizer chooses the pseudonym $h(3|5)$ for the feature, commits it to the pseudonym mapping, provides the salt $\langle h(3|5), 3 \rangle$ in the pseudonymity-layer, and pushes the pseudonym to the stack.

After the transition activation phase, $t_1$ occurs and performs the token binding. When the feature 5 is assigned to the token variable $v$, the corresponding pseudonym $h(3|5)$ is retrieved from the the the stack and $v : h(3|5)$ is appended to the initialized/empty string $a$. The pseudonymizer determines the token identifier using the transition identifier 1 of $t_1$, the former token identifier from the token extension $(NULL)$, and the string of token bindings $a$: $h(1|NULL|v : h(3|5))$. The token identifier is inserted in the pseudonymity-layer and in the token extension. The pseudonymizer also provides appropriate linkage between the token identifier and the current application-layer audit record (not shown in Fig. 28.4).

Using $H$, the pseudonymizer determines the connected component containing $\tau_3$, which represents $t_1$. The connected component is associated with the disclosure context of the disclosure transition $t_2$, represented by $\tau_4$. Since $1 \leq 2$, i.e. the current transition $t_1$ occurs before the disclosure transition $t_2$ occurs, $t_1$ is contained in partition 1 of the disclosure context. Since there is no instantiated scheme for partition 1 in the token extension, a new scheme is generated according to the scheme description of partition 1. The secret of the scheme is copied in the token extension. Then, share $s_1^1 = 82$, which corresponds to $t_1$, is provided in the pseudonymity-layer together with the disclosure transition identifier 2 of the disclosure context: $\langle 2, 82 \rangle$.

For D-feature 5 the disclosure information is computed as $E(10, 5)$, where $10 = 47 \oplus 65 = s^1 \oplus s_2^1 \bmod 100$ (see the black frames in the extension of token 2 in Fig. 28.4). The pseudonym $h(3|5)$ for the corresponding D-feature is retrieved from the stack and inserted in the pseudonymity-layer together with the name $v$ of the variable to which the D-feature is bound: $\langle v, h(3|5), E(10, 5) \rangle$.

Then, the pseudonymizer replaces the feature 5 in the original event with the pseudonym $h(3|5)$, which is popped from the stack. The token with the modified binding and extension is output as token 2 in the output place of $t_1$. This finishes the processing of the first event and the second event is processed.

Since the token variable-value assignment $v : 5$ satisfies the inter-event condition of transition $t_2$, $t_2$ is activated. The pseudonymizer determines that the PL-feature type $(e_2, oid)$ needs to be pseudonymized, fetches the pseudonym $h(3|5)$ from the pseudonym mapping and pushes it on the stack.

After transition activation, $t_2$ occurs for token 2. Since $t_2$ performs no token binding, the string $a$ remains empty, such that the token identifier computes to $h(2|h(1|NULL|v : h(3|5)))$, where $h(1|NULL|v : h(3|5))$ is the former token identifier from the (copy of the) extension of token 2. The token identifier is inserted in the pseudonymity-layer and updated in the token extension.

Then, the pseudonymizer determines that $t_2$ is contained in partition 1 of the disclosure context for $t_2$ (identifier 2). The existing scheme in the token extension is used to provide the share $s_2^1 = 65$ in the pseudonymity-layer, because it represents the occurrence of $t_2$: $\langle 2, 65 \rangle$.

Since the action of $t_2$ uses the variable $v$ as a parameter, but not a feature from $e_2$, no disclosure information needs to be provided in the pseudonymity-layer. The disclosure information for $v$ was already provided when $e_1$ was processed (see above).

Finally, the token together with its extension is placed as token 3 in the output place of $t_2$. After $t_2$ occurred, the pseudonym is popped from the stack and replaces the original feature in $e_2$.

Figure 28.4 depicts the disclosure requirements graph $H$ for the serial signature-net $n_1$ and the connected component of $H$, as well as the partitioning and the scheme description for the disclosure context of the connected component. Also, $n_1$ and its marking are depicted together with the token extensions for the marking after the processing of the two events. Finally, the two events in their original form and in the pseudonymized form as well as the corresponding pseudonymity-layer data are shown.

## 28.6 Operation of the Analysis Engine

In the following, the operation of audit data analysis is described for pseudonymous application-layer audit data, considering the aspects of pseudonym linkability and pseudonym disclosure. Only the necessary extensions are described, which need to be made to the analysis engine, such that it can analyze pseudonymized audit data and disclose D-features before transition actions are executed. The analysis engine is supposed to disclose pseudonyms of D-features before action execution. Pseudonyms of non-D-features, which have been manually specified to be subject to organizational purpose binding, are not disclosed by the analysis engine, because it has no grounds to decide, in what cases disclosure should be performed (see case (2) in Sect. 28.4.1).

The analysis engine requires a specification of the format of pseudonymity-layer data. The analysis engine also needs to know, which pseudonyms of D-features need to be disclosed subject to technical purpose binding and which D-feature pseudonyms need to be disclosed subject to organizational purpose binding.

Note, that the latter are those D-features that need to be disclosed immediately (see case (1) in Sect. 28.4.1). For testing CL-features, the analysis engine also needs to know, which CL-features are pseudonymized.

In order to extract shares for threshold schemes and to recover secrets, the analysis engine needs to know the disclosure requirements, the disclosure contexts and the threshold scheme descriptions. While this knowledge is manually provided in the set-based approach, here it is automatically derived from the models of misuse scenarios during initialization. To do this, the analysis engine constructs the disclosure requirements graph $H$ as described in Sect. 28.1 and generates threshold scheme descriptions with a slightly different meaning as described in Sect. 28.3:

- The shares $s_1^i, \ldots, s_{t^i-1}^i$ are extracted from the pseudonymity-layer. For the last partition the share $s_{t^i}^i$ is also extracted from the pseudonymity-layer. For all other partitions, the share is a copy of the reconstructed secret of the next partition: $s_{t^i}^i := s^{i+1}$.

- The secret of a threshold scheme for partition $i$ is computed as $s^i := \sum_{j=1}^{t^i} s_j^i$.

Pseudonym disclosure requires additional state. Since pseudonym disclosure is tied to individual tokens, each token is associated with its own token extension. A token extension comprises the following elements:

- the token identifier (see Sect. 28.4),

- for each D-feature variable binding the disclosure information that has been extracted from the pseudonymity-layer and recovered from the threshold schemes (see Sect. 28.4.2),

- for each disclosure context (identified by its disclosure transition identifier $m$) (see Sect. 28.3) the shares for all partitions, which have been extracted from the pseudonymity-layer (see Sect. 28.4.2).

When a token is generated from scratch, also a token extension is generated, its fields are initialized with fixed $NULL$ values, and the extension is associated with the token. It is important that token identifiers are initialized with the same $NULL$ values as used by the pseudonymizer. When a token is generated as a copy of a parent token, also the parent token's extension is copied and this copy is associated with the token copy.

For a given current audit record, the analysis engine executes the process of transition activation. Transition activation considers virtual copies of the tokens from the input place of the transitions. During transition activation the analysis engine must take care of pseudonymized CL-features as described in Sect. 27.4. When a (unified) token meets the inter-event conditions, an actual copy is made, including the associated token extension. The transition occurrence is processed on this copy, including the associated copy of the token extensions.

After the transition activation phase, the transition occurrence phase is processed. For a given activating (unified) token for a given transition with identifier $l$ the extraction and use of disclosure information comprises four phases:

1. determining the token identifier,

2. extracting shares for each disclosure context,

3. extracting (encrypted) features, and

4. disclosing original D-features.

The first phase of determining the token identifier can be hooked into the execution of token bindings. The string $a$ of token bindings is initialized as an empty string. When a feature $F$, which may be a pseudonym, is assigned to a token variable $v$, $\langle v : F \rangle$ is concatenated to the end of $a$. After all token bindings have been performed, the token identifier for the (unified) token is updated to $o_{out} := h(l|o_{in}|a)$ in the token extension, where $o_{in}$ is the former token identifier. Before any (encrypted) features or shares can be extracted, the token identifier $o_{out}$ is located in the pseudonymity-layer data. The analysis engine knows, which shares and D-feature disclosure information it can expect in the pseudonymity-layer and can notify the SSO, if the expected data is not found.

In the second phase, the occurrence of the current transition is accounted for by extracting the corresponding share for each disclosure context containing the transition. Each extracted share is labeled with the transition identifier of the disclosure transition of the associated disclosure context: $\langle m, s_j^i \rangle$. Using $m$, the share $s_j^i$ is associated with the correct disclosure context in the token extension. Using $l$, the share $s_j^i$ is inserted at the correct position in the threshold scheme. For each disclosure context, the shares for the schemes of all partitions are held in the token extension, such that the secrets can later be recovered on demand.

In the third phase, the disclosure information for D-features is extracted from the pseudonymity-layer. Escrow data for pseudonym disclosure subject to organizational purpose binding is only extracted and used when D-features need to be immediately disclosed. Also, the pseudonyms $p$ in the disclosure information are used only in case a D-feature is immediately disclosed without previously being assigned to a variable (see phase four below). Note, that immediate D-feature disclosure implies that the current transition executes actions that are parameterized with a feature type of the current event.

Summarizing, the following information is extracted from the pseudonymity-layer for a given D-feature type that is assigned to a variable: $\langle v, E(k^i, F) \rangle$, $\langle v, F \rangle$, or $\langle v, E(\tilde{k}_o, F) \rangle$.

The fourth phase can be hooked in right before the execution of actions. For each pseudonymous parameter of an action the following disclosure procedure is used. If the D-feature is not assigned to a variable, its pseudonym $p$ is looked up in the pseudonymity-layer and a pair $\langle p, F \rangle$ or $\langle p, E(\tilde{k}_o, F) \rangle$ is extracted. Either the clear-text feature $F$ can be directly used as a parameter, or it must be disclosed subject to organizational purpose binding as described in Sect. 16.6.1 or Sect. 16.6.2.

If the D-feature pseudonym is assigned to a variable $v$, the disclosure information in the token extension is used. If for $v$ the (cached) clear-text value is available, it is used as the parameter for the action. If the variable value is disclosed by the same transition that has assigned the value to $v$, the value either is available in clear-text $\langle v, F \rangle$ or needs to be disclosed subject to organizational purpose binding as described in Sect. 16.6.1 or Sect. 16.6.2: $\langle v, E(\tilde{k}_o, F) \rangle$. Otherwise the variable value needs to be disclosed subject to technical purpose binding: $\langle v, E(k^i, F) \rangle$. The current transition identifier $l$ directly identifies the relevant disclosure context in the token extension. All shares for the schemes of the disclosure context should now be available for secret recovery. Beginning with the last partition, the secrets are recovered according to the scheme description. The secret $s^1$ of the first scheme, as well as the last shares $s^i_{t_i}$ of all schemes, are stored with the respective schemes in the token extension. Using $H$, the identifier of the transition where the D-feature is assigned to $v$ is determined, and from the scheme of partition $i$ containing the binding transition the share $s^i_{t_i}$ is retrieved. Then, $k^i := s^1 \oplus s^i_{t_i}$ is calculated and used to decrypt $E(k^i, F)$, yielding $F$. Then, $F$ is cached with the corresponding variable in the token extension for the use as a parameter of actions of later disclosure transitions.

When all pseudonymous action parameters have been disclosed, the action is executed. After action execution the (unified) token may be placed in the output place of the current transition. In two cases, no output token is generated, and the token is removed: First, if the output place is an escape place. Second, if the token identifier equals the token identifier of another token that resides in the output place (duplicate token). Finally, if the input edge of the current transition is a consuming edge, the input token is removed from the input place. Removing a token implies also discarding the associated token extension.

This process is performed for all activating (unified) tokens for all activated transitions. After the transition occurrence phase the current event has been completely processed, and the next event from the queue is processed.

### 28.6.1 Example Operation of the Analysis Engine

Continuing the example from Sect. 28.5.1, we consider that the pseudonymized audit data and the pseudonymity-layer data has been made available to the analysis engine for misuse detection. The basic functionality of the analysis engine is described by the given serial signature-nets. For the example, we focus on the serial signature-net $n_1$ in Fig. 28.5.

During initialization, the analysis engine loads the a priori knowledge including serial signature-nets. Then, the analysis engine constructs the disclosure requirements graph $H$. Using $H$, the analysis engine associates the connected compo-

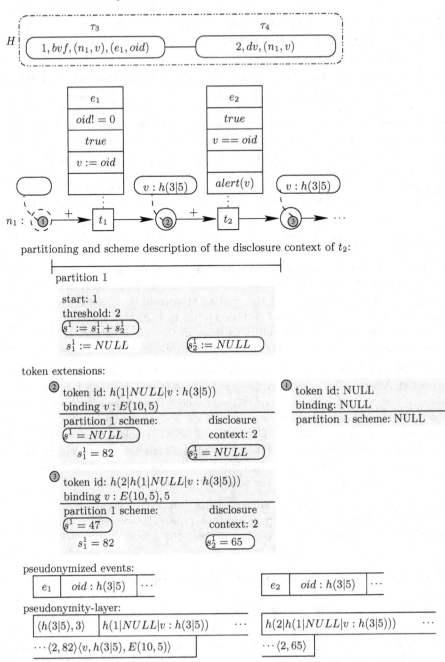

Fig. 28.5. Example operation of the analysis engine (linkability and disclosure)

nent with the disclosure context of $t_2$, determines the partition of the disclosure context and generates the scheme description for the partition. Then, token 1 in the initial place is associated with an initialized token extension. The white fields in the scheme description in Fig. 28.5 show the shares that are extracted from the pseudonymity-layer during audit data processing, and the white field in the token extensions show, which shares have already been extracted. After initialization, the analysis engine is ready to process incoming pseudonymized audit records.

When the first pseudonymized event is processed, the analysis engine detects that the event type $e_1$ is relevant for transition $t_1$ and that $t_1$ evaluates an intra-event condition using the pseudonymized CL-feature $h(3|5)$. Thus, the analysis engine uses $h(3|5)$ and the linkage between the pseudonym in the current application-layer audit record and the pseudonymity-layer data (not shown in Fig. 28.5) to locate the salt $s = 3$ in the pseudonymity-layer, pseudonymizes the constant value as $h(3|0)$ and evaluates the intra-event condition as described in Sect. 27.4.1. The result is, that $t_1$ is activated. After the transition activation phase is finished, transition $t_1$ occurs.

When $t_1$ occurs and performs the token binding, the pseudonym $h(3|5)$ is assigned to the token variable $v$ and $v : h(3|5)$ is appended to the initialized/empty string $a$. The analysis engine determines the token identifier using the transition identifier $(1)$, the previous token identifier $(NULL)$, and the string of token bindings $a$: $h(1|NULL|v : h(3|5))$. The token identifier is updated in the token extension and located in the pseudonymity-layer leveraging the linkage between the token identifier and the current application-layer audit record (not shown in Fig. 28.5).

Accounting for the occurrence of $t_1$, the analysis engine extracts the pair $\langle 2, 82 \rangle$ for the disclosure context of $t_2$ (transition identifier 2) from the pseudonymity-layer. Using the current transition identifier $l = 1$ and the disclosure context identifier 2 (for $t_2$), the analysis engine locates the partition containing $t_1$. Since there is no instantiated scheme for partition 1 in the token extension, a new scheme is initialized according to the scheme description of partition 1. Then $s_1^1 = 82$ is inserted in the scheme of partition 1.

After share extraction, the analysis engine extracts the disclosure information from the pseudonymity-layer: $\langle v, h(3|5), E(10,5) \rangle$. $E(10,5)$ is inserted in the token extension. Since there is no action to be executed for $t_1$, the transition occurrence phase is finished, and the next event is processed.

Since the event type $e_2$ is relevant for transition $t_2$, the inter-event condition of $t_2$ is evaluated as described in Sect. 27.4.1, and $t_2$ is activated. After transition activation, $t_2$ occurs for token 2. Since $t_2$ performs no token binding, the string $a$ remains empty, such that the token identifier computes to $h(2|h(1|NULL|v : h(3|5)))$, where $h(1|NULL|v : h(3|5))$ is the former token identifier from the token extension. The token identifier is updated in the token extension and located in the pseudonymity-layer. Then, share $s_2^1$ is extracted from the pseudonymity-layer and inserted in the token extension: $\langle 2, 65 \rangle$.

After share extraction, the parameter $v$ of the action of $t_2$ needs to be disclosed subject to technical purpose binding. Using $H$, the identifier of the transition (1) that assigned the D-feature pseudonym to $v$ is determined as well as the disclosure context (2). In the token extension the secret is determined as $s^1 :=$ $47 = 82 + 65 = s_1^1 + s_2^1 \bmod 100$. Then, the decryption key is computed as $k^1 := 10 = 47 \oplus 65 = s^1 \oplus s_2^1 \bmod 100$ and used to decrypt $E(10, 5)$, yielding the original D-feature 5. The disclosed D-feature is cached for $v$ in the token extension for later transitions that may use $v$ as an action parameter. Finally, $alert(5)$ is executed.

Figure 28.5 depicts the disclosure requirements graph $H$ for the serial signature-net $n_1$ and the connected component of $H$, as well as the partitioning and the scheme description for the disclosure context of the connected component. Also, $n_1$ and its marking are depicted together with the token extensions for the marking after the processing of the two pseudonymous events. Finally, the two pseudonymous events and the corresponding pseudonymity-layer data are shown.

# Summary

This book presents novel solutions to the problem that audit data for misuse detection contains personal data, such that audit data collection and processing generally conflict with user expectations and pertinent legislation w.r.t. privacy. This conflict can be solved by appropriately replacing personal data with pseudonyms. Central to the solution is the concept of technical purpose binding, warranting that the original personal data concealed by the pseudonyms can only be revealed for an a priori specified purpose. The foundation of the solution is laid by three key contributions:

- It is shown that audit data pseudonymization is a viable short-term solution for lawful personal data protection, and that this solution is preferable over other pseudonymization approaches w.r.t. cost of deployment.

- A novel approach for pseudonymizing audit data is presented, demonstrating that pseudonymized audit data can be analyzed for misuse as effectively as the original audit data.

- This is the first pseudonymization approach that effectively and efficiently enforces purpose binding, such that the information provided by pseudonyms is reduced to the amount necessary for misuse detection, and original personal data can only be revealed, if a detected misuse warrants a response.

The presented solutions provide privacy protection officials (PPOs) with the means to officiate the responsibility for personal data protection w.r.t. audit data, while acquitting the site security officers (SSOs) from the conflict between security objectives and statutorily required restrictions w.r.t. personal data. Moreover, users can rely on the protection of their personal data recorded in audit data, and SSOs can respond timely and autonomously to detected misuse.

It has been shown how such a solution can be validated constructively, analytically, and experimentally by providing appropriate models and algorithms, evaluating the soundness of the design, implementing a toolkit for pseudonymization, and evaluating the performance of the toolkit.

A further major contribution of this book is the proposed architecture model for secure and privacy-respecting authorizations. The model provides a systematic view on architectures for secure and privacy-respecting authorizations, as well as on their generic high-level properties. Starting from a set of required properties it allows to compare and select suitable architectures, either for designing authorization systems from scratch, or to guide product selection. For each architecture the control requirements are made explicit, such that they can be taken into account during design, or can be used to verify the appropriateness of control conditions in products.

Two major conclusions can be drawn from the work described in this book and will hopefully be instrumental in advancing the state of the art in privacy-respecting misuse detection:

Full vs. necessary linkability: It is not a necessary prerequisite of misuse detection that the amount of linkability in the original audit data is retained during pseudonymization. The solutions presented in this book show that the amount of linkability can be reduced in a fully automated way to the amount necessary for the purpose of audit data analysis for misuse detection, thereby potentially greatly reducing the working surface of an attacker. The presented solutions are based on a general and carefully adapted framework for modeling misuse scenarios, which has also been developed in this book.

Organizational vs. technical purpose binding: If the purpose binding for revealing original personal data is enforced externally w.r.t. the technical system, it results in additional work load of the personnel and in a potential delay of appropriate response to detected misuse. The solutions presented in this book show that purpose binding can be securely enforced within and by the system, thereby allowing for a timely and fully automated response.

# A

## Threshold Schemes
## for Cryptographic Secret Sharing

In this appendix we briefly summarize the relevant fundamentals of the threshold schemes we used in Part II and Part V for cryptographic secret sharing. Refer to Stinson [211] for a more detailed exposition.

A $(t, n)$-*threshold scheme* is a specific cryptographic secret sharing scheme that aims at sharing a secret $s \in \mathcal{K}$ among a set of $n$ participants $P_i$, denoted as $\mathcal{P} = \{P_i : 1 \leq i \leq n\}$, such that any $t$ participants can reconstruct $s$, but no group of $t - 1$ or fewer participants can do so.

A *dealer* $D \notin \mathcal{P}$ chooses $s$, and to share $s$ among the participants in $\mathcal{P}$ he secretly provides to each participant some partial information called a *share* ($y_i \in \mathcal{S}$), such that no participant knows the share given to another participant.

Later, a subset of participants $B \subseteq \mathcal{P}$ may attempt to combine their shares to reconstruct $s$. This should work for $|B| \geq t$, but not for $|B| < t$.

In Sect. A.1 and Sect. A.2 we describe two methods of constructing $(t, n)$-threshold schemes, which we adapted and used in Part II and Part V, respectively.

## A.1 Scheme of Shamir

For the scheme of Shamir we have a finite field $\mathcal{K} = \mathcal{S} = \mathbb{Z}_P$, where $P \geq n + 1$ is prime.

During the initialization phase $D$ chooses distinct public values $x_i \in \mathbb{Z}_P, x_i \neq 0$, and provides $x_i$ to $P_i, 1 \leq i \leq n$.

For share distribution $D$ secretly chooses (independently at random) $a_1, \ldots, a_{t-1} \in \mathbb{Z}_P$ for a polynomial $p(x) = s + \sum_{j=1}^{t-1} a_j \cdot x^j \bmod P$, computes the shares $y_i = p(x_i)$ and provides $y_i$ to $P_i, 1 \leq i \leq n$.

A subset $B \subseteq \mathcal{P}$ of $t$ participants can reconstruct $p(x)$ and thus $s$ by means of Lagrange interpolation:

$$p(x) = \sum_{j=1}^{t} y_{i_j} \prod_{1 \leq o \leq t, o \neq j} \frac{x - x_{i_o}}{x_{i_j} - x_{i_o}}.$$

However, the participants do not need to know the whole polynomial $p(x)$. It is sufficient to reconstruct $s = p(0)$ by substituting $x = 0$ into the Lagrange interpolation formula:

$$s = \sum_{j=1}^{t} y_{i_j} \prod_{1 \leq o \leq t, o \neq j} \frac{x_{i_o}}{x_{i_o} - x_{i_j}}.$$

In the traditional application of Shamir's scheme we can precompute and publish for $1 \leq j \leq t$:

$$b_j = \prod_{1 \leq o \leq t, o \neq j} \frac{x_{i_o}}{x_{i_o} - x_{i_j}},$$

Then we have

$$s = \sum_{j=1}^{t} b_j y_{i_j}.$$

However, this optimization does not hold for the way Shamir's scheme is used in the solutions proposed in this book.

## A.2 Scheme of Karnin, Greene and Hellman

A simplified construction for threshold schemes with $\mathcal{K} = \mathcal{S} = \mathbb{Z}_P$ is possible in the special case $n = t$.

For share distribution $D$ secretly chooses (independently at random) the shares $y_1, \ldots, y_{t-1} \in \mathbb{Z}_P$, computes the share $y_t = s - \sum_{j=1}^{t-1} y_j \bmod P$, and provides $y_i$ to $P_i, 1 \leq j \leq t$.

In order to reconstruct $s$ the $t$ participants compute

$$s = \sum_{j=1}^{t} y_j \bmod P.$$

# References

1. Mark S. Ackerman, Lorrie F. Cranor, and Joseph Reagle. Privacy in e-commerce: Examining user scenarios and privacy preferences. In *Proceedings of the 1st ACM Conference on Electronic Commerce*, pages 1–8, Denver, Colorado, USA, 1999.
2. T. Alamaki, M. Björksen, P. Dornbach, C. Gripenberg, N. Gyórbíró, G. Márton, Z. Németh, T. Skyttä, and M. Tarkiainen. Privacy enhancing service architectures. In R. Dingledine and P. Syverson, editors, *Proceedings of the International Workshop on Privacy Enhancing Technologies*, number 2482 in Lecture Notes in Computer Science, pages 99–109, San Francisco, California, USA, April 2002. Springer.
3. J. Allen, A. Christie, W. Fithen, J. McHugh, P. Pickel, and E. Stoner. State of the practice of intrusion detection technologies. Technical Report CMU/SEI-99-TR-028, ESC-99-028, Carnegie Mellon University, Software Engineering Institute, January 2000.
4. Christian Altenschmidt, Joachim Biskup, Ulrich Flegel, and Yücel Karabulut. Secure mediation: Requirements, design and architecture. *Journal of Computer Security*, 11(3):365–398, June 2003.
5. James P. Anderson. Computer security threat monitoring and surveillance. Technical report, James P. Anderson Co., Fort Washington, Pennsylvania, USA, April 1980.
6. Stefan Axelsson. Research in intrusion detection systems: A survey. Technical Report 98-17, Department of Computer Engineering, Chalmers University of Technology, Sweden, August 1999. Revised version.
7. Stefan Axelsson, Ulf Lindquist, and Ulf Gustafson. An approach to Unix security logging. In *Proceedings of the 21st National Information Systems Security Conference*, pages 62–75, Crystal City, Arlington, Virgina, USA, October 1998.
8. Rebecca Gurley Bace. *Intrusion Detection*. Macmillan Technical Publishing, 2000.
9. Bernd Baumgarten. *Petri-Netze: Grundlagen und Anwendungen (in German)*. BI-Wissenschaftsverlag, 1990.
10. Oliver Berthold, Hannes Federrath, and Marit Köhntopp. Project "Anonymity and unobservability in the internet". In *Proceedings of the Workshop on Freedom and Privacy by Design / Conference on Freedom and Privacy*, pages 57–65, Toronto, Canada, April 2000. ACM.

11. Matt Bishop. A standard audit trail format. In *Proceedings of the 18th National Information Systems Security Conference*, pages 136–145, Baltimore, Maryland, USA, October 1995.

12. Joachim Biskup and Ulrich Flegel. On pseudonymization of audit data for intrusion detection. In H. Federrath, editor, *Proceedings of the First International Workshop on Privacy Enhancing Technologies*, number 2009 in Lecture Notes in Computer Science, pages 161–180, Berkeley, California, USA, July 2000. ICSI, Springer.

13. Joachim Biskup and Ulrich Flegel. Threshold-based identity recovery for privacy enhanced applications. In S. Jajodia and P. Samarati, editors, *Proceedings of the 7th ACM Conference on Computer and Communications Security*, pages 71–79, Athens, Greece, November 2000. ACM SIGSAC, ACM Press.

14. Joachim Biskup and Ulrich Flegel. Transaction-based pseudonyms in audit data for privacy respecting intrusion detection. In H. Debar, L. Mé, and S. F. Wu, editors, *Proceedings of the Third International Symposium on Recent Advances in Intrusion Detection (RAID 2000)*, number 1907 in Lecture Notes in Computer Science, pages 28–48, Toulouse, France, October 2000. Springer.

15. Joachim Biskup and Ulrich Flegel. Ausgleich von Datenschutz und Überwachung mit technischer Zweckbindung am Beispiel eines Pseudonymisierers (in German). In S. Schubert, B. Reusch, and N. Jesse, editors, *Informatik bewegt, Proceedings of the 32nd Annual GI Conference on Informatics (Informatik 2002)*, number P-19 in Lecture Notes in Informatics, pages 488–494, Dortmund, Germany, October 2002. GI, GI LNI.

16. Joachim Biskup, Ulrich Flegel, and Yücel Karabulut. Secure mediation: Requirements and design. In S. Jajodia, editor, *Proceedings of the 12th international IFIP TC11 WG 11.3 Working Conference on Database Security*, pages 127–140, Chalkidiki, Greece, July 1998. IFIP, Kluwer Academic Publishers.

17. Joachim Biskup, Ulrich Flegel, and Yücel Karabulut. Towards secure mediation. In A. Böhm, D. Fox, R. Grimm, and D. Schoder, editors, *Security and Electronic Commerce*, DuD-Fachbeiträge, pages 93–106, Essen, Germany, October 1999. Vieweg.

18. Joachim Biskup and Yücel Karabulut. A hybrid PKI model with an application for secure meditation. In S. Shenoi, editor, *Proceedings of the 16th Annual IFIP WG 11.3 Working Conference on Data and Application Security*, pages 271–282, Cambridge, England, July 2002. Kluwer.

19. Joachim Biskup and Yücel Karabulut. Mediating between strangers: A trust management based approach. In *Proceedings of the 2nd Annual PKI Research Workshop*, pages 80–95, Gaitherburg, Maryland, USA, April 2003. NIST.

20. Dan Boneh and Matt Franklin. Anonymous authentication with subset queries. In *Proceedings of the 6th ACM Conference on Computer and Communications Security*, pages 113–119, Kent Ridge Digital Labs, Singapore, November 1999. ACM SIGSAC, ACM Press.

21. Grady Booch, James Rumbaugh, and Ivar Jacobson. *Unified Modeling Language User Guide*. Object Technology Series. Addison Wesley, 2005.

22. J. J. Borking, B. M. A. van Eck, and P. Siepel. Intelligent software agents and privacy. Technical report, Registratiekamer Netherlands and Information and Privacy Commissioner Ontario, Canada, Achtergrondstudies en Verkenningen 13, The Hague, 1999.

23. John Borking. Der Identity Protector (in German). *Datenschutz und Datensicherheit*, 20(11):654–658, November 1996.

24. Stefan A. Brands. *Rethinking Public Key Infrastructures and Digital Certificates: Building in Privacy.* MIT Press, Cambridge, Massachusetts, USA, 2000.
25. Lars Brückner. Aktiver Datenschutz mit Datajournals (in German). *Datenschutz und Datensicherheit,* 27(5):300, May 2003.
26. Bundesamt für Sicherheit in der Informationstechnik, Godesberger Allee 185-189, 53133, Bonn, Germany. *Einführung von Intrusion-Detection-Systemen – Rechtliche Aspekte (in German),* October 2002. http://www.bsi.de/literat/studien/ids02/dokumente/Rechtv10.pdf.
27. Der Deutsche Bundestag. Gesetz über den Datenschutz bei Telediensten (TDDSG) (in German). *Bundesgesetzblatt, Teil I,* (70):3721, December 2001. http://bundesrecht.juris.de/bundesrecht/tddsg/.
28. Der Deutsche Bundestag. Grundgesetz für die Bundesrepublik Deutschland (GG) (in German). *Bundesgesetzblatt, Teil I,* (53):2863, July 2002. http://bundesrecht.juris.de/bundesrecht/gg/.
29. Der Deutsche Bundestag. Bundesdatenschutzgesetz (BDSG) (in German). *Bundesgesetzblatt, Teil I,* (3):66, January 2003. http://bundesrecht.juris.de/bundesrecht/bdsg_1990/.
30. Der Deutsche Bundestag. Gesetz über Rahmenbedingungen für elektronische Signaturen (SIGG) (in German). *Bundesgesetzblatt, Teil I,* (1):2, January 2005. http://bundesrecht.juris.de/bundesrecht/sigg_2001/.
31. Thomas Butzlaff, Florian Jäger, Björn Röber, David Weber, and Andreas Wilms. Marktchancen von Anonymisierung (in German). *Datenschutz und Datensicherheit,* 27(3):146–149, March 2003.
32. Roland Büschkes and Dogan Kesdogan. Privacy enhanced intrusion detection. In G. Müller and K. Rannenberg, editors, *Multilateral Security in Communications,* Information Security, pages 187–204. Addison Wesley, 1999.
33. Jan Camenisch and Anna Lysyanskaya. Efficient revocation of anonymous group membership certificates and anonymous credentials. http://eprint.iacr.org/2001, December 2001.
34. Jan Camenisch and Anna Lysyanskaya. An efficient system for non-transferable anonymous credentials with optional anonymity revocation. In B. Pfitzmann, editor, *Advances in Cryptology – EUROCRYPT 2001,* number 2045 in Lecture Notes in Computer Science, pages 93–118, Austria, May 2001. Springer.
35. Jan Camenisch, Ueli Maurer, and Markus Stadler. Digital payment systems with passive anonymity-revoking trustees. In E. Bertino, H. Kurth, G. Martella, and E. Montolivo, editors, *Proceedings of the 4th European Symposium on Research in Computer Security (ESORICS'96),* number 1146 in Lecture Notes in Computer Science, pages 33–43, Rome, Italy, September 1996. Springer.
36. Jan Camenisch and Markus Stadtler. Efficient group signature schemes for large groups. In B. S. Kaliski, editor, *Proceedings of the Conference on Advances in Cryptology (CRYPTO'97),* number 1294 in Lecture Notes in Computer Science, pages 410–424, Santa Barbara, California, USA, August 1997. Springer.
37. National Computer Security Center. US DoD Standard: Department of Defense Trusted Computer System Evaluation Criteria. DOD 5200.28-STD, Supercedes CSC-STD-001-83, dtd 15 Aug 83, Library No. S225,711, December 1985. http://csrc.ncsl.nist.gov/secpubs/rainbow/std001.txt.
38. National Computer Security Center. Audit in trusted systems. NCSC-TG-001, Library No. S-228,470, July 1987. http://csrc.ncsl.nist.gov/secpubs/rainbow/tg001.txt.

39. Privacy survey results, January 2002. `http://www.cdt.org/privacy/survey/findings/`.

40. Yuen-Yan Chan. On privacy issues of internet access services via proxy servers. In R. Baumgart, editor, *Proceedings of the Congress on Secure Networking – CQRE[Secure]'99*, number 1740 in Lecture Notes in Computer Science, pages 183–191, Düsseldorf, Germany, November 1999. secunet, Springer.

41. David Chaum. Untraceable electronic mail, return addresses, and digital signatures. *Communications of the ACM*, 24(2):84–88, February 1981.

42. David Chaum. Security without identification: Transaction systems to make big brother obsolete. *Communications of the ACM*, 28(10):1030–1044, October 1985.

43. David Chaum. Showing credentials without identification – signatures transferred between unconditionally unlinkable pseudonyms. In *Advances in Cryptology – EUROCRYPT 1985*, number 219 in Lecture Notes in Computer Science, pages 241–244, Linz, Austria, April 1986. Springer.

44. David Chaum. Security without identification – card computers to make big brother obsolete. `http://www.chaum.com/articles/Security_Wthout_identification.htm`, 1987. Extended version of [42].

45. David Chaum. Showing credentials without identification: Transferring signatures between unconditionally unlinkable pseudonyms. In J. Seberry and J. Pieprzyk, editors, *Proceedings of the Conference on Advances in Cryptology (AUSCRYPT'90)*, number 453 in Lecture Notes in Computer Science, pages 246–264, Sydney, Australia, January 1990. Springer.

46. David Chaum and Jan-Hendrik Evertse. A secure and privacy-protecting protocol for transmitting personal information between organizations. In A. M. Odlyzko, editor, *Proceedings of the Conference on Advances in Cryptology (CRYPTO'86)*, number 263 in Lecture Notes in Computer Science, pages 118–167, Santa Barbara, California, USA, August 1987. Springer.

47. David Chaum, Amos Fiat, and Moni Naor. Untraceable electronic cash. In S. Goldwasser, editor, *Proceedings of the Conference on Advances in Cryptology (CRYPTO'88)*, Lecture Notes in Computer Science, pages 319–327, Santa Barbara, California, USA, August 1988. Springer.

48. Benny Chor, Oded Goldreich, Eyal Kushilevitz, and Madhu Sudan. Private information retrieval. *Journal of the ACM*, 45(6):965–981, November 1998.

49. Søren Christensen and Niels Damgaard Hansen. Coloured petri nets extended with place capacities, test arcs and inhibitor arcs. In M. A. Arsan, editor, *Proceedings of the 14th International Conference on Application and Theory of Petri Nets*, number 691 in Lecture Notes In Computer Science, pages 186–205. Springer, June 1993.

50. Joris Claessens, Bart Preneel, and Joos Vandewalle. Anonymity controlled electronic payment systems. In *Proceedings of the 20th Symposium on Information Theory in the Benelux*, pages 109–116, Haasrode, Belgium, May 1999.

51. Sebastian Clauß and Marit Köhntopp. Identity management and its support of multilateral security. *Computer Networks*, 37(2):205–219, 2001.

52. Sebastian Clauß, Andreas Pfitzmann, Marit Hansen, and Els Van Herreweghen. Privacy-enhancing identity management. In *IPTS Report Vol. 67*, pages 8–16. Institute for Prospective Technological Studies (IPTS) of the Joint Research Center (JRC) of the European Commission, Seville, Spain, September 2002. `http://www.jrc.es/pages/iptsreport/vol67/english/IPT2E676.html`.

53. Common Criteria Implementation Board. Common criteria for information technology security evaluation — part 2: Security functional requirements, version

3.1, revision 1. Technical Report CCMB-2006-09-002, National Institute of Standards and Technology, September 2006. http://www.commoncriteriaportal. org/public/files/CCPART2V3.1R1.pdf.

54. Lorrie Cranor, Marc Langheinrich, Massimo Marchiori, Martin Presler-Marshall, and Joseph Reagle. The Platform for Privacy Preferences 1.0 (P3P1.0) specification, September 2001. http://www.w3.org/TR/2001/WD-P3P-20010928/.

55. Lorrie F. Cranor. Agents of choice: Tools that facilitate notice and choice about web site data practices. In *Proceedings of the 21st International Conference on Privacy and Personal Data Protection*, pages 19–25, Hong Kong SAR, China, September 1999.

56. Frédéric Cuppens and Rodolphe Ortalo. Lambda: A language to model a database for detection of attacks. In H. Debar, L. Mé, and S. F. Wu, editors, *Proceedings of the Third International Symposium on Recent Advances in Intrusion Detection (RAID 2000)*, number 1907 in Lecture Notes in Computer Science, pages 197–216, Toulouse, France, October 2000. Springer.

57. M. Dacier, editor. *Proceedings of the First International Symposium on Recent Advances in Intrusion Detection (RAID'98)*, Lovain-la-Neuve, Belgium, September 1998. http://www.zurich.ibm.com/~dac/Prog_RAID98/Table_of_content. html.

58. Ivan Damgard. Payment systems and credential mechanisms with provable security against abuse by individuals. In S. Goldwasser, editor, *Proceedings of the Conference on Advances in Cryptology (CRYPTO'88)*, Lecture Notes in Computer Science, pages 328–335, Santa Barbara, California, USA, August 1988. Springer.

59. Herbert Damker, Ulrich Pordesch, and Martin Reichenbach. Personal reachability and security management. In G. Müller and K. Rannenberg, editors, *Multilateral Security in Communications*, Information Security, pages 95–111. Addison Wesley, 1999.

60. Rene David and Hassane Alla. *Petri Nets and Grafcet: Tools for Modelling Discrete Event Systems*. Prentice-Hall, 1992.

61. George Davida, Yair Frankel, Yiannis Tsiounis, and Moti Yung. Anonymity control in e-cash systems. In R. Hirschfeld, editor, *Proceedings of the First International Conference on Financial Cryptography (FC'97)*, number 1318 in Lecture Notes in Computer Science, pages 1–16, Anguilla, British West Indies, February 1997. Springer.

62. B. De Win, V. Naessens, C. Díaz, S. Seys, C. Goemans, J. Claessens, B. De Decker, J. Dumortier, and B. Preneel. Anonymity and privacy in electronic services (APES) Deliverable 3 – Technologies overview. Technical report, K. U. Leuven, November 2001.

63. Hervé Debar, Marc Dacier, and Andreas Wespi. Towards a taxonomy of intrusion-detection systems. Technical Report 93076, IBM Research Division, Zurich Research Laboratory, 8803 Rüschlikon, Switzerland, June 1998.

64. Arbeitskreis Technik der Konferenz der Datenschutzbeauftragten des Bundes und der Länder. Datenschutzfreundliche Technologien in der Telekommunikation (in German), October 1997. Revised version.

65. Enquete-Kommission "Zukunft der Medien in Wirtschaft und Gesellschaft". Deutschlands Weg in die Informationsgesellschaft (Schlussbericht) (in German). Bundestags-Drucksache 13/11004, June 1998.

66. Erster Senat des Bundesverfassungsgerichts. Urteil vom 15. Dezember 1983 zum Volkszählungsgesetz - 1 BvR 209/83 u.a. (in German). *Datenschutz und*

292    References

*Datensicherheit*, 84(4):258–281, April 1984. http://www.datenschutz-berlin.de/gesetze/sonstige/volksz.htm.

67. Yvo Desmedt and Yair Frankel. Threshold cryptosystems. In G. Brassard, editor, *Proceedings of the Conference on Advances in Cryptology (CRYPTO'89)*, number 435 in Lecture Notes in Computer Science, pages 307–315, Santa Barbara, California, USA, August 1989. Springer.

68. Staatsvertrag über Mediendienste (MDStV) (in German). http://www.iid.de/iukdg/gesetz/mdstv.html, February 1997.

69. Alexander Dix. Privacy Respecting Incident Management – Die Datenschutzsicht (in German). *Datenschutz und Datensicherheit (DuD)*, 29(7):389–392, July 2005.

70. C. Díaz, V. Naessens, J. Claessens, B. De Win, S. Seys, B. De Decker, and B. Preneel. Anonymity and privacy in electronic services (APES) Deliverable 5 – Tools for technologies and applications. Technical report, K. U. Leuven, November 2002.

71. Claudia Díaz, Joris Claessens, and Bart Preneel. APES — Anonymity and privacy in electronic services. *Datenschutz und Datensicherheit (DuD)*, 27(3):143–145, March 2003.

72. Claudia Eckert. *IT-Sicherheit: Konzepte – Verfahren – Protokolle.* Oldenbourg, second edition, 2003.

73. Claudia Eckert and Alexander Pircher. Internet anonymity: Problems and solutions. In M. Dupuy and P. Paradinas, editors, *Proceedings of the IFIP TC11 16th International Conference on Information Security (Sec'01)*, pages 35–50, Paris, France, June 2001. IFIP, Kluwer Academic Publishers.

74. Steven T. Eckmann, Giovanni Vigna, and Richard A. Kemmerer. STATL definition. Technical Report TRCS20-19, Reliable Software Group, Department of Computer Science, University of California, Santa Barbara, California, USA, June 2001.

75. Terry Escamilla. *Intrusion Detection: Network Security Beyond the Firewall.* Wiley Computer Publishing. John Wiley & Sons, Inc., first edition, 1998.

76. Directive 95/46/EC of the European Parliament and of the Council of 24 october 1995 on the protection of individuals with regard to the processing of personal data and on the free movement of such data. Official Journal L 281, October 1995. http://europa.eu.int/eur-lex/en/lif/dat/1995/en_395L0046.html.

77. Herbert Fiedler. Der Staat im Cyberspace (in German). *Informatik Spektrum*, 24(5):309–314, 2001.

78. Herbert Fiedler. Cyber-libertär (in German). *Informatik Spektrum*, 25(3):215–219, 2002.

79. Simone Fischer-Hübner. *IDA (Intrusion Detection and Avoidance System): Ein einbruchsentdeckendes und einbruchsvermeidendes System (in German).* Reihe Informatik. Shaker, 1993.

80. Simone Fischer-Hübner. *IT-Security and Privacy: Design and Use of Privacy-Enhancing Security Mechanisms.* Number 1958 in Lecture Notes in Computer Science. Springer, 2001.

81. Simone Fischer-Hübner and Klaus Brunnstein. Opportunities and risks of intrusion detection expert systems. In *Proceedings of the International IFIP-GI-Conference Opportunities and Risks of Artificial Intelligence Systems (ORAIS'89)*, Hamburg, Germany, July 1989. IFIP.

82. Ulrich Flegel. Pseudonyme für Datenschutz und Überwachung: Anforderungen, Ansatz, Implementierung und Analyse (in German). In *Proceedings of the GI Conference Informatics Days 2002*, pages 307–311, Bad Schussenried, Germany, November 2002. GI, Konradin.

83. Ulrich Flegel. Pseudonymizing Unix log files. Technical report, Dept. of Computer Science, Chair VI - Information Systems and Security, University of Dortmund, D-44221 Dortmund, Germany, May 2002. http://ls6-www.cs.uni-dortmund.de/issi/archive/literature/2002/Flegel:2002a.pdf. Extended version of [84].

84. Ulrich Flegel. Pseudonymizing Unix log files. In G. Davida, Y. Frankel, and O. Rees, editors, *Proceedings of the Infrastructure Security Conference (InfraSec2002)*, number 2437 in Lecture Notes in Computer Science, pages 162–179, Bristol, United Kingdom, October 2002. Springer.

85. Ulrich Flegel. Anonyme Audit-Daten im Überblick (in German). *Datenschutz und Datensicherheit (DuD)*, 27(5):278–281, May 2003.

86. Ulrich Flegel. Ein Architektur-Modell für anonyme Autorisierungen und Überwachungsdaten (in German). Technical report, Dept. of Computer Science, Chair - VI Information Systems and Security, June 2003. http://ls6-www.cs.uni-dortmund.de/issi/archive/literature/2003/Flegel:2003d.pdf. Extended version of [87].

87. Ulrich Flegel. Ein Architektur-Modell für anonyme Autorisierungen und Überwachungsdaten (in German). In R. Grimm, H. B. Keller, and K. Rannenberg, editors, *Mit Sicherheit Informatik, Proceedings of the First GI Conference on Security – Protection and Reliability (Sicherheit 2003)*, number P-36 in Lecture Notes in Informatics, pages 293–304, Frankfurt, Germany, September 2003. GI, GI LNI.

88. Ulrich Flegel. Praktikabler Datenschutz für Log-Daten (in German). In R. Schaumburg and M. Thorbrügge, editors, *Proceedings of the 10th DFN-CERT Workshop on Security in Network Systems*, DFN-CERT publications, pages F1–F20, Hamburg, Germany, February 2003. DFN-CERT, Books on Demand.

89. Ulrich Flegel. Datenschutzfreundliche Missbrauchsentdeckung (in German). *Digma*, 5(4):168–171, December 2005.

90. Ulrich Flegel. Evaluating the design of an audit data pseudonymizer using basic building blocks for anonymity. Technical report, Dept. of Computer Science, Chair - VI Information Systems and Security, January 2005. http://ls6-www.cs.uni-dortmund.de/issi/archive/literature/2005/Flegel:2005a.pdf. Extended version of [91].

91. Ulrich Flegel. Evaluating the design of an audit data pseudonymizer using basic building blocks for anonymity. In H. Federrath, editor, *Proceedings of the Second GI Conference on Security – Protection and Reliability (Sicherheit 2005)*, number P-62 in Lecture Notes in Informatics, pages 221–232, Regensburg, Germany, April 2005. GI, GI LNI.

92. Ulrich Flegel. Mit Affen-Spielzeug etwas über Haustiere lernen – Evaluierung von PETs mittels APES-Bausteinen (in German). *Datenschutz und Datensicherheit (DuD)*, 29(7):410–414, July 2005.

93. Ulrich Flegel. *Pseudonymizing Audit Data for Privacy Respecting Misuse Detection*. PhD thesis, University of Dortmund, Dept. of Computer Science, January 2006.

94. Ulrich Flegel and Joachim Biskup. Requirements of information reductions for cooperating intrusion detection agents. In Günter Müller, editor, *Proceedings of the International Conference on Emerging Trends in Information and Communication Security (ETRICS 2006)*, number 3995 in Lecture Notes in Computer Science, pages 466–480, Freiburg, Germany, June 2006. Springer.

95. Ulrich Flegel and Michael Meier, editors. *Proceedings of the First GI Conference on Detection of Intrusions and Malware & Vulnerability Assessment (DIMVA*

*2004)*, number P-46 in Lecture Notes in Informatics, Dortmund, Germany, July 2004. GI SIG SIDAR, GI LNI.

96. Ulrich Flegel and Michael Meier. Herausforderungen für eine effektive, effiziente und datenschutzgerechte IT-Frühwarnung (in German). In *Proceedings of the BSI Workshop on Early Warning Systems*, pages 39–42, Bonn, Germany, July 2006. BSI, BSI.

97. Internet Engineering Task Force. Security issues in network event logging (syslog), July 2001. http://www.ietf.org/html.charters/syslog-charter.html.

98. Lothar Fritsch and Heiko Rossnagel. Die Krise des Signaturmarktes: Lösungsansätze aus betriebswirtschaftlicher Sicht (in German). In H. Federrath, editor, *Proceedings of the Second GI Conference on Security – Protection and Reliability (Sicherheit 2005)*, number P-62 in Lecture Notes in Informatics, pages 315–326, Regensburg, Germany, April 2005. GI, GI LNI.

99. Eran Gabber, Phillip B. Gibbons, David M. Kristol, Yossi Matias, and Alain Mayer. Consistent, yet anonymous, web access with LPWA. *Communications of the ACM*, 42(2):42–47, February 1999.

100. Eran Gabber, Phillip B. Gibbons, David M. Kristol, Yossi Matias, and Alain Mayer. On secure and pseudonymous client-relationships with multiple servers. *ACM Transactions on Information and System Security*, 2(3):390–415, November 1999.

101. Eran Gabber, Phillip B. Gibbons, Yossi Matias, and Alain Mayer. How to make personalized web browsing simple, secure and anonymous. In R. Hirschfeld, editor, *Proceedings of the First International Conference on Financial Cryptography (FC'97)*, number 1318 in Lecture Notes in Computer Science, pages 17–32, Anguilla, British West Indies, February 1997. Springer.

102. Daniela Gerd tom Markotten and Uwe Jendricke. Identitätsmanagement im E-Commerce (in German). *it+ti Informationstechnik und Technische Informatik*, 43(5):236–245, October 2001.

103. Ariel Glenn, Ian Goldberg, Frédéric Légaré, and Anton Stiglic. A description of protocols for private credentials. http://eprint.iacr.org/2001, October 2001.

104. Ian Goldberg. Privacy-enhancing technologies for the internet, II: Five years later. In R. Dingledine and P. Syverson, editors, *Proceedings of the International Workshop on Privacy Enhancing Technologies*, number 2482 in Lecture Notes in Computer Science, pages 1–12, San Francisco, California, USA, April 2002. Springer.

105. Ian Goldberg, David Wagner, and Eric Brewer. Privacy enhancing technologies for the internet. In *Proceedings of the COMPCON'97*, San Jose, California, USA, February 1997. IEEE. http://www.cs.berkeley.edu/~daw/privacy-compcon97-www/privacy-html.html.

106. Claudia Golembiewski. Das Recht auf Anonymität im Internet (in German). *Datenschutz und Datensicherheit*, 27(3):129–133, March 2003.

107. Dieter Gollmann. *Computer Security*, chapter 10.2.1: Kerberos, pages 168–171. John Wiley & Sons, Inc. 1999.

108. Torbjörn Granlund. *The GNU Multiple Precision Arithmetic Library*. GNU, 3.1.1 edition, September 2000. http://www.gnu.org/manual/gmp/index.html.

109. Dimitris Gritzalis, Konstantinos Moulinos, John Iliadis, Costas Lambrinoudakis, and Steven Xarhoulakos. Pythia: Towards anonymity in authentication. In M. Dupuy and P. Paradinas, editors, *Proceedings of the IFIP TC11 16th International Conference on Information Security (Sec'01)*, pages 1–17, Paris, France, June 2001. IFIP, Kluwer Academic Publishers.

110. Ben Handley. Resource-efficient anonymous group identification. In Y. Frankel, editor, *Proceedings of the 4th International Conference on Financial Cryptography (FC'00)*, number 1962 in Lecture Notes in Computer Science, pages 295–312, Anguilla, British West Indies, February 2000. Springer.

111. Marit Hansen. Identitätsmanagement (in German). *Datenschutz und Datensicherheit*, 27(5):306, May 2003.

112. Marit Hansen and Martin Rost. Nutzerkontrollierte Verkettung (in German). *Datenschutz und Datensicherheit*, 27(5):293–296, May 2003.

113. Shouichi Hirose and Susumu Yoshida. A user athentication scheme with identity and location privacy. In V. Varadharajan and Y. Mu, editors, *Proceedings of the 6th Australasian Conference on Information Security and Privacy (ACISP 2001)*, number 2119 in Lecture Notes in Computer Science, pages 235–246, Sydney, Australia, July 2001. Springer.

114. Donna L. Hoffman, Thomas P. Novak, and Marcos A. Peralta. Information privacy in the marketspace: Implications for the commercial uses of anonymity on the web. *The Information Society*, 15(2):129–140, April 1999. http://elab.vanderbilt.edu/research/papers/html/manuscripts/anonymity/anonymity2_nov10.htm.

115. Alex Iliev and Sean Smith. Privacy-enhanced credential services. In *Proceedings of the 2nd Annual PKI Research Workshop*, Gaitherburg, Maryland, USA, April 2003. NIST.

116. Louis Harris & Associates Inc. IBM multi-national consumer privacy survey. Technical Report 938568, IBM Global Services, 1999.

117. Sun Microsystems Inc. *Solaris 2.6 System Administrator Collection*, volume 1, chapter SunSHIELD Basic Security Module Guide. Sun Microsystems, Inc., 1997.

118. R. H. Irving, Christopher A. Higgins, and Frank R. Safayeni. Computerized performance monitoring systems: Use and abuse. *Communications of the ACM*, 29(8):794–801, 1986.

119. Stefan Jaeger. Verbotene Protokolle (in German). *Zeitschrift für Kommunikations- und EDV-Sicherheit (KES)*, 2000(5):6–12, 2000.

120. Stefan Jaeger. Wie viel Logfile ist erlaubt? Nach wie vor Rechtsunsicherheit bei Protokoll-Dateien (in German). *Zeitschrift für Kommunikations- und EDV-Sicherheit (KES)*, (4):65–66, 2004.

121. Björn Markus Jakobsson. *Privacy vs. Authenticity*. PhD thesis, University of California San Diego, 1997.

122. Uwe Jendricke and Daniela Gerd tom Markotten. Identitätsmanagement: Einheiten und Systemarchitektur (in German). In D. Fox, M. Köhntopp, and A. Pfitzmann, editors, *Proceedings of Verläßliche IT-Systeme - Sicherheit in komplexen Infrastrukturen*, DuD-Fachbeiträge, pages 77–85, Wiesbaden, Germany, September 2001. GI, Vieweg.

123. Kurt Jensen. *Coloured Petri Nets: Basic Concepts, Analysis Methods and Practical Use*, volume 1 of *EATCS Monographs on Theoretical Computer Science*. Springer, 1992.

124. Ari Juels. Targeted advertising ... and privacy too. In D. Naccache, editor, *Proceedings of The Cryptographers' Track at RSA Conference 2001 - Progress in Cryptology (CT-RSA 2001)*, Lecture Notes in Computer Science, pages 408–424, San Francisco, California, USA, April 2001. Springer.

125. Yücel Karabulut. *Secure Mediation Between Strangers in Cyberspace*. PhD thesis, University of Dortmund, Dortmund, Germany, September 2002.

126. E. D. Karnin, J. W. Greene, and M. E. Hellman. On secret sharing systems. *IEEE Transactions on Information Theory*, (29):35–41, 1983.

127. Stephen Kent and Randall Atkinson. *RFC 2401: Security Architecture for the Internet Protocol*, November 1998. http://www.ietf.org/rfc/rfc2401.txt.
128. Dogan Kesdogan, Roland Büschkes, and Jan Egner. Stop-and-go-mixes providing probabilistic anonymity in an open system. In *Proceedings of the 2nd Workshop on Information Hiding (IHW'98)*, number 1525 in Lecture Notes in Computer Science, pages 83–98. Springer, 1998.
129. Joe Kilian and Erez Petrank. Identity escrow. Theory of Cryptography Library, August 1997. http://theory.lcs.mit.edu/pub/tcryptol/97-11.ps.
130. Joe Kilian and Erez Petrank. Identity escrow. In H. Krawczyk, editor, *Proceedings of the Conference on Advances in Cryptology (CRYPTO'98)*, number 1462 in Lecture Notes in Computer Science, pages 196–185, Santa Barbara, California, USA, August 1998. Springer.
131. Christopher Krügel, Fredrik Valeur, and Giovanni Vigna. *Intrusion Detection and Correlation – Challenges and Solutions*, volume 14 of *Advances in Information Security*. Springer, 2005.
132. Sandeep Kumar. *Classification and Detection of Computer Intrusions*. PhD thesis, Purdue University, West Lafayette, Indiana, USA, 1995.
133. Christel Kumbruck. Verwirrungen um die Identität beim pseudonymen elektronischen Einkaufen (in German). *Datenschutz und Datensicherheit*, 27(5):287–292, May 2003.
134. Marit Köhntopp. Technischer Datenschutz in offenen Netzen (in German). In *Proceedings of the 7th DFN-CERT Workshop on Sicherheit in vernetzten Systemen*, DFN-Bericht, Hamburg, Germany, March 2000. DFN-CERT.
135. Marit Köhntopp and Oliver Berthold. Identity management based on P3P. In H. Federrath, editor, *Proceedings of the First International Workshop on Privacy Enhancing Technologies*, number 2009 in Lecture Notes in Computer Science, pages 141–160, Berkeley, California, USA, July 2000. ICSI, Springer.
136. Stefand Köpsell and Tobias Miosga. Strafverfolgung trotz Anonymität (in German). *Datenschutz und Datensicherheit (DuD)*, 29(7):403–409, July 2005.
137. Jia-Ling Lin, X. Sean Wang, and Sushil Jajodia. Abstraction-based misuse detection: High-level specifications and adaptable strategies. In *Proceedings of The 11th Computer Security Foundations Workshop*, pages 190–201, Rockport, Massachusetts, USA, June 1998. IEEE, IEEE Press.
138. Ulf Lindqvist and Phillip A. Porras. Detecting computer and network misuse through the production-based expert system toolset (P-BEST). In *Proceedings of the IEEE Symposium on Research in Security and Privacy*, pages 146–161, Los Alamitos, California, USA, May 1999. IEEE, IEEE Press.
139. C. Lonvick. *RFC 3164: The BSD syslog Protocol*, August 2001. http://www.ietf.org/rfc/rfc3164.txt.
140. Norbert Luckhardt. Aufsichtsbehörden bekennen Farbe (in German). *Zeitschrift für Kommunikations- und EDV-Sicherheit (KES)*, (4):2004, 67-69 2004.
141. Emilie Lundin and Erland Jonsson. Privacy vs. intrusion detection analysis. In D. Frincke, editor, *Proceedings of the Second International Symposium on Recent Advances in Intrusion Detection (RAID'99)*, West Lafayette, Indiana, USA, September 1999.
142. Emilie Lundin and Erland Jonsson. Some practical and fundamental problems with anomaly detection. In *Proceedings of NORDSEC'99*, Kista Science Park, Sweden, November 1999.
143. Emilie Lundin and Erland Jonsson. Anomaly-based intrusion detection: privacy concerns and other problems. *Computer Networks*, 34(4):623–640, October 2000.

144. Teresa F. Lunt, R. Jagannathan, Rosanna Lee, Sherry Listgarten, David L. Edwards, Peter G. Neumann, Harold S. Javitz, and Al Valdes. IDES: The enhanced prototype, a real-time intrusion-detection expert system. Technical Report SRI-CSL-88-12, SRI Project 4185-010, Computer Science Laboratory SRI International, 1988.

145. Anna Lysyanskaya, Ronald L. Rivest, Amit Sahai, and Stefan Wolf. Pseudonym systems. In H. Heys and C. Adams, editors, *Proceedings of the 6th Annual International Workshop on Selected Areas in Cryptography (SAC'99)*, pages 184–199, Kingston, Ontario, Canada, August 1999. Springer.

146. Greg Maitland and Colin Boyd. Fair electronic cash based on a group signature scheme. In S. Qing, T. Okamoto, and J. Zhou, editors, *Proceedings of the Third International Conference on Information and Communications Security (ICICS 2001)*, number 2229 in Lecture Notes in Computer Science, pages 461–465, Xian, China, November 2001. Springer.

147. John McHugh. Intrusion and intrusion detection. *International Journal of Information Security*, 1(1):14–35, 2001.

148. Michael Meier. A model for the semantics of attack signatures in misuse detection systems. In K. Zhang and Y. Zheng, editors, *Proceedings of the 7th International Information Security Conference (ISC 2004)*, number 3225 in Lecture Note in Computer Science, pages 158–169, Palo Alto, California, USA, September 2004. Springer.

149. Michael Meier. *Intrusion Detection effektiv! Modellierung und Analyse von Angriffsmustern (in German)*. X.systems.press. Springer, 2007.

150. Michael Meier, Niels Bischof, and Thomas Holz. Shedel – a simple description language for specifying attack signatures. In A. Ghonaimy, M. El-Hadidi, and H. K. Aslan, editors, *Proceedings of the IFIP TC11 17th International Conference on Information Security (Sec'02)*, Cairo, Egypt, May 2002. IFIP, Kluwer Academic Publishers.

151. Michael Meier and Thomas Holz. Sicheres Schlüsselmanagement für verteilte Intrusion-Detection-Systeme (in German). In P. Horster, editor, *Systemsicherheit*, DuD-Fachbeiträge, pages 275–286, Bremen, Germany, March 2000. GI-2.5.3, ITG-6.2, ÖCG/ACS, TeleTrusT, Vieweg.

152. Michael Meier, Sebastian Schmerl, and Hartmut König. Improving the efficiency of misuse detection. In K. Julisch and C. Krügel, editors, *Proceedings of the Second GI Conference on Detection of Intrusions and Malware & Vulnerability Assessment (DIMVA 2005)*, number 3548 in Lecture Notes in Computer Science, pages 188–205, Vienna, Austria, July 2005. GI SIG SIDAR, Springer.

153. Alfred J. Menezes, Paul C. van Oorschot, and Scott A. Vanstone. *Handbook of Applied Cryptography*. Discrete Mathematics and its Applications. CRC Press, Inc., Boca Raton, Florida, USA, 1997.

154. Alfred J. Menezes, Paul C. van Oorschot, and Scott A. Vanstone. *Handbook of Applied Cryptography*, chapter 9: Hash Functions and Data Integrity. Discrete Mathematics and its Applications. CRC Press, Inc., Boca Raton, Florida, USA, 1997.

155. Cédric Michel and Ludovic Mé. ADeLe: An attack description language for knowledge-based intrusion detection. In M. Dupuy and P. Paradinas, editors, *Proceedings of the IFIP TC11 16th International Conference on Information Security (Sec'01)*, pages 353–368, Paris, France, June 2001. IFIP, Kluwer Academic Publishers.

156. Greg Minshall. Tcpdpriv. http://ita.ee.lbl.gov/html/contrib/tcpdpriv. html, August 1997.

157. Abdelaziz Mounji. *Languages and Tools for Rule-Based Distributed Intrusion Detection*. PhD thesis, Facultés Universitaires Notre-Dame de la Paix, Namur, Belgium, 1997.

158. Klaus Möller. Syslog: Praxis und kommende Standards (in German). In R. Schaumburg and M. Thorbrügge, editors, *Proceedings of the 10th DFN-CERT Workshop on Security in Network Systems*, DFN-CERT publications, pages I1–I14, Hamburg, Germany, February 2003. DFN-CERT, Books on Demand.

159. Frank Müller. Schwellenwertsysteme mit mehreren Geheimnissen und ihre Anwendungen (in German, diploma thesis). Master's thesis, University of Dortmund, Dept. of Mathematics, Dortmund, Germany, November 2001.

160. Frank Müller. Secure share invalidation in specialized threshold schemes. Memo for internal discussion, 2005.

161. Toru Nakanishi, Nobuaki Haruna, and Yuji Sugiyama. Unlinkable electronic coupon protocol with anonymity control. In M. Mombo and Y. Zheng, editors, *Proceedings of the Second International Workshop on Information Security (ISW'99)*, number 1729 in Lecture Notes in Computer Science, pages 37–46. Springer, November 1999.

162. Heike Neumann. Anonyme Zahlungssysteme (in German). *Datenschutz und Datensicherheit*, 27(5):270–273, May 2003.

163. Heise Newsticker. 13. WWW-Benutzer-Analyse von Fittkau & Maaß (in German). http://www.ct.heise.de/newsticker/data/anw-26.11.01-001/, November 2001.

164. Peter Niebert. Petrinetze – Ein anschaulicher Formalismus der Nebenläufigkeit (Teil 1) (in German). *at - Automatisierungstechnik*, 51(3):A5–A8, 2003.

165. Peter Niebert. Petrinetze – Ein anschaulicher Formalismus der Nebenläufigkeit (Teil 2) (in German). *at - Automatisierungstechnik*, 51(4):A9–A12, 2003.

166. *OpenSSL cryptographic library*, December 2001. http://www.openssl.org/docs/crypto/crypto.html.

167. *OpenSSL SSL/TLS library*, December 2001. http://www.openssl.org/docs/ssl/ssl.html.

168. Thomas Ottman and Peter Widmayer. *Algorithmen und Datenstrukturen (in German)*. Informatik. BI-Wissenschaftsverlag, second edition, 1993.

169. Ruoming Pang and Vern Paxson. A high-level programming environment for packet trace anonymization and transformation. In *Proceedings of the 2003 Conference on Applications, Technologies, Architectures, and Protocols for Computer Communications*, pages 339–351, Karlsruhe, Germany, August 2003. ACM SIG-COMM, ACM Press.

170. Vern Paxson. Bro: A system for detecting network intruders in real-time. In *Proceedings of the 7th USENIX Security Symposium*, San Antonio, Texas, January 1998.

171. Holger Petersen. Faires elektronisches Geld (in German). In *Mit Sicherheit in die Informationsgesellschaft*, pages 427–444, Bonn, Germany, April 1997. Bundesamt für Sicherheit in der Informationstechnik, SecuMedia, Ingelheim.

172. Markus Peuhkuri. A method to compress and anonymize packet traces. In *Proceedings of the 1st ACM SIGCOMM Workshop on Internet Measurement*, pages 257–261, San Francisco, California, USA, November 2001. ACM SIGCOMM, ACM Press.

173. Andreas Pfitzmann. Multilateral security: Enabling technologies and their evaluation. In R. Wilhelm, editor, *Informatics: 10 Years Back. 10 Years Ahead.*, number 2000 in Lecture Notes in Computer Science, pages 50–62. Springer, 2001.

174. Andreas Pfitzmann and Marit Hansen. Anonymity, unlinkability, unobservability, pseudonymity, and identity management - a consolidated proposal for terminology. dud.inf.tu-dresden.de/literatur/Anon_Terminology_v0.28.pdf, May 2006.

175. Birgit Pfitzmann, Michael Waidner, and Andreas Pfitzmann. Secure and anonymous electronic commerce: Providing legal certainty in open digital systems without compromising anonymity. Technical Report RZ 3232 (#93278) 05/22/00, IBM Zurich Research Lab, May 2000.

176. David Pointcheval. Self-scrambling anonymizers. In Y. Frankel, editor, *Proceedings of the 4th International Conference on Financial Cryptography (FC'00)*, number 1962 in Lecture Notes in Computer Science, pages 259–275, Anguilla, British West Indies, February 2000. Springer.

177. Jean-Philippe Pouzol and Mireille Ducassé. From declarative signatures to misuse IDS. In W. Lee, L. Mé, and A. Wespi, editors, *Proceedings of the Fourth International Symposium on Recent Advances in Intrusion Detection (RAID 2001)*, number 2212 in Lecture Notes in Computer Science, pages 1–21, Davis, California, USA, October 2001. Springer.

178. Katherine E. Price. Host-based misuse detection and conventional operating systems' audit data collection. Master's thesis, Purdue university, December 1997.

179. Pew Internet & American Life Project. Trust and privacy online: Why americans want to rewrite the rules. http://www.pewinternet.org/reports/pdfs/PIP_Trust_Privacy_Report.pdf, August 2000.

180. Kai Rannenberg, Andreas Pfitzmann, and Günter Müller. IT security and multilateral security. In G. Müller and K. Rannenberg, editors, *Multilateral Security in Communications*, Information Security, pages 21–29. Addison Wesley, 1999.

181. Darren Reed. IP Filter. http://coombs.anu.edu.au/~avalon/ip-filter.html, 2001.

182. Darren Reed. Nsyslogd, 2001. http://coombs.anu.edu.au/~avalon/nsyslog.html.

183. Virginia E. Rezmierski, Marshall R. Reese, and Nathaniel St. Clair II. University systems security logging: who is doing it and how far can they go. *Computers & Security*, 21(6):557–564, 2002.

184. Virginia E. Rezmierski and Nathaniel St. Clair II. Final report NSF-Lamp project: Identifying where technology logging and monitoring for increased security end and violations of personal privacy and student records begin. Technical Report CSD1702, American Association of Collegiate Registrars and Admissions Officers, 2001. http://www.aacrao.org/publications/catalog/NSF-LAMP.pdf.

185. Konrad Rieck. *Konzept zur datenschutzorientierten Verarbeitung von Solaris-BSM-Audit-Daten (in German)*. Fachbereich Mathematik und Informatik, Institut für Informatik, Freie Universität Berlin, January 2003. http://www.roqe.org/bsmpseu.

186. Martin Roesch. Snort – lightweight intrusion detection for networks. In *Proceedings of LISA'99: 13th Systems Administration Conference*, pages 229–238, Seattle, Washington, November 1999. The Usenix Association, Usenix.

187. Martin Roesch. *Snort Users Manual – Snort Release: 1.8.2*, October 2001. http://www.snort.org/docs/SnortUsersManual.pdf.

188. Marshall T. Rose. *The Open Book: A Practical Perspective on OSI*. Prentice-Hall, Englewood Cliffs, N. J., 1990.

189. Jarek Rossignac et al.    GVU's 10th WWW User Survey, December 1998.    http://www.cc.gatech.edu/gvu/user_surveys/survey-1998-10/graphs/graphs.html#privacy.

190. Alexander Roßnagel. Freiheit im Cyberspace (in German). *Informatik Spektrum*, 25(1):33–38, 2002.

191. Alexander Roßnagel and Philip Scholz. Datenschutz durch Anonymität und Pseudonymität (in German). *Zeitschrift für Informations-, Telekommunikations- und Medienrecht (MMR)*, 2000(12):721–732, 2000.

192. James Rumbaugh, Ivar Jacobson, and Grady Booch. *Unified Modeling Language Reference Manual*. Object Technology Series. Addison Wesley, 2004.

193. Stuart Schechter, Todd Parnell, and Alexander Hartemink. Anonymous authentication of membership in dynamic groups. In M. Franklin, editor, *Proceedings of the Third International Conference on Financial Cryptography (FC'99)*, number 1648 in Lecture Notes in Computer Science, pages 184–195, Anguilla, British West Indies, February 1999. Springer.

194. Sebastian Schmerl. Entwurf und Implementierung einer effizienten Analyseeinheit für Intrusion-Detection-Systeme (in German, diploma thesis). Master's thesis, Brandenburgische Technische Universität Cottbus, October 2004.

195. Michael Schneider and Ulrich Pordesch. Identitätsmangement. *Datenschutz und Datensicherheit*, 22(11):645–649, 1998.

196. Bruce Schneier. *Angewandte Kryptographie (in German)*. Addison-Wesley, Bonn, first edition, 1996.

197. Bruce Schneier and John Kelsey. Cryptographic support for secure logs on untrusted machines. In Dacier [57]. http://www.zurich.ibm.com/~dac/Prog_RAID98/Table_of_content.html.

198. Thomas Schoen. Rechtliche Rahmenbedingungen zur Analyse von Log-Files (in German). *Datenschutz und Datensicherheit (DuD)*, 29(2):84–88, February 2005.

199. S. Seys, C. Díaz, Bart De Win, V. Naessens, C. Goemans, J. Claessens, W. Moreau, B. De Decker, J. Dumortier, and B. Preneel. Anonymity and privacy in electronic services (APES) Deliverable 2 – Requirement study of different applications. Technical report, K. U. Leuven, May 2001.

200. Adi Shamir. How to share a secret. *Communications of the ACM*, 22:612–613, 1979.

201. Victor Shoup. NTL: A library for doing number theory. http://www.shoup.net/ntl/, 2003.

202. Stephen E. Smaha. SVR4++, A common audit trail interchange format for Unix. Technical report, Haystack Laboratories, Inc., Austin, Texas, USA, October 1994. Version 2.2.

203. Michael Sobirey. Aktuelle Anforderungen an Intrusion Detection-Systeme und deren Berücksichtigung bei der Systemgestaltung von AID$^2$ (in German). In H. H. Brüggemann and W. Gerhardt-Häckl, editors, *Proceedings of Verläßliche IT-Systeme*, DuD-Fachbeiträge, pages 351–370, Rostock, Germany, April 1995. GI, Vieweg.

204. Michael Sobirey. *Datenschutzorientiertes Intrusion Detection (in German)*. DuD-Fachbeiträge. Vieweg, 1999.

205. Michael Sobirey, Simone Fischer-Hübner, and Kai Rannenberg. Pseudonymous audit for privacy enhanced intrusion detection. In L. Yngström and J. Carlsen, editors, *Proceedings of the IFIP TC11 13th International Conference on Information Security (SEC'97)*, pages 151–163, Copenhagen, Denmark, May 1997. IFIP, Chapman & Hall, London.

206. Michael Sobirey, Birk Richter, and Hartmut König. The intrusion detection system AID – Architecture and experiences in automated audit trail analysis. In P. Horster, editor, *Proceedings of the IFIP TC6/TC11 International Conference on Communications and Multimedia Security*, pages 278–290, Essen, Germany, September 1996. IFIP, Chapman & Hall, London.

207. Gerald Spiegel. Spuren im Netz (in German). *Datenschutz und Datensicherheit*, 27(5):265–269, May 2003.

208. Sarah Spiekermann. Die Konsumenten der Anonymität (in German). *Datenschutz und Datensicherheit*, 27(3):150–154, March 2003.

209. Markus Stadtler, Jean-Marc Piveteau, and Jan Camenisch. Fair blind signatures. In F. Pichler, editor, *Advances in Cryptology – EUROCRYPT 1995*, number 219 in Lecture Notes in Computer Science, pages 209–219, Linz, Austria, April 1995. Springer.

210. Sandra Steinbrecher and Stefan Köpsell. Modelling unlinkability. In R. Dingledine, editor, *Proceedings of the International Workshop on Privacy Enhancing Technologies*, number 2760 in Lecture Notes in Computer Science, pages 32–47, Dresden, Germany, March 2003. Springer.

211. Douglas Robert Stinson. *Cryptography — Theory and Practice*, chapter Secret Sharing Schemes, pages 326–331. Discrete mathematics and its applications. CRC Press, first edition, 1995.

212. Stuart G. Stubblebine and Paul F. Syverson. Authentic attributes with fine-grained anonymity protection. In Y. Frankel, editor, *Proceedings of the 4th International Conference on Financial Cryptography (FC'00)*, number 1962 in Lecture Notes in Computer Science, pages 276–294, Anguilla, British West Indies, February 2000. Springer.

213. Stuart G. Stubblebine, Paul F. Syverson, and David M. Goldschlag. Unlinkable serial transactions: Protocols and applications. *ACM Transactions on Information and System Security*, 2(4):354–389, November 1999.

214. *syslog.conf*. Manual Page.

215. Jaques Traoré. Group signatures and their relevance to privacy-protecting offline electronic cash systems. In J. Pieprzyk, R. Safavi-Naini, and J. Seberry, editors, *Proceedings of the 4th Australasian Conference on Information Security and Privacy (ACISP'99)*, number 1587 in Lecture Notes in Computer Science, pages 228–243, Wollongong, NSW, Australia, April 1999. Springer.

216. Els Van Herreweghen. Secure anonymous signature-based transactions. In G. Goos, J. Hartmanis, and J. van Leeuwen, editors, *Proceedings of the 6th European Symposium on Reserach in Computer Security (ESORICS 2000)*, number 1895 in Lecture Notes in Computer Science, pages 55–71, Toulouse, France, October 2000. Springer.

217. Henk van Rossum, Huib Gardeniers, John Borking, et al. Privacy-enhancing technologies: The path to anonymity, volume ii. Technical report, Registratiekamer Netherlands and Information and Privacy Commissioner Ontario, Canada, Achtergrondstudies en Verkenningen 5B, Rijswijk, Netherlands, August 1995.

218. Giovanni Vigna, Steven T. Eckmann, and Richard Kemmerer. Attack languages. In *Proceedings of the IEEE Information Survivability Workshop*, Boston, Maryland, USA, October 2000.

219. Giovanni Vigna, Richard A. Kemmerer, and Per Blix. Designing a web of highly-configurable intrusion detection sensors. In W. Lee, L. Mé, and A. Wespi, editors,

*Proceedings of the Fourth International Symposium on Recent Advances in Intrusion Detection (RAID 2001)*, number 2212 in Lecture Notes in Computer Science, pages 69–84, Davis, California, USA, October 2001. Springer.

220. Samuel D. Warren and Louis D. Brandeis. The right to privacy. *Harvard Law Review*, (5):193–220, 1890-91.

221. webwasher.com AG. Den Überblick behalten, Reporting mit WebWasherEE (in German). `http://www.webwasher.com/product_pdf/deutsch/Produktblatt_Reporting.pdf`, January 2003.

222. Alan Westin. *Privacy and Freedom*. Bodley Head, New York, 1987.

223. Jun Xu, Jinliang Fan, Mostafa Ammar, and Sue B. Moon. On the design and performance of prefix-preserving IP traffic trace anonymization. In *Proceedings of the 1st ACM SIGCOMM Workshop on Internet Measurement*, pages 263–266, San Francisco, California, USA, November 2001. ACM SIGCOMM, ACM Press.

224. Detlef Zimmer. *A Meta-Model for the Definition of the Semantics of Complex Events in Active Database Management Systems*. PhD thesis, University of Paderborn, 1998.

225. Detlef Zimmer and Rainer Unland. On the semantics of complex events in active database management systems. In *Proceedings of the 15th International Conference on Data Engineering*, pages 392–399. IEEE, IEEE Press, 1999.

# Index

abstract event, 147
accountable, 47
accuracy, 39
action, 214
activating token set, 216
activating unified token, 216
activity, 203
activity level, 46, 98, 253, 254
agent, 49
AID, 73, 83
alarm, 58, 207
analysis component, 58
analysis context, 58
ANIDA, 84
anonymity, 33
    conditional, 181
    unconditional, 171
anonymous, 47
Anonymouse, 74
Apache, 193
appearance, 173
application-layer, 104
attacker, 49
attacker model, 57
attribute
    dependable, 66
    of property, 13
    of property statement, 16
audit component, 58, 92
audit data, 29, 98, 203
    in ASCII format, 147
    of syslog, 29, 147
audit record, 58, 98, 147, 203
    of syslog, 148, 151

of syslog pseudonymized, 151
audit service, 137
authentication of property statement, 13,
    16
authentication server of Kerberos, 23, 72
authenticator, 68
authorization, 15
authorizer, 15
avoidance of data, 39

basic event, 206
billing data, 37
bound property, 15
bound step, 206
BROanonymize, 74
broker
    of identity, 68
    of profile, 68
bsmpseu, 74
building block, 172
    application level, 175
    connection level, 173

census decision, 35
certificate, 14
certification, 14
certifier, 15
child token, 257
CL-feature, 234
clarity of law, 34
clear-text-linkable feature, 234
clue, 58
compatible shares, 110
completeness of misuse detection, 203

complex event, 206, 208
complex event instance, 207
complex event occurrence, 207
concurrency, 208
condition of disclosure, 46, 253, 254
conditional anonymity, 181
conjunction, 208, 220
consuming activity, 209
consuming edge, 212
context
    of analysis, 58
    of disclosure, 46, 253, 254
continuity, 208, 221
control block, 260
controlled disclosure of a pseudonym, 48
correctness of misuse detection, 203
credential, 71
    one-show, 72

D-feature, 248
data avoidance, 39
data quality, 39, 41
dependable attribute, 66
DIMVA, 3
disclosure condition, 46, 98, 253, 254
disclosure context, 46, 97, 204, 253, 254
disclosure feature, 248
disclosure of a pseudonym, 45, 48
disclosure scenario, 204, 253, 254
disclosure transition, 248
disjunction, 208, 220

edge, 210, 211
    consuming, 212, 220
    input, 211
    non-consuming, 212, 220
    output, 211
entity, 13, 14, 17
    property, 14
escape place, 212
escape transition, 214
escrow data, 133, 134
event, 98, 147, 203
    abstract, 147
    basic, 206
    designator, 98
    type, 98, 208, 213
event designator, 98
    of syslog, 148

event report, 58

facility of syslog, 141
fairness, 39, 41
feature, 99
    CL-, 234
    clear-text-linkable, 234
    D-, 248
    disclosure, 248
    PL-, 234
    pseudonym-linkable, 234
feature designator, 98
feature type, 99
final place, 212
flow, 173
free property, 14

giver, 11
global setup, 175
group pseudonym, 48

ID, 47
IDA, 73, 82
identifiability of a person, 44
identity, 99
identity broker, 68
identity management
    privacy-enhancing, 69
identity protector, 69
independence of infrastructure, 68
independence of service, 66
independence of user, 67
infomediary, 70
information of data subject, 39
informational self-determination, 31
informed consent, 39
initial marking of signature-net, 215
initial place, 212
input edge, 211
input place, 212, 213
input token set, 216
instance of complex event, 207
inter-event condition, 209, 213, 220
interior place, 212
intra-event condition, 209, 213, 220
intrusion detection
    signature, 204
IP filter, 139
IPSEC, 143

Kerberos, 23
  authentication server, 23, 72
  ticket granting server, 23, 72, 85

legal purpose, 34
linkable, 47
Linux, 160
local setup, 174

manifestation, 203
marking, 215
  stable, 216
  unstable, 216
match
  valid, 110
mismatch, 110
misuse detection, 203
  completeness, 203
  correctness, 203
  signature, 204
misuse scenario, 203
misuse scenario semantics
  concurrency, 208
  conjunction, 208, 220
  continuity, 208, 221
  disjunction, 208, 220
  inter-event condition, 209, 220
  intra-event condition, 209, 220
  negation, 208, 221
  repetition, 208, 221
  sequence, 208, 220
  simultaneous, 208, 221
  step instance consumption, 209, 221
  step instance selection, 209, 221
multilateral security, 43, 66

necessity, 39
negation, 208, 221
non-consuming activity, 209
non-consuming edge, 212
notification of data subject, 39

object, 47
  accountable, 47
  anonymous, 47, 48
  linkable, 47
  pseudonymized, 48
  pseudonymous, 48
  reidentified, 48
  unlinkable, 47

observation of activity, 46, 97, 203
OpenBSD, 160
organizational purpose binding of
    pseudonym disclosure, 49
output edge, 211
output place, 212, 213

parent token, 257
personal identifiability, 44
Petri-net, 210, 212
PIM, 69
PL-feature, 234
place, 210, 212
  escape, 212
  final, 212
  initial, 212
  input, 212, 213
  interior, 212
  output, 212, 213
principal, 13, 14, 47
priority of syslog, 141
privacy, 34
profile broker, 68
property, 13
  attribute, 13
  bound, 15
  free, 14
  of entity, 14
property statement, 13, 17
  attributes, 16
  authentication, 13, 16
  certification, 14
  component, 15
  responsible agent, 13, 15
  subject, 13, 15, 16
  validity, 13, 16
  verification, 17
proportionateness, 34, 36
protector of identity, 69
Pseudo/CoRe, 159, 180
pseudonym, 47
  of group, 48
  verifiable, 67
pseudonym disclosure, 45, 48
  controlled, 48
  uncontrolled, 53
pseudonym mapping, 44, 48, 92
pseudonym-linkable feature, 234
pseudonymity-layer, 104

pseudonymization, 48
    direct, 77
    indirect, 75
pseudonymize, 47
pseudonymizer, 92, 178
pseudonymizers
    AID, 73, 83
    ANIDA, 84
    Anonymouse, 74
    BROanonymize, 74
    bsmpseu, 74
    IDA, 73, 82
    Lundin, 73, 84
    Pseudo/CoRe, 74, 159, 180
    WebWasher, 74
purpose binding, 36, 40
    organizational
        of pseudonym disclosure, 49
    technical, 67
        of pseudonym disclosure, 46, 50
        of pseudonym linkability, 53
purpose of analysis, 58

quality of data, 39, 41

RAID, 3
redirector, 145
reduction of data, 39
regular transition, 214
reidentification, 48
reidentifier, 187
repetition, 208, 221
response component, 58
responsible agent, 15
    of property statement, 13, 15
rule of law, 34

safeguard, 36, 41
scheme description, 261
security multilateral, 43, 66
sensitivity of personal data, 36
separation of power, 36
sequence, 208, 220
serial signature-net, 223
severity of syslog, 141
sibling token, 257
signature, 204
signature-net, 210
    edge, 210, 211

consuming, 212, 220
input, 211
non-consuming, 212, 220
output, 211
marking, 215
    initial, 215
    stable, 216
    unstable, 216
place, 210, 212
    escape, 212
    final, 212
    initial, 212
    input, 212, 213
    interior, 212
    output, 212, 213
serial, 223
token, 214
    child, 257
    parent, 257
    sibling, 257
transition, 210, 212
    action, 214
    activating token set, 216
    activating unified token, 216
    disclosure, 248
    escape, 214
    input token set, 216
    inter-event condition, 213
    intra-event condition, 213
    regular, 214
    spontaneous, 214
    token binding, 213
    token variable, 213
    unifiable token set, 216
    unified token, 216
simultaneous, 208, 221
site security officer, 58
Snort, 143
Solaris, 160
spontaneous transition, 214
SSO, 58
STAT, 143
statement of property, 13
step, 208
    bound, 206
    instantiated, 207
    of complex event, 206
step instance consumption, 209, 221
step instance selection, 209, 221

stock data, 36
subject, 49
   of property statement, 13, 15, 16
syslog, 29, 139, 141, 193
syslog API, 145, 158, 161
syslog audit data, 29, 142, 147
syslog audit record, 142
syslog facility, 141
syslog options, 165
syslog priority, 141
syslog protocol, 143
syslog severity, 141
syslogd, 145

taker, 11
technical purpose binding, 67
   of pseudonym disclosure, 46, 50
   of pseudonym linkability, 53
ticket granting server of Kerberos, 23, 72,
   85
token, 214
   child, 257
   parent, 257
   sibling, 257
token binding, 213
token variable, 213
transition, 210, 212
   action, 214
   activating token set, 216

activating unified token, 216
disclosure, 248
escape, 214
input token set, 216
inter-event condition, 213
intra-event condition, 213
regular, 214
spontaneous, 214
token binding, 213
token variable, 213
unifiable token set, 216
unified token, 216
transparency, 36, 39
trust, 13

unconditional anonymity, 171
uncontrolled disclosure of a pseudonym,
   53
unifiable token set, 216
unified token, 216
unlinkable, 47
usage data, 37

validity of property statement, 13, 16
verifiable pseudonym, 67
verification of property statement, 17

WebWasher, 74